Money, Income, and Wealth

Money, Income and Wealth

The Macroeconomics of a Monetary Economy

BRIAN MOTLEY   University of Kentucky

D.C. HEATH AND COMPANY

Lexington, Massachusetts | Toronto

339
M919m

Published simultaneously in Canada.

Printed in the United States of America.

International Standard Book Number: 0-669-95794-1

Library of Congress Catalog Card Number: 76-14634

79-4333

To my wife, FRANCES,
and my four boys,
ANDREW, JONATHAN,
SIMON, and TIMOTHY.

Preface

This book is designed to provide undergraduate and beginning graduate students with a simple but relatively comprehensive exposition of the fundamentals of modern macroeconomic theory. It has evolved over several years of teaching macroeconomics at both the graduate and undergraduate levels.

Traditionally, the emphasis of macroeconomics texts has been on the relationships among the various *flow* variables in the economy: income, consumption, investment, etc. The only explicit discussion of a *stock* variable comes in the analysis of the demand for and supply of money. The fact that a modern economy contains a myriad of different assets — of which money is but one — among which investors must choose is rarely mentioned and certainly plays little role in analysis.

This book seeks to correct this overemphasis on the flow variables by giving equal time both to the behavior of the *spenders* in the economy — whose decisions determine the flow variables — and to that of the *wealth holders*, who make decisions about stock variables.* The book emphasizes that these are different kinds of decisions, that they are made subject to different kinds of constraints, but that they impinge on each other in all kinds of ways. In particular, the portfolio decisions of the wealth holders in the economy affect asset prices and rates of return, which in turn have an impact on spending decisions. This emphasis on the role played by the asset markets and asset prices is a feature that is common both to the Monetarist school, represented by such theorists as Milton Friedman, and to the neo-Keynesian approach of James Tobin and his colleagues.

In the early sections of the book money is treated as an asset that is produced exclusively by the government. However, Part 4, Money and Banking, contains a somewhat lengthier treatment of the banking system and the supply of money than is typical in books of this type. As a result, it may prove valuable to teachers and students of

---

*To avoid severe problems of repetition and inept wording, the generic *he* has been used to refer to theoretical individuals, spenders, etc. The reader should understand the masculine pronoun to refer to both males and females in all cases.

monetary theory as well as to those of general macroeconomics. In this part the emphasis is on the behavior of banks as profit-maximizing, risk-averting institutions rather than on the institutional setup of the American financial system. This approach, which is usually described as the "new view" of the money supply process, represents a natural extension of the models of asset markets developed earlier.

Throughout the book the emphasis is on *policy*. Theoretical models are in most cases illustrated by considering how they respond to changes in policy variables such as tax rates, the stocks of money and government bonds, and government expenditures. In addition, the analysis seeks to describe how these models behave as the economy moves from one equilibrium position to another as well as what those equilibria look like when the economy reaches them. Hopefully these features will make the bare bones of the theory come alive for the reader.

The exposition of the book is largely verbal and geometric. Algebra is used to represent functional relations but rarely to derive conclusions. Thus the analysis should be accessible to readers with only a limited mathematical background.

This book has been in process for several years. During its long gestation period I have received helpful comments and advice from students and colleagues at the Universities of Wisconsin, Rochester, and Kentucky. Particularly valuable have been the detailed criticisms of the complete manuscript by Roger Waud of the Federal Reserve System and Dwayne Wrightsman of the University of New Hampshire as well as critiques of portions of the manuscript by Donald Nichols, Stuart Greenbaum, and David Laidler. The comments of the editorial staff at D. C. Heath have also been helpful. Lois Engelhart and Judy Pittenger did valiant service in typing and retyping the manuscript. Of course, no one but I bears any responsibility for any errors of fact or analysis that remain.

Finally, I must thank my wife and family for their continuing support throughout this period and especially during the last few months when publisher's deadlines have compelled me to spend less time with them than I would have wished. Without that support the writing process would have been longer and the pains of authorship greater.

BRIAN MOTLEY
Lexington, Kentucky

Contents

Part Five   Prices, Output, and Employment 311

14 Prices and Aggregate Demand 313

15 Wages, Prices, and Employment 336

16 The Variable-Price Economy 361

Part One

Introduction

Introduction

1

As their science has developed, economists have found it useful to divide their studies into two broad categories: *microeconomics,* or price theory, and *macroeconomics,* sometimes known as aggregative economics or income theory. Microeconomists are concerned mainly with the activities of single households or firms and with how these entities interact through markets to determine prices and outputs of individual commodities. Macroeconomists, on the other hand, generally are interested in the behavior of various economic variables that refer to the economy as a whole. They ask such questions as What determines the level and rate of growth of total production in our economy? or What determines the average level of prices and the rate at which they rise or fall? rather than What determines the output and price of peanuts?, which is a microeconomic question.

Although this distinction between macroeconomics and microeconomics has proved very fruitful, the two areas are not independent fields of study. Indeed, one of the most important developments in macroeconomics during the last quarter century has been the increasing application of microeconomic concepts to macroeconomic problems. In Chapters 7 and 8, for example, the microeconomic theories of consumer choice and of cost-minimizing production are employed to study the determinants of aggregate consumption and investment.

An area of economics that does not fit conveniently into the twofold division between micro- and macroeconomics and that has shown especially rapid development in recent years is that known as *capital theory.* The special province of the capital theorist is the study of the implications of the fact that the decisions of all economic agents are influenced both by their inheritances from the past and by their expectations of the future. Capital theory is, in a sense, the *economics of time.*

With respect to the past the capital theorist points out that the familiar adage that "bygones are bygones" does not mean that decisions made in the past are irrelevant to discussions of the present. If past decisions resulted in the accumulation of machines, buildings, and other forms of tangible capital or of corporate securities, bank deposits, and other types of financial assets, the outcome of decisions made today is inevitably influenced by those made in the past. The output that a firm is able to produce today, for example, obviously depends on the number and type of machines that it possesses, which in turn reflects the investment decisions that it made in the past.

Similarly, the decisions that economic agents make today will determine the amount and type of both financial and physical assets that they or their heirs will inherit in the future. As long as economic agents recognize this fact, their present decisions are bound to be influenced by their expectations of the future. To take another example, the amount of its income that a household saves this year and the manner in which it invests its savings will affect the amount of consumption it will be able to enjoy in future years. Hence its saving and investment decisions today are likely to be influenced by its expectations of both future needs and future income.

These examples suggest that capital theory also may be thought of as the study of the economic implications of the existence of long-lived commodities, or *assets,* as they are commonly called. This is because these commodities—which include not only tangible items like machines, automobiles, and homes but also financial assets such as common stocks, government securities, and bank loans—serve as the links between past, present, and future.

In line with the development of macroeconomic theory in recent years, the role of assets in the current decisions of economic agents receives considerable emphasis in this book. More and more, macroeconomics is becoming a part (or at least an application) of capital theory, and this book reflects this tendency.

Of all the assets in the economy, one has been singled out for special attention by economists. This is the asset that we call *money.* The theoretical discussions in this book will suggest that the behavior of such important national aggregates as total production, employment, and level of prices is likely to be profoundly influenced by what happens to the supply of money. Moreover, American economic history supports this theoretical conclusion. All major depressions and inflations have been associated with large changes in the amount of money in circulation. For example, during the Great Depression of the early thirties, the stock of money fell by a quarter at the same time that output declined by a third and prices by more than 20 percent. Similarly, the sharp increase in the rate of inflation after 1965 was accompanied by an acceleration in the rate of growth of the money supply.

However, these facts do not prove that depressions and inflations are *caused* by changes in the stock of money. It might be the other way around. In fact, the role of money in the economy remains the subject of intense debate among economists. One of our objectives in this book is to present a framework within which this issue may be examined.

The Concept of Equilibrium

You are probably familiar with the notion of *equilibrium*. An economic system is usually described as being in equilibrium when the values of certain key variables do not change as time passes. A market for a single commodity, for example, is in equilibrium when the price of that commodity and the amount that is bought and sold do not change over time.

This definition of equilibrium, which is analogous to that used in the physical sciences, has the disadvantage of not explaining why these key variables remain unchanged. A more satisfactory definition would describe economic equilibrium as a situation in which the plans and expectations of all the economic agents involved are exactly realized. As a result, none of the agents have any reason to alter their plans or behavior, and since the behavior of individuals does not change, neither does that of the economic system as a whole.

We may illustrate this approach to the concept of equilibrium by a simple example involving the market for a single commodity, say, wheat. Consider Figure 1.1. In this figure *DD* represents the demand curve for wheat; at any price this curve shows how much wheat buyers will want to purchase per day. Similarly, *SS* represents the supply curve for wheat; at any price it shows how much wheat sellers will offer for sale per day.

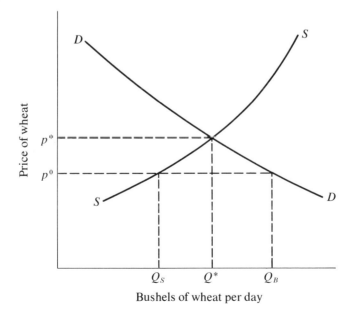

FIGURE 1.1 The market for wheat
When the price of wheat is p^*, buyers want to buy and sellers want to sell the same amount of wheat, namely, Q^* bushels per day. Their plans are consistent and the market is in equilibrium.

When the price of wheat is p^*, the amount of wheat suppliers want to sell per day is equal to the amount purchasers want to buy. Since plans of the sellers are consistent with those of the buyers, both sides find their expectations realized. Suppliers are able to sell and purchasers are able to buy the amount of wheat they anticipated at the price p^*. Thus the market is in equilibrium.

Contrast this situation with one in which the price is less than p^*, say, p^0. At this price the amount of wheat buyers want to purchase, Q_B, exceeds the amount sellers are prepared to supply, Q_S. In this situation the market is in disequilibrium, since the buying plans of the purchasers are not consistent with the selling plans of the suppliers. Either buyers must purchase less than they had planned or sellers must sell more. Since their plans and expectations are not realized, one side or the other (or both) is likely to change its behavior.

Economists generally assume that economic systems are always either in equilibrium or at least moving toward equilibrium. It is this assumption that enables us to make predictions about how an economy will behave. In the case of our wheat market example, this assumption enables us to predict that the price of wheat will settle at p^* rather than at some other price, such as p^0.

The assumption that economic systems move toward positions of equilibrium is derived from a more basic assumption, namely, that when a system is *not* in equilibrium, there are forces at work that tend to push it toward equilibrium. Again, consider the situation in the wheat market when the price is p^0. At that price some buyers will find that they are unable to obtain the quantities of wheat they had planned to purchase. They will be willing to pay more than p^0 in order to obtain more wheat. Conversely, sellers will find that they are being called upon to supply larger quantities of wheat than they had planned to offer and will realize that their customers are willing to buy the same quantity of wheat at a price above p^0. Thus, on both sides of the market, forces are at work that tend to produce an increase in the price of wheat. These forces will continue to operate as long as the price of wheat is less than p^*. As the price rises, both buyers and sellers will modify their plans (buyers plan to purchase less and suppliers plan to offer more) until, when the price reaches p^*, their plans are mutually consistent.

The exact mechanism by which this price rise comes about varies from one market to another. In some markets (auctions, for example) prices rise as a result of buyers bidding them upward. In other markets (including most of those in which households purchase consumer goods) it is the sellers who post the higher prices. However, knowledge of the exact process by which equilibrium is restored is generally less important than the fact that it will be restored somehow. It is this fact that enables us to focus our attention on equilibrium situations, confident in the knowledge that the actual situation will always be close to, and moving toward, that equilibrium.[1]

---

[1] In Part 4 we will encounter an example of a market—the market for bank deposits—that frequently remains out of equilibrium because of government regulation of the price.

Functional Relations

Frequently in economics we want to discuss situations in which one variable depends on or is related to some other variable or group of variables. The supply and demand relations introduced in the previous section are examples: the quantities of wheat that suppliers want to offer and that buyers want to purchase are both dependent on the market price.

It is convenient to describe this kind of situation using the mathematical concept of a *function*.[2] When some variable, say Y, is systematically related to some other variable, say, X, in such a way that to every value of X within some range there corresponds a value of Y, we say that Y is *a function of* X and write

$$Y = f(X)$$

Note that this definition does not say that changes in X *cause* changes in Y, but only that X and Y are related to one another in some systematic way. In later chapters we will encounter several examples of functions that do not represent cause-and-effect relationships.

Generally we need to indicate that certain variables are related as well as to specify the nature of that relationship. If, for example, the relationship is *direct*, we write

$$\frac{\Delta Y}{\Delta X} > 0$$

to indicate that a change in X is associated with a change in Y in the same direction. Conversely, if a change in X is associated with a change in Y in the opposite direction (that is, the relationship is an *inverse* one), we write

$$\frac{\Delta Y}{\Delta X} < 0$$

Sometimes a given variable is functionally related to a number of other variables rather than to just one. In this case we might write

$$Y = g(V, W, X)$$

indicating that Y is related to V and W as well as X. Again, we need to specify the nature of the relation and can do it in the same manner as before. Thus if we write

$$\frac{\Delta Y}{\Delta V} > 0, \qquad \frac{\Delta Y}{\Delta W} < 0, \qquad \frac{\Delta Y}{\Delta X} > 0$$

then Y will increase if either V or X increases or if W decreases (*while at the same time the other two variables remain constant*).[3]

---

[2] Strictly speaking, the definition given is that of a *relation*. Mathematicians reserve the word *function* for situations in which for every value of X there corresponds a *unique* value of Y. In most cases the relations we study in this book are functions in this strict mathematical sense.
[3] This qualification is important. If, for example, both X and W increase, the effect on Y cannot be predicted without more information.

Stocks and Flows

In economic theory—and especially in macroeconomics—it is important to draw a distinction between variables that are *flow variables* and those that are *stock variables*. This distinction depends on the dimension of the variables. Specifically, a stock variable is one that is measured as a given quantity *on a particular date* whereas a flow variable is one that is measured as a given quantity *over some given period.*

For example, the quantity of water in a reservoir on any given day is a stock variable; it has the dimension "gallons." By contrast, the amounts of water entering and leaving the reservoir are flow variables; they must be measured in gallons over some time interval, since it makes no sense to say that the quantity of water flowing into or out of the reservoir is a certain number of gallons unless we indicate whether this particular quantity flows in a day, a week, or some other time interval. Similarly, total employment, which measures the number of persons at work on a specific date, is a stock variable, having the dimension "workers" whereas "new hires" and "separations," which measure the numbers of persons obtaining and losing jobs, are both flow variables, since both must be measured over some time interval.[4]

In practice, flow variables are normally measured in the form of a *periodic rate;* we say that on a given date workers are hired at a rate of so many workers per day or per week. The choice of the time period is purely a matter of convenience. If, for example, 280 persons are hired during the month of February, we can describe hiring as proceeding at the rate of 10 workers per day, 70 workers per week, or 280 workers per month. Obviously, it makes no substantive difference which units we choose.

In this book we will be concerned with both stock variables and flow variables (as well as with other variables—prices, for example—that are neither stocks nor flows). When a new variable is introduced, you will find it helpful to ask yourself whether it is a stock variable or a flow variable.

Let us take a closer look at a pair of concepts that will play a key role in the analysis of following chapters: *income* and *money supply*. Income is a flow variable: An individual's income is the amount received per month or per year, and the national income is the aggregate of the incomes of all the persons and businesses in the economy over some period of time.[5] The supply of money is a stock variable: On a particular date a certain amount of money, in the form of notes, coin, and checking accounts, is outstanding, and each individual and business in the economy holds a given stock.

Many students find it difficult to understand the distinction between in-

---

[4] The examples used have the special property that the *change* in the level of the stock variable over some interval is equal to the difference between the two flow variables. For example, the change in total employment over some period, say, a month, is equal to new hires minus separations during that month. We will encounter a number of examples of such accounting relations in later chapters.

[5] A more precise definition of the national income will be given in Chapter 2.

come and the money stock, and as a result they confuse the two concepts. One possible reason for this difficulty may be that incomes are typically paid in the form of money.[6] However, not all incomes are paid in money. Some individuals receive part of their incomes in nonmonetary form; the food, clothing, and shelter received by military employees is one obvious example. Again, not all receipts of money represent income; if you sell your holdings of government securities and receive $500 in one-dollar bills, this receipt of money is not income. Such a transaction changes the *form* in which you are holding your accumulated assets (you have depleted your stock of securities and increased your stock of money) but it does not add to your total stock of assets as does the receipt of income.

Another possible reason why money and income are frequently confused is that for many households the amount of money in their checking accounts on payday is equal to their incomes. Each month these households deposit their salaries into their accounts and then proceed to spend them. By the time the next payday comes around, their money stocks are down to zero. For such a household an increase in its income means an increase in its holdings of money. However, this is because the household's income and its stock of money are functionally related to one another[7]—not because they are the same concept.

Individuals, businesses, and governments make decisions with respect to both stock variables and flow variables. A household, for example, decides how to allocate its income between consumption and saving; this is a decision involving *flows*. In addition, it decides how to allocate its total assets between, say, bank deposits, corporate bonds, and government securities; this is a decision involving *stocks*. Note that these decisions are not, in general, independent of one another, if only because total assets will rise if consumption expenditures are less than income over some given period and will fall if those expenditures exceed income.

Even the impoverished household whose money stock falls to zero at the end of each month has to make both types of decisions. That household chooses to save nothing over the month as a whole and to hold its assets exclusively in the form of money. As a result, the household's income and money holdings are closely related to one another. A world in which all economic agents operated like this household would not be very interesting to the economic theorist; for in such a world the relation between the level of income and the amount of money the public would want to hold would be purely a matter of arithmetic. The theory of the role of money becomes

---

[6] In common language we often say that Mr. X makes a lot of money in his job. By this we do not mean that Mr. X is employed by the Mint making quarters and dimes but that he earns a large income. The reader should be careful not to allow such loose language to lead him into confusing money and income.

[7] In fact the householder's money stock on any date depends on his income, the frequency with which he receives his paycheck, and the pattern of his expenditures over time. This situation will be studied in considerable detail in Chapter 9.

interesting, and the distinction between money and income becomes crucial, when it is recognized that for most economic agents money is but one form in which they may hold their accumulated savings. Stocks of currency and bank deposits are assets, just as homes, cars, and holdings of common stock or U.S. Savings Bonds are assets. The proportion of total assets that an economic agent chooses to hold in the form of money depends on the relative attractiveness of the assets that are available. Income and spending habits are relevant to this decision (since most receipts and payments are made in money) but are not the whole story.

Markets for Assets

The types of stock variables with which we are chiefly concerned are those that represent stocks of commodities. The stocks of money and other financial assets feature prominently in the analyses of the following chapters, as do the quantities of various tangible assets. At this point, therefore, it is useful to examine the behavior of markets in these commodities and to contrast it with that of markets in flow commodities.

Figure 1.2 depicts a market for a typical flow commodity, taxicab trips. Note that since this is a flow commodity, its dimension is expressed in the form of a rate, namely, trips per week. The curve DD represents the demand for trips. At any fare per trip it shows the number of trips per week that cab users will wish to take. The downward slope of DD reflects the fact that at lower fares users will take more taxicab trips per week in preference to using other forms of transportation (e.g., bus, subway, etc.). Similarly, SS represents the supply of trips by cab operators and slopes upward since presumably at high fares they will be willing to work longer hours and make more trips per week than at low fares.[8]

The market for taxicab trips is in equilibrium when the number of trips riders wish to take each week is equal to the number that taxi owners are willing to supply. Equilibrium occurs when the fare per trip is p; at this fare the number of trips demanded and supplied each week is T. As long as there is no shift in either the supply curve or the demand curve, the market remains in equilibrium and the same transactions will be repeated every week. This repetition of transactions is a characteristic of a flow market that is not shared by markets for stock commodities.

Now consider Figure 1.3, which depicts the market for a typical stock commodity, namely, taxicabs. That this is a stock commodity is shown by the fact that it is measured in terms of the number[9] of taxis on a specified

---

[8] If you have some knowledge of price theory you will recognize that the explanations given for the slopes of the supply and demand curves are not the only ones possible.

[9] A five-year-old taxi is not the same thing as a new taxi. Hence it may be more useful to measure the stock in *new taxi equivalents*. For example, one new taxi may be equivalent to two five-year-old taxis or three ten-year-old taxis, etc. With this method of measurement the stock of taxis need not take only integer values (1, 2, 3, etc.). It is perfectly possible to own five-sixths of a taxi by holding one five- and one ten-year-old taxi.

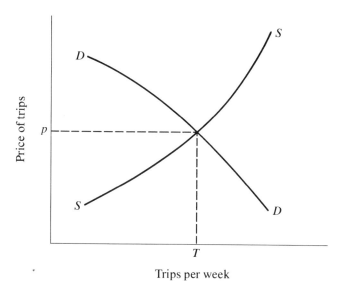

Trips per week

FIGURE 1.2 The market for taxicab trips

date. In Panel A of this figure *dd* represents the demand to own taxis by an individual wealth holder. At any price this curve shows the stock of taxis that an individual will wish to own.[10] Its downward slope reflects the fact that a taxi becomes a less attractive asset to own in comparison with other types of assets, when its price increases. By aggregating the stock that each individual wealth holder will wish to own at each possible price, we obtain the total demand to own taxis: this is represented by *DD* in Panel B.

On any specified date both the aggregate stock of taxis and the holdings of every individual wealth owner are given. These quantities are represented by *OS* and *Os* in the figure. The supply curves faced by wealth holders as a group and by each individual are *SS* and *ss*. These supply curves are vertical straight lines reflecting the fact that on a given date the supply is fixed and given.[11]

The market for taxis is in full equilibrium when wealth holders are both collectively and individually content to hold the existing supplies. Figure 1.3 represents such an equilibrium. At the price *q* wealth holders as a group are willing to hold just the total stock of taxis in existence. This is shown by

---

[10] Clearly the demand to own taxis is related to the fare of taxicab trips. A rise in the fare, for example, will increase the return obtainable from owning a taxi. An increased return will in turn cause owners to wish to add their fleets; that is, it will shift *dd* in Figure 1.3 to the right.

[11] As time passes the stock of taxis changes. New taxis are produced while old ones are scrapped. Moreover, the change in the stock is affected by the current price. For example, if the price of used taxis is high, many wealth holders who want to add to their stocks will prefer to buy new taxis rather than used ones; as a result, the stock will rise. At present these considerations are firmly ignored. They will be discussed in Chapter 8 when we take up the theory of investment. The advantage of proceeding in this way is that the discussion of decisions about *flows* is kept rigidly separate from that of *stock* decisions.

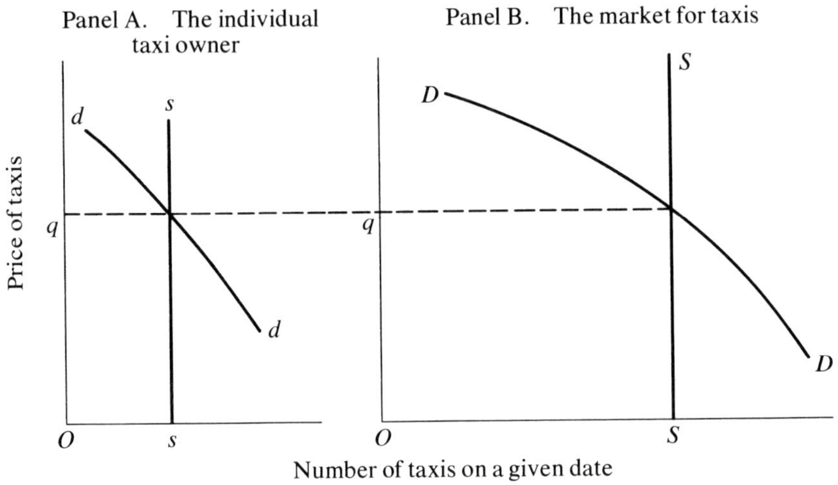

Panel A. The individual
taxi owner

Panel B. The market for taxis

FIGURE 1.3 The market for taxis

the fact that the aggregate supply and demand curves—*SS* and *DD*—
intersect at this price. In addition, each individual wealth holder is satisfied
with his particular share of this total stock. This is shown by the fact that *dd*
and *ss* also intersect at the price *q*. Hence, in contrast to the situation in
flow markets, when the market for a stock commodity is in full equilibrium,
no further transactions occur. Each wealth holder is content with his stock
of commodity and so does not wish either to buy or sell at the prevailing
market price.

It is of course possible for a market to be in equilibrium at the aggregate
level but out of equilibrium at the level of some individual wealth holders. If
this occurs, transactions between individuals will take place with no change
in the market price. At the going price Mr. X may decide he wants to hold
one more taxi while at the same time Mr. Y decides he wants to hold one less
taxi. In terms of Figure 1.3 the demand curve of Mr. X will shift to the right,
the demand curve of Mr. Y will shift to the left, but the aggregate demand
curve, *DD*, will be unaffected. Both Mr. X and Mr. Y will be out of
equilibrium. However, since Mr. X is willing to buy one taxi and Mr. Y is
willing to sell one taxi at price *q*, this transaction can be negotiated between
the two parties without affecting any other wealth holder and without dis-
turbing the aggregate equilibrium of the market.

This situation is, in fact, typical of that in the markets for most stock
commodities. During any given trading session large numbers of individual
transactions may be negotiated with little or no change in the market price.[12]
These transactions occur as a result of the continuing shifts in the demand
curves of individual wealth holders. If these shifts in demand were to cease,

---

[12] The New York Stock Exchange is a classic example of this phenomenon. On any day the
volume of dealing is very large in relation to the size of any price changes that occur.

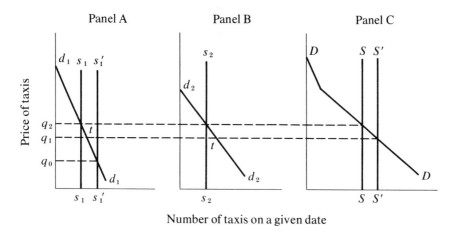

FIGURE 1.4 Trading in the taxi market

trading would come to a halt and the market would settle into full equilibrium. This situation contrasts with the one in flow markets where dealing continues even after the market has come to equilibrium. Note also that in a flow market the amount of the commodity changing hands is represented by the intersection of the demand and supply curves but that this is not the case in a market for a stock commodity.

It is instructive to examine how the market for a stock commodity responds to change in supply. Such an examination gives us additional insight into the nature of equilibrium in such markets. Consider Figure 1.4.

For diagrammatic simplicity, assume (in this figure) that there are only two individuals in the market.[13] Their demand curves for taxi holdings are represented by $d_1 d_1$ and $d_2 d_2$ in Panels A and B. DD in Panel C represents the aggregate demand for taxis. The two individuals initially hold stocks of s_1 and s_2 taxis, respectively, and the market is in full equilibrium with the two individuals individually and collectively content to hold the existing stock at price q_2.

Suppose now that the first individual receives an increase in his stock of taxis from s_1 to s'_1. This is represented in Panel A by a shift to the right of the supply curve from $s_1 s_1$ to $s'_1 s'_1$. As a result, this individual is out of equilibrium. At the current price q_2, his stock of taxis exceeds his demand to hold them. Thus he is willing to retain the entire addition to his stock only if the price falls from q_2 to q_0. At prices between q_0 and q_2, he is willing to sell part of his holdings, since at those prices his demand for taxis is less than his newly augmented stock.

From Panel B, however, we see that at prices below q_2 the second

---

[13] However, we will assume that each individual acts *as though* there were a large number of other participants in the market.

individual is willing to buy additional taxis, since at those prices his demand exceeds his present supply. We conclude, therefore, that there is scope for a mutually advantageous exchange between the two individuals. At prices between q_0 and q_2 one individual wishes to buy and the other wishes to sell. In particular, at price q_1 the first individual is willing to sell and the second is willing to buy t taxis. As a result, t taxis will change hands at that price. The market then will return to a new full equilibrium in which the price is lower (q_1 is less than q_2), all market participants are holding increased stocks of the commodity (taxis), and no further transactions occur. In particular, in the new equilibrium situation the first individual holds $s'_1 - t$ taxis and the second individual holds $s_2 + t$ taxis.

Note that the same final conclusion can be obtained simply by observing the aggregate situation. The increase in the total stock is represented by the shift in the total supply curve from SS to $S'S'$. With an unchanged aggregate demand the price must fall from q_2 to q_1 if market participants collectively are to be willing to hold this addition to the total stock. However, the manner in which the stock is allocated *between* participants and the trading that takes place before equilibrium is restored cannot be inferred from these aggregate relationships.[14]

References

Ackley, Gardner. *Macroeconomic Theory*, Chapter 1. New York: Macmillan, 1961.

Smith, Warren L. *Macroeconomics*, Chapter 1. Homewood, Illinois: Richard D. Irwin, 1970.

Both these texts provide excellent introductions to the scope and method of macroeconomics.

Questions for Classroom Discussion

1. Give examples of three *stock* and three *flow* concepts in economics.
2. In what ways may a household change its economic position in the future by decisions it makes today? What about a business firm? A state or local government?
3. Suppose a hitherto unknown Cézanne painting is discovered. Explain the market process by which the market prices of all Cézanne paintings are affected by this discovery. For simplicity, you may assume all Cézanne paintings are identical.

---

[14] In this chapter we have employed several notational conventions, which we will continue to use throughout the chapters that follow. The symbol p will always represent the price of some flow variable. Similarly, q will stand for the price of some asset. Finally, if we introduce a variable that takes a series of values, their relative magnitudes in most cases will be indicated by the use of subscripts. Thus p_0 is less than p_1, which in turn is less than p_2.

Social Accounting

2

Every month a huge volume of statistical data is published by governmental and other agencies. For economists, government officials, and others seeking to understand what is going on in our economy there is assuredly no scarcity of prompt and accurate factual information.[1] To cite a few widely used data series we now have monthly (and in some cases weekly) information on such important variables[2] as retail sales, employment and unemployment, consumer and wholesale prices, factory orders, inventories and sales, and the quantities of demand deposits and currency outstanding.

However, the most comprehensive bodies of economic data available are the National Income and Product Accounts, prepared by the U.S. Department of Commerce, the Flow-of-Funds Accounts, which are constructed and published by the Federal Reserve System, and several sets of national balance sheets, prepared both by private researchers and by the Federal Reserve System. An important advantage of viewing the performance of our economy through these three sets of social accounts is that the data are presented in a logical and internally consistent scheme. Macroeconomists and monetary theorists have found that this scheme is particularly useful in developing theories about how our economy works.

The National Income and Product Accounts

These accounts document the flows of new commodities produced in the economy and the corresponding flows of income received. To begin our discussion of these accounts, consider for a moment the situation of Robinson Crusoe alone on his island. Suppose that Robinson owns a plow, and with its aid grows 2,000 pounds of yams a year. (Assume that yams are the sole product of the island.) If he sets the price[3] of yams at 50 cents a pound, then the value of the gross island *product* is $1,000 per year. Imagine now

---

[1] This does not mean we are satisfied; it seems that the more data we have, the greater is our appetite for more!

[2] What is the dimension of each of these variables? Are they stocks, flows, or neither?

[3] Since there is only one commodity and Robinson is the sole inhabitant of his island, there is no need for him to invent money. For stylistic reasons we suppose that he does his accounts in terms of dollars, although the price he chooses to put on yams is of course arbitrary.

that he sets up a corporation, RC Inc., with himself as sole employee, sole supplier of plow services,[4] sole owner, and sole customer. RC Inc. produces 2,000 pounds of yams in a year, which are valued at $1,000. In his role of consumer, Robinson purchases these yams from their producer, RC Inc. Thus, the gross island *product* and the gross island *expenditure* each amount to $1,000. From the proceeds of the sale of yams, RC Inc. pays wages to its employee, Robinson Crusoe, and rents to its supplier of plow services, also Robinson Crusoe. The surplus after meeting these outlays is profit, which is paid to the owner of RC Inc., who is, of course, Robinson Crusoe. Thus the gross island *income*[5] (wages plus rents plus profits) is also $1,000. Since yams are the only commodity, Robinson spends the whole of his income on them.

This simple example illustrates the fundamental identities among gross product, expenditure, and income. The accounts of a more complex economy preserve these identities, the principal complications being the existence of indirect taxes, imports, intermediate products, depreciation, and inventories. Notwithstanding these complications, total activity in the economy may be measured in the same three ways: by adding the value of the net *output* of all productive enterprises, by adding total *spending* on newly produced products by all households, firms, foreigners, and governments, or by adding the *incomes* of all factors of production in the economy.

As a somewhat more complicated example, consider the purchase of a new suit of clothes by a household[6] from a retail store for $100. Such a purchase is a component of gross national expenditures.[7] Part of this sum, say, $60, goes to buy the suit from the manufacturer. The remaining $40 is paid out by the retail store in wages, rent, interest, and profits and thus forms part of the gross national income. The retail store is a productive enterprise, its product being the service of getting the suit from the manufacturer to the final purchaser. The value of this product is equal to the increase in the value of the suit ($40) as it passes through the store's hands. Note that this *value added* to the suit is identically equal to the income arising in the retail store.

Of the $60 received by the suit manufacturer, part (say, $25) goes to buy cloth, buttons, and other materials, and the remainder is paid out in wages, rent, interest, and profits. Once again the value added to the materials in transforming them into the suit ($35) equals the income arising in the suit-manufacturing enterprise.

Without proceeding further with the story of the suit it should be clear that at each stage of the manufacturing process, the sum of all incomes arising from the production of the suit must equal the value added to the suit at that

---

[4] That is, Robinson Crusoe leases his plow to RC Inc.
[5] In this simple economy the division of income between wages, rents, and profits is arbitrary.
[6] In fact, the following discussion does not depend on whether the buyer of the suit is a household, a business, a government, or a foreigner.
[7] Specifically, in the United States accounts such a purchase would be classified as part of "Personal Consumption Expenditures."

stage. In addition, the total of all incomes arising at all stages of production must be equal to the final expenditure on the suit, namely, $100. Thus if over a period of a month ten suits were produced and sold, the accounts might appear as in Table 2.1.

In this table total income is subdivided according to the *industry* (retailing, manufacturing, etc.) in which it is earned. A second method of organizing the accounts is to break the total down by *type of income* (wages, rents, profits, etc.). An example of such a classification is shown later in Table 2.4. The United States accounts provide both types of classification. In addition, gross income may be classified according to its *recipients* (households, businesses, governments, and foreigners). The Department of Commerce does not publish data for this classification, but it can readily be derived from the available data.

In the example just given, it was assumed that the suit of clothes was produced exclusively in the United States and all income generated in its production was received by U.S. residents. In reality, many commodities—including raw materials, semifinished goods, and final products—are imported from abroad. The production of these commodities does not generate income here but it does in foreign countries. Clearly, these items do not belong in the gross national product of the United States.

Thus, in terms of our accounting framework, spending on imported commodities must be excluded from gross expenditures if the identities among output, income, and expenditures are to be maintained. If, for example, all buttons come from abroad, the accounts of our imaginary suit-making economy will appear as in Table 2.2. In this table, imports are deducted from the expenditures side of the accounts. Income from button manufacture no longer appears since it does not accrue in the United States. Throughout the remainder of this chapter and in most of the book the words *expenditure* and *spending* should be taken to mean outlays only on U.S.-produced commodities and to exclude all imports.

Up to now it has been assumed that the entire market price paid by the purchaser of a suit (or any other commodity) accrued to the seller. This will not be the case if there are *indirect taxes or subsidies*. The sales taxes levied by many state and local governments are examples of such taxes. As a

Table 2.1 Income and Product Accounts—Suit Manufacture

	Dollars		*Dollars*
Purchases of suits	1,000	Income from retailing	400
		Income from suit manufacture	350
		Income from cloth manufacture	100
		Income from button manufacture	50
		Income from earlier stages	100
Gross Expenditure	1,000	Gross Income	1,000

Table 2.2 Income and Product Accounts—Suit Manufacture with Imported Buttons

	Dollars		Dollars
Purchases of suits	1,000	Income from retailing	400
		Income from suit manufacture	350
Imports of buttons	−50	Income from cloth manufacture	100
		Income from earlier stages	100
Gross Expenditure on U.S. Products	950	Gross Income accruing in United States	950

result of these taxes and subsidies, the sums paid by the buyers of commodities differ from those received by the sellers.[8] However, it is these latter sums that generate the incomes of factors of production. If, for example, the price of a suit includes indirect taxes of $10,[9] only $90 are available for payments to the factors of production.

Two other minor complications should also be mentioned at this point. First, National Income in the United States is defined to exclude the incomes of government-operated businesses, such as the Postal Service. Second, if businesses use part of their sales incomes to make gifts, these funds are not available for payments to factors of production. However, the gifts themselves are not treated as incomes of the recipients since they are not given in return for any services rendered. Hence National Income also excludes business transfer payments. When these complications are taken into account, the basic equalities become:

> Gross national expenditures at market prices
> = Gross national product at market prices
> = Gross national product at factor cost
>   + Indirect business taxes
>   − Subsidies.

> Gross national product at factor cost
>   − Surplus of government enterprises
>   − Business transfer payments
> = Gross national income.

In the discussion so far, no reference has been made to the role of

---

[8] Expenditures valued at the prices paid by purchasers are termed expenditures *at market prices*. When evaluated at the prices received by sellers, they are described as expenditures *at factor cost*. However, the phrases *at market prices* and *at factor cost* are not used by the compilers of the U.S. accounts. In the United States the aggregate that is referred to as the gross national product (GNP) is, in fact, gross national expenditure at market prices; that is, it is constructed by adding up everyone's expenditures rather than by adding everyone's product.
[9] Note that this sum includes any indirect taxes imposed on materials incorporated in the suit as well as those levied directly on the finished product.

inventories. However, if the retail store purchases a suit from the manufacturer and adds it to its stock of suits rather than selling it, this transaction will generate the same amount of income during the month as does a sale to a household. Conversely, if the retailer sells a suit out of inventory and does not replace it within the month, the transaction produces no income since no production takes place. The same thing is true of stocks of raw materials and semifinished products. If the suit manufacturer adds to its inventory of cloth, this generates income in cloth manufacture, but if buttons are supplied out of stock, no income arises in the button-making industry.

In order to preserve the identity between income and expenditure and yet take account of the role of stocks of commodities, inventory changes must be treated as a component of gross expenditures. In effect, businesses that accumulate stocks of commodities are treated as *purchasing* these goods from themselves at the going market price. To preserve symmetry, reductions in inventories are regarded as *negative expenditures.* The net change in business inventories may be positive or negative.

Hence as an accounting identity we have

Gross national product at market prices
= Gross final purchases by households, businesses,
governments, and foreigners
+ Net additions to business inventories.

Table 2.3 provides an example. In this table we assume that suit retailers, in addition to selling 10 suits to households, also add 4 suits to their inventories; that is, they purchase 4 suits from themselves. Thus a total of 14 suits is produced and sold. During the same period suit manufacturers supply all their raw material needs (for 14 suits at $25 a suit) by reducing

Table 2.3 Income and Product Accounts—The Role of Inventory Change

	Dollars		*Dollars*
Expenditures on suits by final purchasers	1,000	Income in retailing	560
Net change in business inventories	50	Income in manufacture	490
Inventory accumulation by retailers	400	Income in earlier stages	0
Inventory decumulation by manufacturers	−350		
Gross Expenditures	1,050	Gross Income	1,050

NOTE: For simplicity we assume there are no imports, no indirect taxes or subsidies, no government enterprises, and no business transfers.

their stocks of these goods. Hence no production occurs in cloth or button manufacture or in any earlier stages of the productive process. Thus net additions to inventories are $50, consisting of a positive item of $400 (representing stock accumulation by the retailers) and a negative item of $350 (representing stock decumulation by suit manufacturers). Thus, gross expenditures, product and income, are each larger by this amount.

Apart from the change in inventories of raw materials and semifinished goods, gross national expenditures include only purchases of newly produced final products. Spending on intermediate products is excluded since we would be doublecounting if, for example, we included both the expenditure on the suit (which is a final product) and the expenditure on the cloth (which is an intermediate product). Expenditure on used commodities is excluded because this does not generate income: When Mr. A sells his car to Mr. B, each experiences a change in the form in which he is holding his wealth, but neither receives any income.[10]

A difficulty we glossed over in the previous paragraph is the question of the appropriate definition of an intermediate product. From one point of view (not a very helpful one) virtually all purchases are of intermediate products. For example, an automobile is not wanted for its own sake but because when used in conjunction with various other intermediate products (gasoline, oil, etc.) it "produces" a new commodity, namely, automobile services. Even if production is viewed in the more usual sense as an activity that is carried on in firms, the definition of intermediate products remains necessarily arbitrary: There is, for example, no essential difference between the cloth, buttons, and thread used in the production of a suit and the sewing machine used by the tailor. To resolve this difficulty national income accountants have adopted two conventions. First, all expenditures by households, foreigners, and governments are treated as spending on final products. Second, for purchases by productive enterprises a commodity is treated as an intermediate product if it is used up in less than a year and as a final product if it lasts more than a year. The choice of a year as the cutoff period is dictated by the fact that the accounting period is also a year. Under this convention cloth purchased by a suit manufacturer would be treated as an intermediate product but a sewing machine would be regarded as a final product.

In the process of producing goods and services, part of the nation's stock of capital goods is used up. Hence part of current output should be set aside and used to maintain the capital stock intact. For example, if Robinson Crusoe eats all of his yam crop, leaving none for planting next year, he will find his future consumption sharply reduced. An advanced economy is in a

---

[10] When a dealer acts as an intermediary, he will make a profit, which is part of gross national income. In this case Mr. B's expenditure has two components: the cost of the car and the cost of the dealer's services. Those services are a newly produced final product and the part of Mr. B's total outlay that represents the purchase of those services is included in gross national expenditures.

Table 2.4 Simplified Income and Product Accounts

Expenditures on newly produced final products by households, businesses, foreigners, and governments	Compensation of employees
− Imports of goods and services	+ Corporate profits
+ Net additions to business inventories	+ Income of noncorporate business
= Gross national expenditures at market prices	+ Rental income of persons
= *Gross national product at market prices*	+ Net interest income of persons
− Indirect business taxes	= *National income*
+ Subsidies	
= Gross national product at factor cost	
− Capital consumption allowances	
= Net national product at factor cost	
− Business transfer payments	
− Surplus of government-owned enterprises	
− Statistical discrepancy	
= *National income*	

similar (though less precarious) situation. Unless it uses part of its current output to replace worn-out factories, machines, homes, etc., its standard of living will be lower in the future.[11]

For this reason the term *income* is reserved for that portion of gross output that may safely be consumed without reducing the nation's stock of capital. The portion set aside to maintain capital intact is known as the *capital consumption allowance, or depreciation.*[12] This allowance is deducted from the gross product in order to arrive at the net national income.

In the United States separate estimates of gross national expenditures and of net national income are prepared. The discussion of the past several pages has been concerned with the relation between these two aggregates. Table 2.4 shows the reconciliation in tabular form. Although the estimates of expenditures and income are made from quite different sets of data, the statistical discrepancy that is unaccounted for is usually not large.

In principle all final expenditures (excluding inventory changes) may be divided into purchases of goods and services that are consumed immediately (*consumption*) and purchases of long-lived commodities that yield a stream

---

[11] When present needs are extremely pressing, for example, in war time, the nation may choose not to replace capital. In this case it is, in a very real sense, mortgaging the future to win the war in the present.

[12] In the national product accounts prepared by the U.S. Department of Commerce, no deduction is made for depreciation on consumer durables (cars, furniture, appliances, etc.). Estimates of this item are available in the flow-of-funds accounts and in a number of private sources.

of services over a period of time (*fixed capital formation*). In practice this distinction (like that between final products and intermediate goods) is necessarily arbitrary.

Business expenditures on final products, excluding inventory accumulation, are exclusively capital formation since firms (by definition) do not consume and since their purchases of short-lived commodities are not a part of final product because (again by definition) such goods are intermediate products.

Households engage in both consumption and capital formation. In the official Department of Commerce accounts, only purchases of new homes are treated as capital formation; all other household spending on newly produced goods and services is regarded as consumption. However, in this book we will follow the convention adopted in the flow-of-funds accounts, treating household purchases of other types of durable goods (including cars, furniture, and appliances as well as new homes) as a part of fixed capital formation.

Governments also engage in both capital formation and consumption. Some of their purchases are for immediate use—the services of government employees, for example—while others are for commodities such as roads, office buildings, and military hardware that will yield flows of services over many years. Although in recent years the Commerce Department has published data on government capital formation, the distinction between current and capital spending is not carried over into the aggregate accounts nor into the flow-of-funds accounts. In these accounts all government outlays are treated, in effect, as a form of consumption. In addition, the data on capital consumption allowances do not include depreciation on government-owned capital goods but only that on capital owned by the private sector.

When speaking of government spending it should also be noted that *transfer payments,* such as social security and welfare outlays and interest payments on the public debt, are not treated as part of final expenditures. The justification for this is that such outlays (unlike payments to civil servants) are not payments for services rendered.[13] That is, no additional production results.

To the extent that a household owns durable assets it receives a flow of services from those assets, which is part of its income even though it does not accrue in the form of money receipts.[14] This type of income is known as *imputed income.* Correspondingly, there is of course an equal amount of imputed consumption of durable-good services. The official accounts in-

---

[13] Interest payments by households and governments are also not regarded as outlays for services rendered and hence are not part of gross national product or of national income. Hence the item *net interest income* consists only of income received from businesses and foreigners.

[14] In Chapter 1 we mentioned another type of income that did not accrue in the form of money. What was it?

Table 2.5 Components of National Expenditure and Product

Personal consumption expenditures
+ Imputed value of services of household durables[a]
+ Government purchases of final products
    Government capital formation
    Compensation of employees
    Other current items
+ Exports minus imports of goods and services
+ Gross private capital formation
    Business purchases of plant and equipment
    Business residential construction
    Household purchases of new homes
    Household purchases of other durables
+ Additions to business inventories
= *Gross national expenditure at market prices*
= *Gross national product at market prices*
    − Business capital consumption
    − Household capital consumption[b]
= *Net national product at market prices*

---

[a] In the official accounts only the services of owner-occupied homes are included in this item.
[b] This item includes only depreciation on owner-occupied homes in the official accounts.

clude estimates of the value of housing services consumed by owner-occupiers.[15] However, if purchases of other types of durable commodities by households are treated as capital formation, consistency requires that the flow of services that these commodities yield should be added to consumption. No official estimates of the value of this flow are available, but a number of private researchers have made estimates. If this item were included in the official statistics, the measured gross national product would be correspondingly increased.

In the light of this discussion the expenditures side of the accounts may be expanded as shown in Table 2.5.

The gross product of Robinson Crusoe's island was 2,000 pounds of yams, which were valued at 50 cents a pound. Similarly, the gross national product of a more complex economy has an *output* dimension and a *price* dimension. However, since there are many commodities, neither output nor prices can be measured in terms of physical units (like pounds of yams). Nonetheless, the change in physical output between two periods may be measured by estimating how much expenditures would have changed *if* prices had remained constant.

In the United States, the Department of Commerce prepares estimates of gross national expenditures both at current prices and at prices that pre-

---

[15] In the case of nonfarm households these estimates are incorporated in the item, *rental income of persons*. Services from farm homes are included in *income from noncorporate business*.

vailed in some specified base period. At present the base period in use is 1972. Thus in 1975 the gross national product was $1,516 billion when valued at current prices but only $1,192 billion at 1972 prices. Thus actual expenditures were $1,516 billion, but if the same goods and services had been bought at 1972 prices, expenditures would have amounted to only $1,192 billion. The corresponding figures for 1974 were $1,413 billion and $1,214 billion. Thus between the two years, the total increase in GNP amounted to $103 billion, but this increase was entirely due to a sharp increase in prices, and the real output of goods and services actually fell.

By dividing GNP at current prices by GNP at 1972 prices we obtain the so-called *implicit price deflator,* which measures the extent to which prices have, on the average, changed since the base period. By this measure prices rose by more than 27 percent between 1972 and 1975 and by about 9 percent between 1974 and 1975 alone.[16] The deflator is a slightly different type of price index from others in common use, such as the consumer price, or cost-of-living, index.[17] The latter indicates by how much the cost of a *fixed bundle* of commodities has changed whereas the former refers to the cost of a *changing bundle,* since the composition of the GNP is continually varying.[18]

If we represent gross national product (or expenditure) at current prices by Y, gross output (or GNP at constant prices) by Q, and the average level of prices (measured by the deflator) by p, we have

$$Y = p \cdot Q$$

Any change in Y may be divided into the change due to varying Q and the change due to varying p. In later chapters we will analyze the factors that determine this division.[19]

National Balance Sheets

The items in the national income and product accounts refer exclusively to the flows of income, output, and expenditure over some specified accounting period. In macroeconomics and especially in monetary theory, we are also

---

[16] Check these calculations to be sure that you understand the process.

[17] It also differs in terms of coverage, since it purports to measure the average prices of all commodities entering into gross expenditures, whereas the CPI, for example, only refers to the items bought by an average middle-income household.

[18] In technical terms the implicit price deflator is a *variable-weighted price index* while the consumer price index is a *fixed-weighted price index.*

[19] In principle, gross (or net) national income could also be divided into price and quantity components. For simplicity, for example, we might assume that there are only two factors of production, labor and capital, the owners of which, laborers and capitalists, receive income in the form of wages and rent. Changes in aggregate income can occur as a result of either changes in the prices of the factors of production (the wage of labor and the rental of capital) or changes in the quantities in use. If we could obtain data on these prices, the division of income into its components could be made. For an example of an attempt to carry out this exercise, see L. R. Christensen and D. W. Jorgenson, "U. S. Real Product and Real Factor Input, 1929–1967," *The Review of Income and Wealth,* Vol. XVI, Number 1 (March 1970).

Table 2.6 Accounting Framework for a National Balance Sheet*

Assets	Private Sectors				Total Private Sector	Total Government Sector	Total Net Supply
	1	2	. . .	*m*			
1							
2							
.							
.							
.							
n							
Sector net worth					Private net worth	Government net worth	National wealth

* We assume a closed economy; that is, there are no outstanding net claims on foreigners.

interested in the stocks of the various types of assets and liabilities that exist in the economy on a given date. National balance sheets attempt to document this type of information. At present no complete series of balance-sheet data are available on a regular basis from official sources.[20] The Federal Reserve system publishes partial balance sheets—detailing the stocks of *financial* assets and liabilities—in conjunction with the flow-of-funds accounts. A number of private researchers[21] have constructed complete sets of accounts, including both financial and tangible assets, but these are not updated on a regular basis. Nonetheless, the basic *accounting framework* of a national balance sheet is not complicated and can be described briefly in terms of Table 2.6.

Each column in Table 2.6 represents a given *sector* of the economy. The number of sectors that are useful to distinguish in a particular balance sheet will depend on the problem at hand. As a minimum we would require two sectors—the private sector and the government sector. Most actual balance sheets distinguish three government sectors—the federal government, the Federal Reserve System, and the state and local governments—and at least three private sectors—households, financial business, and nonfinancial business. Frequently, they provide considerable detail on the assets and liabilities of the financial business sector.

Each row represents a particular type of asset, which may be a physical

[20] This is partly due to the severe estimation problems involved. However, the fact that macroeconomic theorizing has, until recently, emphasized the relationships among *flow variables* and has tended to neglect *stock variables* has meant that there has been less impetus to the development of this type of data.

[21] See, for example, Raymond W. Goldsmith and Robert Lipsey, *Studies in the National Balance Sheet of the United States,* 2 vols. (Princeton: Princeton University Press, 1963).

asset (for example, plant and equipment) or a financial asset (for example, government securities or savings deposits). A positive entry in the table indicates that the sector in question is a *net holder* of the asset indicated, while a negative entry means that it is *net issuer*.

The sum of the entries across any row is the *net supply* of the asset concerned. Since all financial assets held by one sector are necessarily issued by other sectors, the net supply of each financial asset is zero. This is simply another way of saying that all financial instruments are simultaneously claims on some sectors and claims by other sectors.

The sum down any column is the net worth, or wealth, of the sector concerned and consists of its holdings of physical assets plus its claims on all other sectors minus claims by all other sectors on it. Total private net worth (private wealth), obtained by adding net worth across the private sectors of the economy, is then equal to the value of the stock of all privately owned physical assets plus private net claims on the government. This is because, for the private economy as a whole, all financial instruments issued by one private sector and held by another cancel out against each other. Moreover, since all businesses are ultimately owned by households, so that the latter have a residual claim on all business assets, the only sectors with a nonzero net worth are the household sector and the government sector. Hence private net worth coincides with household net worth.

Finally, note that the national wealth, obtained by adding the net worth of the private and government sectors of the economy, consists only of tangible assets. This is because claims by the private sector on the government are exactly balanced by the latter's liability to meet those claims.

As an example of a national balance sheet, consider the simple matrix shown in Table 2.7. There are four sectors and four types of assets. All private sectors own tangible assets.[22] Bonds are issued by the government and nonfinancial businesses and are held by households and financial institutions. Deposits are issued by financial institutions and are held by households, nonfinancial businesses, and governments. The equity of businesses belongs to households. Private net worth comprises physical assets, valued at $900, plus net claims on the government of $250. Since all businesses are owned by households, private net worth is equal to household net worth.

Entries in the balance-sheet matrix may change between a pair of dates for four reasons: (1) a change in the market value of existing assets, (2) trading between sectors in existing physical or financial assets, (3) the issue (production) of new financial assets, and (4) the production of new physical assets. The flow-of-funds accounts (to be discussed in the next section) document

---

[22] National balance sheets typically ignore government-owned tangible assets. This is partly because these assets are in many cases difficult to evaluate. For example, how does one go about valuing the Lincoln Memorial or the nation's strategic missile force? In addition, however, the value of these items, in sharp contrast to the value of assets owned by the private sector, does not influence the behavior of governments, and hence their value is of less interest to the macroeconomic theorist seeking to explain the behavior of economic agents.

Table 2.7 Hypothetical National Balance Sheet

	Households	*Non-financial Business*	*Financial Business*	*Total Private Sector*	*Govern-ment*	*Total Net Supply*
Physical assets	+300	+500	+100	+900	0	+900
Bonds	+100	−50	+250	+300	−300	0
Deposits	+200	+50	−300	−50	+50	0
Equity of business	+550	−500	−50	0	0	0
Net worth	+1,150	0	0	+1,150	−250	+900

the changes in the balance-sheet matrix that result from the last three of these factors. From the point of view of macroeconomic theory and policy, there is particular interest in point (4), since the production of tangible assets generates income and provides employment in the economy.

The Flow-of-Funds Accounts

As indicated in our discussion of income and product accounts, the gross national product may be divided into personal consumption, government expenditures, and gross private investment,[23] which includes both fixed capital formation and net additions to business inventories.

$$Y \equiv C + G + I \qquad (2.1)$$

If we describe that portion of gross output that is not consumed (either by households or by governments[24]) as *gross saving, S*, this identity may be written in equivalent form as

$$S \equiv Y - C - G \equiv I$$

In this form the identity states that gross saving is equal to gross investment. Finally, if capital consumption allowances are deducted, we see that *net saving* is necessarily equal to *net investment*.

---

[23] From now on, exports and imports are ignored.

[24] In this section we treat all government outlays as forms of consumption. If the distinction between government consumption and government investment were introduced, we would have

$$G \equiv C^G + I^G$$

and the identity between saving and investment would become

$$S = S^P + S^G \equiv Y - C^P - C^G \equiv I^P + I^G = I$$

where the superscripts refer to the private and government sectors respectively.

$$S_{\text{NET}} = Y - CCA - C - G = I - CCA = I_{\text{NET}}$$

where $Y - CCA$ is net national product at market prices. This identity demonstrates that the economy's net output must be either consumed or added to the stock of tangible assets, including inventories. Incidentally, it also shows that the economy as a whole can save only by accumulating tangible commodities. Although a single individual can save for the future by accumulating paper claims on other individuals, the economy as a whole cannot do this.[25]

Each sector of the economy receives a certain share of the gross national product. Gross saving by a sector is equal to the portion of the GNP that accrues to it minus its consumption. Net saving is equal to gross saving minus the depreciation that occurs in the sector's stock of physical assets.

The share of any sector in the GNP is equal to the income that it receives from the production of final goods and services plus or minus any transfers received from or paid to other sectors. The business share of GNP is equal to the portion of gross profits that is neither paid to governments in taxes nor paid to households in dividends.[26] Moreover, since businesses (by definition) do not consume, business saving is equal to business income. The government's share of total product is equal to its total tax receipts minus its expenditures on transfer payments (such as welfare and social security benefits) and on interest payments. Government saving is equal to its share of product minus its outlays on goods and services. Since no attempt is made to estimate depreciation on government assets, no distinction is made between net and gross government saving. All product not appropriated by business and government accrues to households. Thus gross household saving is equal to this share of total product minus expenditures on personal consumption.[27]

To the extent that any sector does not spend its share of the gross national product on consumption, it must either add to its holdings of assets or reduce its liabilities. Thus, as with the economy as a whole, saving and investment by any sector are necessarily equal. In the case of a single sector, however, investment consists not only of its acquisitions of newly produced tangible assets (so-called real investment) but also of its net *financial* investment.[28] Unlike the economy as a whole, a single sector *can*

---

[25] This conclusion is not true in the case of an open economy—one that trades with other economies. An open economy can save by accumulating claims against foreigners.

[26] Noncorporate businesses are assumed, by the flow-of-funds statisticians, to pay out all their net income to their owners. Hence their retentions consist only of their capital consumption allowances. The reason for this convention is that owners of noncorporate businesses rarely maintain separate household and business accounts; that is, they do not pay dividends to themselves.

[27] Remember that household consumption includes only expenditures on nondurable goods and services. Spending on durables (homes, cars, etc.) is treated as a form of saving. In principle, household income and consumption spending should include imputed expenditures on the services of durables. In the United States accounts, data are presented only for the services of owner-occupied homes.

[28] In principle, a sector may also use its saving to purchase existing physical assets from other

save by adding to its stock of financial assets. Net financial investment by any sector comprises the additions to its financial assets minus the additions to its liabilities.

Thus for any sector, say, sector m, the identity between saving and investment takes the following form:

> Gross saving by sector m
> = Gross investment by sector m
> = Gross purchases of real assets by sector m
>   + Net purchases [29] by sector m of claims issued by other sectors (net lending)
>   − Net issues[30] to other sectors of claims on sector m (net borrowing)

The flow-of-funds accounts provide a detailed description of the financial transactions (the last two lines) of this identity. Altogether some twenty sectors and more than thirty classes of assets are distinguished.

The national balance sheet shows the asset holdings of the various sectors of our economy. The flow-of-funds accounts document the changes in these asset holdings. Since the net change in the total assets of any sector is equal to that sector's net saving, the flow-of-funds accounts may be thought of as describing the link between the income and product accounts, which document the sources of saving, and the balance sheets, which document the assets in which accumulated savings are held.

The flow-of-funds accounts may be set out in a matrix form similar to Table 2.6. This is done in Table 2.8. Assuming no change in asset prices, the change in the net worth of each sector is equal to its net saving. This in turn is equal to gross real investment, including additions to inventories, minus capital consumption allowances on physical assets plus net financial investment. Net financial investment by each sector is equal to its purchases of financial instruments issued by other sectors minus its sales of instruments issued by other sectors and minus its net sales of instruments issued by itself. For the economy as a whole, net financial investment is zero so that the change in national wealth over any accounting period is necessarily equal to real investment minus depreciation. These relationships are shown in Table 2.8. The national totals shown in this matrix will coincide with the corresponding aggregates in the income and product accounts.

In the following four chapters we will be concerned with an economy that comprises only two sectors: a private sector and a government sector. We

---

sectors (for example, household purchases of used cars from businesses). However, the amount of such intersector trading is probably small and it is ignored.

[29] Net purchases of financial assets comprises gross purchases minus gross sales; only the net flows are recorded in the accounts.

[30] Net issues of financial assets comprises gross issues minus gross redemptions; only the net flows are recorded in the accounts.

Table 2.8 Specimen Flow-of-Funds Matrix

Transactions	*Private Sectors*				*Total Private Sector*	*Total Government Sector*	*National Totals*
	1	2	. . .	m			
Gross saving							Gross national saving
− Capital consumption							− Total capital consumption
= Net saving							= Net national saving
= Gross real investment							= Gross real investment
− Capital consumption							− Total capital consumption
+ Net financial investment							+ Zero
Net acquisitions of claims on other sectors							Net lending
Net issue of claims to other sectors							Net borrowing
Change in net worth*					Change in private net worth	Change in government net worth	Change in national wealth

* Assuming no change in asset prices over the accounting period.

will find that the basic flow-of-funds indentities play an important role in the analysis of the economy.

For the private sector of the economy, the basic flow-of-funds identity between saving and investment appears as

> Gross national product at market prices (Y)
> − Tax payments to government (T)
> + Transfers received from government (R)
> − Personal consumption (C)
> = Private saving (S^P)
> = Gross real investment (I)
> + Net private financial investment

The private sector as a whole can engage in financial investment only by acquiring claims issued by the government. These claims consist of notes and coin (M) and interest-yielding securities (B). Hence net private financial investment must equal the change in the amounts of government securities and currency outstanding.

Writing this flow-of-funds identity symbolically, we have [31]

$$Y - T + R - C = I + \Delta M + \Delta B$$

or

$$Y - T + R = C + I + \Delta M + \Delta B \qquad (2.2)$$

In this form the identity shows that the private share of gross output may either be consumed, invested in new physical assets, or used to add to private holdings of government-issued money or securities.

For the government sector the corresponding identity states that

> Taxes received from the private sector (T)
> − Transfer payments to the private sector (R)
> − Government consumption (G)
> = Government saving
> = Net government financial investment

Positive government financial investment implies that the liabilities of the government to the private sector are reduced. Net financial investment by the government is, therefore, equal to the net decrease in the private sector's holdings of claims against the government.

Symbolically, this second identity may be written

$$T - R - G = -\Delta M - \Delta B$$

or

$$T = R + G - \Delta M - \Delta B \qquad (2.3)$$

---

[31] The symbol Δ means *change in*.

In this form the identity shows that the government may use its tax receipts to make transfer payments, to purchase newly produced goods and services, or to reduce its monetary or bond liabilities.

Finally, we note that identities (2.1), (2.2), and (2.3) are not independent of one another. For example, if (2.2) and (2.3) are added together, we obtain

$$(Y - T - R - C) + T = (I + \Delta M + \Delta B) + (R + G - \Delta M - \Delta B)$$

which, when simplified, reduces to (2.1), $Y = C + I + G$. This simply reflects the fact that gross national saving and investment are equal to the sums of saving and investment by the individual sectors.

References

Federal Reserve Bulletin. Board of Governors of the Federal Reserve System, Washington, D. C.: Monthly.

Complete data on flow-of-funds accounts are published in the October issue each year.

Flow of Funds Accounts, 1945–68. Board of Governors of the Federal Reserve System, Washington, D. C.: 1970.

An explanation of the flow-of-funds accounts with historical data.

Kendrick, John W. *Economic Accounts and Their Uses.* New York: McGraw-Hill, 1972.

An excellent text covering all aspects of social accounting.

National Income. U.S. Department of Commerce, Office of Business Economics, Washington, D. C.: 1954.

A detailed description of the methods and sources used in constructing income and product accounts.

Survey of Current Business. U.S. Department of Commerce, Bureau of Economic Analysis, Washington, D. C.: Monthly.

Complete data on income and product accounts are published in the July issue each year.

Questions for Classroom Discussion

1. Define *gross national saving.* Define *gross national investment.* Why are saving and investment always equal?

2. Why is it that the total output of our economy is equal to the sum of everybody's expenditures?

3. My checking account at the bank might increase because (a) I sold my car and put the proceeds in the bank or (b) my income over some period exceeded my consumption expenditures. Which of these transactions involves an increase in my net worth? Does either of them involve an increase in the national wealth? Explain.

4. Do you think (a) expenditures on commuting to work, (b) the output of housewives, and (c) interest payments on government debt should be included in the GNP? Why or why not? How are each of these items treated in the U.S. accounts?

Appendix   Social Accounts for 1973

The purpose of Chapter 2 was not to provide a detailed guide to the social accounts of the United States but rather to bring out their principal characteristics. Particular attention has been paid to the important accounting identities and to the interrelationships among the income and product accounts, the flow-of-funds accounts, and the national balance sheet.

In this appendix we show the actual accounts for 1973.* In order to bring out the points made earlier in Chapter 2, the data have been put in a somewhat different format, and some changes in terminology have been made from that in the officially published statistics.

---

* Since the tables in this appendix were prepared, the Department of Commerce has undertaken a revision of the National Income and Product Accounts. Details of this revision were published in the *Survey of Current Business* (January 1976 and July 1976). At the time the book went to press (September 1976), the Federal Reserve System had not issued the corresponding revisions to the Flow-of-Funds Accounts. Since the purpose of this appendix is to illustrate the relationships between the income accounts and the flow-of-funds accounts, we have retained the unrevised figures. If the reader wishes to obtain revised and updated tables, he should contact the author.

Table 2A.1   United States Income and Product Accounts, 1973

Expenditures on Product	*$ Billion*		*Incomes Generated*	*$ Billion*
Personal expenditures on non-durable goods and services*	674.9		Compensation of employees	786.0
			Proprietors' income*	96.1
Private gross fixed domestic investment	324.3		Rental income of persons*	26.1
Expenditures on producers' durable equipment		89.8	Corporate profits and inventory valuation adjustment	105.1
Expenditures on nonresidential construction		47.0	Net interest	52.3
			National income	1,065.6
Expenditures on household durable equipment		130.3	Business transfer payments	4.9
			Indirect business taxes plus surplus of government enterprises minus subsidies	119.8
Expenditures on residential construction		57.2	
Government purchases of goods and services	276.4		Capital consumption allowances	110.8
			Statistical discrepancy	−5.0
Government fixed capital formation		42.0	
Compensation of employees		148.5	
Other		85.9	
Net exports of goods and services	3.9		
Total final purchases	1,279.6		
Change in business inventories	15.4		
Gross national product at market prices	1,294.9		*Gross national product at market prices*	1,294.9

SOURCE: *Survey of Current Business* (July 1974).

*Excludes imputed income from services of consumer durables except owner-occupied houses.

Table 2A.2 Appropriation of Gross National Product, 1973

	$ Billion	
Gross product accruing to business		124.0
*Corporate profits and inventory valuation adjustment	105.1	
Capital consumption allowances on business assets	98.3	
Less: Profits tax liability	−49.8	
Less: Dividends	−29.6	
Gross product accruing to governments		279.9
Profits tax accruals	49.8	
Personal taxes	151.3	
Contributions to social insurance	91.2	
Indirect business taxes	119.2	
Surplus of government enterprises	3.7	
Less: Transfers to households	−113.0	
Less: Transfers to foreigners	−2.6	
Less: Net interest paid on government debt	−15.4	
Less: Subsidies	−4.3	
Gross product accruing to households		892.1
*Compensation of employees	786.0	
*Proprietors' income**	96.1	
*Rental income of persons**	26.1	
Dividend income	29.6	
*Net interest income from business and foreigners	52.3	
Net interest income from governments	15.4	
Transfers from government	113.0	
Transfers from business	4.9	
Capital consumption allowances on household assets**	12.5	
Less: Household transfers to foreigners	−1.3	
Less: Personal taxes	−151.3	
Less: Contributions to social insurance	−91.2	
Gross product accruing to foreigners		3.9
Household transfers to foreigners	1.3	
Government transfers to foreigners	2.6	
Statistical discrepancy		−5.0
Gross national product at market prices		1,294.9

SOURCES: *Survey of Current Business* (July 1974); *Federal Reserve Bulletin* (October 1974).

*These items make up the National Income.
**Excludes imputed income from and depreciation on household durables apart from owner-occupied homes. The Federal Reserve System estimated capital consumption allowances on consumer durables in 1973 as $103.3 billion.

Table 2A.3 Saving and Investment by Sector, 1973 ($ Billion)

Transaction Category	Household Sector	Government Sector	Business Sector[a]	Domestic Economy	Foreign Sector	Total Economy
Product accruing to sector	892.1	279.9	124.0	1,296.0	3.9	1,299.9
Consumption	−674.9	−234.4	0	−909.3	−3.9	913.2
Capital gains dividends	0.9	—	−0.9	0	—	0
Credits from government insurance	11.5	−11.5	—	0	—	0
Gross saving	229.6	34.0	123.1	386.8	−0.1	386.7
Gross investment	235.6	28.9	112.5	377.2	2.1	379.3
Real investment	174.1	42.0	165.5	381.7	0	381.7
Financial investment	61.5	−13.1	−53.0	−4.6	2.1	−2.4
Sector discrepancy[b]	−6.0	5.1	10.6	9.6	−2.2	7.4

SOURCES: *Survey of Current Business* (July 1974); *Federal Reserve Bulletin* (October 1974).

[a]Includes Federal Reserve System.
[b]The statistical discrepancy in the income and product accounts was $5 billion (see Table 2A.1). In this table, this total appears as the sum of the sector discrepancies ($7.4 billion) plus aggregate financial investment, which is shown as −$2.4 billion but should be zero for the economy as a whole.

Table 2A.4 Financial Investment By Sector 1973[a] ($ Billion)

Transaction Category	Household Sector	Government Sector	Business Sector[b]	Domestic Economy	Foreign Sector	Total Economy
Net financial investment[c]	61.5	−13.1	−53.0	−4.6	2.1	−2.4
Net acquisition of financial claims	130.8	12.2	261.7	404.7	17.4	422.1
Demand deposits and currency	13.1	−2.1	2.1	13.1	2.5	15.5
Time and savings accounts	67.7	7.0	1.5	76.2	2.9	79.1
Life insurance and pension funds reserves	31.7					31.7
Corporate shares	−8.2		13.4	5.2	2.8	8.0
Government bonds	24.7	0.4	17.7	42.8	0.3	43.1
Corporate and foreign bonds	1.1		11.3	12.4	0.1	12.5
Mortgages	0.5	−0.6	72.0	71.9		71.9
Consumer credit, bank loans, and other loans	3.5	3.6	96.6	103.5	0.3	103.8
Other	−3.1	4.1	47.3	48.3	8.6	56.7
Net issue of financial claims	69.3	25.3	314.6	409.2	15.3	424.1
Demand deposits and currency			16.0	16.0		16.0
Time and savings accounts			79.1	79.1		79.1
Life insurance and pension funds reserves		2.2	29.5	31.7		31.7
Corporate shares			8.2	8.2	−0.2	8.0
Government bonds		21.7	21.4	43.1		43.1
Corporate and foreign bonds			11.5	11.5	1.0	12.5
Mortgages	45.6	−0.1	26.3	71.9		71.9
Consumer credit, bank loans, other loans	27.2	0.3	69.6	97.1	6.7	103.8
Other	−3.6	1.2	53.1	50.7	7.8	58.6

SOURCE: *Federal Reserve Bulletin* (October 1974).

[a]Table 2A.3 and this table comprise the Flow-of-Funds Accounts.
[b]Includes Federal Reserve System.
[c]From Line 8 of Table 2A.3.
NOTE: Components may not add up to totals because of rounding.

Part Two

Macroeconomics with Fixed Prices

The accounting scheme outlined in Chapter 2 emphasized the formal, or *accounting,* relationships among expenditure, output, and income (the income and product accounts) and among saving, investment, and the accumulation of tangible and financial assets (the flow-of-funds accounts and national balance sheets). However, the relations among these variables are more than a matter of accounting. Many variables are connected by behavioral relations and equilibrium conditions as well as by accounting relations. For example, household consumption is related to the national income and product in the accounting sense (that it is a component of that product), in the behavioral sense (that the amount of consumption which households want to do is affected by their incomes) and in the equilibrium sense (that certain levels of consumption and income are consistent with equilibrium in the economy while others are not).

With this in mind, we now direct our attention away from accounting toward the factors that *determine* the levels of the many stock and flow variables we have introduced. Our method of approach will be through the construction of a series of theoretical *models* of the economy.

An economic model is a simplification of the real-world economy. It focuses attention on a limited number of relationships and ignores much of the rich institutional and factual detail of an actual economy. The art of constructing an economic model lies in selecting those relations (whether of accounting or of behavior) in the real world that are crucial; that is, those that determine the direction in which such important economic variables as output, employment, and prices change over time. An economic model cannot by its very nature explain everything about the real-world economy, but it can help us to understand the major forces that determine the way in which our economy behaves. We are particularly concerned with developing models that assist us in analyzing the impact of government policy on the overall working of the economy.

The first model developed is quite simple; thus its capacity to explain real world events is limited. Later, as more details are added, the model becomes more complicated, and the number of variables involved becomes larger. At the same time, as the model becomes more complete, it becomes possible to provide answers to more questions and to more sophisticated questions as well.

In the next three chapters we develop a simple model that economists have found useful in analyzing the determinants of total income and output. Our analysis begins with a number of intuitively plausible hypotheses concerning the behavior of economic agents in their roles as both spenders and wealth holders and proceeds to develop the implications of these propositions for the behavior of the economy as a whole. In Part 3 we examine these propositions in more detail, and in Part 4 we discuss how our simple model must be modified to take account of the existence of financial institutions and particularly of commercial banks and the Federal Reserve System.

Throughout the analysis of these chapters we assume that *newly produced commodities are always forthcoming in response to demand with no change in their prices*. Producers are assumed always to be both able and willing to supply the goods and services their customers demand with no changes in their unit costs of production and so to have no incentive to raise or lower prices in response to increases or decreases in demand. As a result, prices at which newly produced* commodities are sold remain fixed and constant: All changes in the gross national product are reflected in the *quantity* dimension and none in the price dimension. Hence there is no need to make a distinction between variables measured in current prices (*nominal* magnitudes) and those measured in constant prices (*real* magnitudes).

---

* Although the prices of *newly produced* goods and services are held constant, the same is not true of the prices of *existing assets*. In fact, in Chapter 4 and in succeeding chapters we assume that the prices of both financial and tangible assets adjust rapidly to bring the markets for these *stock* variables into equilibrium.

Such a fixed-price situation is most likely to be realized in an economy in which there are unemployed supplies of men and machines that can be brought into use when required. The macroeconomics of situations in which prices vary and the economy is operating at close to full employment is taken up in Part 5. In that part we will be particularly interested in the causes and effects of inflation and in the relation between the level of employment in our economy and the rate at which prices tend to rise.

A Simple Model of the Economy:
(1) The Behavior of Spenders

In most transactions involving the production and sale of goods and services, the initiative comes from the individuals who do the buying rather than from those who do the selling. Hence, if we want to know why the value of output (and hence of income) is what it is, we should examine the behavior of the spenders in the economy. The present chapter is concerned with this behavior.

Assume that there is no foreign trade. (Initially we will also ignore the government.) Hence the only sources of expenditure are consumption and investment. The accounting identities between net national product Q, national income Y, and net national expenditures X, may be written

$$Q = Y = X = C + I \tag{3.1}$$

Investment consists of both expenditures on fixed capital formation and the change in business inventories. We ignore capital consumption allowances by assuming that capital formation is measured net of depreciation.

Suppose that production cannot take place instantaneously. Each period firms produce output in the expectation of selling it in the succeeding period. The exact length of the *period* is not important for theoretical purposes: A month would probably be about right in most sectors of the economy. Thus in January the amount of output available for sale is fixed and given by the decisions made in December. In January firms make decisions that will determine the output available in February. These decisions will be based on firms' forecasts of the demand for their products in February.

However, a firm's expectations may turn out to be mistaken: The demand for its products in any month may exceed or fall short of the level it expected when it made its production plans. If demand in a particular month exceeds current production, the firm may be able to supply its customers from its inventories. If it cannot do this,[1] potential custom-

---

[1] This may be because its accumulated inventories are insufficient to meet demand or because its products are not storable. Commodities that are *services* rather than goods (for example,

ers must be turned away, or the firm may accept orders for future delivery. Thus when demand exceeds current output, there must be either an unanticipated reduction in business inventories or an unanticipated increase in the volume of orders on hand. Conversely, if current output exceeds demand, including planned deliveries of goods ordered earlier, the excess either may be used to supply orders sooner than had been planned or must be added to inventories. In this case, therefore, there will be either an unanticipated reduction in the volume of unfilled orders or an unanticipated addition to inventories.

The relationships between what businesses and households expect when they make their spending and production plans and what actually happens may be shown by a series of accounting identities.[2]

First, firms will set their output equal to the amount they expect to sell, including the delivery of goods ordered earlier, plus any addition to their inventories they plan to make:

> Output of final products
> = Planned sales of final products
> + Planned additions to inventories

Second, if realized sales fall short of planned sales, firms experience an unanticipated increase in their inventories. Conversely, if they sell more than expected, there is an unanticipated reduction in inventories:

> Planned sales of final products
> = Realized sales of final products
> + Unplanned additions to inventories

This pair of identities relating to firm behavior may be combined to give:

> Output of final products
> = Realized sales of final products
> + Planned additions to inventories
> + Unplanned additions to inventories

In this form the identities simply state that all output must either be sold or be added to business inventories.

Third, we have an identity referring to buyers' behavior. If firms are unable to supply the goods and services their customers planned to buy, realized purchases will fall short of planned purchases and the difference will be added to firms' order books. Conversely, if firms are able to supply more than their customers planned to buy, realized purchases will exceed planned purchases and order books will be reduced.[3]

---

airline transportation or physicians' services) obviously cannot be stored. Goods that must be custom built (certain types of machine tools, for example) also cannot be stored though, in some cases, their components can be.

[2] For simplicity, inventories of and unfilled orders for intermediate goods are ignored.

[3] This case corresponds to the situation in which producers find that they are able to supply the

> Planned purchases of final products
> = Realized purchases of final products
> + Unplanned additions to order books

Realized purchases and sales must of course be equal to each other, so this identity may also be written:

> Realized sales of final products
> = Planned purchases of final products
> − Unplanned additions to order books

Finally, this last identity may be combined with those relating to firm behavior to give:

> Output of final products
> = Planned purchases of final products
> + Planned additions to inventories
> + Unplanned additions to inventories
> − Unplanned additions to order books

Thus the difference between realized expenditures, which in the aggregate is equal to the net national product (NNP), and planned expenditures consists of (a) unplanned additions to inventories minus (b) unplanned additions to order books.

Algebraically, we write this relation between planned and realized quantities as

$$Q \equiv Y \equiv X \equiv C + I$$
$$\equiv C^P + I^P + \Delta\text{Inv} - \Delta\text{Ord} \tag{3.2}$$

where C^P and I^P denote planned consumption and planned investment, including planned additions to inventories, and ΔInv and ΔOrd represent unplanned inventory accumulation and unplanned additions to unfilled orders; either or both of these last two items may of course be negative.

In any accounting period, both consumption and investment may differ from their planned levels. Households' consumption plans may be thwarted by the firms' inability to supply; in this case there will be an unexpected increase in order books for consumption goods. Actual investment may differ from planned investment for two reasons. First, some purchasers of investment goods may be unable to obtain the goods they want; that is, there may be an unexpected increase in investment good orders. Second, if any unplanned change in inventories occurs, this change is a component of actual investment that will therefore differ from the level that firms had expected.

When producers and spenders simultaneously find that their plans are realized, the economy is in *equilibrium*. Firms experience neither an unex-

---

commodities they have on their order books at an earlier date than they and their customers had anticipated.

pected change in their backlogs of unfilled orders nor an unplanned change in their inventories. The demands of spenders can be met without delay from current production. Hence producers have no incentive to change their production levels, and spenders have no incentive to alter their expenditure plans. When plans are not realized, however, there are forces at work inducing businesses to change their production plans. The economy is in *disequilibrium* and the level of output changes from one period to another as firms seek to match their production to the demands of their customers.

Equilibrium in a Two-Sector Economy

We now introduce our first intuitively plausible proposition: *The amount households plan to spend on consumption depends on their incomes.* We write this algebraically as

$$C^P = C(Y) \tag{3.3}$$

To be specific we suppose that planned consumption in a given period, say, a month, depends on income in the *same* period.

This relationship between the level of income and the planned level of consumption was first introduced into economics by the English economist John Maynard Keynes. It has come to be known as the *consumption function*. Keynes proposed two hypotheses concerning the form of this relationship. First, he suggested that when their incomes increase, households will wish to increase their consumption spending. Second, he suggested that households will also wish to save more when their incomes increase and hence that the rise in consumption spending will be less (in *dollar* amount) than the increase in income. Thus if income rises by $100, consumption will increase by less than $100. The proportion of each additional dollar of income that is spent on consumption is termed the *marginal propensity to consume* (MPC). Thus Keynes's two hypotheses are that the MPC is positive but less than one. Algebraically, these hypotheses may be written as

$$0 < \frac{\Delta C^P}{\Delta Y} < 1$$

This relation between planned consumption and income is illustrated by the curve CC in Figure 3.1. Our twin hypotheses[4] imply that this curve is upward sloping but has a slope of less than 45°.

Suppose planned investment (that is, planned net capital formation plus

---

[4] Figure 3.1 also incorporates two other hypotheses regarding planned consumption. First, the proportion of income spent on consumption, which is usually described as the *average propensity to consume*, declines as income increases. Second, the fact that CC is drawn as a straight line implies the hypothesis that the marginal propensity to consume is constant. We will incorporate these hypotheses in our diagrams since there is some empirical support for them, but at the same time we note that none of our results depend on them.

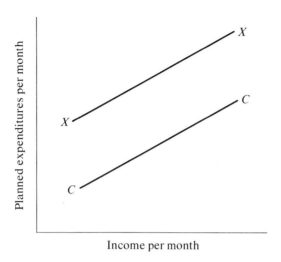

FIGURE 3.1 Income and planned spending
CC represents the Keynesian consumption function relating income and
planned consumption. *XX* represents the aggregate expenditure line. The
vertical distance between these curves represents planned investment
spending, I^P, which is assumed to be constant.

planned additions to inventories) is fixed at some level I^P. Then there is a
relationship between total planned spending and total income. Algebraically,

$$X^P = C^P + I^P = C(Y) + I^P$$

This relationship is shown also in Figure 3.1 where it is labeled *XX*. We call
this line the *aggregate expenditure line*.

So far we have been concerned only with the behavioral relationship
between planned spending and income. In addition, however, there is an
accounting relation requiring that actual expenditures must be equal to
income. In diagrammatic terms, this means that when plotted against income, actual expenditures must lie on a 45° ray from the origin.

When all plans are realized, the economy will be in equilibrium with
planned expenditures equal to actual expenditures and hence equal to output. To locate the level of output at which this equilibrium occurs we simply
superimpose a 45° ray on the previous diagram. This is done in Figure 3.2.
In this figure *XX* again represents the relation between planned spending and
income. The 45° ray is labeled $X = Y$, since at points on this ray expenditures are equal to income.

Equilibrium occurs at the intersection of the aggregate expenditure line
with the 45° ray. If firms produce a level of output Q^*, and hence generate a
level of income Y^* $(=Q^*)$, the aggregate expenditure line *XX* shows that
planned expenditures will be X^*. This level of spending is precisely equal to

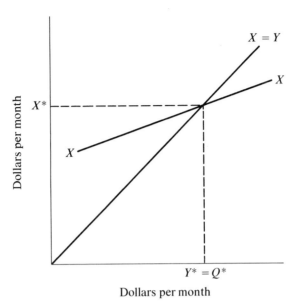

FIGURE 3.2 Equilibrium in a simple economy

the volume of output ($X^* = Q^*$). Producers will experience no unforeseen changes in either their order books or their inventories. Spenders will find that their demands can be met out of current production and will not find it necessary to wait for delivery. As a result, neither households nor firms will be under any pressure to alter their production or expenditure plans, so that income and expenditures will remain at the same level. Thus the economy will be in equilibrium.

The nature of this equilibrium can be seen more clearly if we examine the behavior of the economy when it is *out* of equilibrium and analyze the forces at work that act to push the economy toward equilibrium.

Consider Figure 3.3. Suppose that the aggregate expenditure line is $X_0 X_0$ and that the economy is in equilibrium with planned and actual expenditures equal to net output at level Q_0^* ($=Y_0^* = X_0^*$). Assume now that planned investment rises (for some unspecified reason), so that the aggregate expenditure line shifts upward from $X_0 X_0$ to $X_1 X_1$. In this new situation the level of output and income at which planned and actual expenditures are equal is Q_1^* ($=Y_1^*$). Initially, however, firms will be producing a level of output Q_0^* and hence generating a level of income Y_0^*, which is *below* this equilibrium level. This is because output cannot be adjusted instantaneously.

We see from the diagram that when income is accruing at a rate of Y_0^*, planned expenditures by households and businesses will total X_1^P, which exceeds the amount of goods and services available from current production (Q_0^*). As a result, firms will be forced either to draw down their inventories or to add to their order books.

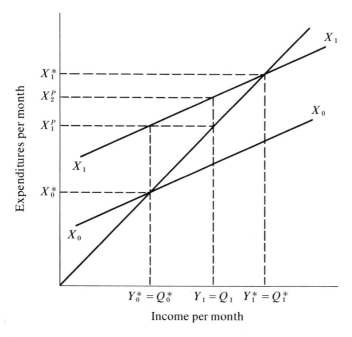

FIGURE 3.3   The approach to equilibrium in a simple economy

Our accounting scheme requires that *actual* spending must be equal to output:

$$\text{Actual expenditures } (X_0^*) = \text{Planned expenditures } (X_1^P)$$
$$- \text{ Additions to unfilled orders}$$
$$- \text{ Unplanned reductions in}$$
$$\text{inventories}$$
$$= \text{Output } (Q_0^*)$$
$$= \text{Income } (Y_0^*)$$

Actual spending falls short of its planned level for two reasons. First, some potential buyers find that they are unable to make the purchases they planned because the sellers are unable to deliver the commodities they are demanding. Second, some suppliers are able to meet demand only by depleting their inventories; this inventory reduction represents negative spending, which partially offsets the expenditures of the final purchasers. In our simple model we cannot predict the amounts of unanticipated inventory decumulation and order accumulation separately. Presumably these will depend on such factors as the amount of inventories on hand and the insistence of customers on immediate delivery. However, the total of these two items is equal to the difference between planned spending and actual output, namely, $X_1^P - X_0^*$.

Firms will respond to their lengthened order books and depleted inventories by expanding their output in the next period. Without more information we cannot predict precisely how much output will be increased. For simplicity, let us suppose that producers increase their output in the second period by the same amount as they underestimated sales in the first period (that is, by $X_1^P - X_0^*$). This will enable businesses to supply goods ordered and to replace inventories depleted in the first period.

On this assumption output will rise in the second period from Q_0^* to Q_1, which is equal to X_1^P. However, this increase in production generates a corresponding rise in income to Y_1, and this rise in income will lead to a further rise in planned expenditures from X_1^P to X_2^P. Once again, planned spending will exceed the amount of output currently available, and further additions to order books and inventory depletions will occur. The amount involved is given by $X_2^P - X_1^P$ in the figure. Firms will increase their outputs for a second time, but the corresponding increase in income will lead to yet another rise in planned spending.

This process will be repeated until the level of output and income finally converges to Q_1^* ($=Y_1^*$). At each stage firms increase their output because the demand for their products has risen. However, each rise in output generates a corresponding rise in income, which leads in turn to a further rise in planned spending. When output finally rises to Q_1^* and income to Y_1^*, planned expenditures will equal current output and, hence, there will be no further incentive for firms to change their production levels. The economy will again be in equilibrium.[5] Note that this final equilibrium is unaffected by the assumption we make about how firms adjust their production levels when current demand exceeds output. This assumption determines the *path* by which the economy moves to equilibrium but has no affect on the equilibrium position itself.[6]

A number of complications may be added to the preceding analysis without altering its essential character. The distinction between consumption and investment expenditures is not crucial to the analysis. All that is required is that total planned spending is a function of income. For example, some classes of investment spending may respond to the level of output; this possibility will be discussed in more detail in Chapter 8. The rate of

---

[5] If you have mastered the last few paragraphs, you should now be able to analyze the converse case—that in which the aggregate expenditure line shifts *downward* so that the initial level of output lies *above* the equilibrium level.

[6] This statement is not quite accurate. In the analysis in the text, firms have lower inventories and longer order books at the end of the process than at the beginning. Because of this it might be more realistic to assume that firms increase their output in each period by more than the current output deficiency in order to catch up on the deficiencies remaining from earlier periods. In this case output may for a time exeed Y_1^* before falling back to the equilibrium level, and it is possible that the economy may never attain equilibrium. Income may oscillate endlessly about Y_1^* but never converge to it. Though theoretically possible, this does not seem to be a very likely situation. For an exhaustive analysis of the various possibilities, see Lloyd A. Metzler, "The Nature and Stability of Inventory Cycles," *The Review of Economic Statistics*, Vol. XXIII (August 1941).

spending by governments may be affected by their tax revenues and hence by the income of their citizens. You can probably think of other examples.

In this more general case in which nonconsumption expenditures also respond to changes in aggregate income, the response of total planned spending to a change in income might be termed (by analogy with the marginal propensity to consume) the *marginal propensity to spend on newly produced domestic output*. As long as this marginal propensity is less than one (so that the aggregate expenditure curve *XX* has a slope of less than 45°) the analysis of Figures 3.2 and 3.3 may simply be extended to the more general case in which other classes of spending as well as consumption are related to total income. This is possible because at no time in that analysis did we use the assumption that consumption was the only class of spending that was related to income.

The Role of Government

The spending and taxing activities of governments may be introduced into our simple model with no great difficulty. Government spending on goods and services is a component of net national expenditure, while government tax revenues are a claim on the net national product. Private spending on goods and services will now depend on income *after taxes;* that is, on the share of the national product that is appropriated by the private sector.

As an example of the effect of the introduction of governments, consider the following situation. Suppose total private planned expenditures (consumption plus investment) depend on income after taxes. For simplicity, let us assume that this relation is a linear one and write it as

$$C^P + I^P = \alpha + \beta (Y - T)$$

The coefficient β represents the proportion of each additional dollar of after-tax income the private sector will plan to spend; that is, β is the marginal propensity to spend after-tax income. Total planned spending is equal to the sum of private and government spending:

$$X^P = C^P + I^P + G^P = \alpha + \beta (Y - T) + G^P$$

which can be rearranged in the form

$$X^P = (\alpha + G^P - \beta T) + \beta Y \tag{3.4}$$

This equation now represents a relation between total planned expenditures and the level of pretax income. Although apparently more complicated, the model is essentially the same as that analyzed earlier. As long as β is less than unity, the relation between planned spending and income can be represented by a line such as *XX* in Figure 3.2. Hence the equilibrium level of income can be located in exactly the same way as in the simpler case analyzed above. However, this time let us find the equilibrium income algebraically.

Since Eq. (3.4) is true for all levels of income, it must be true for the equilibrium level of income Y^*. Thus

$$X^P* = (\alpha + G^P - \beta T) + \beta Y^*$$

Moreover, in equilibrium, planned and actual expenditures are equal:

$$X^P* = X^*$$

Finally, actual expenditures are necessarily always equal to income and hence

$$X^* \equiv Y^*$$

Combining these three relationships, we have

$$Y^* = (\alpha + G^P - \beta T) + \beta Y^*$$

which can also be written as

$$Y^* = \frac{\alpha + G^P - \beta T}{1 - \beta} \qquad (3.5)$$

This equation enables us to predict the effect of a number of possible tax and expenditure policies.[7] An increase in government spending (G^P) or a reduction in government tax revenues (T) will each lead to a rise in the level of equilibrium output. In fact, this simple model has provided the basic rationale for the taxing and spending policies of most recent American governments.[8]

Note that other complications could be introduced. For example, government tax revenues T are not in practice independent of income. Governments fix tax *rates,* but the amount of tax that citizens actually pay depends on both the tax laws and their incomes. One simple case is that in which tax revenues are proportional to income:

$$T = tY$$

In this case Eq. (3.4) must be modified and becomes

$$X^P = \alpha + G^P - \beta tY + \beta Y$$

or

$$X^P = (\alpha + G^P) + \beta(1 - t)Y \qquad (3.4a)$$

---

[7] If government expenditures exceed tax revenues, the question arises, Where does the government get the money to pay its bills? Similarly, if revenues exceed expenditures, the question is, What does the government do with the surplus? These questions will be dealt with in Chapter 5. Until then they are simply ignored. Because of this, the conclusions of the present section must be regarded as provisional and subject to alteration later.

[8] The 1975 tax cut, for example, was advocated on grounds very similar to the analysis above. See *Economic Report of the President, 1975* (Washington, D. C.: February 1975).

Once again we note that the relation between planned spending and income is not *essentially* different from that in the original model. However, in this case the marginal propensity to spend out of national income, $\beta(1 - t)$, depends on the tax rate. Changes in this rate will alter the *slope* of the aggregate expenditure line.

By a procedure analogous to that used above, we can show[9] that equilibrium income is given by

$$Y^* = \frac{\alpha + G^P}{1 - \beta(1 - t)} \tag{3.5a}$$

Again we note that increases in government expenditures will lead to an increase in the level of equilibrium income. Increases in the tax rate, on the other hand, will lead to a lowering of equilibrium income.

The various complications introduced so far do not alter the essential character of the model. This is because the key assumption, that total planned spending depends only on the level of income and on no other variable, was not altered by those complications. As long as that assumption is maintained, the equilibrium level of income may always be located either by a geometric argument like that used in Figure 3.3 or by an algebraic approach such as that used to derive Eq. (3.5). Similarly, the behavior of the model when it is out of equilibrium will remain essentially unchanged as long as income remains the only independent variable affecting spending decisions. The story will change—and the model will be radically altered—only if some other independent variable affecting spending is introduced.

Spending and the Rate of Interest

It is now time to introduce a new independent variable by proposing a second intuitively plausible hypothesis. At any level of income we hypothesize that *planned spending will be negatively related to the rate of interest on securities.*[10] This proposition will be considered in more detail in Chapters 7 and 8 when we discuss the determinants of consumption and fixed investment. So far as fixed investment spending is concerned, the hypothesis may be justified initially as follows.

If a business or household uses part of its resources to purchase capital goods, those funds are not available to buy securities and hence the interest income that those securities would yield must be sacrificed. A rise in the rate of interest increases the amount of interest income that must be sacrificed if resources are invested in physical assets rather than in securities. In economics jargon, a rise in the interest rate increases the *opportunity cost* of

---

[9] You are left to carry out the calculations as an exercise.

[10] For simplicity, we assume there is only one type of income-bearing financial asset in the economy. We describe the rate of return on this asset as *the* rate of interest. In any actual economy there are, of course, many types of financial assets, each with its own unique characteristics and yielding its own particular rate of return.

holding wealth in the form of material capital (homes, machines, etc.) rather than in the form of securities. Hence an increase in the interest rate will cause households and firms to wish to hold less of their total wealth in the form of physical assets and more in the form of financial assets. As a result, expenditures on newly produced physical assets (that is, investment) will tend to decline.

Under this second hypothesis, total planned expenditures (by households, businesses, and governments) during any period depend on both the level of income and the rate of interest. This situation is illustrated in Figure 3.4. There is now a different relationship between income and planned spending at each level of the rate of interest. In Figure 3.4 the lines labeled $X(Y, i_0)$ and $X(Y, i_1)$ represent the relations between planned spending and income when the rate of interest is i_0 and i_1, respectively. Our second hypothesis implies that i_0 is less than i_1; that is, the effect of a reduction in the rate of interest is to increase planned expenditures at each level of income. For simplicity, we assume that the marginal propensity to spend is constant and independent of the rate of interest so that the effect of a reduction in the rate of interest is to shift the aggregate spending line upward without altering its slope. Although, in general, we might expect a change in the rate of interest to alter the marginal propensity to spend, the special assumption that it does not will simplify our argument without changing our conclusions.

Suppose the interest rate is i_0 and planned and actual expenditures are equal at the level X_1 $(= Y_1)$. The economy is in equilibrium. Our earlier analysis implies that an increase in the rate of interest to i_1 will, *if perma-*

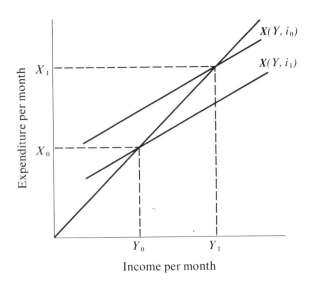

FIGURE 3.4 Spending and the rate of interest

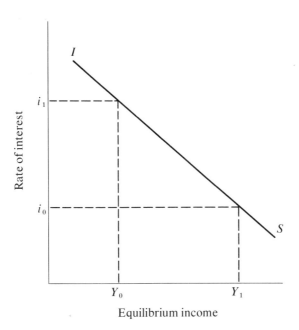

FIGURE 3.5 The *IS* curve

nent,[11] set off a series of downward adjustments in expenditures and output until a new equilibrium is reached at a lower level of spending X_0 (= Y_0).

Thus, in contrast to the simple model analyzed earlier, there is now no unique equilibrium level of income at which all spending plans are realized. If the interest rate is i_1, the equilibrium level of income is Y_0, while a lower level of the interest rate, i_0, is associated with a higher level of equilibrium income, Y_1.

In fact, since there is a relationship between planned spending and income at every level of the rate of interest (and not just at i_0 and i_1), there is a continuous relation between the rate of interest and the equilibrium level of income. This relation is shown in Figure 3.5; this diagram incorporates the conclusion derived from Figure 3.4 that (Y_0, i_1) and (Y_1, i_0) represent two pairs of values for income and the rate of interest at which the economy may reach equilibrium.

The relation between equilibrium income and the rate of interest depicted in Figure 3.5 was first developed by J. R. Hicks and is known as the *IS curve*. At all points on this curve, the economy is in equilibrium in the sense that planned expenditures equal actual expenditures, so that firms are under no pressure to alter the level of output. Our twin hypotheses that planned

---

[11] We emphasize this qualification, since the argument of Chapters 4 and 5 will suggest that as the adjustment process continues, further changes in the interest rate will occur.

spending responds positively to the level of income and negatively to the rate of interest together imply that the *IS* curve slopes downward to the right.

It is important not to interpret the *IS* curve as showing the level of income as *determined* by the rate of interest or vice versa. Rather it shows those pairs of values of the rate of interest and of income that are *consistent* with one another in the sense that only at those values can the economy be in equilibrium with planned expenditures equal to actual expenditures. When the economy is not in equilibrium (when planned spending is not equal to actual spending, so that output is changing as firms respond to unexpected changes in their inventories or order books), it will be "off the *IS* curve." If the adjustment process described earlier in this chapter (see pages 46–48) were very slow, so that most of the time the economy were out of equilibrium, the *IS* curve would not be a useful technique for analyzing the economy. Those economists who employ the *IS* curve in their analysis are, in effect, assuming that adjustment to equilibrium is sufficiently rapid that the behavior of income and output can be adequately approximated by supposing that the economy is always "on the *IS* curve."

Changes in the behavioral relations among spending, income, and the rate of interest lead to shifts in the *IS* curve. We illustrate this by a simple extension of the algebraic model introduced in the previous section.

Suppose that private planned spending depends on both the level of income after tax and the rate of interest. Again we will suppose that this relation is linear and that the government's tax revenues are independent of income. Then

$$C^P + I^P = \alpha + \beta(Y - T) - \gamma i$$

Total planned spending is equal to private spending plus government spending and hence may be written

$$X^P = \alpha + \beta(Y - T) - \gamma i + G^P$$
$$= (\alpha - \gamma i + G^P - \beta T) + \beta Y \qquad (3.6)$$

Note the similarity between this equation and Eq. (3.4).

In equilibrium, planned spending is equal to actual spending and hence equal to income. Thus we can write

$$X^{P*} = Y^* = (\alpha - \gamma i + G^P - \beta T) + \beta Y^*$$

which can also be written in the form

$$Y^* = \frac{\alpha + G^P - \beta T}{1 - \beta} - \frac{\gamma}{1 - \beta} i \qquad (3.7)$$

This is the equation of the *IS* curve. In this special case it is a straight line. Since $-\gamma/(1 - \beta)$ is negative, a rise in the rate of interest is associated with a fall in the equilibrium level of income; that is, the *IS* curve slopes downward to the right.

In Eq. (3.7) the coefficient on government spending G^P is positive while that on tax revenues T is negative. An increase in government spending or a reduction in tax revenues therefore increases the level of equilibrium income at all levels of the rate of interest; that is, it shifts the *IS* curve to the right.

In Chapter 5 we will be particularly interested in the situation in which both government spending and government tax revenues increase (or decrease) by the same dollar amount. To investigate the effect of such a change in government policy, suppose that government expenditures increase from G^P to $G^P + \Delta G$ while at the same time tax receipts rise from T to $T + \Delta T$.

At the new levels of spending and taxing, the equation of the *IS* curve is

$$Y^{**} = \frac{\alpha + G^P + \Delta G - \beta(T + \Delta T)}{1 - \beta} - \frac{\gamma}{1 - \beta} i$$

We are assuming that the increases in expenditures and in taxes are equal, $\Delta G = \Delta T$, so this equation may also be written

$$Y^{**} = \frac{\alpha + G^P - \beta T}{1 - \beta} + \frac{\Delta G - \beta \Delta G}{1 - \beta} - \frac{\gamma}{1 - \beta} i \qquad (3.8)$$

Finally, subtracting Eq. (3.7) from (3.8), we find that

$$Y^{**} - Y^* = \frac{\Delta G(1 - \beta)}{1 - \beta} = \Delta G$$

This equation shows that when both government expenditures and tax revenues increase (or decrease) by the same dollar amount, the level of equilibrium income associated with any given rate of interest increases (or decreases) by that amount; that is, the *IS* curve shifts to the right (or left) by the amount of the increase (or decrease) in expenditures and revenues. This result is known as *the balanced budget multiplier theorem.*[12]

Conclusion

This completes our discussion of the behavior of spenders in a simple economy. Our results are, of course, inconclusive. When spending plans depend not only on income but also on the rate of interest, there is no unique level of income at which the economy will be in equilibrium. There is a whole series of possible equilibria, each associated with a particular rate of interest on securities. If we are to discover which of these equilibria will actually prevail in any particular circumstances, we need to consider the factors that determine the rate of interest. We turn to this problem in the next chapter.

---

[12] The case when tax revenues depend on income is somewhat more complicated and will not be pursued here. You will find a discussion of this case in William A. Salant, "Taxes, Income Determination and the Balanced Budget Theorem," *The Review of Economics and Statistics,* Vol. XXXIX (May 1957).

References

Hicks, John R. "Mr. Keynes and the 'Classics': A Suggested Interpretation." *Econometrica,* Vol. V (April 1937).
A classic article in which the *IS* curve (and the *LM* curve, which is discussed in Chapter 4) was first developed.

Metzer, Lloyd A. "The Nature and Stability of Inventory Cycles." *The Review of Economic Statistics,* Vol. XXIII (August 1941).

Samuelson, Paul A. "The Simple Mathematics of Income Determination," *Income, Employment and Public Policy, Essays in Honor of Alvin H. Hansen.* New York: W. W. Norton, 1948.
A comprehensive treatment of the model developed in this chapter using simple algebra.

Questions for Classroom Discussion

1. Consider the simple model economy in which there is no government, consumption depends on income, and planned investment is some fixed constant. Suppose the economy is in equilibrium when there is a decline of $1 million in investment spending. By how much will equilibrium income fall? By more than $1 million? By less than $1 million? Describe in some detail the process by which the economy moves to its new equilibrium.

2. Suppose government tax revenues depend on the level of income, $T = tY$, where t is the tax rate. Derive the *IS* curve using this hypothesis, and show how it will be affected by an increase in the tax rate. Be specific about both the position and the slope of the curve.

3. Under what assumptions will the *IS* curve be close to horizontal? Do these assumptions seem plausible to you? Under what assumptions will it be vertical? Are these assumptions plausible?

Appendix   The *IS* Curve

If you have some knowledge of calculus you may be interested in the algebraic derivation of the *IS* curve. We have three basic relations. First, there is an accounting identity between actual expenditures, income, and output. This must hold at all levels of the variables and hence, in particular, it holds at the equilibrium levels:

$$X^* = Y^* = Q^* \tag{3A.1}$$

Second, planned spending depends on income and the rate of interest:

$$X^{P*} = X(Y^*, i) \tag{3A.2}$$

Finally, in equilibrium, actual spending must be equal to planned spending:

$$X^{P*} = X^* \tag{3A.3}$$

Simple substitution enables us to collapse these three equations into a single relation:

$$Y^* = X(Y^*, i) \tag{3A.4}$$

This equation defines (implicitly) a relation between equilibrium income Y^* and the rate of interest i. This is the equation of the *IS* curve shown graphically in Figure 3.5. It is important to remember that, although Eq. (3A.1) and (3A.2) hold for *all* values of income, Eq. (3A.3) is an *equilibrium condition* that holds only for the equilibrium values of income and spending. The *IS* curve represents a relationship between income and the rate of interest that holds *only when planned and actual spending are equal*.

By implicitly differentiating Eq. (3A.4), we find that

$$\frac{di}{dY} = \frac{1 - (\delta X/\delta Y)}{\delta X/\delta i} = \text{slope of } IS \text{ curve}$$

By the first hypothesis the marginal propensity to spend, $\delta X/\delta Y$, lies between zero and one. Hence the numerator of this expression is positive. Our second hypothesis states that the response of spending to the rate of interest, $\delta X/\delta i$, is negative. Thus the slope of the *IS* curve is *negative* as we found graphically.

A Simple Model of the Economy:
(2) The Behavior of Wealth Holders

4

In Chapter 3 we dealt exclusively with flow variables. We examined how a number of important flow aggregates—income, consumption, investment, and so on—are affected by the decisions of spenders in the economy. Our principal conclusion was that only certain values of income and the rate of interest—those represented by points on the *IS* curve—are consistent with flow equilibrium in the economy, in the sense that the actual flows of spending are equal to the planned flows.

In this chapter we turn our attention from the behavior of spenders to that of *wealth owners* and from flow variables to *stock variables*. In particular we are concerned with the decisions that wealth owners make about how to allocate their total wealth among the various assets available and with the implications of these decisions for the economic system as a whole. The equilibrium positions we describe are *stock equilibria;* that is, they are situations in which the actual stocks of assets in the hands of wealth owners are equal to the desired stocks.

Analyzing the behavior of spenders and wealth holders separately does not, of course, mean that these are different groups of people. In reality, all economic units function in both capacities. In their roles as spenders, individuals decide how much to spend, how much to save, and hence how much wealth to accumulate. As wealth owners they decide how to allocate the wealth they have accumulated among the various available assets and liabilities. However, macroeconomists have found it useful to assume that spending decisions and portfolio decisions can be separated—that decisions about how much wealth to *accumulate* are made independently of decisions about how to *distribute* that wealth once it has been accumulated.

Like many assumptions in economics this one cannot be justified by its realism but only by its convenience. When a household reduces current consumption and buys a new car, it is making both a saving and a portfolio decision. Clearly these decisions are not independent of one another. As we will see, however, the assumption that spending and portfolio decisions can be separated greatly simplifies our analysis and enables us to arrive at a number of plausible conclusions. A more realistic model in which spending and portfolio decisions are made simultaneously rather than sequentially might be so complicated that we could draw no useful conclusions from it. In addition, the fact that conclusions drawn from the simple model seem to be consistent with our observations of the real world suggests that this simplifying assumption is less serious than it might first appear.

The Arithmetic of Asset Prices and Yields[1]

An asset, whether it is a physical good, such as a car, or a financial claim, such as a corporate bond, is a long-lived commodity that can be purchased for a certain price and that yields a stream of income or services over a series of years. In deciding how to allocate his total resources among the various assets available, a wealth owner will be interested both in the price of each asset and in the flow of income it is expected to yield. The relation between these two quantities can be conveniently summarized in the form of the *rate of return* on the asset. However, this rate may be defined in a number of ways.

Suppose an asset is expected to yield a flow of returns, $x_1, x_2, \ldots, x_M$, over the next M years. Suppose further that its current price is q_{0M}.[2] Then the *internal rate of return*[3] $\bar{i}$ on the asset is defined by the equation[4]

$$q_{0M} = \frac{x_1}{1 + \bar{i}} + \frac{x_2}{(1 + \bar{i})^2} + \cdots + \frac{x_M}{(1 + \bar{i})^M} \tag{4.1}$$

This internal rate is a form of average rate of return that the asset yields *over its entire M-year lifetime.*

---

[1] This section and the one that follows contain a fair amount of time-consuming arithmetic. Since mastery of the details is not essential to the understanding of the argument that follows, you may prefer to skim over these sections at first and return to them later to pick up the details.

[2] Throughout this book the prices of assets (stocks) are represented by the symbol q, while the prices of newly produced goods and services (flows) are represented by the symbol p. The first subscript on q_{0M} refers to the present date (year zero), and the second subscript refers to the number of years until the asset matures (M years).

[3] The concept represented by the symbol $\bar{i}$ in Eq. (4.1) is known by a variety of names in economics and finance. Financial analysts concerned with security prices and yields generally use the expression, *yield to maturity.* When the asset involved is a piece of tangible capital, economists frequently describe $\bar{i}$ as the *marginal efficiency of capital.* The term *internal rate of return* is found in the literature of both economics and finance.

[4] We are glossing over a mathematical difficulty. For certain values of $x_1, x_2, \ldots, x_M$, and q_{0M}, there may be no value of $\bar{i}$ that makes the right-hand side of Eq. (4.1) equal to the left-hand side. Alternatively, there may be *several* values of $\bar{i}$ that are acceptable. This means that in any particular case, the internal rate of return either may not exist or may be nonunique. These problems will be ignored. It can be shown that as long as q_{0M} and $x_1, x_2, \ldots, x_M$ are all *positive,* these algebraic difficulties cannot arise. In effect, we assume that all these quantities are, indeed, positive. For an exhaustive discussion of the issues raised in this note, see J. Hirshleifer, *Investment, Interest and Capital* (Englewood Cliffs: Prentice-Hall, 1970), Chapter 3.

The *one-period rate of return,* on the other hand, is the ratio of the total dollar return on the asset during a *single period* to the market price of the asset at the beginning of the period. Thus if R_{tM} is the return an asset holder expects to receive on an M-year asset during the year ending at date t, the one-year rate of return over that period is

$$i_{t-1} = \frac{R_{tM}}{q_{t-1\ M}} \tag{4.2}$$

The return that an asset holder receives during a given period comprises two components. First, he receives a flow of income in the form either of money or services. This is the flow that was represented by $x_1, x_2, \ldots x_M$ in Eq. (4.1). Second, he obtains a gain (or suffers a loss) if the market price of the asset rises (or falls). Thus the *total* return during year t is equal to the income or services he receives, x_t, plus the change in the market price of the assets between the beginning of the year (date $t - 1$) and the end of the year (date t):[5]

$$R_{tM} = x_t + q_{t\ M-1} - q_{t-1\ M} \tag{4.3}$$

For the current year, Eqs. (4.2) and (4.3) specialize to

$$i_{01} = R_{1M}/q_{0M}$$
$$R_{1M} = x_1 + q_{1\ M-1} - q_{0M} \tag{4.4}$$

It is important to realize that the one-period rate of return and the internal rate of return are different concepts[6] and will, in general, have different values. They are, however, closely related. In particular if the internal rate remains constant over any single period, it will be equal to the one-period rate over that same period.

To demonstrate this fact, suppose that between date zero and date one there is no change in the internal rate of return. Then the price *at date one* of the asset represented in Eq. (4.1) will be[7]

$$q_{1\ M-1} = \frac{x_2}{1 + \bar{i}} + \frac{x_3}{(1 + \bar{i})^2} + \cdots + \frac{x_M}{(1 + \bar{i})^{M-1}}$$

$$= \sum_{m=2}^{M} \frac{x_m}{(1 + \bar{i})^{m-1}} \tag{4.5}$$

In general $q_{1\ M-1}$ may be either smaller or larger than q_{0M}; that is, even

---

[5] An asset that has a maturity of M years at date $t - 1$ will have a maturity of $M - 1$ years one year later. Hence its prices at the beginning and end of the year are denoted $q_{t-1\ M}$ and $q_{t\ M-1}$, respectively.

[6] In particular, the one-period rate of return always exists and is unique even in cases where the internal rate either does not exist or is nonunique.

[7] If you are unfamiliar with the use of the symbol Σ to denote summation, check that you thoroughly understand its use in this expression.

though the internal rate of return remains constant, the market price of any asset may either rise or fall as time passes.

If we substitute Eqs. (4.1) and (4.5) into Eq. (4.4), we obtain[8]

$$R_{1M} = x_1 + \sum_{m=2}^{M} \frac{x_m}{(1 + \bar{i})^{m-1}} - \sum_{m=1}^{M} \frac{x_m}{(1 + \bar{i})^{m}}$$

$$= \sum_{m=1}^{M} \frac{x_m}{(1 + \bar{i})^{m-1}} - \sum_{m=1}^{M} \frac{x_m}{(1 + \bar{i})^{m}}$$

$$= \bar{i} \cdot \sum_{m=1}^{M} \frac{x_m}{(1 + \bar{i})^{m}} = \bar{i} \cdot q_{0M}$$

Hence

$$\bar{i} = R_{1M}/q_{0M} = i_{01} \tag{4.6}$$

Thus we have shown that if the internal rate $\bar{i}$ remains constant, it is equal to the one-period rate.[9]

This is an important result. In the real world the rates of return that are quoted (in the media, for example) are generally *internal* rates. However, much of the analysis in this and later chapters is cast in terms of *one-period* rates of return. In effect we assume that investors make their portfolio decisions at the beginning of each period on the basis of the one-period rates of return that they expect to prevail during the period. However, Eq. (4.6) shows that if, in fact, investors respond to the internal rate—but always assume that rate will remain constant over the following period—they will behave in precisely the same way as if they responded to the one-period rate.

Types of Assets

A bewildering variety of different types of assets are available to the average wealth holder in the real world. In our economic model, however, we assume that there are only three types: money, bonds, and physical capital.

In this part of the book *money* consists only of currency that is printed and issued by the central government. It yields no return and is used as a medium of exchange. There are no checking accounts and no commercial banks in the economy. In Part 4 the role of banks will be examined and the model extended to take account of their activities.

Bonds are financial claims (I.O.U.s) that yield a fixed and certain dollar

---

[8] If you have difficulty understanding the following calculation, you may find it helpful to write out the various summations in full.

[9] We might mention that the converse of this statement is not necessarily true. In any period the internal rate may be equal to the one-period rate and yet may change over the period.

return in each time period. This return is termed the *coupon*. In addition, bonds have a specified maturity value. Bonds are issued both by the government and by private borrowers. We assume that wealth holders regard private and government bonds as identical. This means that the two classes of bonds must yield the same rate of return if wealth holders are to be willing to hold both in their asset portfolios.[10] As we saw in Chapter 2, the net supply of private bonds in the hands of private wealth holders is necessarily zero, since the assets of the *holders* of private bonds are exactly balanced by the liabilities of the *issuers* of such bonds. As a result, the net stock of *all* bonds outstanding is equal to the stock of government bonds and is under the full control of the authorities.

The total bond stock includes bonds with various maturity dates. We denote the present price of an M-year bond by q_{0M}^B and the number of such bonds outstanding by B_{0M}. Then the value of the stock of M-year bonds is $q_{0M}^B B_{0M}$. The value of all bonds outstanding is simply the sum of the values of the various maturity groups:[11]

$$q_0^B B_0 = q_{01}^B B_{01} + q_{02}^B B_{02} + \cdots + q_{0M}^B B_{0M} + \cdots \qquad (4.7)$$

$$= \sum_{M=1}^{\infty} q_{0M}^B B_{0M}$$

where q_0^B is the price of an average bond and B_0 is the total number of bonds outstanding. Rearranging this equation gives

$$q_0^B = \sum_{M=1}^{\infty} \frac{B_{0M}}{B_0} q_{0M}^B \qquad (4.8)$$

Thus the price of an average bond, q_0^B, is a weighted average of the prices of different maturities where the weights are the proportions of the total stock that are in the various maturity groups.

We assume that these proportions do not change as time passes. If 15-year bonds represent one-tenth of the total bond stock this year, they will represent one-tenth of the total next year.[12] This assumption is introduced only for arithmetic simplicity and could easily be abandoned with no effect on our conclusions. The effect of the assumption is to ensure that as long as the prices of the various maturity groups (q_{01}^B, q_{02}^B, ...) do not change, neither does the price of the average bond.

---

[10] If private bonds were to yield a higher rate of return, wealth holders would attempt to sell government bonds in order to buy private bonds. This would raise the prices of private bonds (lowering their rate of return) and lower the price of government bonds (increasing their rate of return) until these rates of return were equalized.

[11] We leave this summation open-ended to allow for the case of bonds that have no maturity date and will never be redeemed by the issuer. Some bonds of this type, which are known as *consols*, are outstanding in Britain. At present, there are no consols outstanding in the United States.

[12] Of course, these are not the same bonds. Those which will be 15-year bonds *next* year are 16-year bonds *this* year.

Bonds yield both a coupon and a capital gain (or loss). Thus the return from an M-year bond may be written:

$$R_{1M}^B = c + q_1^B{}_{M-1} - q_{0M}^B$$

The total return yielded by the aggregate stock of bonds is simply the sum of the returns produced by the various maturity groups,

$$R_1^B B_0 = \Sigma R_{1M}^B B_{0M}$$

which may also be written

$$R_1^B = \Sigma \frac{B_{0M}}{B_0} R_{1M}^B \tag{4.9}$$

Thus the dollar return on an average bond is a weighted average of the returns on bonds of various maturities.

We assume that investors treat bonds with differing maturity dates as identical; that is, wealth holders will only be willing to hold bonds of differing maturity dates if they promise the *same* one-period rate of return.[13] Since the one-period rates of return on bonds of differing maturity must be equal, it is clear that the one-period rate on an average bond i_{01}^B must be the same[14] as that on bonds of any given maturity:

$$\frac{R_{1M}^B}{q_{0M}^B} = i_{01}^B = \frac{R_1^B}{q_0^B} \qquad (M = 1, 2, \ldots) \tag{4.10}$$

We saw previously (pages 60–61) that for assets of any given maturity, if the internal rate does not change, then the one-period rate is equal to the internal rate. Equation (4.10) implies that this conclusion also holds true for the rate of return on an average bond.[15]

In addition to money and bonds there are also tangible assets or *capital* in the economy. Like bonds, these assets yield an income[16] (or *rental*) to their owners and may also produce gains or losses as a result of increases or decreases in their prices. Unlike bonds, tangible assets depreciate; that is, the rental income that they yield typically declines as they become older.

---

[13] The branch of monetary theory that treats the determination of the rates of return on bonds of varying maturities is called the theory of the term structure of interest rates. For a complete survey of this theory, see Jacob B. Michaelson, *The Term Structure of Interest Rates* (New York: Intext, 1973).

[14] You are left to demonstrate this proposition.

[15] However, the analogy between a single bond of a given maturity and the average bond is not exact since, in general, the dollar return on the latter is not given by

$$R_1^B = c + q_1^B - q_0^B$$

This minor difficulty is ignored in later chapters when we examine the price of and rate of return on the aggregate bond stock.

[16] The income from capital may be in the form of money (as when a firm uses a machine that enables it to earn a flow of money profits or when the owner rents it to another individual in return for a money payment) or it may be in the form of services (as in the case of the service yield obtained from owner-occupied homes and other household durables).

For example, the services yielded by a ten-year-old car are less than those given by a new car.

It is convenient (and also approximately accurate) to assume that depreciation occurs geometrically; that is, the value of the services yielded by a particular piece of capital declines by the same proportion during each year of its lifetime. This proportion is usually described as the *depreciation rate*. As an example, suppose that a new car yields services that are valued at $1000 a year and that the depreciation rate is 10 percent. These services will be worth only $900 when it is one year old, $810 when it is two years old, $729 when it is three years old, and so on. Finally, the value of the services becomes essentially[17] zero, at which point the car is scrapped. We will assume that capital assets have no scrap value.

Algebraically, this assumption may be represented as follows. If the rental yielded by a new piece of capital is represented by r and the depreciation rate by δ, then the rental on a v-year-old piece of capital is $r(1 - \delta)^v$. Thus the stream of income yielded by a piece of capital over its lifetime is

$$r, r(1 - \delta), r(1 - \delta)^2, \ldots$$

The relation between the price of capital and its internal rate of return is the same as in the case of any other asset. Specifically, if the price at data zero of a v-year-old piece of capital is deonted[18] q_{0v}^K then[19]

$$q_{0v}^K = \frac{r(1 - \delta)^v}{1 + \bar{i}} + \frac{r(1 - \delta)^{v+1}}{(1 + \bar{i})^2} + \cdots \tag{4.11}$$

Similarly, the price of a $(v + 1)$-year-old piece of capital will be

$$q_{0\,v+1}^K = \frac{r(1 - \delta)^{v+1}}{1 + \bar{i}} + \frac{r(1 - \delta)^{v+2}}{(1 + \bar{i})^2} + \cdots$$

$$= (1 - \delta)q_{0v}^K$$

Thus there is a simple arithmetic relation between the prices of capital goods of various ages.[20] In particular, there is a relation between the price of a v-year-old piece of capital and that of a new piece of capital:

---

[17] Mathematically our assumption implies that the rental never falls exactly to zero.

[18] A word on notation may be useful at this point. In the case of bonds, it is more important to know the maturity date than to know the issue date. This is because two bonds with the same maturity date will have the same price irrespective of their issue dates. In the case of capital, the reverse is true: The date when the item was produced is crucial. This is because the flow of services that a capital good will yield depends on its age.

Our notation reflects these considerations; q_{0M}^B represents the price now (date zero) of a bond that will mature M periods from now (in the future), and q_{0v}^K represents the price now of a capital asset that was produced v periods ago (in the past).

[19] This equation is simply a special case of Eq. (4.1). A v-year-old piece of capital will yield $r(1 - \delta)^v$ in the present year, $r(1 - \delta)^{v+1}$ next year, and so on. Since capital has no maturity date, there is an infinite number of terms in this sum.

[20] This conclusion depends on the implicit assumption that wealth holders are not concerned with the age of an asset *per se* but only with the services it yields. If, for example, the services yielded by a ten-year-old car are one-half of those yielded by a new car [$(1 - \delta)^{10} = 1/2$], the

$$q_{0v}^K = (1 - \delta)^v \, q_{00}^K \tag{4.12}$$

If you own a car, this tendency for the market price of a capital good to decline as it gets older will be well known to you.

The total value of the capital stock is simply the aggregate of the values of tangible capital of various ages:

$$q_0^K K_0 = \sum_{v=0}^{\infty} q_{0v}^K K_{0v} = \Sigma \, q_{00}^K \, (1 - \delta)^v K_{0v}$$

It is convenient to measure the quantity of capital in any age group in terms of new capital equivalents.[21] The price of all capital is then equal to the price of new capital and the total quantity of capital is a weighted sum of the quantities in the various age groups. This procedure[22] means that q_0^K and K_0 are defined as

$$q_0^K = q_{00}^K$$
$$K_0 = \Sigma(1 - \delta)^v \, K_{0v}$$

Note that this procedure in the exact opposite of the procedure used in the case of bonds. In that case, the total *stock* of bonds was the aggregate of the number of bonds of all maturities, and the *price* of an average bond was a weighted average of the prices of the different bonds outstanding.

As in the case of bonds, the one-period return on a capital asset consists of the rental plus the change in the asset's market value. Thus the return in the current period on a v-year-old piece of capital is

$$R_{1v}^K = r(1 - \delta)^v + q_{1\,v+1}^K - q_{0v}^K$$

Since $q_{1\,v+1}^K = q_{1v}^K (1 - \delta)$, we can rewrite this as

$$R_{1v}^K = r(1 - \delta)^v + q_{1v}^K (1 - \delta) - q_{0v}^K$$
$$= r(1 - \delta)^v + (q_{1v}^K - q_{0v}^K) - \delta q_{1v}^K \tag{4.13}$$

Thus the annual dollar return on a v-year-old piece of capital has three components. First, there is the rental $r(1 - \delta)^v$. This is analogous to the coupon yielded by a bond. Next there is the gain or loss that accrues when the price of assets of a *given age* rises or falls. This is analogous to the gain (or loss) experienced by a bondholder when the price of a bond of a given maturity rises (or falls). As long as the rental on capital[23] r and the internal

---

assumption is that the price investors will pay for a ten-year-old car will be one-half the price of a new car. Alternatively, we may say that investors will be indifferent between one new car and two ten-year-old cars.

[21] This procedure was used in Chapter 1, where the stock of taxis was measured in new taxi equivalents.

[22] An example may help. Suppose the total stock of cars consists of a new car valued at $1000 and a ten-year-old car valued at $500. This $500 may be viewed in two possible ways. It may be treated as the cost of one car with a price equal to one-half the price of a new car or as the cost of one-half of a car with the same price per car as a new car. Our procedure corresponds to the second way of viewing the situation. The total stock is valued at $1500 and consists of one and one-half cars with a price per car of $1000.

[23] In this and the next chapter we assume rentals on capital are constant. The determinants of capital rentals are considered in Chapter 8.

rate of return $\bar{i}$ both remain constant, this portion of the total return will be zero. Finally, there is the loss that is attributable to depreciation. This is somewhat analogous to the change in the value of a bond that occurs as its maturity date approaches.[24]

As a special case of Eq. (4.13), the dollar return on new capital is

$$R_{10}^K = r + (q_{10}^K - q_{00}^K) - \delta q_{10}^K$$

so that, using Eq. (4.13) we find that

$$R_{1v}^K = (1 - \delta)^v R_{10}^K \qquad (4.14)$$

Combining Eqs. (4.12) and (4.14), we find

$$\frac{R_{1v}^K}{q_{0v}^K} = \frac{(1 - \delta)^v R_{10}^K}{(1 - \delta)^v q_{00}^K} = \frac{R_{10}^K}{q_{00}^K}$$

This result shows that the one-period rate of return on a new capital asset is the same as that on a v-year-old asset (for any v). Hence the rate of return on *all* capital is also the same as the rate on new capital. Given our convention of measuring all capital in terms of new capital equivalents, so that the price of all capital is set equal to the price of new capital, we can write the rate of return on capital as

$$i_{01}^K = \frac{r + (q_1^K - q_0^K) - \delta q_1^K}{q_0^K}$$

We may summarize this discussion by saying that there are *two* broad classes of earning assets in our model economy. Although there are bonds of various maturities and capital assets of various ages, their quantities, prices, and rates of return may be aggregated successfully under the assumptions we have introduced. The one-period rates of return on bonds and capital may be written[25]

$$i_1^B = R^B/q^B$$
$$i_1^K = R^K/q^K$$

In general, the returns from an asset cannot be predicted with certainty when the asset is purchased. For example, the returns from both classes of asset include an uncertain capital gain or loss; the rental that will accrue from ownership of a piece of capital is inherently uncertain; and the coupon on bonds is subject to some risk. As a result, the one-period rates of return that actually materialize may differ from the rates the holder expected when he bought the bond. Moreover, wealth holders' decisions on how many assets they wish to hold are based not on the actual rates but on the expected rates.

---

[24] The analogy is not perfect. The market price of a bond may either rise or fall as maturity approaches, whereas in the case of capital, depreciation always causes the price to decline.
[25] From now on we drop the subscripts that denote the current date. The 1 subscripts on i_1^B and i_1^K remain to remind us that these are one-period rates of return.

Monetary theorists have only recently begun to grapple with the many difficult theoretical issues that flow from this apparently simple observation. In this chapter, we avoid all these difficulties by supposing that wealth owners always assume that the prices of bonds and capital assets of any given maturity or age will remain constant. An M-year bond will be an $(M - 1)$–year bond one year from now. Our assumption is that wealth holders expect its price next year to be the same as the present price of an $(M - 1)$–year bond. Similarly, a v-year-old capital asset will be a $(v + 1)$-year-old asset next year, and we assume that its price then will be the same as the present price of an asset of that age. This assumption corresponds to the assumption that wealth holders always expect that the internal rate of return will remain constant. In addition, we further assume that both the rental on capital and the coupon on bonds are fixed and constant. The effect of these assumptions is to ensure that the one-period dollar return on both classes of assets is fully known at the beginning of the period.

The Demand for Assets

We turn now to the determinants of the demand for assets by wealth holders. As in Chapter 3, we content ourselves at first with the introduction of a number of intuitively plausible hypotheses. With regard to the demand for money, these hypotheses will be discussed in considerable detail later.

For now, we will assume that wealth holders regard bonds and tangible capital as identical in the sense that they will be indifferent between holding a bond and holding a piece of capital if both are expected to yield the same one-period rate of return, and that they will always prefer the asset that promises the higher return. This is clearly an unrealistic assumption. In many cases bonds are more marketable and offer a more certain return than does tangible capital. Hence wealth holders are often willing to hold bonds even though they yield a lower rate of return than tangible assets. The implications of dropping this assumption are examined in Chapter 6, where an economy that contains three distinct assets is analyzed.

The assumption that bonds and capital are regarded as identical by wealth holders means that the rate of interest on bonds must always be equal to the rate of return on capital.[26] If the bond rate were to exceed the rate on capital, many wealth holders would seek to sell capital and buy bonds. As a result, the price of bonds would tend to rise (thus lowering the rate of interest on bonds) and the price of capital would tend to fall (thus raising the rate of return on capital). These price changes would continue until the two rates of return were equalized.

It will also be arithmetically convenient to assume that both bonds and capital yield a return of one dollar a year:[27]

---

[26] Where there is no possibility of confusion, the phrases *rate of return* and *rate of interest* will be used instead of the clumsy (but more accurate) expression *one-period rate of return*.

[27] The units in which bonds and capital are measured are quite arbitrary. If a given asset yields

$$R^B = R^K = 1$$

With these two assumptions we can write

$$i_1^B = i_1^K = i$$
$$q^B = q^K = q$$

and

$$i = 1/q$$

where i and q represent, respectively, the rate of return on and the price of all nonmoney assets.

The total wealth, or net worth, of the private sector is the sum of its holdings of money, bonds,[28] and tangible capital.

$$W = M + q^B B + q^K K \qquad (4.15)$$

Since money functions as the unit of account, the price of money is fixed at one. For any individual, bond holdings may be positive (if he is a bond-*holder*) or negative (if he is a bond *issuer*). However, for all private individuals as a group, holdings of private bonds add to zero and hence $q^B B$ represents the value of the stock of government bonds outstanding. Given our assumptions about asset prices and yields, this expression for total wealth may also be written as

$$W = M + q(B + K) \qquad (4.16)$$

or

$$W = M + (B + K)/i$$

We now consider the demand for money. Money is an asset and hence, in discussing the demand for money, we are considering the factors that determine how much money the public wishes to hold in its total portfolio of wealth. We suggest three plausible hypotheses in this area. (Each of these will be discussed in greater detail later.)

First, we hypothesize that an increase in the public's total wealth will lead to an increase in the demand for both money and nonmoney assets. Thus if total wealth increases by, say, $100, the demand for money will rise, but by less than $100. As a result, individuals will want to hold some, but not all, of any addition to their total wealth in the form of money.

Second, we suggest that at high levels of current income the public will want to hold a larger share of its total wealth in the form of money than at low levels of income. The reason for this is that at higher levels of income individuals are likely to be engaging in more and larger transactions (purchases and sales) and, since money is the medium of exchange, they will require larger holdings of money to carry through these transactions.

---

a return of, say, $3, it may be treated as three assets each of which yields $1. Hence this is an unimportant simplification.

[28] The assertion that money and government bonds represent wealth to the private sector has been the subject of some controversy among economists. This issue is treated briefly in Appendix B.

Finally, we hypothesize that, *at any level of total wealth,* the public will want to hold more money at a low rate of interest than at a high rate. This is because the rate of interest represents the income a wealth holder sacrifices when he holds a dollar's worth of wealth in the form of money[29] rather than in the form of securities or tangible capital.[30] When this sacrifice is small, the individual is likely to hold more money than when it is large.

A reduction in the rate of interest will lead to an increase in the amount of money that wealth owners wish to hold, for two reasons. First, using our third hypothesis, a decline in the interest rate will cause the average wealth owner to substitute money for nonmoney in his portfolio. In addition, however, a decrease in the rate of interest implies a rise in the price of nonmoney assets and hence an increase in total wealth. Under our first hypothesis, this increase, also leads to a rise in the demand for money.

Since all wealth must be held in the form of either money or nonmonetary assets, our three hypotheses may be restated in terms of the demand for nonmoney assets. First, an increase in total wealth leads to a rise in the demand for nonmonetary assets. Second, an increase in the level of income will, with wealth constant, lead to a decrease in the demand for nonmoney. Finally, again with wealth constant, a rise in the rate of interest will increase the demand for nonmoney.[31]

The three hypotheses regarding the demand for money may be represented algebraically as

$$M^D = M(W, Y, i) \tag{4.17}$$

where

$$1 > \frac{\Delta M}{\Delta W} > 0$$

$$\frac{\Delta M}{\Delta Y} > 0$$

$$\frac{\Delta M}{\Delta i} < 0$$

Since wealth not held in money must be held in nonmoney, the demand for nonmoney may be written

$$qN^D = N(W, Y, i) \tag{4.18}$$
$$= W - M(W, Y, i)$$

so that

---

[29] Recall that money itself yields no income.

[30] One bond or one unit of capital costs q dollars and yields an annual return of $1. Hence the return from one dollar's worth of either of these nonmoney assets is $1/q$ or i dollars.

[31] If wealth is *not* held constant, however, the effect of a rise in the rate of interest may be to increase or decrease the demand for nonmoney. This is because, in addition to causing wealth holders to substitute nonmoney for money in their portfolios, it implies a reduction in total wealth. These two factors have opposite effects on the demand for nonmoney.

$$1 > \frac{\Delta N}{\Delta W} > 0$$

$$\frac{\Delta N}{\Delta Y} < 0$$

$$\frac{\Delta N}{\Delta i} > 0$$

Since any increase in wealth must be held either in money or in non-money, it must be true that

$$\frac{\Delta M}{\Delta W} + \frac{\Delta N}{\Delta W} = 1$$

Similarly, if there is no change in wealth and either income rises or the rate of interest falls, the increase in the demand for money must be exactly equal to the decrease in the demand for nonmoney:

$$\frac{\Delta M}{\Delta Y} + \frac{\Delta N}{\Delta Y} = 0$$

$$\frac{\Delta M}{\Delta i} + \frac{\Delta N}{\Delta i} = 0$$

It will simplify our verbal and geometric argument if we assume that the demand for money relationship represented by Eq. (4.17) takes a particular form, namely,

$$M^D = m(Y, i) \cdot W \tag{4.19}$$

or

$$M^D/W = m(Y, i)$$

Of course, this means that the demand for nonmoney may be written similarly as

$$qN^D/W = n(Y, i) \tag{4.20}$$

These equations embody the assumption that the desired ratios of money and nonmoney holdings to total wealth, M^D/W and qN^D/W, depend only on income and the rate of interest and are independent of the level of wealth itself. If income and the rate of interest remain unchanged while total wealth, say, doubles, this assumption states that the amount of money (and hence the amount of nonmoney) that wealth holders will want to hold will also double.[32] This assumption may appear somewhat arbitrary and im-

---

[32] If you have some knowledge of price theory you should be able to realize that the assumption may be stated in another way, namely, that the wealth elasticity of demand for money is equal to one:

$$\frac{M^D}{W} \cdot \frac{W}{M} = 1$$

It is in this form that the hypothesis has been tested empirically.

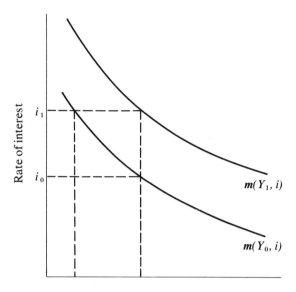

Desired money-wealth ratio

FIGURE 4.1   The demand for money

plausible a priori; however, there is some evidence that it is approximately true in practice. More important, the assumption is introduced only to simplify the verbal and especially the geometric argument that follows, and the main conclusions of that argument do not depend on the validity of the assumption. This is demonstrated in Appendix A to this chapter.

Our hypotheses are represented graphically in Figure 4.1. In this figure the curves labeled $m(Y_0, i)$ and $m(Y_1, i)$ represent the desired money-wealth ratios when income is accruing at Y_0 and Y_1, respectively. At any given interest rate, say, i_1, the public will want to hold a larger share of its wealth in the form of money when income is accruing at the rate of Y_1 dollars a year[33] than when it is accruing at the lower rate of Y_0 dollars a year. At any given income level, say, Y_0, the public will demand a larger money-wealth ratio when the interest rate is low (i_0) than when it is high (i_1). However, the money-wealth ratio depends only on income and the rate of interest, and not on the level of wealth itself.

Equilibrium in the Asset Markets

On any given date there will be given stocks of money and nonmoney in existence. Then equilibrium in the markets for assets requires that the

---

[33] The demand for money is a stock concept, since it refers to a specific date, whereas income is a flow over some period. Hence the demand for money depends on the rate (per period) at which income is accruing on the date in question.

levels of income and the rate of interest be such that the public is willing to hold those existing stocks—since all money, bonds, and capital must be held by someone. Figure 4.2 illustrates this argument.

In this figure we show the supply of and demand for money. The curve OM represents the ratio of the actual supply of money to the value of total wealth. Since the value of wealth falls as the interest rate rises, this curve slopes upward to the right. In fact, given the stock of money in existence, the actual money-wealth ratio approaches unity as the interest rate becomes very large, and it approaches zero as the interest rate becomes very small. This is because at high interest rates the value of nonmoney assets becomes very small, while at low interest rates it is very large. Algebraically, we have

$$\frac{M}{W} = \frac{M}{M + (B + K)/i}$$

As i rises this ratio also rises. In fact, when i becomes large, $(B + K)/i$ becomes small, so that the ratio approaches M/M, or one. When i becomes small, $(B + K)/i$ becomes very large, and the ratio approaches zero.

The curves labeled $m(Y_0, i)$ and $m(Y_1, i)$ represent the demand for money when income is accruing at Y_0 and Y_1, respectively. These curves slope downward reflecting our hypothesis that the desired money-wealth ratio rises as the interest rate falls.

Points A and B represent levels of income and the rate of interest at which the *desired* money-wealth ratio is equal to the *actual* ratio. Such pairs of

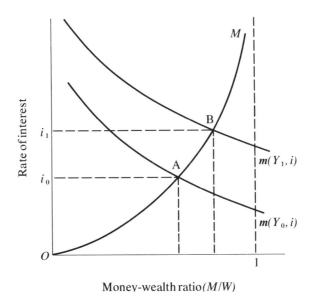

FIGURE 4.2   Equilibrium in the money market

values of income and the interest rate are possible positions of stock equilibrium in the economy. Our hypotheses imply that at higher levels of income the public will remain willing to hold the existing money stock only if the interest rate is also higher. Point B, for example, corresponds to a higher level of income and a higher interest rate than point A. If we construct the set of all possible income-interest rate combinations at which the actual and desired money-wealth ratios are equal, we obtain an upward sloping relationship such as that illustrated in Figure 4.3. This relation, which, like the *IS* curve, was introduced into monetary economics by J. R. Hicks, is known as the *LM* curve.

The *LM* curve may also be derived by considering the supply of and demand for nonmoney assets. This is illustrated in Figure 4.4, which shows the actual and desired ratios of nonmoney to wealth as functions of income and the price of nonmoney assets.

In this figure the curve *ON* represents the actual nonmoney-wealth ratio. This ratio rises as the price of nonmoney assets rises. The curves labeled $n(Y_0, q)$ and $n(Y_1, q)$ represent the desired nonmoney-wealth ratio when income is accruing at the rates Y_0 and Y_1, respectively. As our hypotheses require, an increase in the price of nonmonetary assets (from q_1 to q_0) at any income level and an increase in the level of income (from Y_0 to Y_1) at any asset price level, both lead to a *decline* in the desired nonmoney-wealth ratio.

Given the existing stocks of the two classes of assets, the asset markets will be in equilibrium at levels of income and of price of nonmoney assets at

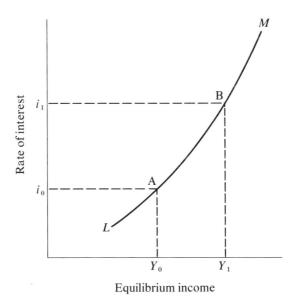

FIGURE 4.3   The *LM* curve

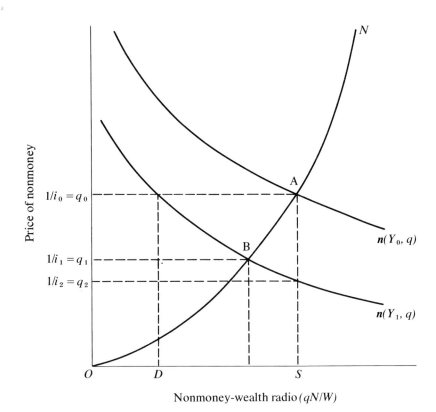

FIGURE 4.4 Equilibrium in the market for nonmoney

which the actual and desired nonmoney-wealth ratios are equal. Points A and B represent possible points of equilibrium and thus correspond to points on the *LM* curve.

Figures 4.2 and 4.4 are not independent. They show the same information in different forms. To every value of i in Figure 4.2 there corresponds a value of q ($= 1/i$) in Figure 4.4. To every value of M/W in Figure 4.2 there corresponds a value of qN/W ($= 1 - M/W$) in Figure 4.4. Hence the equilibrium positions (such as A and B) represented in the two diagrams are identical. Traditionally, economists, unlike specialists in finance, for example, have viewed asset market equilibrium in terms of the supply of and demand for money. However, you may find the equilibrium represented by the *LM* curve easier to understand when viewed in terms of the supply of and demand for nonmoney.

Assume that on a given date the rate of interest is i_0, so that the price of nonmoney assets is q_0 ($= 1/i_0$). Then we see from curve *ON* in Figure 4.4 that the *actual* nonmoney-wealth ratio is *OS*. Suppose, however, that income is accruing at the rate Y_1, so that the *desired* ratio is *OD*. The average wealth owner has more nonmoney assets (and hence less money) than he wants at the present levels of wealth, income, and the rate of interest. As a group wealth holders will want to reduce their *net* holdings of bonds and capital[34] and increase their holdings of money. In fact, the average wealth holder would be prepared to sell a marginal unit from his portfolio of bonds and capital at a price of q_2, which is less than the prevailing market price of q_0. In addition, wealth owners who are net issuers of private bonds would be prepared to issue bonds at a price of q_2, but will actually be able to issue them at a higher price, q_0.[35]

Although any *individual* wealth holder can reduce his holdings of bonds and capital and increase those of money, wealth holders *as a group* cannot do this. The stock of capital in existence is determined by past investment decisions; the stocks of money and government bonds are determined by government rather than private decisions, and the net stock of private bonds in the hands of the private sector is necessarily zero. As a result, when most wealth owners are seeking to switch out of nonmoney into money, competition to sell capital and bonds drives the prices of these assets downward. This decline in asset prices leads to a decrease in the demand for money both by making nonmoney assets relatively more attractive and by reducing the total value of the average wealth holder's portfolio. As a result, wealth holders become less and less anxious to switch out of nonmoney into money. Finally, when asset prices have fallen to q_1, the desired and actual holdings of the two classes of assets are equal, and wealth holders (at least in the aggregate) will no longer wish to alter the composition of their portfolios. Thus at income level Y_1 the price of nonmoney assets must be q_1 and the rate of interest $i_1 (= 1/q_1)$ if wealth owners as a group are to be willing to hold the existing net stocks of money, capital, and bonds. Hence the income-interest rate pair (Y_1, i_1) represents a situation of equilibrium in the asset markets and thus corresponds to a point on the *LM* curve.

Shifts in the LM Curve

As explained in the preceding section, the *LM* curve depicts the levels of income and the rate of interest at which the public is willing to hold the existing stocks of money, bonds, and capital. Hence changes in the stocks of these assets will lead to shifts in the *LM* curve. In this section we examine the effects of changing the stocks of money and/or bonds. The effects of changing the stock of capital are analogous: investigation of those effects is left as an exercise.

The stock of money outstanding may be increased either by the government's buying bonds and paying for them with new money or by its buying

---

[34] At price q_0, holders of capital and bonds wish to sell part of their holdings, thus reducing their nonmoney assets while issuers of bonds wish to issue more bonds, thus increasing their nonmoney liabilities.

[35] Put somewhat differently, this means that borrowers would be prepared to borrow at an interest rate of $i_2 (= 1/q_2)$, but can actually borrow at a lower rate, $i_0 (= 1/q_0)$.

goods and services from or making transfer payments to members of the public with newly printed money. In the first case the stock of money is increased and the stock of bonds is decreased by equal dollar amounts. At the price of bonds at which this transaction takes place, there is no change in the public's wealth.[36] In the second case there is no offsetting change in the bond stock and hence, at the price of bonds at which the transaction takes place, the value of the public's wealth increases by the amount of the new money issed.[37]

Conversely, the money stock in the hands of the public may be reduced either by the government's selling bonds for money or by its leaving unspent the money received from the public in tax payments. At the price of assets at which these transactions occur,[38] the first case involves no change in the wealth of the private sector, while the second involves a reduction in private wealth.

Finally, the bond stock outstanding may be increased by the government's selling bonds to the public and spending the proceeds, and may be decreased by using tax receipts to redeem outstanding government debt. In each case there is no change in the money stock, and hence the change in private wealth is equal to the change in the stock of bonds.[39]

An increase in the stock of money or a decrease in the stock of bonds causes the *LM* curve to shift downward;[40] that is, at any given level of income, the public will be willing to hold more money or fewer bonds only if the return on nonmoney assets is lowered. However, the amount of this shift in the *LM* curve depends on the method by which the money and/or bond stocks are changed. This is illustrated in Figure 4.5.

Suppose that the stocks of money, bonds, and capital are M_0, B_0, and K_0, respectively. Then the money-wealth ratio at any interest rate i is

$$\left(\frac{M}{W}\right)_0 = \frac{M_0}{M_0 + (B_0 + K_0)/i}$$

This ratio is represented by the curve OM_0. At income level Y the interest rate must be i_3 for the public to be willing to hold the existing stocks of assets.

The authorities may simultaneously increase the money stock and reduce the bond stock by purchasing bonds from members of the public and paying for them with new money. If the stock of money is increased from M_0 to M_1

---

[36] As we will see, however, the transaction leads to a change in asset prices. This change does imply a change in wealth.

[37] In this case also, the transaction leads to a change in asset prices. This change implies a change in wealth in addition to the increase referred to in the text.

[38] But see footnotes 36 and 37.

[39] Again, see footnote 37.

[40] In the next few paragraphs we will discuss the forces that lead to downward shifts in the *LM* curve. When you have mastered this material, check that you can repeat the arguments for the converse case of an upward shift.

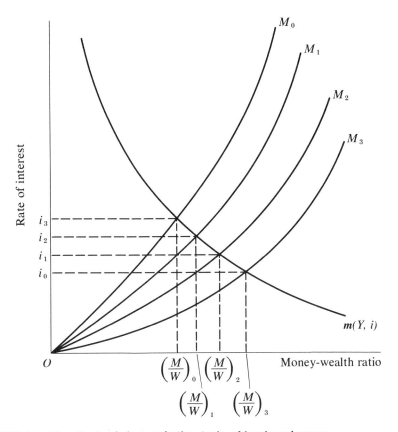

FIGURE 4.5 The effects of changes in the stocks of bonds and money

and the number of bonds outstanding is simultaneously reduced from B_0 to B_1, the money-wealth ratio will rise to

$$\left(\frac{M}{W}\right)_3 = \frac{M_1}{M_1 + (B_1 + K_0)/i}$$

This ratio is represented by the curve OM_3 in Figure 4.5. In order to induce wealth holders to sell bonds in exchange for money, the rate of interest must be reduced; that is, bond prices must rise. From the figure we see that the interest rate must fall from i_3 to i_0 to induce the public to sell the required number of bonds. In common-sense terms this simply means that private citizens are unwilling to reduce their bond holdings unless an increase in bond prices makes it worth their while. Since this government operation leads to a decline in the rate of interest, it causes a downward shift in the *LM* curve.

The value of the bonds purchased by the government at the interest rate at which the purchase occurs, i_0, must be equal to the increase in the stock of money. This implies that

$$M_1 - M_0 = \frac{B_0 - B_1}{i_0}$$

An increase in the stock of money from M_0 to M_1 may also be accomplished by the government's purchasing consumption goods and paying for them with new money. This operation increases total wealth (at any given interest rate) by the same dollar amount. Hence the money-wealth ratio rises to

$$\left(\frac{M}{W}\right)_2 = \frac{M_1}{M_1 + (B_0 + K_0)/i}$$

This ratio is represented by OM_2 in Figure 4.5. This second method of increasing the money supply involves a smaller increase in the money-wealth ratio than the first method; that is, since B_0 is greater than B_1,

$$\left(\frac{M}{W}\right)_2 = \frac{M_1}{M_1 + (B_0 + K_0)/i} < \frac{M_1}{M_1 + (B_1 + K_0)/i} = \left(\frac{M}{W}\right)_3$$

Thus OM_2 lies to the left of OM_3.

At income level Y and with interest rate i_3, members of the public will be unwilling to hold the whole of this increment to their wealth in the form of money. Hence wealth holders will attempt to add to their holdings of nonmoney assets, that is, to reduce the money-wealth ratio. In the aggregate, wealth holders cannot do this, and hence the prices of these assets will be driven up and the interest rate will be driven down. This process will continue until the interest rate falls to i_1, at which point the public is willing to hold the larger stock of money. Again, this decline in the interest rate implies a downward shift in the LM curve. However, since the initial increase in the money-wealth ratio is smaller than in the first case, this second method causes a smaller decline in the interest rate ($i_1 > i_0$) and a lesser shift in the LM curve.

The LM curve will also be shifted downward by a reduction in the stock of bonds that is not accompanied by an increase in the money stock. The authorities can accomplish such a reduction by using tax revenues to redeem government debt. If the stock of bonds is reduced in this way from B_0 to B_1, the money-wealth ratio rises to

$$\left(\frac{M}{W}\right)_1 = \frac{M_0}{M_0 + (B_1 + K_0)/i}$$

In Figure 4.5 this ratio is represented by the curve OM_1.

As in the first case, purchases of bonds by the authorities drive up their price. The public will be content to hold a smaller stock of bonds only if their rate of return is reduced from i_3 to i_2. However, the reduction in the rate of interest (and hence the size of the downward shift in the *LM* curve) is less when bonds are redeemed out of tax revenues than when they are redeemed in exchange for new money. This is because the effect on the money-wealth ratio is smaller in the former case, that is, since M_0 is less than M_1,

$$\left(\frac{M}{W}\right)_1 = \frac{M_0}{M_0 + (B_1 + K_0)/i} < \frac{M_1}{M_1 + (B_1 + K_0)/i} = \left(\frac{M}{W}\right)_3$$

Thus OM_1 lies to the left of OM_3 and hence i_2 exceeds i_0.

Whether a reduction in the stock of bonds or an equal increase in the stock of money has the greater effect on the interest rate cannot be specified a priori. However, as long as the stock of money is smaller (in dollar terms) than the stock of nonmoney—which it is in the United States—an addition to the money stock leads to a larger increase in the money-wealth ratio than does a decrease in the bond stock. Since the proof of this fact is lengthy, it is relegated to a footnote.[41] As a result, the reduction in the rate of interest, and hence the downward shift in the *LM* curve, is greater when the money stock is increased than when the bond stock is decreased. In terms of Figure 4.5, OM_2 lies to the right of OM_1 and hence i_1 is less than i_2.

Conclusion

This completes our discussion of the workings of the asset markets in our simple economy. The principal conclusion of this discussion is that certain

---

[41] Since we are considering equal changes in the money and bond stocks, we know that

$$M_1 - M_0 = q \cdot (B_0 - B_1)$$

So

$$M_1 = M_0 + q \cdot (B_0 - B_1)$$

Using the fact that $i = 1/q$, $(M/W)_1$ and $(M/W)_2$ may be written

$$\left(\frac{M}{W}\right)_1 = \frac{M_0}{M_0 + q \cdot (B_1 + K_0)}$$

$$\left(\frac{M}{W}\right)_2 = \frac{M_0 + q \cdot (B_0 - B_1)}{M_0 + q \cdot (B_0 - B_1) + q \cdot (B_0 + K_0)}$$

If we subtract $(M/W)_1$ from $(M/W)_2$, we obtain

$$\frac{M_0 + q \cdot (B_0 - B_1)}{M_0 + q \cdot (B_0 - B_1) + q \cdot (B_0 + K_0)} - \frac{M_0}{M_0 + q \cdot (B_1 + K_0)}$$

After some manipulations this expression reduces to

$$\left(\frac{M}{W}\right)_2 - \left(\frac{M}{W}\right)_1 = \frac{q \cdot (B_0 - B_1) \cdot (q B_1 + q K_0 - M_0)}{[M_0 + q \cdot (B_0 - B_1) + q \cdot (B_0 + K_0)] \cdot [M_0 + q (B_1 + K_0)]}$$

We know that $q \cdot (B_0 - B_1)$ is positive. Also, the denominator of the expression is the product of two positive terms and hence is positive. The second term in the numerator, $(qB_1 + qK_0 - M_0)$, is also positive as long as the value of nonmoney exceeds that of the money stock. Hence $(M/W)_2$ exceeds $(M/W)_1$ if the money stock is less than the nonmoney stock.

pairs of values of income and rate of interest (those represented by the *LM* curve) are consistent with stock equilibrium in the sense that wealth owners are willing to hold the existing stocks of money, bonds, and capital.

As was the case with the argument of Chapter 3, these results are inconclusive when taken by themselves. They do not enable us to predict what the levels of income and the rate of interest will be in any particular circumstances. However, when combined with the analysis of the previous chapter, they will enable us to locate a unique equilibrium for the economy and to predict how that equilibrium may be affected by government policy. These topics are the subject of Chapter 5.

References

Hicks, John R. "Mr. Keynes and the 'Classics': A Suggested Interpretation." *Econometrica,* Vol. V (April 1937).

Patinkin, Don. "Money and Wealth: A Review Article." *Journal of Economic Literature,* Vol. VII, Number 4 (December 1969).

An advanced discussion of the controversy over whether bank money should be treated as wealth, together with an analysis of the implications of this controversy for macroeconomic theory.

Rousseas, Stephen W. *Monetary Theory.* New York: Alfred A. Knopf, 1972.

Chapter 6 provides a derivation of the *LM* curve. However, as is the case in most textbook presentations, the role of the wealth holder's net worth in determining his demand for money is ignored.

Silber, William L. "Fiscal Policy in *IS–LM* Analysis: A Correction." *Journal of Money Credit and Banking,* Vol. II (November 1970).

Until recently, macroeconomists generally failed to recognize that changes in the stock of bonds (or of capital) produce shifts in the *LM* curve. This article was one of the first to point this out.

Questions for Classroom Discussion

1. Suppose the government finances a budget deficit by selling government securities. How will this affect the *LM* curve? Provide an intuitive explanation of your answer.

2. Suppose the government issues new government securities and simply destroys the money (currency notes) it received in exchange. How will this affect the *LM* curve? Contrast the effect with that in Question 1.

3. One of the hypotheses about behavior suggested in this chapter was that an increase in income will reduce the demand for bonds by a typical wealth holder. John Paul Getty owned more bonds than I do and also had a bigger income. Does this fact contradict the hypothesis? Why or why not?

4. Under what circumstances will the *LM* curve be (a) vertical (b) horizontal? Do these situations seem plausible to you? Explain.

Appendix A   The *LM* Curve

The purpose of this appendix is to show that the results reached earlier with regard to the *LM* curve do not depend on the restrictive assumption embodied in Eq. (4.19). We write the demand for money function as

$$M^D = M(W, Y, i)$$

We write the partial derivatives of this function thus:

$$\frac{\partial M}{\partial Y} \equiv M_Y$$

$$\frac{\partial M}{\partial i} \equiv M_i$$

$$\frac{\partial M}{\partial W} \equiv M_W$$

We can state our three hypotheses with regard to the demand for assets in mathematical terms:

$$0 < M_W < 1$$
$$M_Y > 0$$
$$M_i < 0$$

At any date the stocks of bonds, capital, and money are B, K, and M, respectively. Hence total wealth is

$$W = M + (B + K)/i$$

In stock equilibrium the demand for and supply of money must be equal. Thus

$$M = M[M + (B + K)/i, Y, i] \qquad (4A.1)$$

Given, M, B, and K, this equation describes a relationship between income Y and the rate of interest i. Thus this is the equation of the *LM* curve written in implicit form.

By implicit differentiation, we find

$$\frac{\partial Y}{\partial i} = \frac{M_W(B + K)/i^2 - M_i}{M_Y} > 0$$

Thus the *LM* curve slopes upward.

To show how the *LM* curve shifts for various changes in the stocks of bonds and money, we take the total differential of Eq. (4A.1).

$$dM = M_Y \, dY + M_i \, di + M_W \, dW$$
$$= M_Y \, dY + M_i \, di + M_W\left[dM + d\left(\frac{B}{i}\right) + d\left(\frac{K}{i}\right)\right]$$
$$= M_Y \, dY + M_i \, di + M_W\left[dM + \frac{dB}{i} + \frac{dK}{i} - (B + K) \, di/i^2\right]$$

We wish to show how the interest rate responds to specified changes in B and M. Hence we set $dY = dK = 0$. This yields

$$dM = [M_i - M_W(B + K)/i^2] \, di + M_W \, dM + M_W \frac{dB}{i} \qquad (4A.2)$$

Case 1

Assume the purchase of outstanding bonds with new money. Mathematically, this case implies

$$dM = \frac{-dB}{i}$$

Substituting this expression into Eq. (4A.2) gives

$$dM = [M_i - M_W(B + K)/i^2] \, di$$

so that

$$\frac{di}{dM} = \frac{1}{M_i - M_W(B + K)/i^2} < 0$$

Thus an increase in the money supply engineered by purchasing bonds reduces the interest rate. The public must be induced to sell bonds by bidding their price upward. The *LM* curve shifts downward.

Case 2

Assume the issue of new money to finance government spending. Mathematically, this case implies $dB = 0$. Under this restriction, we find

$$dM = [M_i - M_W(B + K)/i^2] \, di + M_W \, dM$$

so that

$$\frac{di}{dM} = (1 - M_W)/[M_i - M_W(B + K)/i^2] < 0$$

Again the interest rate falls and the *LM* curve is shifted downward. Note that

$$0 > (1 - M_W)/[M_i - M_W(B + K)/i^2] > 1/[M_i - M_W(B + K)/i^2]$$

Thus the reduction in the rate of interest that results from an increase in the money stock is greater when the increase is accomplished by the purchase of bonds than when money is issued to finance government spending. This corresponds to the conclusion yielded by Figure 4.5 that i_1 is greater than i_0.

Case 3

Assume the issue of new bonds to finance government spending. Mathematically, this case implies $dM = 0$, and this restriction yields

$$0 = [M_i - M_W(B + K)/i^2] \, di + M_W \, dB/i$$

so that

$$\frac{di}{dB} = \frac{-M_W}{i} \bigg/ [M_i - M_W(B + K)/i^2]$$

To find the effect of increasing the stock of bonds by one dollar, we compute

$$\frac{di}{d(B/i)} = \frac{di}{dB} \cdot \frac{dB}{d(B/i)} = i \, \frac{di}{dB}$$

$$= - M_W/[M_i - M_W(B + K)/i^2] > 0$$

Thus an increase in the bond supply causes a rise in the interest rate and an upward shift in the *LM* curve. Hence the redemption of bonds causes a downward shift:

$$- \frac{di}{d(B/i)} = M_W/[M_i - M_W(B + K)/i^2] < 0$$

Note that

$$1/[M_i - M_W(B + K)/i^2] < M_W[M_i - M_W(B + K)/i^2] < 0$$

Thus the purchase of bonds with new money (Case 1) produces a greater downward shift in the *LM* curve than bond redemption out of tax receipts (Case 3). This result corresponds to the conclusion that i_0 is less than i_2 in Figure 4.5.

We cannot determine a priori whether the issue of new money to finance expenditures (Case 2) or the redemption of bonds out of taxes (Case 3) produces the larger decrease in the rate of interest. That is,

$$[1 - M_W]/[M_i - M_W(B + K)/i^2]$$

may be greater or smaller than

$$M_W/[M_i - M_W(B + K)/i^2]$$

However, it is clear that if $M_W < 1/2$, the interest-rate reduction is larger in Case 2. This is the generalization of the conclusion reached earlier (in footnote 41), since in the special case treated in the text $M_W = M/W$.

Appendix B   A Note on the Definition of Wealth

In Chapter 4 we defined the total wealth of the private sector to include its holdings of tangible capital, government bonds, and government-issued money. This definition followed from the accounting conventions adopted in the discussion of national balance sheets in Chapter 2. A number of economists have challenged this definition and have argued that government bonds or money or both should not be regarded as a part of total wealth.

From the point of view of society as a whole it is clear that no financial assets[1] represent net wealth, since they are simultaneously assets to their holders and liabilities to their issuers. The existence of financial claims does not (by itself) make it possible for us to enjoy more consumption in total.[2] Society as a whole can add to its consumption (either now or in the future) only by increasing its capacity to produce goods and services. This capacity alone constitutes the true wealth of a society.

Clearly this argument also applies to financial instruments issued by governments. The mere existence or issue of government securities does nothing directly to add to the productive capacity of the economy. Hence government securities are not a component of the national wealth. A much more difficult and controversial question, however, is whether government securities should be treated as part of the wealth of the private sector, that is, of the nongovernment part of the economy.

The existence of a government debt implies that the private sector has a claim on the government sector. However, it also implies that the government must levy taxes in order to meet its obligations to pay interest and repay principal. If members of the public recognize that the existence of a government debt not only implies future payments of interest by the government to them but also necessitates additional tax payments by them to the government, and if they treat these two types of claims in a symmetrical way, they will not regard the debt as part of their wealth. On the other hand, if private individuals are myopic and treat their holdings of government securities as part of their assets, but ignore the corresponding liabilities to pay taxes in the future,[3] they will regard the government debt as a part of their wealth. This is an issue on which economists are divided, though the majority probably takes the second position. In this book we will accept this second view: the wealth of the private sector will be defined to include their claims on the government. The liability to pay taxes in the future will not be regarded as a claim against the total wealth of the public.

The issue of whether money should be regarded as a part of total wealth has provoked even more controversy among economists than that regarding

---

[1] Except financial claims on foreigners.
[2] This is not to deny that the financial system makes a contribution to the overall productivity of the economic system, but simply to point out that financial assets are merely pieces of paper that are not themselves productive.
[3] In large part these taxes will be paid by future generations. Thus myopia means that individuals do not treat claims on their children's children as indirect claims on themselves.

government debt. From the point of view of the individual, money is one form in which he or she may hold wealth. There is no doubt that as far as individuals are concerned, holdings of coin, Federal Reserve notes, and demand deposits are a part of their wealth just as are their homes, their cars, and their holdings of corporate stock. Much less obvious, however, is the question of whether the total stock of money in circulation should be considered part of the wealth of the public taken as a whole.

In the case of demand deposits at commercial banks, it seems clear that the answer should be in the negative.[4] Commercial banks are part of a broader class of institutions known as financial intermediaries. They have deposits of various kinds as liabilities, and claims on households, businesses, and governments as assets. Hence demand deposits are ultimately claims on the assets of the individuals and institutions who own or are indebted to banks. If we include demand deposits in our definition of the public's wealth, we will be guilty of double counting, since we will be counting *claims* to certain assets as well as the assets themselves.

Notes and coins are claims on the U.S. government and thus form part of the government debt. However, unlike government securities, they do not yield interest and hence do not give rise to any offsetting tax liability. This suggests that these forms of (government-issued) money should be included in our definition of private wealth. On the other hand, the government is not obligated to redeem notes and coin in gold or some other physical asset. Although a $10 bill is a claim on the Federal Reserve system, it is one that can be met simply by the issue of, say, two $5 bills. It might be argued that a financial instrument that is merely a claim to another instrument bearing a different number should not properly be regarded as a part of the wealth of the private sector.

One way out of this dilemma is to argue that since notes and coin function as a medium of exchange, they represent claims to goods and services. Clearly, the mere issue of notes and coin does nothing directly to add to the total flow of goods and services. Hence this form of money should not be regarded as a part of the public's wealth if by "the public" we mean all generations, present and future. On the other hand, currency may also be regarded as a claim on the next generation: The issue of notes and coin does add to the purchasing power of those alive today, since it can be spent on goods produced by the next generation. From the point of view of the present generation, therefore, notes and coins are a part of their wealth. In this book we adopt this second position and treat notes and coin issued by the government as part of the wealth of the private sector.

---

[4] A few monetary economists would not agree with this assertion.

Equilibrium in the Fixed-Price
Economy: The Role of Government

5

In Chapters 3 and 4 we considered separately the conditions for flow equilibrium and stock equilibrium in our model economy. It is now time to draw these results together.

The conditions for flow equilibrium embodied in the *IS* curve and for stock equilibrium represented by the *LM* curve yield two relations between the equilibrium level of income and the equilibrium rate of interest. The economy will be in full equilibrium when both sets of conditions are simultaneously satisfied. This equilibrium is illustrated in Figure 5.1.

In Panel A the *IS* and *LM* curves are shown. At income level Y^* and rate of interest i^*, planned and actual spending are equal; the economy is "on the *IS* curve." At the same time, actual holdings of money and nonmoney assets are equal to those desired by wealth holders; the economy is "on the *LM* curve."

Panels B and C show these equilibria in more detail. When the interest rate is i^*, the relation between planned spending and the level of income is that represented by $X(Y, i^*)$ in Panel B. Hence flow equilibrium, with planned spending equal to actual spending, occurs at income level Y^*. Similarly, when income accrues at the rate Y^*, the relation between the interest rate and the desired money-wealth ratio is that shown by $m(Y^*, i)$ in Panel C. Given the existing stocks of money, capital, and bonds, the actual money-wealth ratio is represented by OM, and hence wealth holders will be in stock equilibrium if the rate of interest is i^*.

Thus spenders and wealth holders are simultaneously in stock and flow equilibrium if and only if the levels of income and the rate of interest are Y^* and i^*, respectively. At any other levels of income and the rate of interest, either planned spending will diverge from actual spending (so that producers or spenders will be dissatisfied with the situation and will wish to change it) or actual asset holdings will differ from those desired by wealth holders (so that the latter will wish to rearrange their portfolios, thus causing changes in asset prices).

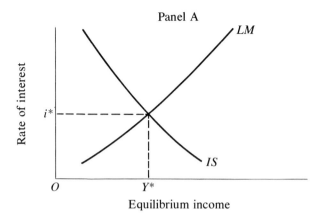

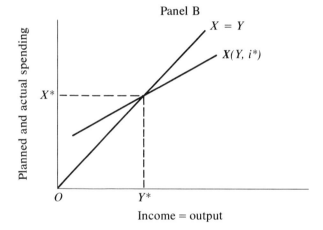

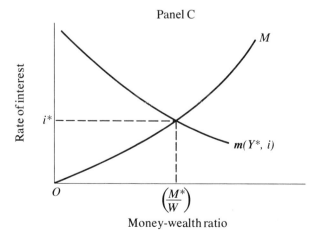

FIGURE 5.1 Full equilibrium in a simple economy

It is worth pointing out that the intersection of the *IS* and *LM* curves represents a position of short-run equilibrium in the economy. The fact that the economy is in full equilibrium in a given period does not guarantee that the levels of income and the rate of interest will remain unchanged in the succeeding period. The reason for this is that although the flow variables are constant when the economy is in equilibrium, the stock variables are likely to be changing. As we saw in the previous chapter, when the stocks of assets in the economy change, the *LM* curve in Figure 5.1 shifts.

The change in the stock of tangible capital over any period is equal to the flow of net real investment over that period. There is nothing in the *IS–LM* equilibrium conditions that requires net investment to be zero; and hence, in general, the stock of capital will be changing. Similarly, the change in the outstanding stocks of money and bonds is equal to the amount of government dissaving (that is, to the amount of the government deficit).[1] Unless the government's budget is in balance, either the stock of money or the stock of bonds (or both) must be changing. Again, there is nothing in the *IS–LM* equilibrium that implies that the government's budget is balanced. We conclude that even though the economy may be in full equilibrium on a given date, this does not guarantee that it will remain in equilibrium. As time passes, the stocks of capital,[2] bonds, and money will change, the equilibrium of wealth holders will be disturbed, and the *LM* curve will shift.[3]

The theoretical apparatus that we have developed provides a useful framework in which to begin the study of the impact of various types of government policy on aggregate income and output.[4] Three principal classes of government action may be distinguished: (1) pure monetary policy, (2) pure fiscal policy, and (3) mixed fiscal-debt policies. In order to examine the effects of each of these policy types, we will assume that initially the government budget is in balance ($G = T$) and the economy is in both stock and flow equilibrium with given quantities of money, bonds, and capital[5] in existence.

Pure Monetary Policy

We use this term to refer to government actions that alter the *composition* of the public's portfolio of wealth but do not change its total value at any given

---

[1] See Eq. (2.3) on page 31.

[2] In Chapter 4 the effects on the *LM* curve of changes in the stocks of money and bonds were discussed in detail. The reader should be able to satisfy himself that additions to the capital stock lead to a *leftward* shift in the *LM* curve.

[3] In this discussion we have drawn attention only to the fact that the *LM* curve is likely to shift as time passes. In addition, if net real investment is not zero, the stock of physical capital will be changing, and this is likely to affect the amount of investment that spenders will want to undertake at given levels of income and the rate of interest and thus to cause a shift in the *IS* curve. This possibility, as well as the effects on the *LM* curve of changes in the capital stock, will be ignored at present.

[4] Recall the assumption that prices are constant. Until this assumption is relaxed, our analysis will remain incomplete.

[5] In addition, we will ignore the effects via both the *LM* and *IS* curves of changes in the stock of capital that occur as long as net investment is not zero.

interest rate.[6] The authorities may increase the money stock by purchasing bonds from the public and paying for them with newly printed money. Conversely, they may decrease the money stock by selling government bonds and destroying the money they receive in exchange. Since in each case the change in the stock of money is exactly balanced by the change in the bond stock, these actions leave total wealth unaltered.

Pure monetary[7] policy initially affects only the stock variables in the economy and hence causes shifts in the *LM* curve while leaving the *IS* curve unaffected. As we showed in Chapter 4 (pp. 76–77), an increase in the money stock at the expense of bonds shifts the *LM* curve downward. At any given level of income, the rate of interest must fall (and the price of bonds must rise) if wealth holders are to be willing to reduce their holdings of bonds in exchange for new money. Conversely, a reduction in the money stock brought about by the sale of new bonds shifts the *LM* curve upward. In order to persuade wealth holders to add to their bond holdings, bonds must be made relatively more attractive; that is, their price must fall and their rate of return must increase.

The effects of a decrease in the money stock engineered by pure monetary policy are analyzed in Figure 5.2. Initially, the economy is in equilibrium with income accruing at the rate Y_2 and with the rate of interest i_0. The authorities now pursue a policy of selling bonds in exchange for money. The *LM* curve shifts upward from LM_0 to LM_1. As Panel A of the figure shows, the effect of this policy is to reduce the level of income to Y_1 and raise the rate of interest to i_1.

These changes in income and the rate of interest will not occur instantaneously. Hence it is useful to attempt to describe the dynamic process through which the economy adjusts to the new equilibrium. This process cannot be analyzed in terms of the *IS–LM* curve apparatus since it depends on how the economy behaves when it is out of equilibrium. In particular, it depends on the speeds with which the level of output and the rate of interest change when planned and actual spending are unequal (the economy is "off the *IS* curve") or when the actual holdings of money, bonds, and capital differ from those desired by wealth holders (the economy is "off the *LM* curve").

Since money and bonds are traded regularly in highly developed financial markets, we would expect interest rates to respond rapidly to changes in supply and demand conditions in these markets. Changes in the level of income, on the other hand, are likely to occur much less rapidly not only because production cannot adjust instantaneously to changes in planned spending, but also because expenditure plans themselves may respond rather slowly to changes in income and the rate of interest.[8] This argument

---

[6] As we will see, pure monetary policies involve changes in asset prices and interest rates and hence in the *value* of the existing stocks of assets. This is the reason for the qualifying phrase *at any given interest rate* in the definition of a pure monetary policy.

[7] Since this type of policy also involves a change in the stock of bonds, it might also be described as a *pure bond policy*.

[8] In Chapter 3 we assumed that production cannot adjust instantaneously to changes in planned

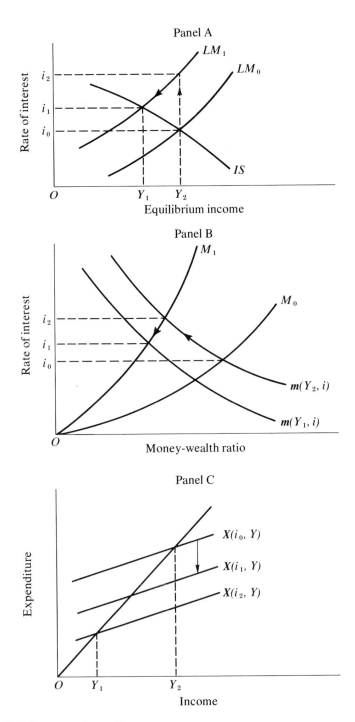

FIGURE 5.2 Pure monetary policy

implies that the initial effect of a pure monetary policy is likely to take the form of a change in the rate of interest with no change in the level of income.

If the authorities sell bonds in exchange for money, this reduces the stock of money, leaving total wealth unchanged, and hence lowers the money-wealth ratio at any interest rate. In Panel B of Figure 5.2 the curve representing this ratio shifts leftward from OM_0 to OM_1. The interest rate rises from i_0 to i_2. In common sense terms, if the government is to persuade wealth holders to purchase bonds in exchange for money, the price of bonds must be bid downward. Income is unchanged, however, because firms cannot adjust their production schedules instantaneously and the economy remains "on the *LM* curve" but "off the *IS* curve."

This rise in the rate of interest that results from the authorities' operations in the bond market will cause the expenditure plans of firms, households, and (perhaps) governments to be revised downward. This is shown in the downward shift[9] in the spending schedule from $X(i_0, Y)$ toward $X(i_2, Y)$ in Panel C of Figure 5.2. As a result, firms find that the demand for their products decreases; inventories begin to accumulate while order books shorten. Producers are likely to respond to this situation by reducing their output, thus causing corresponding declines in income and employment.

As incomes fall, however, the demand for money will also decrease. This follows from our second hypothesis of the previous chapter: Since incomes are lower, wealth holders require less cash to carry on their transactions.[10] Panel B shows this effect in the leftward move of the demand-for-money function from $m(Y_2, i)$ toward $m(Y_1, i)$. As a result, the interest rate will now begin to decline from i_2 toward i_1 as wealth holders bid up the prices of nonmoney assets. This downward tendency in the interest rate will in turn moderate the tendency for spending plans to be cut back. In terms of the diagram, the spending line will fall only to $X(i_1, Y)$ rather than to $X(i_2, Y)$.[11]

Thus there is likely[12] to be a period in which both the level of output and

---

spending. As a result, it was possible for actual output to differ from planned spending, and hence income could diverge from its equilibrium level. In the interest of simplicity, however, it was assumed in that chapter that spending plans responded instantaneously to changes in their determinants. In discussing the consumption function, for example, it was assumed that planned consumption in any period depends on income in that same period. We now wish to point out that there may be time lags between changes in income or the rate of interest and the resulting revisions in spending plans as well as between changes in plans and the resulting changes in output.

[9] If plans were adjusted instantaneously, the spending line would immediately shift downward from $X(i_0, Y)$ to $X(i_2, Y)$. In practice, plans are adjusted slowly, so that the spending line moves downward *toward* $X(i_2, Y)$ but may never reach that level. See footnote 11.

[10] In particular, as output contracts, firms' needs for working capital are reduced. As a result, business borrowing (the issue of private bonds) decreases, so that interest rates on loans tend to fall.

[11] If plans were adjusted instantaneously to changes in the rate of interest, the spending line would first fall to $X(i_2, Y)$ and later rise to $X(i_1, Y)$. In practice, it seems more likely that the spending line will simply shift slowly downward toward the $X(i_1, Y)$ level.

[12] The paths of income and the rate of interest suggested in this paragraph are those that appear most likely in practice. These paths depend on the speed with which spending plans are revised

the rate of interest are declining. During this phase of the adjustment process, the economy remains in stock equilibrium (on the *LM* curve) at every point in time. This is because as income falls the rate of interest adjusts sufficiently rapidly to make the desired amounts of money, bonds, and capital always equal to the actual amounts determined by government policy. However, the economy remains out of equilibrium in the flow sense (and hence off the *IS* curve) because actual and planned expenditures are changing continuously as spenders adjust their plans to falling levels of income and the interest rate, while producers endeavor to match their output levels to the decreasing demands of their customers.

Finally, a position of full equilibrium is reached in which wealth holders are content with the new quantities of money and bonds in existence and in which the spending plans of the public exactly match the production plans of business firms. Comparing this final equilibrium with the initial situation, we find that output (Y_1) is lower and the interest rate (i_1) is higher (though it is below the peak reached immediately after the policy action).

The analysis of the response of the economy to an increase in the stock of money produced by the purchase of government bonds is analogous to that presented in the last few paragraphs. The final results of such a policy (an increase in the level of income and a decrease in the interest rate) can be seen directly from the *IS–LM* curve diagram.[13] However, if you have mastered the preceding discussion of the dynamics of adjustment, you should have no difficulty in describing the details of the adjustment process and you are strongly advised to do so.

Pure Fiscal Policy

By pure fiscal policy we mean government actions that alter the levels of government expenditures or tax revenues, but leave the public's wealth portfolio unchanged. Thus these policies initially affect only the flow variables, and leave the stock variables unaffected. Such actions may be of two types. First, the government may alter the composition of either its expenditures or its tax revenues, leaving the totals unchanged. Examples are the shifting of expenditures from military to civilian purposes and the replacement of one type of tax, for example, an income tax, by another type, such as a sales tax. The analysis of the aggregate implications of this type of policy is customarily treated within the branch of economics known as *public finance*. A second type of pure fiscal policy is that in which total government expenditures and tax revenues are increased or decreased by

---

and with which firms respond to the changing demand for their products as well as on the relative shapes of the *IS* and *LM* curves. A priori, it is possible for income and the rate of interest to fluctuate around their final equilibrium values before converging. Under some circumstances the system may not converge at all. These theoretical possibilities are ignored as being unlikely in practice.

[13] The *LM* curve shifts downward, and the *IS* curve remains unaffected.

equal amounts. This policy also leaves the government budget in balance (or leaves the imbalance unchanged) and hence has no effect on the public's wealth portfolio, since the government does not need to issue or redeem either money or bonds. In this chapter, we are concerned only with this second type of policy.

Pure fiscal policies influence the *IS* curve, leaving the *LM* curve unaffected. Specifically, an equal increase in government spending and tax revenues will produce an increase in the equilibrium level of income at any given rate of interest; that is, it shifts the *IS* curve to the right. This result, the so-called balanced budget theorem, was demonstrated in Chapter 3.[14]

Figure 5.3 illustrates the impact of a pure fiscal policy that increases both expenditures and revenues. Once again, the analysis of the converse case is analogous and is left as an exercise. Assume that initially the economy is in full equilibrium at income level Y_0 and interest rate i_0. The budget remains in balance throughout, and hence the stocks of money and bonds remain unchanged. As Panel A of the figure shows, the effect of an expansive fiscal policy is to shift the *IS* curve to the right and hence to increase both the level of income and the rate of interest. Income rises from Y_0 to Y_1, and the rate of interest increases to i_1 from i_0.

The process through which the economy adjusts to the new equilibrium may be described quite briefly. The impact effect of an equal increase in government spending and tax revenues is to increase total planned spending. The aggregate expenditure line shifts upward from $X_0(i_0, Y)$ to $X_1(i_0, Y)$.[15] This is because the marginal propensity to spend is less than unity, so that for each dollar of additional taxes it pays, the private sector reduces its planned spending by less than a dollar. Part of the added tax burden falls on saving. At the same time government outlays rise by a full dollar, and hence total (public and private) spending increases.[16]

From Panel B we see that at the original level of income, Y_0, planned expenditures will now total X_1^P and hence will exceed available output. Firms will experience unexpected reductions in their inventories and additions to their orders on hand. As a result, they will be induced to expand their production levels. When output rises, income does also, and as a result wealth holders will want to hold a larger proportion of their wealth in the form of cash, and hence will attempt to sell their bonds in exchange for

---

[14] See page 55.

[15] As in the monetary policy case discussed above, it seems likely that this shift will not occur instantaneously because spending plans will not be adjusted immediately. As a result, the planned spending line will move upward toward $X_1(i_0, Y)$, but may not reach that level.

[16] As an example, consider the linear model discussed on pages 54–55. The spending line is given by Eq. (3.6).

$$X^P = (\alpha - \gamma i + G^P - \beta T) + \beta Y$$

where β represents the marginal propensity to spend. At any given interest rate, say i_0, this equation describes a relation between planned spending X^P and income Y. An equal increase in G^P and T causes this relation to shift upward.

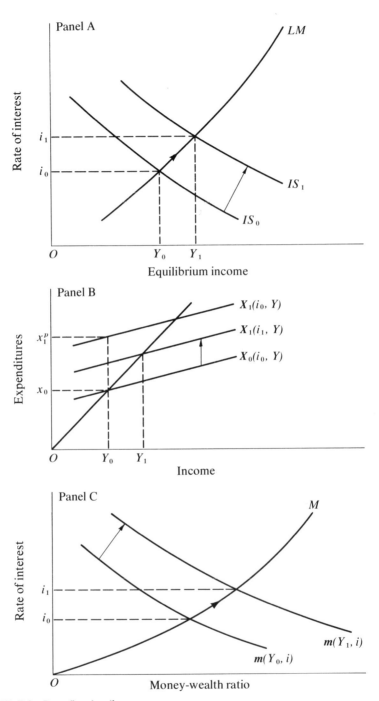

FIGURE 5.3 **Pure fiscal policy**

money.[17] This increase in the demand for money is represented in Panel C by the rightward shift of the demand-for-money function.

In the aggregate, however, this attempt on the part of the public to add to its money holdings cannot succeed because the actual stock of money is controlled by the central authorities, who do not allow it to increase. Hence pressure to sell bonds has the effect only of lowering the price of bonds and raising the interest rate. Given our assumption that asset prices adjust rapidly, the economy remains in stock equilibrium (on the *LM* curve) but out of equilibrium in the flow sense (off the *IS* curve).

This rise in interest rates moderates the initial upward shift in planned expenditures resulting from the government's fiscal actions. That is, the change in government spending and taxation policy tends to stimulate aggregate demand, but the ensuing rise in bond interest rates tends to depress it.[18] In terms of Panel B of Figure 5.3 this means that the planned spending line rises only to $X_1(i_1, Y)$ rather than to $X_1(i_0, Y)$.[19]

As long as planned outlays exceed the level of current production, firms will experience rising order books and declining inventories and hence will continue to expand their output. As a result, income and interest rates will rise steadily. This is represented by the movement up the *LM* curve in Panel A. Finally, the economy will converge[20] to a new equilibrium in which actual and desired spending are brought into equality at level Y_1.

Fiscal-Debt Policies

As noted in the previous section, fiscal policies that change the *flows* of government spending and tax revenues but have no effect on the private

---

[17] One aspect of this portfolio shift is that business will seek to borrow more (issue more private bonds) in order to finance the rising levels of output and sales.

[18] As their incomes rise, wealth holders might also seek to add to their money holdings by selling *capital*. This would tend to depress the prices of existing ("used") capital relative to the cost of new capital and so to reduce fixed investment. However, this effect would occur only if (as we are assuming throughout this chapter) the rental of capital remained constant. It seems more plausible to assume that capital rentals will rise during periods of business expansion, and if they do, the amount of investment that firms and households want to do may rise rather than fall. These issues cannot be treated fully within the present framework. They will be examined in more detail in Chapter 8.

[19] If spending plans adjust instantaneously, the spending line shifts upward to $X_1(i_0, Y)$ and then downward to $X_1(i_1, Y)$. If adjustment takes time, spending rises steadily, but (because of the interest rate effect) it increases only to $X_1(i_1, Y)$ rather than to $X_1(i_0, Y)$.

[20] Two qualifications are necessary. First, if the spending line first rises and later falls (see footnote 19), it is theoretically possible for planned spending to be depressed below actual output, thus provoking a temporary decline in the latter. As in the case of monetary policy, this possiblity for oscillation is ignored. Second, if rising incomes provoke an increase in capital rentals (see footnote 18), the resulting rise in fixed investment implies a further increase in planned expenditures. The spending line may shift upward from $X_1(i_0, Y)$ rather than downward. This possibility of a secondary source of expansion is frequently emphasized by advocates of expansionary fiscal actions. See, for example, *Economic Report of the President* (Washington, D.C.: January 1963), p. 49. In terms of our model this possibility implies that the *IS* curve may shift continually rightward, so that the economy does not converge to an equilibrium.

sector's wealth portfolio require that the government's budget remain continually in balance. Normally, changes in government receipts and outlays do not occur in this way but instead involve either a budget surplus or a budget deficit. Hence the analysis of changes in the government's fiscal stance requires us to pay attention not only to their effect on aggregate planned expenditures but also to the changes in the asset portfolio of the public that follow from the resulting surplus or deficit.

We consider two polar cases: an increase in government expenditures financed by printing new money and an equal increase financed by the issue of new government bonds. You should have no difficulty analyzing intermediate cases once you understand the principles involved. Similarly, the analysis of the effects of changes in tax revenues is analogous to that of expenditure changes and is left as an exercise.

Consider first the case of an increase in government spending financed by the sale of bonds. Assume that the economy is initially in full equilibrium with the government budget in balance ($G = T$). Income is accruing at the rate Y_2 and the rate of interest on nonmoney assets is i_1. In Figure 5.4 this initial situation is represented by the intersection of IS_0 and LM_0.

The authorities now increase their purchases of goods and services but do not raise taxes. The resulting budget deficit is financed by borrowing from private wealth holders by the issue of new government securities.[21]

The effects of this policy on the level of income cannot be predicted with certainty. The fiscal aspect of the policy (increased government spending) causes a rightward shift in the IS curve from IS_0 to IS_1. The financing aspect (sales of new government bonds to the public) shifts the LM curve to the left from LM_0 to LM_1. As a result, the net effect may be to raise or lower total income. In the figure these two possibilities are denoted the expansionary and contractionary cases, respectively. In the contractionary case income falls from Y_2 to Y_0. In the expansionary case income rises from Y_2 to Y_4. As with the policies analyzed earlier, it is enlightening to attempt to describe how the economy moves toward the new equilibrium.

Since this policy involves a change in the stock of bonds, it is more convenient to analyze it in terms of the supply of and demand for bonds than of the supply of and demand for money. Panel B of Figure 5.4 shows the actual and desired bond-wealth ratios as functions of the price of bonds. The actual ratio of the bond stock to total wealth is $qB/(M + qB + qK)$, which rises as the price of bonds q rises. This ratio is represented by the curve OB_0. The desired stock of bonds relative to wealth may be written

$$\frac{qB^D}{W} = b(q, Y)$$

By our hypotheses of the last chapter, this desired bond-wealth ratio will

---

[21] The government cannot, of course, pay for goods and services with government bonds, since these are not a medium of exchange. First it must sell bonds for money and then spend that money on goods and services. We assume that these two transactions occur rapidly enough to allow us to ignore the intermediate stage (after the bonds have been sold but before the proceeds have been spent). Note that the stock of money is left unchanged by this combined transaction.

increase when either the price of bonds or the level of income declines. At the initial level of income Y_2, the desired bond-wealth ratio is that represented by the curve labeled $b(q, Y_2)$, and the asset markets are in equilibrium at asset price q_1, which is equal to $1/i_1$. Thus the economy is on the LM_0 curve at the point (Y_2, i_1).

Panel C shows the relation between income and planned spending at various rates of interest. In the initial equilibrium, the interest rate is i_1 and the relation of income to spending is that represented by $X_1(i_1, Y)$. The economy is in flow equilibrium (on the IS_0 curve) at income level Y_2.

The government now sells bonds to finance a higher level of spending. The immediate effect of this action is to lower bond prices and increase the rate of interest. This is because bonds must become more attractive, that is, cheaper, if private wealth holders are to be willing to hold more of them. In terms of Panel B of the figure, the actual bond-wealth curve shifts rightward from OB_0 to OB_1, and as a result the price of bonds falls from q_1 to q_3 ($=1/i_3$). In Panel A of the figure this bond sale is represented by the upward shift in the LM curve. Since there is initially no change in income, the interest rate rises to i_3 ($=1/q_3$).

Immediately on selling these bonds the government increases its expenditures on goods and services. Taken alone, this fiscal aspect of the policy would shift the planned spending schedule in Panel C upward from $X_1(i_1, Y)$ to $X_2(i_1, Y)$.[22]

At the same time as government is increasing its expenditures, however, the rise in the interest rate resulting from the sale of bonds will lead to a reduction in planned expenditures by the private sector of the economy. Thus the fiscal and financing aspects of the policy have opposing effects on spending plans. The fiscal aspect implies an increase in government spending, but the associated rise in interest rates leads to a contraction in private spending.

Hence the net effect of the policy on total planned expenditures (government and private) cannot be predicted with any certainty. If bond demand is rather unresponsive to the rate of interest, so that wealth holders require a large increase in the interest rate to induce them to purchase the new bonds (i_3 is substantially above i_1), while at the same time planned expenditures by the private sector are very responsive to the interest rate, so that a given rise in the interest rate produces a substantial decline in private spending, the contractionary impact of the bond sale on private spending plans will be large. In this case, the net effect of the combined policy may be to reduce total spending. This is the case we describe as the *contractionary case* and illustrate on the left side of Figure 5.4. The expenditure line at the new higher interest rate is denoted $X_2(i_3, Y)$ in Panel C and lies *below* the original expenditure line $X_1(i_1, Y)$.[23]

---

[22] Where the difference between $X_2(i_1, Y)$ and $X_1(i_1, Y)$ is equal to the increase in government spending.

[23] Thus the vertical distance between $X_2(i_3, Y)$ and $X_2(i_1, Y)$ represents the reduction in private spending produced by the rise in the interest rate from i_1 to i_3.

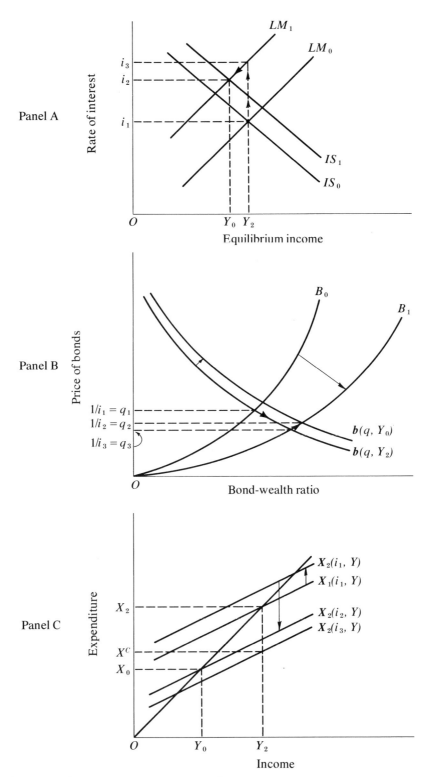

CONTRACTIONARY CASE

FIGURE 5.4 Government spending financed by borrowing

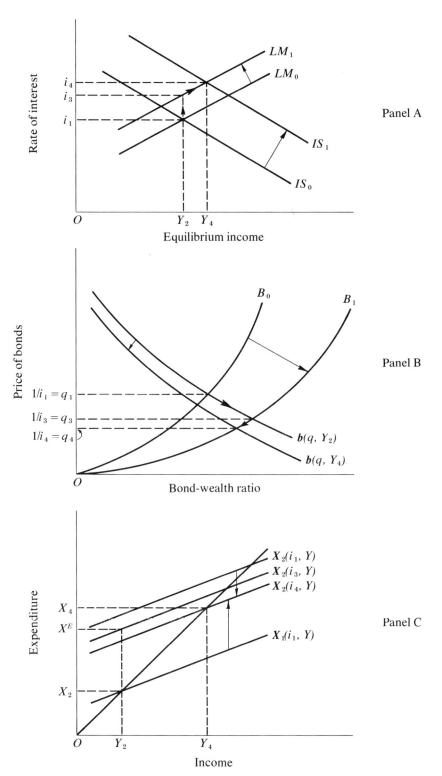

EXPANSIONARY CASE

Panel A

Panel B

Panel C

FIGURE 5.4 (cont'd)

If, on the other hand, bond demand is very responsive to the interest rate, so that wealth holders are willing to hold more bonds with only a small increase in the interest rate (i_3 is only slightly above i_1), while private spending is rather unresponsive to the interest rate, so that any rise in the interest rate produces only a small decline in private spending, the contractionary effect of the bond sale on private spending plans will be minor. In this case—*the expansionary case*—the net effect of the combined policy will be to increase total spending. This case is illustrated on the right side of Figure 5.4. The expenditure line at the new interest rate is again denoted $X_2(i_3, Y)$, but in this case it lies above $X_1(i_1, Y)$.[24]

Consider first the expansionary case in which the cutback in private spending is less than the increase in government spending, so that total planned expenditures rise. In this case desired outlays X^E, at the original level of income Y_2, exceed the output available from current production. This is illustrated in the right side of Panel C by the fact that X^E is greater than Y_2. As a result, firms find their orders rising and their inventories contracting and hence will begin to increase their output.

As in the case of pure fiscal policy, the resulting increase in income will lead to a desire on the part of wealth owners to reduce their holdings of bonds (and to issue new private bonds) in exchange for money. This is shown in the leftward shift in the demand-for-bonds schedule in Panel B. Thus bond prices decline further and there is a further rise in the interest rate. As a result, private demand is again reduced and the aggregate spending schedule shifts downward[25] from $X_2(i_3, Y)$ toward $X_2(i_4, Y)$. However, as long as total planned expenditure remains above the actual level of output, income and the rate of interest continue to rise. Finally, the economy converges to a position of stock and flow equilibrium with both income Y_4 and the rate of interest i_4 higher than in the initial situation. The path that the key variables follow is shown by the arrow in Panel A of the figure.

The analysis of the contractionary case is similar and is illustrated on the left side of Figure 5.4. Since the net effect of the combined policy is to reduce planned expenditures, firms find that they are unable to sell the whole of their output (Y_2 exceeds X^C). Thus output and income fall, wealth holders attempt to shift out of money into bonds (the demand-for-bonds schedule shifts to the *right*), and the interest rate declines. This decrease in the rate of interest moderates the decline in private spending so that the total spending line shifts upward[26] from $X_2(i_3, Y)$ toward $X_2(i_2, Y)$. However, as long as

---

[24] Again the vertical distance between $X_2(i_3, Y)$ and $X_2(i_1, Y)$ represents the reduction in private spending caused by the interest-rate effect, but in this case this reduction is small and does not offset the rise in government expenditures.

[25] If planned spending does not respond instantaneously to income and the rate of interest, it may, in fact, never reach the levels represented by $X_2(i_3, Y)$, but instead may simply drift slowly up from $X_1(i_1, Y)$ to $X_2(i_4, Y)$.

[26] Alternatively, if spending responds rather slowly to income and the interest rate, the downward shift in the spending line toward $X_2(i_3, Y)$ will be halted before that position is reached. See the preceding footnote.

total planned expenditures remain below the level of current output, both the level of income and the rate of interest continue to decline until a new equilibrium is reached. In this final situation the rate of interest i_2 is higher, but the level of income and output Y_0 is lower than in the initial equilibrium. Thus we see that an expansive fiscal policy (an increase in government spending) may actually lead to a contraction in the economy if it is inappropriately financed.

Up to now we have considered only fiscal policies financed by changes in the stock of bonds. However, the government may also finance its budget deficits or surpluses by changes in the stock of money.

In the United States, control over the stock of money is vested in the Federal Reserve System. The stock of bonds in the hands of the public is jointly controlled by the Treasury and the Federal Reserve System. For example, if the Treasury sustains a deficit in its budget over a certain period, it will normally finance it by borrowing from the public. Thus the usual case is that in which fiscal changes are associated, at least initially, with changes in the stock of bonds. If, however, the authorities fear that the resulting rise in interest rates will unduly restrict private demand, the Federal Reserve System may respond by purchasing bonds from the public and paying for them with new money, that is, by pursuing an expansionary pure monetary policy. The net effect of these two actions—a budget deficit financed by bond creation and an expansionary pure monetary policy—is equivalent to a budget deficit financed by money creation. In what follows we ignore these institutional details and assume that budget deficits are financed simply by printing new money.

Suppose, then, that the authorities increase their purchases of goods and services and pay for them by printing new money. The increased expenditures cause the *IS* curve to shift to the right; this is the *fiscal* impact of the policy. The increase in the stock of money leads to a rightward shift in the *LM* curve; this is the financing or *monetary* impact of the policy. In contrast to the case of bond financing, both aspects of the policy are expansionary, so the equilibrium level of income will certainly rise.[27] This is shown in the increase in income from Y_0 to Y_1 in Figure 5.5. No description of the dynamic process through which the economy moves toward the new equilibrium will be provided for this case. The provision of such a description, which will draw on the knowledge gained from the argument of the past several pages, is left as an exercise.

Before leaving the subject of combined fiscal and debt policies, one final point must be made. In the above analysis we considered only a once-and-for-all change in the stocks of bonds and money. However, if the government maintains the flows of its expenditures and receipts unchanged, there

---

[27] In this case, however, the effect of the policy on the rate of interest cannot be predicted with certainty. This is because both the supply of and the demand for money are increased, and hence the effect on the price of money is uncertain.

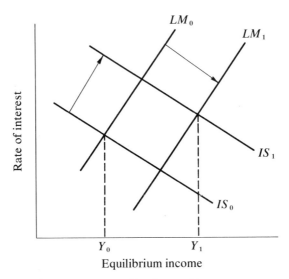

FIGURE 5.5 **Increased government spending financed by new money**

will be a *continuing* deficit or surplus in its budget. Although the flows of taxes and outlays remain the same, the stocks of bonds and/or money will continue to change, since this imbalance of the government budget must be financed *every period*. A continuing deficit, for example, necessitates continual increases in the stocks of money, bonds, or both. If the deficit is financed by money creation, the effect will be expansionary (since the *LM* curve will shift steadily to the right) whereas the issue of bonds will be contractionary (since the *LM* curve will move to the left).

The Monetarists vs. the Keynesians

The argument of the past two sections implies that the impact of a change in government spending or tax revenues, that is, a *fiscal* action, on total output and income depends, in general, on the manner in which it is *financed*. Consider, for example, an increase in the level of government expenditures on goods and services. If such an increase is accompanied by an equal increase in taxes, the balanced-budget multiplier theorem tells us that the net effect will be a modest rise in aggregate income. If, on the other hand, taxes are not raised and the resulting deficit is financed by money creation, the expansionary effect will be much larger. Finally, if the deficit is financed by government borrowing, the net effect is ambiguous, and aggregate income may rise or fall.

In their discussions of government policy, economists frequently disagree as to the relative importance of the fiscal and financing aspects of particular policy actions. In 1964, for example, taxes were cut substantially, and this action was followed by a prolonged period of economic expansion. However, there has been some dispute as to the causes of that expansion. Proponents of the efficacy of fiscal policy argue that the tax cut caused the business advance in the sense that if there had been no tax cut, the expansion would have been shorter and less vigorous. Opponents of this view (notably Milton Friedman) point out that the tax cut was followed by an acceleration in the rate of growth of the money supply and argue that it was this monetary action, rather than the tax cut, that was responsible for the long period of prosperity in the middle sixties.[28]

A similar debate over the relative importance of fiscal and financing policies occurred in 1975. Early in that year many economists were advocating a tax cut in order to stimulate the economy out of the 1974–1975 recession. It was admitted that such a policy would produce massive federal deficits in 1975 and 1976 and hence would necessitate large-scale government borrowing that would tend to raise interest rates. Although most economists took the view that the net effect would be to expand total spending and raise incomes, a few observers[29] argued that the rise in interest rates might be so large that despite the tax-reduction, aggregate private spending would actually decline rather than increase. Hence the business situation might worsen rather than improve.[30] On this occasion it appears that the expansionists were correct.

Disputes of this kind may be regarded as reflecting disagreements about certain vital facts. If, for example, the demand for bonds is rather unresponsive to the rate of interest, a given increase in the stock of bonds will produce a large rise in the interest rate. If, at the same time, private investment and consumption spending are very responsive to the rate of interest, this rise will have a large contractionary effect on total spending and hence on the levels of income and output. Under such circumstances a reduction in government tax receipts accompanied by an equivalent increase in government borrowing (such as was advocated in 1975) is unlikely to have much expansionary effect on the economy and may even, on balance, be contractionary. In the contrary case, where the demand for bonds is very responsive to the interest rate—so that a given volume of government borrowing can be accomplished with very little upward pressure on interest rates—and where private expenditures are not much affected by interest rates anyway, such a policy would have a clear expansionary effect.

The debate within the economics profession over the relative significance of fiscal and monetary actions has led to the emergence of two schools of thought: the *Monetarists* and the *Keynesians*.[31] As a rough approximation,

[28] See Milton Friedman and Walter W. Heller, *Monetary vs. Fiscal Policy* (New York: W.W. Norton, 1969), pp. 55–57, 67–68.

[29] At the time, it was alleged in the media that Treasury Secretary Simon was the chief proponent of this view within the administration.

[30] For an example of a contribution to this debate, see *Monthly Economic Letter,* First National City Bank (April 1975) pp. 3–5.

[31] In a sense this is a misnomer. Keynes himself clearly believed that changes in the stock of money play a crucial role in the overall behavior of the economy. After all, his two most

the Monetarists take the view that unless a fiscal action is financed by a change in the stock of money, it will have little or no effect on total spending.[32] Keynesians, on the other hand, believe that fiscal actions will always have a positive effect on aggregate demand regardless of how they are financed.[33]

The difference between the Monetarist and Keynesian views of the world is illustrated in Figures 5.6 and 5.7. These figures show the effects of a tax cut financed either by borrowing or by money creation.

Monetarists take the position that the amount of money (and hence the amount of nonmoney[34]) that people want to hold is closely related to their incomes but is rather unresponsive to the rate of interest.[35] At the same time they argue that spending is highly sensitive to asset prices and rates of return. These hypotheses imply that the *LM* curve is rather steep and the *IS* curve is rather shallow. This is the situation in the upper portion of the two figures.

Keynesians, by contrast, generally assume that the demands for money and other assets are rather sensitive to the rate of interest but that income is the principal determinant of the level of private expenditures and that rates of return, while not totally irrelevant, play a much more limited role in spending decisions. This Keynesian position is illustrated in the lower portion of the figures: It implies that the *IS* curve is quite steep whereas the *LM* curve is quite shallow.

A tax cut produces a rightward shift in the *IS* curve from *IS* to *I'S'*. If such a cut is financed by money creation, the *LM* curve also shifts rightward from *LM* to *L'M'*. The issue of bonds, on the other hand, implies a leftward shift in the *LM* curve from *LM* to *L''M''*. Since the two schools of thought do not seriously disagree on the role of *income* in the determination of spending and the demand for assets, the *lateral* shifts in the *IS* and *LM* curves are the same in the two scenarios. However, since their slopes differ, the *vertical* shifts in the curves also differ.

In both scenarios the tax cut, taken by itself, stimulates spending. If there

significant publications are *Treatise on Money* (1931) and *The General Theory of Employment, Interest and Money* (1936).

[32] Milton Friedman, in his debate with Walter Heller, points out that if taxes are cut and the resulting deficit financed by the issue of bonds, the taxpayers will have more money, but the bondholders will have less money. He concludes from this that the impact of this policy on total spending cannot be predicted unambiguously. See Friedman and Heller, pp. 53–54.

[33] Most Keynesians agree that a fiscal policy will have a *larger* impact on demand if it is accompanied by a monetary action than if it is not, but they insist that the effect will be significant even if there is no change in the money stock.

[34] Monetarists focus their attention on the money stock and pay little or no attention to the stock of nonmoney. However, as we have seen, the wealth constraint of the private sector implies that any statements about the stock of money may always be translated into statements about the stock of nonmoney.

[35] Monetarists often cast their analysis in terms of the *income velocity* of money, which is the ratio between the stock of money and the level of income. They then assume that velocity is a constant independent of the rate of interest. For an attempt to test this hypothesis, see Milton Friedman, "The Demand for Money: Some Theoretical and Empirical Results," *Journal of Political Economy*, Vol. LXVII (August 1959).

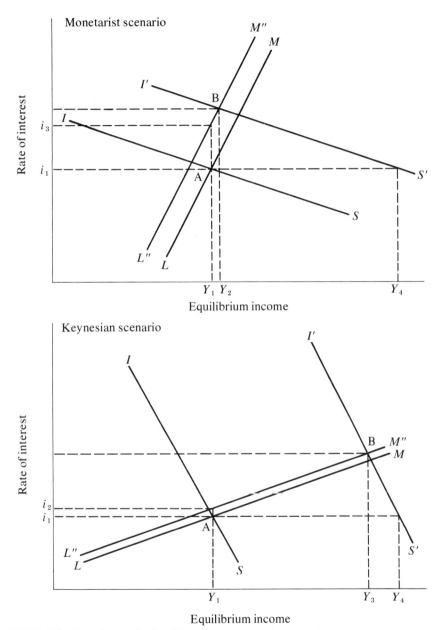

FIGURE 5.6 The effects of a bond-financed tax cut

were no change in the interest rate (it remained at i_1), income would rise from Y_1 to Y_4. In fact, however, the interest rate will, in general, not remain unchanged and, moreover, the direction and extent of any change depends on the method by which the tax cut is financed.

If the tax cut is financed by the issue of bonds, the net effect of the

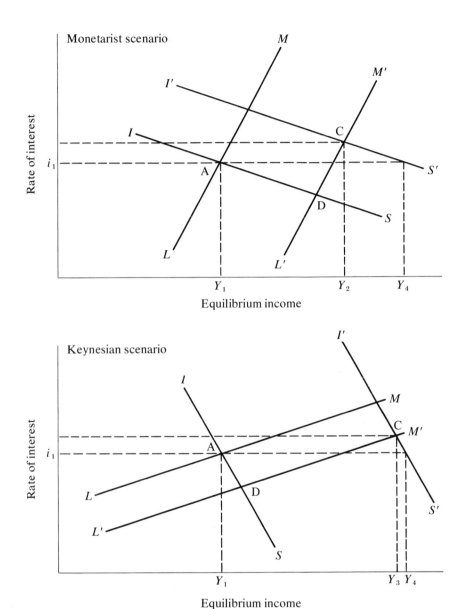

FIGURE 5.7 The effects of a money-financed tax cut

combined fiscal and financing action is to shift the economy from point A to point B in Figure 5.6. Note that the effect of the policy on total income is quite different in the monetarist and Keynesian scenarios. In the money-creation case, Figure 5.7 shows that the action shifts the economy from point A to point C. In this case the total effect on income is similar in the two scenarios, but the relative contributions of the tax cut and the increased stock of money to the final outcome are different.

Consider first the situation in which bonds are issued. In this case the interest rate must rise in order to induce wealth holders to purchase these additional bonds. In the monetarist scenario, because the demand for bonds is rather unresponsive to the interest rate (the *LM* curve is steep), this initial increase in the rate of interest—from i_1 to i_3—is large. Moreover, because private spending is quite sensitive to the interest rate (the *IS* curve is shallow) this sharp increase in the rate of interest has a substantial contractionary effect, which largely offsets[36] the expansionary effect of the tax cut. Instead of increasing from Y_1 to Y_4, income increases by a much smaller amount to Y_2.[37]

Contrast this conclusion with the Keynesian scenario. Since Keynesians assume that the demand for bonds is quite sensitive to the rate of interest (the *LM* curve is shallow), the initial increase in the interest rate—from i_1 to i_2—is quite small. Moreover, since private spending is not very sensitive to the interest rate (the *IS* curve is steep), the contractionary effect of this rise in the interest rate will be modest. As a result, the overall effect of the policy is unambiguously expansionary. Total income increases from Y_1 to Y_3, a much larger increase than in the monetarist case.

Let us turn now to the situation in which the tax cut is accompanied by an increase in the stock of money. In this case the two schools agree that the overall impact of the policy will be expansionary, but disagree on the quantitative significance of the fiscal and monetary aspects.[38]

From Figure 5.7 we see that the overall effect of the policy is to move the economy from A to C. This total move may be decomposed into the movement from A to D, which reflects the shift in the *LM* curve (the monetary effect) and into that from D to C, which results from the shift in the *IS* curve (the fiscal effect).[39] In the monetarist scenario the monetary effect is the dominant force, whereas in the Keynesian world the fiscal effect dominates. This is because monetarists believe that the reduction in the interest rate brought about by the increase in the stock of money is large and has a major impact on spending decisions, whereas Keynesians believe

---

[36] In the figure, we have assumed that the offset is not complete, so that the policy package as a whole does have some small expansionary impact. As we saw in the last section, this is not a necessary result: The net effect may be contractionary rather than expansionary. In this case Y_2 would be less than Y_1.

[37] This scenario represents the view of those economists who opposed the 1975 tax cut on the grounds that it would provide little or no net stimulative effect. See p. 103.

[38] In Figure 5.7 the policy is more expansive in the Keynesian case: Income rises to Y_3 in the Keynesian scenario but only to Y_2 in the monetarist model. This is not a necessary result, but occurs in this example because the rightward shift in the *IS* curve is greater than the shift in the *LM* curve. As a result, the interest rate rises. Since spending is less responsive to the interest rate in the Keynesian scenario, income rises more in that case. If the rightward shift in the *LM* curve had been greater than that in the *IS* curve, the interest rate would have fallen and the monetarist scenario would have shown the greater expansion. Check this argument by algebraic or geometric means. However, in this case the disagreement between the two schools is not over the size and direction of the overall effect, but rather over the roles of the fiscal and monetary actions in producing this effect.

[39] Clearly a similar decomposition is possible in the bond financing case. In that case, the financing effect was negative.

these effects are minor in comparison with the effects of the tax reduction. The dispute between Friedman and Heller over the effects of the 1964 tax cut provides an example of this analysis.

Before leaving the Keynesian–monetarist debate, two other issues require mention. First, in connection with the link between spending and changes in the stock of money, monetarists frequently criticize Keynesians for their alleged overemphasis on the rate of interest on *bonds*. They point out that if wealth holders believe that their holdings of money are too large relative to their other assets, they may shift out of money into *physical capital,* thus pushing up the prices of existing capital goods and stimulating purchases of new capital. They allege that this link between money and expenditures is ignored by Keynesians, who therefore underestimate the impact of changes in the stock of money on spending.[40] While this may have been a legitimate criticism of many early Keynesians (and remains true of many "Keynesian" textbooks), it is much less valid today. Neo-Keynesian economists, such as James Tobin, accept the view that the price of existing capital is a key link[41] between changes in the stock of money and the level of income, but do not conclude from this that the stock of money is the sole (or even the most important) determinant of the level of aggregate spending.

Second, in connection with the Keynesian view of the *LM* curve, we should mention the so-called *liquidity trap*. As we have seen, Keynesians generally assume that the demand for bonds is quite sensitive to the interest rate, so that the *LM* curve is shallow. The liquidity trap is a special limiting case in which the *LM* curve is actually horizontal. The argument leading to this possibility runs as follows. Suppose the interest rate is very low (bond prices are very high), so that all wealth holders believe that bond prices will be lower in the future than they are now. In these circumstances all bondholders would be prepared to sell bonds at a price fractionally above the current market price, but none can find buyers. As a result, when the monetary authorities offer to buy bonds in exchange for new money, they are able to do so without bidding up bond prices. Changes in the stock of money have virtually no effect on bond prices and interest rates: The *LM* curve is, for all practical purposes, horizontal.

In these extreme circumstances the activities of the monetary authorities have no effect on the rate of interest and hence no effect on aggregate spending. The economy behaves in the manner of the simple model developed in the first part of Chapter 3. Fiscal policy works, but monetary policy is impotent.

This case is frequently described in textbooks as the "Keynesian case."

---

[40] In particular, monetarists argue that empirical findings that consumption and investment spending is not very sensitive to the rate of interest on government bonds do not prove that the monetarist position is incorrect.

[41] The *IS–LM* analysis is not a very useful framework in which to analyze this link, however, since it implicitly assumes that there is only one rate of interest and one nonmoney asset in the economy.

Table 5.1 Effects of Various Government Policies

Policy	Income	Rate of Interest
Expansionary pure monetary policy	+	−
Expansionary pure fiscal policy	+	+
Bond financed* expansionary fiscal policy	? (−)	+
Money financed* expansionary fiscal policy	+	? (−)

* The minus signs in parentheses indicate the effects of the policies if they are maintained over a long period of time. See pages 101–102.

This is unfortunate terminology for two reasons. In the first place, modern-day Keynesian economists do not assert that only fiscal policy works and that the financing method employed by the government is irrelevant. Their claim is the more modest one that both fiscal and monetary policy have an impact on spending. Secondly, Keynes himself apparently did not believe in the "Keynesian case" except as a theoretical curiosity! After having mentioned the possibility of the liquidity trap, he went on to say, "I know of no example of it hitherto."[42] Since 1936 a number of attempts have been made empirically to test for the existence of the "trap." Most such attempts have been unsuccessful.

Conclusion

We have now completed our analysis of a simple model economy. The conclusions of our discussion regarding monetary and fiscal policy are summarized in Table 5.1. This table shows the effects of expansionary pure monetary and pure fiscal policies on the equilibrium levels of income and the rate of interest. It also shows the impact of a mixed expansionary[43] fiscal-debt policy both in the short run and in the long run. In cases where the policy impact is uncertain, a question mark is shown.

The analysis of the last three chapters was based on a series of special

---

[42] J.M. Keynes, *The General Theory of Employment, Interest and Money* (London: Macmillan, 1936), p. 207.
[43] That is, a policy in which either government spending is increased or tax revenues are decreased. Note that although we describe this policy as expansionary, its effects (if financed by the issue of bonds) may be contractionary.

assumptions and hypotheses. One of these assumptions was that wealth holders were indifferent between holding bonds and capital as long as they yielded the same rate of return. The implications of dropping that assumption are examined in Chapter 6. However, the analysis of this chapter is more difficult than that of preceding chapters. You may wish to omit it on a first reading and proceed directly to Part 3. In the three chapters of that part our hypotheses with regard to consumption, investment, and the demand for money are examined more carefully.

References

Blinder, Alan S., and Robert M. Solow. "Docs Fiscal Policy Matter." *Journal of Public Economics,* Vol. II, No. 4 (November 1973).
In this article the authors extensively examine the relationship between fiscal and financial policy. Their model is more complex than that used here, since it takes account of the fact that interest receipts are taxable and hence that changes in the interest rate and/or the stock of bonds lead to changes in government tax revenues.

Carlson, Keith M., and Roger W. Spencer. "Crowding Out and Its Critics," *Review.* Federal Reserve Bank of St. Louis, Vol. 57, No. 12, December 1975.
A useful discussion of the dispute over the efficacy of monetary and fiscal policy.

Okun, Arthur M. *The Political Economy of Prosperity.* New York: W.W. Norton, 1970, Chapter 2.

Silber, William L. "Fiscal Policy in *IS-LM* Analysis: A Correction." *Journal of Money, Credit, and Banking,* Vol. II, No. 4 (November 1970).

Questions for Classroom Discussion

1. In the summer of 1968 the U.S. government raised taxes by imposing a surcharge on personal income taxes. This slowed but did not reverse the steady rise in demand for goods and services. Some economists argued that the reason for this was that the money supply continued to rise rapidly. Explain this argument in terms of the analytical framework of this chapter.

2. The following is a quotation from Milton Friedman: "You can have a tax cut, let us say, and finance the resulting deficit by borrowing money . . . . Alternatively, you can have a tax cut and finance the deficit by printing money . . . . The essence of the position that I'm presenting is that those two kinds of tax cut will have very different effects." Explain the argument that underlies Friedman's assertion.

3. If the demand for money is insensitive to the rate of interest, fiscal policy is ineffective. Why? If the demand for bonds is sensitive to their price, fiscal policy is effective. Why?

Portfolio Equilibrium in an Economy with Three Assets*

In Chapters 4 and 5 we assumed that wealth holders regard bonds and capital as perfect substitutes in their portfolios. As a result of this assumption, bonds and capital always yielded the same rate of return and could be treated as the same asset. In effect, our model economy contained only two assets, namely, money and nonmoney.

In this chapter we consider the behavior of asset markets and the nature of asset equilibrium in an economy that contains three assets rather than only two. Bonds and capital will no longer be regarded as perfect substitutes, and hence their rates of return may differ. Our objective is to explain the determination of both these rates of return. As far as possible the method of approach will parallel that used in Chapter 4.

On any given date there exist given stocks of money, bonds, and capital goods. Wealth owners will be in equilibrium when the stock of each of these assets is willingly held, that is, when desired holdings of money, bonds, and capital are each equal to the actual holdings. Thus our analysis must begin by considering the determination of these desired stocks.

The Demand to Hold Assets

We continue to employ the same basic hypotheses we introduced in Chapter 4[1] with regard to the demand for assets. Specifically, we suppose that the demand to hold any asset depends on wealth, income, and the rates of return on bonds and capital.[2]

We assume that an increase in their wealth causes wealth owners to want to hold more of all three types of assets. An investor who obtains an addition to his resources will wish

---

* The material in this chapter is more difficult than that in previous chapters. You may wish to omit it on first reading and proceed directly to Part 3.
[1] See pp. 68–69.
[2] We continue to assume that money yields no interest, or if it does, that the interest rate never changes.

to add to his holdings of money and bonds and capital. This assumption is not only plausible a priori but is also backed by a considerable volume of factual evidence.

A rise in his income will cause the wealth holder to want to add to his stock of money. This is because money is the medium of exchange and is required to make transactions. At higher income levels the volume of transactions is generally larger, and so more money is required to finance them.

If wealth is unchanged, an increase in the demand for money necessarily implies a decrease in the demand for bonds, capital, or both. If a wealth owner wants to hold more money, he must hold less of some other asset. This accounting requirement implies that an increase in income will cause a wealth owner to wish to reduce his holdings of bonds, capital or both.[3]

The final variables affecting the demands for the various assets are their rates of return. An increase in the rate of return on any given asset will make it relatively more attractive to hold and the other two assets relatively less attractive. Thus, if the rate of return on capital increases, the demand to hold capital will rise, and the demand to hold bonds and money will fall. Similarly, an increase in the bond rate of interest will cause the demand for bonds to rise and those for money and capital to fall.

We will continue to assume that the return on a bond (including both the coupon and the expected capital gain) amounts to one dollar per year and remains constant. Hence the rate of return on bonds may be written

$$i_B = 1/q_B$$

Capital goods yield both a rental and a capital gain. The latter will be assumed constant, but in this chapter we drop the assumption that the rental is also fixed. Instead, we now assume that the rental of capital rises when the level of income increases. This is because a rise in income means that output is also higher. Firms need more plant and equipment to produce this higher level of output and will bid up the rentals of these items. Thus the rate of return on capital will now be written

$$i_K = R(Y)/q_K$$

where $R(Y)$ represents the dollar return on a unit of capital and rises when income rises.

These various hypotheses may be summarized in the demand functions for assets, which we write as

$$M^D = M[i_K, i_B, Y, W] = M\left[\frac{R(Y)}{q_K}, \frac{1}{q_B}, Y, W\right] \qquad (6.1)$$
$$\quad - \quad - \quad + \quad +$$

---

[3] This conclusion holds true only if the rates of return on assets remain constant. However, we will argue later that an increase in income is likely to produce a rise in the rate of return on capital and so to have a second, indirect, effect on the demands for assets.

$$q_B B^D = B[i_K, i_B, Y, W] = B\left[\frac{R(Y)}{q_K}, \frac{1}{q_B}, Y, W \right] \qquad (6.2)$$
$$ {\scriptstyle -\ +\ -\ +}$$

$$q_K K^D = K[i_K, i_B, Y, W] = K\left[\frac{R(Y)}{q_K}, \frac{1}{q_B}, Y, W \right] \qquad (6.3)$$
$$ {\scriptstyle +\ -\ -\ +}$$

where W represents total wealth and is given by

$$W = M + q_B B + q_K K \qquad (6.4)$$

The plus and minus signs represent the direction in which the dependent variables will change if the independent variables rise.

We see from these equations that an increase in the level of income has two effects on the demands to hold assets. First, it leads to an increase in the demand for money for transactions purposes and hence to a corresponding decline in the demands for the other two assets. Second, it raises the rate of return on capital [because $R(Y)$ rises when Y rises], which increases the demand for capital and so reduces the demand for money and bonds. In the cases of money and capital, this means that the net effect of an income change is ambiguous in theory.[4]

In reality, however, the transactions effect of a change in income on the demand for capital is probably quite small. Increases in the demand for money for transactions purposes are usually made at the expense of bonds rather than of capital goods. The wealth holder who wishes to add to his money stock to finance a higher level of spending is more likely to do this by selling bonds or by borrowing[5] than by selling his car.[6] Accordingly, we will assume that in the case of capital the rate-of-return effect dominates the transactions effect so that an increase in income causes a rise in the demand for capital. Conversely, in the case of money we will assume that the transactions effect is predominant, so that wealth holders also want to hold more money when their incomes increase. These assumptions are not only plausible but are also backed by a considerable volume of empirical evidence.

As in Chapter 4 we assume that the proportions in which a wealth holder distributes his portfolio between the available assets do not alter when his wealth increases or decreases. This assumption enables us to make use of the same geometric construction that we employed in that chapter. Once again, however, we stress that the assumption is not crucial to the results we

---

[4] In the case of bonds there is no ambiguity. An increase in income reduces the demand to hold bonds.

[5] Borrowing is, of course, the sale of securities issued by oneself.

[6] When put this way the proposition sounds very plausible. However, common stocks are claims to capital goods owned by firms, and the sale of stocks in order to increase money holdings is by no means uncommon.

will obtain.[7] When this assumption is incorporated and the effects of income are collapsed into a single term, our demand functions become

$$M^D = m[q_K, q_B, Y]W \qquad (6.4)$$
$$+ \quad + \quad +$$

$$M^D/W = m[q_K, q_B, Y] \qquad (6.4a)$$
$$+ \quad + \quad +$$

$$q_B B^D = b[q_K, q_B, Y]W \qquad (6.5)$$
$$+ \quad - \quad -$$

$$q_B B^D/W = b[q_K, q_B, Y] \qquad (6.5a)$$
$$+ \quad - \quad -$$

$$q_K K^D = k[q_K, q_B, Y]W \qquad (6.6)$$
$$- \quad + \quad +$$

$$q_K K^D/W = k[q_K, q_B, Y] \qquad (6.6a)$$
$$- \quad + \quad +$$

These equations indicate that the shares of total wealth that wealth owners wish to hold in the form of each asset depend on income (Y) and on the prices of capital and bonds (q_K and q_B).

When the markets for assets are in equilibrium, the actual ratios of each asset to total wealth are equal to the desired ratios.

$$\frac{M}{W} = \frac{M^D}{W}$$

$$\frac{q_B B}{W} = \frac{q_B B^D}{W}$$

$$\frac{q_K K}{W} = \frac{q_K K^D}{W}$$

However, if the markets for two of the assets are in equilibrium, that for the third must also be in equilibrium. This is simply because if wealth owners are satisfied with the shares of their portfolios that are held in the form of any two of the assets, they must be satisfied with the share held in the remaining asset.

We will now examine the conditions under which each market, considered in isolation from the others, may be in equilibrium. Later we will go on to analyze the conditions necessary for equilibrium in all three markets simultaneously.

---

[7] Demonstrate this fact for yourself using methods analogous to those of Appendix A to Chapter 4.

The Supply of and Demand for Money

On any date there exist given stocks of money and other assets and hence a given ratio of the money stock to total wealth:

$$\frac{M}{W} = \frac{M}{M + q_K K + q_B B} \tag{6.7}$$

This ratio will decline when the price of either bonds or capital rises. In particular, the money-wealth ratio will be $M/(M + q_K K)$ when q_B is zero and will approach zero as q_B becomes large. Thus the relation between the actual money-wealth ratio and the price of bonds is the downward-sloping one represented by the curve M/W in Figure 6.1.

The desired money-wealth ratio depends on income and the prices of capital and bonds. In particular, at a given price of capital and a given level of income, the desired money-wealth ratio will rise as the price of bonds rises. This is because an increase in the price of bonds makes them a less attractive asset relative to money and hence induces wealth owners to hold more money and fewer bonds in their portfolios. In Figure 6.1 the desired ratio of money holdings to total wealth is represented by the upward-sloping curve labeled $m(q_K, q_B, Y)$.

Investors will be satisfied with their holdings of money when the actual money-wealth ratio is equal to the desired ratio. In Figure 6.1 this occurs when the price of bonds is q_B^*. At that price the amount of money wealth

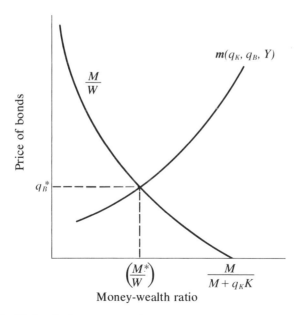

FIGURE 6.1   Equilibrium in the money market

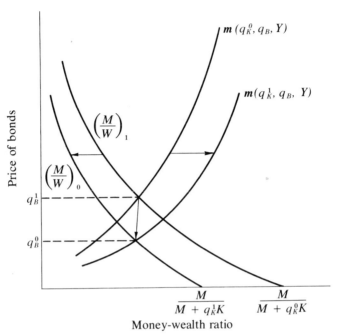

FIGURE 6.2 **The effect of a rise in the price of capital on money-market equilibrium**

owners are holding is just equal to the amount they want to hold. At any higher price of bonds, wealth owners would want to hold more money than there is available. Pressure to switch out of bonds and into money would push the price of bonds downward, and this pressure would continue until the price reached q_B^*. Conversely, if the price of bonds were less than q_B^*, investors would want to switch out of money and into bonds, thus driving the price of bonds upward until it reached q_B^*.

We now wish to examine how this equilibrium price[8] of bonds is affected when either the price of capital or the level of income changes. We consider first the effect of a change in the price of capital.

Suppose the price of capital is initially q_K^0 and now rises to q_K^1. At any given price of bonds, total wealth will increase and hence the actual money-wealth ratio will decline. This effect may be seen directly from Eq. (6.7): When q_K increases, M/W declines. In Figure 6.2 this decline is represented by the leftward shift from $(M/W)_1$ to $(M/W)_0$.

The rise in the price of capital will also affect the share of total wealth that wealth owners will want to hold in the form of money. Specifically, it

---

[8] It is an equilibrium price only in the partial sense that the supply of and demand for money are equal at that price. The true or full equilibrium price will be that at which the supplies of and demands for all assets are equal. This full equilibrium will be derived later in the chapter.

reduces the rate of return on capital and hence makes it a less attractive asset relative to money. Hence investors will want to increase the proportion of their wealth held in the form of money and decrease the proportion held in capital. Thus at any given price of bonds, the desired money-wealth ratio will rise. In Figure 6.2 this increase in the desired money-wealth ratio is represented by the rightward shift from $m(q_K^0, q_B, Y)$ to $m(q_K^1, q_B, Y)$.

Thus the effect of an increase in the price of capital is to reduce the actual money-wealth ratio but to increase the desired money-wealth ratio. As Figure 6.2 demonstrates, the net effect of these changes is to cause a decline in bond prices. When the price of capital increases from q_K^0 to q_K^1, the price of bonds falls from q_B^1 to q_B^0. Let us attempt to provide an intuitive explanation of this result.

A rise in the price of capital leads investors to want to hold *more* money because it makes them wealthier and because it makes money a more attractive asset relative to capital. In fact, however, there is no more money available. Hence something else must happen to make investors want to hold less money so that, on balance, they are content with the existing supply. A fall in the price of bonds has the desired effect: It reduces wealth and also makes money a relatively less attractive asset. As a result, a simultaneous rise in the price of capital and a fall in the price of bonds leave the demand for money unaffected.[9]

Thus we conclude that if the price of capital rises, the price of bonds must fall if investors are to remain content with their existing money holdings. This relation between q_K and q_B is represented by the downward-sloping curve in Figure 6.3. This *mm curve* shows the values of q_K and q_B at which actual and desired holdings of money are equal. By referring to Figure 6.1 you may check that at points to the left of the *mm* curve the price of bonds is below its equilibrium level and the actual money-wealth ratio exceeds the desired ratio, so that there is an excess supply of money (*ESM*). Conversely, at points to the right of the *mm* curve there is an excess demand for money (*EDM*): The actual money-wealth rat o is less than the desired ratio.

Let us now turn to the effect of a change in the level of income on the money market. Suppose incomes rise. At any given set of asset prices, this will cause a rise in the desired money-wealth ratio. As a result the desired ratio will exceed the actual ratio and wealth owners will seek to sell bonds to add to their money holdings. Since the stocks of all assets are fixed in the aggregate, this attempt on the part of wealth holders to rearrange their portfolios will cause bond prices to fall.

This argument is illustrated in Figure 6.4. An increase in income from Y_0 to Y_1 causes a rightward shift in the desired money-wealth ratio from $m(q_K, q_B, Y_0)$ to $m(q_K, q_B, Y_1)$. As a result, the price of bonds declines from q_B^1 to q_B^0.

---

[9] It will not, of course, leave the demand for the other two assets unaffected.

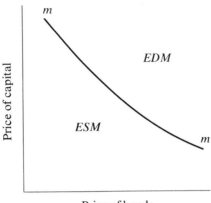

FIGURE 6.3   Equilibria in the money market: The *mm* curve

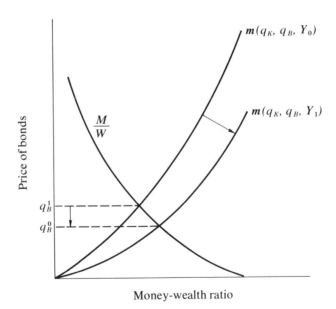

FIGURE 6.4   The effect of a rise in the level of income on money-market equilibrium

We conclude, therefore, that at any given price of capital, if the level of income rises, the price of bonds must fall if equilibrium between the demand for and supply of money is to be maintained. This means that an increase in the level of income implies a *leftward* shift in the *mm* curve, since each value of q_K will now be associated with a lower value of q_B.

The Supply of and Demand for Capital

The analysis of the market for capital goods will parallel that of the market for money and hence can be treated more briefly.

On any date there is a given ratio of capital to total wealth:

$$\frac{q_K K}{W} = \frac{q_K K}{M + q_K K + q_B B}$$

This ratio will fall when the price of bonds rises and will rise when the price of capital rises. In particular, as q_K becomes large the ratio approaches unity, and as q_K approaches zero the ratio also approaches zero. Thus, at any given price of bonds, the actual capital-wealth ratio may be represented by the upward-sloping curve labeled $q_K K/W$ in Figure 6.5.

The desired ratio of capital to wealth declines as the price of capital rises. This is because, at any given level of income and any given price of bonds, a rise in the price of capital makes capital a less attractive asset and hence leads investors to want to hold less capital and more money and bonds. This phenomenon is illustrated in Figure 6.5 by the downward-sloping curve $k(q_K, q_B, Y)$.

If there is to be equilibrium in the market for capital goods, the actual ratio of capital to wealth must be equal to that *desired* by wealth owners. In Figure 6.5 this situation occurs when the price of capital is q_K^*. At higher

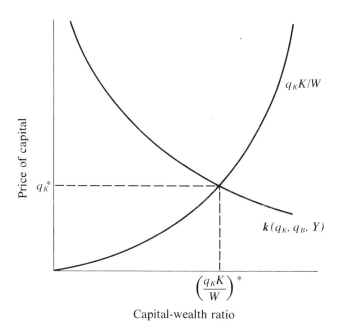

FIGURE 6.5 Equilibrium in the capital market

prices the available supply exceeds the demand, so that the price tends to fall, while at lower prices demand exceeds supply, so that the price tends to rise.

Suppose the price of bonds rises. At any price of capital, bonds become less attractive relative to capital, and the desired ratio of capital to wealth rises. At the same time an increase in q_B implies a rise in the value of wealth and thus a reduction in the *actual* capital-wealth ratio. Thus a rise in the price of bonds causes the demand to hold capital to exceed the available supply. As a result, the price of capital will increase. We conclude that when bond prices rise, the price of capital must also rise if investors are to remain willing holders of the existing capital stock.

This argument is illustrated in Figure 6.6. The price of bonds rises from q_B^0 to q_B^1. As a result, the actual capital-wealth ratio declines from $(q_K K/W)_1$ to $(q_K K/W)_0$ while the desired ratio increases from $k(q_K, q_B^0, Y)$ to $k(q_K, q_B^1, Y)$. As a result, the price of capital at which investors are content to hold the existing stock of capital rises from q_K^0 to q_K^1.

This conclusion implies the existence of a second relation between q_B and q_K. This second relation is represented by the upward-sloping *kk curve* depicted in Figure 6.7. This curve shows the values of q_K and q_B at which the wealth-owning public is willing to hold the existing supplies of capital. You may confirm from Figure 6.5 that at points above the *kk* curve, the price of capital is above its equilibrium level so that the actual capital-wealth

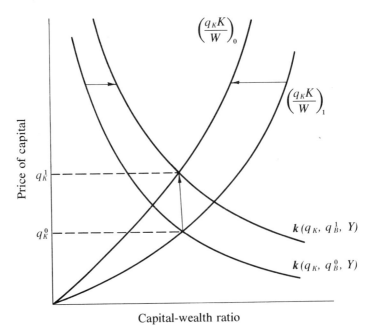

FIGURE 6.6 The effect of a rise in the price of bonds on capital-market equilibrium

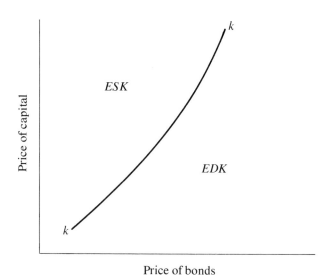

FIGURE 6.7 Equilibria in the capital market: The *kk* curve

ratio is above the desired ratio: There is an excess supply of capital (*ESK*). Conversely, at points below the *kk* curve there is an excess demand for capital (*EDK*).

Before turning to the third market in the economy—the market for bonds—let us examine how the *kk* curve is affected by a change in the level of income. We do this by analyzing how q_K will be affected by a change in Y, assuming that q_B remains unchanged.

Suppose the level of income rises. As a result, the return to capital increases, so that at any given price of capital, wealth holders will want to hold more capital in their portfolios: The desired capital-wealth ratio will exceed the actual ratio. Since the stock of capital is fixed, the price of capital goods will be bid up. This process is illustrated in Figure 6.8. The increase in income from Y_0 to Y_1 causes the price of capital to rise from q_K^0 to q_K^1.

We conlude that when income increases, the price of capital at which the public is willing to hold the existing stock also increases. Since this result is true at any specified price of bonds q_B, it implies that the effect of an increase in income is to cause the *kk* curve to shift upward.

The Supply of and Demand for Bonds

Finally, we come to the market for bonds. Our discussion of this market will be brief for two reasons. First, the discussion will parallel that of the previous two sections. Second, if the markets for both capital and money are in equilibrium, the market for bonds must also be in equilibrium. In a sense, therefore, discussion of this market is redundant, but we include it for the sake of completeness.

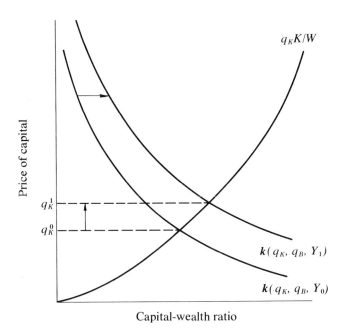

FIGURE 6.8 **The effect of a rise in the level of income on capital-market equilibrium**

At any time there is a given stock of bonds in existence and hence a given bond-wealth ratio

$$\frac{q_B B}{W} = \frac{q_B B}{M + q_K K + q_B B}$$

This ratio rises as the price of bonds rises. Specifically, the ratio is zero when q_B is zero and rises toward unity as q_B becomes large. Hence the actual bond-wealth ratio is given by the upward-sloping curve $q_B B/W$ in Figure 6.9.

The share of wealth that investors want to hold in the form of bonds rises as the price of bonds falls. This is because a decline in q_B implies an increase in the rate of interest on bonds and hence makes bonds a more attractive asset relative to either money or capital. Thus the desired bond-wealth ratio increases as q_B declines. This is shown by the curve $b(q_K, q_B, Y)$ in Figure 6.9.

The bond market is in equilibrium when the price of bonds is q_B^*. At this price the share of their assets that wealth owners wish to hold in the form of bonds is equal to the share they are actually holding.

How is this equilibrium affected by a change in the price of capital? Suppose the price of capital goods rises. This will increase the value of wealth and hence lower the actual bond-wealth ratio. At the same time a rise in q_K reduces the rate of return on capital and hence makes bonds a

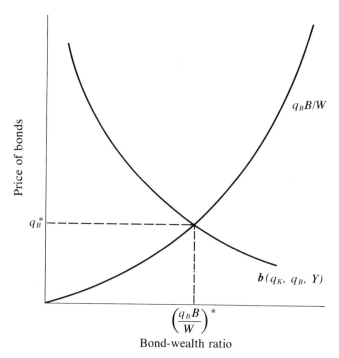

FIGURE 6.9 Equilibrium in the bond market

relatively more attractive asset in which to hold wealth. As a result, the desired bond-wealth ratio will rise. Thus an increase in q_K reduces the actual bond-wealth ratio while raising the desired ratio. Hence the demand for bonds will exceed the supply, and the price of bonds will rise.

This argument is illustrated in Figure 6.10. A rise in the price of capital from q_K^0 to q_K^1 causes the actual bond-wealth ratio to decline from $(q_BB/W)_1$ to $(q_BB/W)_0$, while the desired ratio increases from $b(q_K^0, q_B, Y)$ to $b(q_K^1, q_B, Y)$. As a result, the price of bonds increases from q_B^0 to q_B^1.

We conclude, therefore, that a rise in q_K must be accompanied by a similar rise in q_B if the bond market is to remain in equilibrium. This means that there is a third relationship between q_K and q_B—namely, that associated with bond-market equilibrium. This relation is represented by the upward-sloping *bb curve* in Figure 6.11. Note that at points to the left of the *bb* curve there is an excess demand for bonds (*EDB*) while at points to the right there is an excess supply (*ESB*).[10]

Finally, consider the effect on bond-market equilibrium of an increase in the level of income. Such an increase raises the rate of return on capital and also increases the transactions demand for money. Hence it reduces the attractiveness of bonds relative to both capital and money. The desired

---

[10] Check this assertion by reference to Figure 6.9.

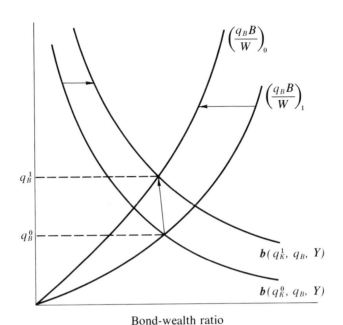

FIGURE 6.10 The effect of a rise in the price of capital on bond-market equilibrium

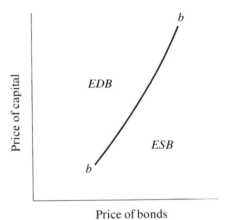

FIGURE 6.11 Equilibria in the bond market: The *bb* curve

bond-wealth ratio contracts. This is shown in Figure 6.12 by the leftward shift from $b(q_K, q_B, Y_0)$ to $b(q_K, q_B, Y_1)$. As a result, the price of bonds falls from q_B^1 to q_B^0. Since this result is true for any value of q_K, we conclude that an increase in the level of income causes a leftward shift in the *bb* curve.

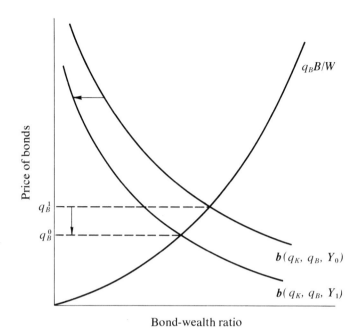

FIGURE 6.12 The effect of a rise in the level of income on bond-market equilibrium

Full Equilibrium in Asset Markets

We have now analyzed the market for each of the three assets in our simple model economy. It is now time to bring these results together.

For any single asset, wealth owners are in equilibrium when their actual holdings are equal to their desired holdings. Hence they will be in *full portfolio equilibrium*[11] when actual and desired holdings of all three assets are equal simultaneously. In this section we first analyze how this equilibrium is attained at any given income level and then discuss how the equilibrium situation changes when the level of income rises or falls.

At a given income level Y, the supply of and demand for money are equal when the prices of bonds and capital (q_B and q_K) are at levels represented by the *mm* curve. Similarly, the market for capital is in equilibrium when the economy is on the *kk* curve. Finally, bond-market equilibrium requires that the economy be on the *bb* curve. It follows, therefore, that full equilibrium in all three markets requires that q_B and q_K take the values yielded by the intersection of these three curves. Figure 6.13 shows this full equilibrium.

This figure shows that at income level Y, wealth owners are content with their existing holdings of assets if and only if the prices of capital and bonds

---

[11] This is, of course, an equilibrium only with respect to the assets in the economy. In this sense it is analogous to the equilibrium represented by a point on the *LM* curve.

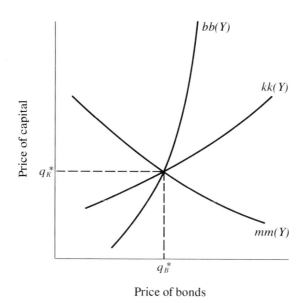

FIGURE 6.13 Equilibrium in a three-asset economy

are q_K^* and q_B^*, respectively. At this set of prices wealth owners are content with their existing holdings of money (since they are "on the *mm* curve"), of capital (since they are "on the *kk* curve") and of bonds (since they are "on the *bb* curve"). At no other set of asset prices is this true.

Two points need to be made about this full equilibrium. First, note that the *mm*, *kk*, and *bb* curves all intersect at the same pair of asset prices. This reflects the fact that if any two markets are in equilibrium, the third market must also be in equilibrium. In terms of the diagram, if wealth holders are simultaneously on the *mm* curve and on the *kk* curve, they must also be on the *bb* curve. Second, in Figure 6.13, note that the *bb* curve has been drawn with a steeper slope than the *kk* curve. However, the arguments of the preceding sections established only that both these curves slope upward. Can we be sure that the *bb* curve is steeper than the *kk* curve?

The answer to this question is yes. In Figure 6.14 the *mm* and *kk* curves alone are shown. The intersection of these two curves divides the diagram into four quadrants. Above the *mm* curve there is an excess demand for money (*EDM*), whereas below it there is an excess supply of money (*ESM*). Similarly, above the *kk* curve there is an excess supply of capital (*ESK*), whereas below it there is an excess demand for capital (*EDK*).

Consider Quadrant I. In this quadrant there is an excess demand for both money and capital. This means that at *all* asset-price combinations represented by points in this quadrant, the shares of wealth held in the form of money and capital are less than those desired by wealth owners. This implies that the share held in the form of bonds must be greater than that

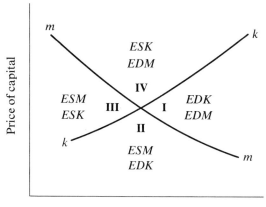

FIGURE 6.14 Supplies of and demands for capital and money

desired. Hence the market for bonds cannot be in equilibrium at any (q_K, q_B) combination that lies in Quadrant I.

A similar argument applies to Quadrant III. In this quadrant there is an excess supply of both money and capital and hence an excess demand for bonds. That is, at all (q_K, q_B) combinations that lie in Quadrant III, the desired bond-wealth ratio exceeds the actual ratio, and hence the bond market is out of equilibrium.

The *bb* curve represents situations of bond-market equilibrium. The argument of the preceding paragraphs establishes that no such equilibrium can occur in the first and third quadrants. Hence the *bb* curve cannot pass through these quadrants and must therefore pass through the second and fourth quadrants. Thus the *bb* curve is necessarily steeper than the *kk* curve.

We are now in a position to examine how asset-market equilibrium is affected by a change in the level of income. We choose to focus our attention on the money and capital markets and to ignore the market for bonds.[12]

Consider Figure 6.15. Suppose that the initial level of income is Y_0. At this income level the *mm* curve is $mm(Y_0)$ and the *kk* curve is $kk(Y_0)$. Full equilibrium in the asset markets requires the prices of capital and bonds to be q_K^1 and q_B^1, respectively.

The level of income now rises from Y_0 to Y_1. From the arguments developed earlier, we know that this increase will cause leftward shifts in both the *mm* and *kk* curves to $mm(Y_1)$ and $kk(Y_1)$, respectively. These shifts reflect the fact that an increase in income makes both money and capital

---

[12] You may wish to incorporate the bond-market adjustments into the following analysis. You may do this by adding the *bb* curve to Figure 6.15 and examining how it shifts in response to income changes. You will find that this addition will merely confirm the conclusions reached.

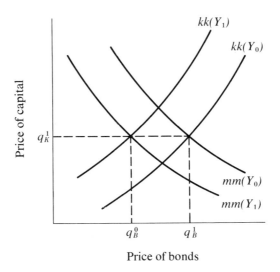

FIGURE 6.15 The effect of a rise in income on asset equilibrium

An increase in income will produce an unambiguous reduction in bond prices. However, the effect on capital-good prices in uncertain: they may rise, fall, or remain unchanged. The last case is illustrated in this figure. You should have no difficulty in illustrating the other two possibilities.

more attractive relative to bonds. Wealth owners will want to increase the shares of their wealth held in the form of these two assets. As a result, at any given price of capital, the price of bonds must decline.

From Figure 6.15 we see that the overall effect of the increase in income is to lower the price of bonds from q_B^1 to q_B^0. However, the effect on the price of capital cannot be predicted from theoretical considerations alone: q_K may rise, fall, or remain unchanged. In the figure this last possibility is illustrated.

The reason for this ambiguity is that we cannot predict how the demand to hold capital will be affected by an increase in income. Such an increase raises capital rentals and hence makes capital more attractive. At the same time, however, it increases the demand for money relative to bonds and causes bond prices to fall. This decline in q_B in turn makes capital less attractive relative to bonds. Thus the net impact of the increase in income on the demand for capital cannot be predicted. As a result, the effect on the price of capital is ambiguous.

Monetary and Debt Policy

In this section we analyze the impact of various government policy actions on asset-market equilibrium. Three types of policy will be considered: (1) the issue of new money to finance a government deficit, (2) the issue of new bonds to finance a government deficit, and (3) the purchase of outstanding bonds with new money. In Chapter 4 these policies were discussed for the case of an economy in which there were only two assets. The results were summarized in terms of the effects of the policies on the *LM* curve.[13] The argument of the present section is essentially a generalization of the analysis of Chapter 4 to the asset markets of an economy containing three assets.

The Effect of an Increase in the Money Stock

The impact of a policy in which the government issues new money to finance a deficit is analyzed in Figure 6.16. In Panels A, B, and C of this figure the markets for money, bonds, and capital, respectively, are illustrated. Panel D depicts the overall equilibrium of the asset markets.

The issue of new money increases the stock of money and total wealth by equal dollar amounts and hence causes a rise in the actual money-wealth ratio. As Panel A shows, such a change causes a rise in the price of bonds at which the public is willing to hold the existing stock of money. The *mm* curve in Panel D shifts rightward. This policy also causes a reduction in the shares of wealth that are held in the forms of both capital and bonds. As Panels B and C show, the actual bond-wealth and capital-wealth ratios both decline. Wealth holders will be content with this situation only if bonds and capital each become less attractive relative to money. Panel B shows that equilibrium in the bond market requires a rise in the price of bonds: This implies a rightward shift in the *bb* curve. Similarly, equilibrium in the market for capital requires a rise in the price of capital: This implies an upward shift in the *kk* curve.

In Panel D the effects of these changes on the overall equilibrium are shown. The prices of bonds and capital both rise. This reflects the fact that total wealth and the demands to hold both these assets have risen, whereas the available supplies have not. Hence their prices have been driven up.

It is worth pointing out that this is the same conclusion as was reached in Chapter 4. In the model of that chapter an increase in the stock of money caused the rate of interest to decline. Since bonds and capital were perfect substitutes and yielded the same dollar return, this meant that the prices of both increased.

The Effect of an Increase in the Stock of Bonds

The issue of new bonds increases the bond stock and total wealth by equal dollar amounts. Hence the actual bond-wealth ratio rises while the

---

[13] You might like to be reminded of the conclusions of that analysis. An increase in the stock of money, whether it is used to finance a deficit or to purchase outstanding bonds, causes a decline in the rate of interest and thus a rise in the price of nonmonetary assets: The *LM* curve shifts downward. An increase in the stock of bonds causes a rise in the interest rate and a fall in the price of nonmoney: The *LM* curve shifts upward.

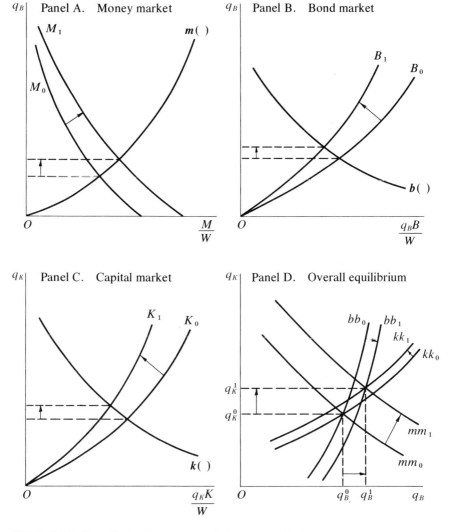

FIGURE 6.16 The effects of an increase in the money stock

money-wealth and capital-wealth ratios both decline. These changes are shown in the upper three panels of Figure 6.17.

At any given price of capital, wealth owners will be willing to hold a larger share of their assets in the form of bonds only if the price of bonds declines. This effect is shown in Panel B of the figure. Thus the policy causes the *bb* curve to shift leftward. Similarly the wealth-owning public will accept a reduction in their money-wealth ratio only if money becomes a relatively less attractive asset. At any given q_K this means that q_B must decline (see

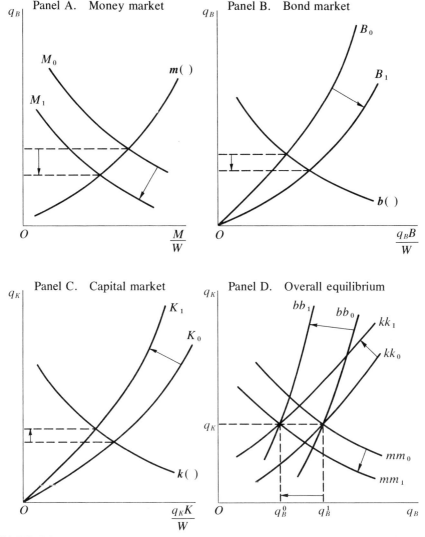

FIGURE 6.17 **The effects of an increase in the bond stock**

Panel A). This implies a leftward shift in the *mm* curve. Finally, wealth owners will be satisfied with a reduction in their capital-wealth ratio only if capital becomes less attractive. This means that the price of capital must rise. At any q_B, capital-market equilibrium requires a higher q_K (see Panel C). This implies an upward shift in the *kk* curve.

Panel D illustrates the implications of these changes for overall equilibrium. From this panel we see that the effect of this policy on the price of bonds is clear: q_B will fall from q_B^1 to q_B^0 in order to induce investors to hold a larger share of their portfolios in the form of bonds. The effect on the price of capital is ambiguous; q_K may rise, fall, or remain unchanged.[14]

The reason for this ambiguity is that we cannot predict the net effect of the policy on the demand for capital. On the one hand the increase in total wealth will cause a rise in the demand to hold capital. On the other hand the fall in bond prices makes capital a less attractive asset relative to bonds: This tends to reduce the demand for capital. We cannot predict which of these effects will dominate, and hence we cannot predict whether the price of capital will rise or fall.

The Effect of Open-Market Bond Purchases

Finally, we consider a policy in which the government purchases outstanding bonds from wealth owners and pays for them with newly printed money. In Chapter 5 such a policy was described as a *pure monetary policy*. The effects of this policy are illustrated in Figure 6.18 on page 134.

The effect of a pure monetary policy is to raise the share of wealth in the form of money and to reduce the share held in bonds. At any given price of capital, wealth holders will hold more money only if bonds become more expensive. This is shown in Panel A. It implies a rightward shift in the *mm* curve. Conversely, at any given q_K, wealth holders will be willing to reduce their holdings of bonds only if bond prices rise. This is shown in Panel B. It implies a rightward shift in the *bb* curve.

Since both the *mm* and *bb* curves shift rightward as a result of the government's action, the price of bonds must rise. This reflects the fact that if the authorities are to induce wealth holders to sell bonds for cash, the price of bonds must be bid up. In Panel D this bidding up is represented by the increase in the bond price from q_B^0 to q_B^1.

Consider now the market for capital and the effect of the policy action on the *kk* curve. We note first that at the price of bonds at which the transaction between bondholders and the government takes place, q_B^1, the value of total wealth is unchanged. This is because the value of the bonds sold by wealth holders is equal to the value of the money they receive in exchange. Hence, at the price of bonds q_B^1, the policy action has no effect on the capital-wealth ratio and hence no effect on the market for capital goods. Therefore the new *kk* curve and the old *kk* curve (labeled kk_1 and kk_0 in Panel D) will intersect at a price of bonds q_B^1.

At the original price of bonds, q_B^0, however, the effect of the transaction is to increase the value of total wealth. This is because at the original, lower price of bonds, the value of the bonds sold by wealth holders is less than the value of the money they receive in exchange.[15]

---

[14] The diagram has been constructed so that q_K does not change. Clearly, however, q_K could rise or could fall.

[15] Consider the value of wealth when the price of bonds is q_B^0. Before the policy action, this value is

Panel C illustrates the market for capital when the price of bonds is q_B^0. Since the open market operation raises total wealth, it causes a reduction in the capital-wealth ratio. As a result, this policy would raise the price of capital if q_B were to remain constant. Thus we conclude that at the price of bonds q_B^0 the new kk curve must lie above the old kk curve.

These conclusions are incorporated in Panel D of the figure. At q_B^1 the old and new kk curves intersect. At q_B^0 the new curve lies above the old curve.[16] From this panel we see that an open-market bond purchase raises not only the price of bonds but also the price of capital. An intuitive explanation of this result is not difficult. Open-market bond purchases cause bond prices to rise. As a result, bonds become a less attractive asset relative to capital and hence wealth owners will wish to shift out of bonds and into capital. Since the available stock of capital is fixed, the price of capital rises.

Conclusion

We have now completed our analysis of portfolio equilibrium in a three-asset economy. In most cases the results obtained are strictly analogous to those reached earlier in the two-asset model. This is reassuring. Frequently the two-asset model is simpler to deal with and to obtain results from than the corresponding three-asset model. This is particularly true when we wish to consider the spending and production sides of the economy in addition to the behavior of asset markets. The results of this chapter suggest that the simplification that is made possible by considering only a two-asset model will in most cases not lead us into serious error. This is the justification for our continued use of the *IS–LM* apparatus.

$$W^0(q_B^0) = M + q_B^0 B + q_K K$$

After the action the value is

$$W^1(q_B^0) = M + \Delta M + q_B^0 (B - \Delta B) + q_K K$$

where ΔM represents the amount of new money issued and ΔB represents the number of bonds the government purchases. The change in the value of wealth is

$$W^1 - W^0 = \Delta M - q_B^0 \Delta B$$

By adding and subtracting $q_B^1 \Delta B$ from this expression, we obtain

$$W^1 - W^2 = \Delta M - q_B^1 \Delta B + (q_B^1 - q_B^0) \Delta B$$

We know, however, that

$$\Delta M = q_B^1 \Delta B$$

so that

$$W^1 - W^0 = (q_B^1 - q_B^0) \Delta B$$

which is positive because q_B^1 exceeds q_B^0. Hence we have proved that at the initial price of bonds the effect of the policy action is to raise the value of total wealth.

[16] *Exercise:* Prove that for prices of bonds above q_B^1 the old kk curve lies above the new kk curve.

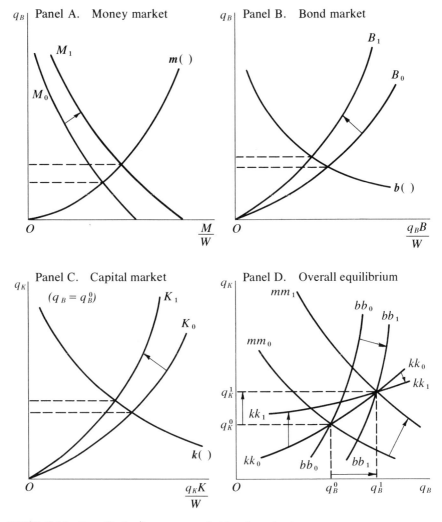

FIGURE 6.18 The effects of an open-market bond purchase

The model of this chapter may be extended to any number of assets. Full equilibrium in asset markets requires that the prices of all assets be such that the available supplies of all assets are willingly held by wealth owners. However, geometric analysis becomes difficult when there are four or more assets in the model. This is because there are then at least three asset prices to keep track of, which cannot be done within the bounds of a two-dimensional diagram. Nonetheless, although the analytical tool must be algebra rather than geometry, the same general approach may be used.

One particular extension of the model occurs when we bring a system of banks—which accept deposits and make loans—into the story. This extension is the subject of Part 4.

Reference

The model of this chapter is based on the work of James Tobin. For a useful summary of Tobin's views, see Tobin, James. "A General Equilibrium Approach to Monetary Theory." *Journal of Money, Credit and Banking,* Vol. I, Number 1 (February 1969).

Questions for Classroom Discussion

1. For many years economists have debated the question of why money plays a special role in our economy. Why is there a subject known as monetary economics but not one dealing with savings-and-loan-share economics or common stock economics? Tobin answers this question as follows: "The essential characteristic . . . [of money] . . . is that the interest rate on money is exogenously fixed by law or convention, while the rate of return on securities is endogenous, market determined. If the roles of the two assets in this respect were reversed, so also would the economic impacts of changing their supplies. Conceivably the government could fix the interest rate on [securities] and let the rate on [money] be determined in the market. Then the way for the [government] to achieve an expansionary monetary impact would be to buy money with securities!"

   Explain this quotation. (*Hint*: Suppose we set i_B equal to some fixed level (zero will do) and introduce i_M as the rate of interest on money that may vary from one time to another. How does this change alter the analysis of this chapter?)

   Are any other characteristics of money (such as the fact that it is used as a medium of exchange) relevant to the conclusions of this chapter?
2. Suppose the rate of interest on money is not zero but is fixed by the government at some nonzero level. Using the framework of this chapter, analyze the effect on capital and bond prices of an increase in the interest rate on money.

Part Three

Studies of Particular Variables

The analysis of our simple model of an economy in Part 2 was based on a series of intuitively plausible hypotheses regarding the behavior of spenders and wealth holders. We now must examine these hypotheses more carefully and critically. Our emphasis will be on the developments in economic theory that have occurred in the past quarter century and especially on those that appear most important from the point of view of monetary economics. In Chapters 7 and 8 we take a closer look at the determinants of two important components of aggregate spending, namely, consumption and tangible investment. In Chapter 9 we turn to the behavior of wealth holders and examine the theory of the demand for money.

The Theory of Consumption

7

When he introduced the consumption function to the economics profession in 1936, John Maynard Keynes argued that the marginal propensity to consume (*MPC*) will be positive but less than unity[1] and that the average propensity to consume (*APC*) will decline as income rises.[2] These suppositions implied the relation between consumption and income that was depicted in Figure 3.1. As income increases, both consumption and saving also increase, so that consumption rises less rapidly than income. Moreover, as income increases, the proportion devoted to current consumption declines.

In the years following the publication of the *General Theory*, economists found that this specification of the consumption function not only had intuitive appeal but also seemed to fit the facts of experience. For example, when real consumption is plotted against after-tax real income for the years 1929–1941, the result is as shown in Figure 7.1. Not only is the relation between income and consumption during this period very close, but it also accords well with Keynes's predictions. The marginal propensity to consume over this period is around 0.7 and the average propensity declines as disposable income rises.

After World War II, however, evidence began to accumulate indicating that there was, in fact, no long-run tendency for the average propensity to consume to decline as incomes rose. For example, the ratio of personal consumption expenditures (including purchases of consumer durables) to after-tax income was approximately the same in the late 1960s as that which had prevailed at the turn of the century.[3]

---

[1] "The fundamental psychological law, upon which we are entitled to depend with great confidence both a priori from our knowledge of human nature and from the detailed facts of experience, is that men are disposed, as a rule and on the average, to increase their consumption as their income increases, but not by as much as the increase in their income." J. M. Keynes, *The General Theory of Employment, Interest and Money* (London: Macmillan, 1936), p. 96.

[2] ". . . it is also obvious that a higher absolute level of income will tend, as a rule, to widen the gap between income and consumption. For the satisfaction of the immediate primary needs of a man and his family is usually a stronger motive than the motives toward accumulation, which only acquire effective sway when a margin of comfort has been attained. These reasons will lead, as a rule, to a greater *proportion* of income being saved as real income increases." *General Theory*, p. 97.

[3] In the five-year period 1897–1901 this ratio was 0.905. After rising during the Great Depression and falling during the war and the immediate post-war years, it returned to 0.907 in the period 1966–1970.

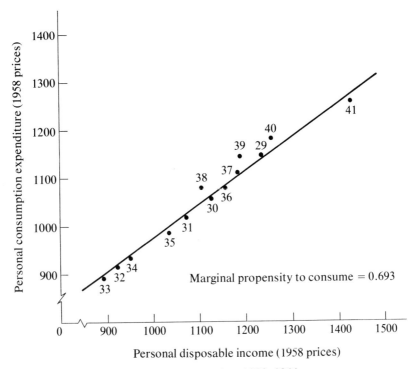

FIGURE 7.1 Per capita income and consumption, 1929–1941

Economists should not have been surprised to find that the facts did not support Keynes's hypothesis of a falling average propensity to consume. For if the consumption-income ratio has always declined as income has risen, then at some date in the past, consumption must have accounted for essentially all of income. For example, the statistical relation shown in Figure 7.1 implies that for levels of income of less than $920 (at 1958 prices), consumption would be greater than income.[4] Since this level of income was reached for the first time in 1915, acceptance of this "Keynesian" consumption function as a description of a long-run relationship between income and consumption would imply that saving had been negative throughout all history up to that date; and obviously such an implication is absurd!

As was pointed out in Chapter 3, acceptance of Keynes's hypothesis of a falling *APC* is not critical to the model of the economy developed in Part 2. Nonetheless, these new data suggested that Keynes's theory of consump-

---

[4] The relation in Figure 7.1 is represented by the equation

$$C = 282.6 + 0.693Y$$

where *C* stands for consumer spending and *Y* stands for income after tax (both in 1958 prices). According to this equation, when *Y* is equal to 920, *C* is also equal to 920.

tion was seriously incomplete. In particular, it failed to explain why the *APC* declined as income rose over relatively short periods (such as 1929–1941, for example) but did not on the average decline over much longer periods. In an attempt to solve this puzzle, economists have been led to investigate the determinants of consumption much more carefully than Keynes did.

The results of this reexamination are a group of theories of household behavior that have come to be known as the *new theories of the consumption function.*[5] Prominent among these new approaches are the *permanent income hypothesis* of Milton Friedman and the *life-cycle hypothesis* of Modigliani, Brumberg, and Ando. Although they differ in their details, the broad outlines of these new approaches are quite similar.

The New Theories of the Consumption Function

The fundamental assumption from which the new consumption theorists begin their analysis is that the typical household plans its consumption spending over a span of time that extends beyond the current year.[6] The amount it decides to spend this year is only one element in this long-term plan and hence depends not only on its income this year but also on the income it expects to earn in future years.

This long-term planning is made possible by the fact that households are able to borrow and lend. By saving (and lending) part of its current income, a household can increase its future consumption at the expense of its present consumption. Conversely, by borrowing or selling assets, a household can increase its current consumption at the expense of a cut in its future consumption. Thus borrowing and lending enable the household to plan a pattern of consumption spending over time that may differ markedly from the pattern of its income.

We will develop the implications of these simple observations in the context of a household that expects to live for only two periods,[7] which, for ease of reference, we will describe as year one and year two. The household expects to have receipts[8] in each period of R_1 and R_2 dollars, respectively.

---

[5] This term was coined by M. J. Farrell. See M. J. Farrell, "The New Theories of the Consumption Function," *Economic Journal*, Vol. LXIX (December 1959).

[6] In the *General Theory*, Keynes did not specify the period over which he expected his consumption function to apply. However, since his analysis was concerned throughout with the short run, it is unlikely that he had in mind a period longer than a year. As an aside, we might mention that there is virtually no stable relation between income and consumption on a quarter-by-quarter basis. This suggests that households plan their spending over a longer time horizon than three months.

[7] This is a less restrictive assumption than it appears at first sight. Although we use the term *years* for convenience, nothing in the succeeding argument requires that the two periods be of equal length. Hence the first period may be interpreted to mean the current year (the present) and the second to mean all subsequent years (the future).

[8] In the diagram and text we assume that both R_1 and R_2 are positive, but this is not essential to the argument.

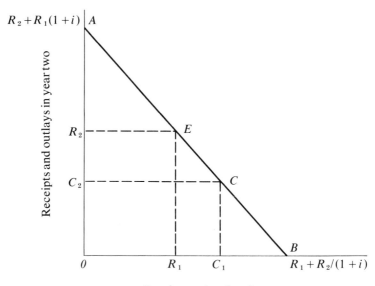

FIGURE 7.2   The choice of a consumption plan

Hence one possible consumption plan is that in which the household's consumption is exactly equal to its receipts in each year. This plan is represented by point E in Figure 7.2.

However, if borrowing and lending are possible, the household is not compelled to consume at a rate exactly equal to its income. Suppose the household can borrow or lend at a fixed rate of interest i. Then for each dollar by which it reduces year-one consumption, the household is able to increase its year-two consumption by $(1+i)$ dollars. Conversely, each one-dollar increase in its year-one consumption (financed either by borrowing or by selling earning assets) requires it to curtail its year-two consumption by $(1+i)$ dollars. As a result, the household can choose any consumption plan that is represented by a point in the triangle OAB in Figure 7.2. This set of possibilities is usually described as the household's *feasible consumption set*. As long as the household always prefers more consumption to less in each year,[9] however, it will always choose a consumption plan that lies on the line AB rather than below it.

In Figure 7.2 we suppose that the household chooses the consumption plan represented by point C. This means that it consumes C_1 in year one and C_2 in year two. In order to finance this plan it must borrow $(C_1 - R_1)$ dollars

---

[9] The assumption that the household prefers more consumption to less in the *last* period of its life implies that it does not wish to leave any bequests to its heirs. If you object to this assumption, you may either interpret R_2 to mean the household's receipts in the second period minus its planned bequests, or define consumption in the second period to include planned bequests.

in year one. Repayment of interest and principal on this loan amounts to $(C_1 - R_1)$ $(1+ i)$ or $(R_2 - C_2)$ dollars in year two. Thus its outlays on consumption and loan repayment in year two are exactly equal to its receipts in year two.

The implication of this discussion is that current consumption is determined by the interaction between the household's total consumption opportunities (that is, its feasible consumption set) and its preferences with regard to present and future consumption. Thus we might write

$$C_1 = f(R_1, R_2, i, u) \tag{7.1}$$

where R_1, R_2, and i together determine the household's feasible consumption set and u represents the whole complex of factors that determine its preferences. The important point to note about this consumption function is that present consumption is made to depend not only on present income but also on future income.

In Eq. (7.1) the household's spending opportunities are represented by three variables, namely, its income in years one and two, R_1 and R_2, and the rate of interest at which it can borrow or lend, i. However, it is clear from Figure 7.2 that the feasible consumption set OAB really depends only on two variables, since the line AB is fully determined by its slope and its intercept with the year-one axis. If R_1 were larger and R_2 smaller, but this intercept and slope were unchanged, then the position of AB, and hence the choice of a consumption plan, would also be unchanged.

The slope of AB represents the amount of consumption the household can obtain in year two if it reduces its year-one consumption by one dollar. Since the interest rate is i, this quantity is $(1 + i)$ dollars. The intercept OB represents the total consumption the household can enjoy in year one if it mortgages the whole of its year-two income; that is, if all its receipts in year two are required to repay debt incurred in year one. This maximum present consumption is equal to its year-one receipts, R_1, plus the maximum amount it can borrow against its future receipts, $R_2/(1 + i)$.[10] Changes in R_1 and R_2 that leave $[R_1 + R_2/(1 + i)]$ unchanged do not alter the household's consumption opportunities and hence do not call for a change in its consumption plan.

Algebraically, the condition that the household's consumption plan must be on the line AB may be represented by the condition[11] that

---

[10] If the household borrows $R_2/(1 + i)$ in the first year, it must repay $iR_2/(1 + i)$ in interest and $R_2/(1 + i)$ in principal in the second year. This total payment is exactly R_2.

[11] This may be demonstrated as follows: The household's savings in year one are equal to its receipts minus its consumption, $R_1 - C_1$. If these are lent out at interest rate i, they will provide a return in principal and interest of $(R_1 - C_1) \cdot (1 + i)$ in year two. Consumption in that year will be equal to receipts in that year, R_2, plus this return from lending. Thus

$$C_2 = (R_1 - C_1)(1 + i) + R_2$$

Dividing through by $(1 + i)$ and rearranging terms yields the expression in the text.

$$C_1 + C_2/(1 + i) = R_1 + R_2/(1 + i) \qquad (7.2)$$

The household seeks values of C_1 and C_2 that satisfy this condition and that it prefers over all other feasible values. Changes in R_1 and R_2 that leave the right side unchanged will not lead to a revision of its consumption plans. Thus we may write Eq. (7.1) in an alternative form as

$$C_1 = F[R_1 + R_2/(1 + i), i, u] \qquad (7.3)$$

The feasible consumption set now is represented by only two variables, $R_1 + R_2/(1 + i)$ and i. In his pioneering work on the consumption function, Milton Friedman described the quantity $R_1 + R_2/(1 + i)$ as the household's total wealth. However, to avoid confusion with the narrower concept of wealth used in earlier chapters, the term *total resources*[12] will be used here. Denoting total resources by $\mathcal{V}$, we write

$$C_1 = F[\mathcal{V}, i, u] \qquad (7.3a)$$

Consumption and Income

In the formulation of the consumption function represented in Eq. (7.3a), consumption is made to depend on total resources, the interest rate, and the tastes of the household as between current and future consumption. The level of current income (which was the main determinant of consumption in the Keynesian formulation) does not appear explicitly. This does not, of course, mean that current consumption is unaffected by changes in current income but that such changes influence consumer behavior only via their effect on total resources. In the first place, current income is a component of total resources, so that if the household's current income changes, its total resources will also change.[13] In the second place, however, a change in current income will have an additional effect on total resources if it leads the household to revise its expectations of its future income.

Because of the importance of expectations of future income in determining consumption, the approach to consumer behavior that emphasizes total resources, rather than current income alone, predicts that an increase in income that is expected to be permanent will lead to a larger increase in consumption than will one that is assumed to be only temporary. This is because a permanent increase in income implies a larger rise in total resources than does one that is temporary.

---

[12] In earlier chapters the term *wealth* was used to mean the value of the stock of tangible and financial assets. The concept of wealth used here is broader than that used earlier, since it includes not only assets that yield property income but also the amount that the household can borrow against its labor income. To avoid confusion this broader concept will be described as *total resources* and denoted $\mathcal{V}$, and the narrower concept will be termed *nonhuman wealth* (or simply wealth if there is no possibility of confusion) and denoted W.

[13] Except in the case in which the change in current income is regarded as purely transitory. See the following discussion.

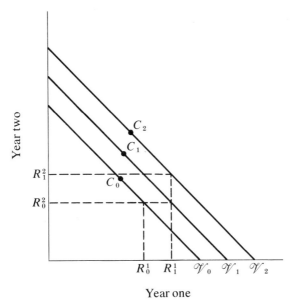

FIGURE 7.3   Permanent and temporary income increases

Consider Figure 7.3. Suppose the household has receipts of R_0^1 and R_0^2 and hence has total resources[14] of $\mathcal{V}_0$. In this situation it chooses the consumption plan represented by the point C_0. Suppose current income rises from R_0^1 to R_1^1. The effect of this increase in income on the amount of current consumption depends on the extent to which it leads the household to revise its estimate of its total resources.

One possibility is that the household regards the increase in income as a permanent one. This implies that future income is also expected to increase (from R_0^2 to R_1^2) and hence that the household's estimate of its total resources rises from $\mathcal{V}_0$ to $\mathcal{V}_2$. In this case, current consumption will rise to, say, C_2. A second possibility is that the increase in current income is regarded as a purely temporary one. This implies that expected future income remains unchanged at R_0^2 and hence that estimated total resources rise only to $\mathcal{V}_1$, which is less than $\mathcal{V}_2$. Current consumption rises only to C_1 in this case. Friedman[15] has suggested that such temporary increases in current income should be termed *windfalls*.[16] Finally, the rise in income may be regarded as a purely random event that leads to no change in the household's estimate of its resources and hence to no change in its current consumption.

This last possibility may require some further explanation, since in terms

---

[14] $\mathcal{V}_0 = R_0^1 + R_0^2/(1 + i)$.
[15] Milton Friedman, "Windfalls, the 'Horizon,' and Related Concepts in the Permanent Income Hypothesis," in *Measurement in Economics*. C. Christ *et al.* (Stanford, California: Stanford University Press, 1963).
[16] Temporary decreases in income are *negative windfalls*.

of Figure 7.3 it implies that current income can rise from R_0^1 to R_1^1 without there being an increase in total resources $\mathcal{V}_0$. Many households experience fluctuations in their incomes for reasons that are largely outside their control. The construction worker and the farm worker, whose weekly paychecks are affected by the vagaries of the weather, are examples of this phenomenon. Although such persons cannot predict their current income accurately on a week-to-week basis, they generally can form fairly good estimates of their average income over the longer term and hence can estimate their total resources. Random variations in current income around this average do not lead these households to revise their estimates of their long-run situation and hence do not lead to any change in the rate of current consumption. In terms of Figure 7.3 this means that R_0^1 and R_0^2 are both subject to random fluctuations, but these tend to offset one another, so that $\mathcal{V}_0$ does not vary.[17] Friedman describes these random variations in current income around its average level—which may, of course, be rising or falling as time passes—as *transitory income*.[18]

This discussion has implications for the conduct of fiscal policy by the government. Suppose the government raises taxes on household income. In the analysis of Chapter 3 and again in Chapter 5, it was assumed that consumption depends on after-tax income and hence that a tax increase will lead households to reduce their consumption. It now appears that the amount of this reduction depends on how the tax increase is viewed by the average household. Specifically, if households assume that the tax change is a temporary measure that will be reversed in the near future, it will have a much smaller effect on consumption than if it is regarded as a permanent change. The failure of the 1968 tax increase to have a significant effect on household spending is ascribed by some economists[19] to the fact that it was advertised as a temporary surcharge that would be removed later. In the terminology introduced above, the tax change was viewed as a *negative windfall*. If the authorities get in the habit of changing tax rates very frequently, the general public may even come to regard these changes as essentially random events that should not be allowed to influence the rate of household spending. We do not seem to have reached this stage in the United States, but the argument does suggest that "fiscal activism" may be subject to diminishing returns.

Consumption and the Rate of Interest

We now turn our attention to the effects of changes in the rate of interest on consumption. We will find that an increase[20] in the interest rate has three

---

[17] Some weeks are fair and others are foul, but the construction worker recognizes this and does not allow it to affect his consumption planning.

[18] Current income in any period may be above or below its average level, and hence transitory income may be positive or negative.

[19] Robert Eisner, "Fiscal and Monetary Policy Reconsidered," *American Economic Review*, Vol. LIX (December 1969), pp. 897–900.

[20] Throughout this section we consider only the effects of an interest rate increase. As a test of

types of effects on the level of current consumption. First, a rise in the interest rate means that each dollar saved in year one makes possible a larger increase in consumption in year two; that is, the terms on which the household can increase consumption in year two by reducing its consumption in year one are improved. This *substitution effect* will tend to cause the household to reduce current consumption in order to take advantage of these better terms. Second, a rise in the rate of interest may reduce the prices of any assets the household has accumulated in the past and so cause the value of its total resources to decline. This *capital-loss effect* will tend to reduce not only current, but also future consumption. Finally, an interest-rate increase may raise the income the household receives both from the assets it has accumulated in the past and from any new assets it purchases in the current period. This *property-income effect* makes the household better off and thus, in contrast to the substitution and capital-loss effects, will tend to encourage the householder to increase his current consumption.[21]

The previous paragraph indicates that the total effect of an interest-rate increase is complex and may be ambiguous. It is ambiguous because the substitution and capital-loss effects operate to reduce current consumption, whereas the property-income effect acts to increase[22] it. As we will see, this ambiguity can be resolved only in certain special circumstances. Specifically, the combined impact of the property-income and capital-loss effects depends on whether the household is a borrower or a lender and on the types of assets it has accumulated in the past.

Up to now we have not considered the nature of the household's resources in any detail. In this section we will suppose that the householder expects to earn labor income (wages, salaries, etc.) of ℓ_1 dollars in year one and ℓ_2 dollars in year two. He also owns nonhuman wealth valued at W_1 in year one and W_2 dollars in year two.[23]

The nature of the nonhuman assets owned by the household is important. If they are in the form of savings-and-loan shares, bank accounts, and similar deposit-type assets, their current value, W_1, does not depend on the interest rate. This is because the price of a one-dollar deposit is always exactly one dollar. Changes in the interest rate do affect W_2, since they alter the return yielded by this class of assets. If the rate of interest between year one and year two is i, then we may write

$$W_2 = W_1 + iW_1 = W_1(1 + i) \qquad (7.4a)$$

since the value of deposits in year two is equal to their value in year one plus the interest income they will yield.

---

your understanding of the analysis you should attempt to duplicate the argument for the case of a decrease.

[21] This is not true if the household is a net debtor rather than a net creditor. In that case a rise in the interest rate makes the household worse off and so tends to reduce consumption.

[22] But see the previous footnote.

[23] Interest income received during year one is also included in ℓ_1. Interest income received in year two, however, is included in W_2.

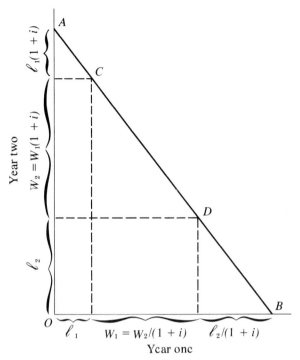

FIGURE 7.4 The nature of total resources

If nonhuman wealth is held in the form of securities or other bond-type assets that yield a fixed coupon, its future value does not depend on the current rate of interest.[24] In this case, however, changes in the interest rate do affect the current market value of these assets.[25] Hence it is more satisfactory to write

$$W_1 = W_2/(1 + i) \tag{7.4b}$$

Equations (7.4a) and (7.4b) are identical in an algebraic sense but must be interpreted differently. The first equation says that W_2 depends on W_1 and the interest rate, whereas the second equation states that W_1 depends on W_2 and the interest rate.

The feasible consumption set of the household is illustrated in Figure 7.4. The household has labor income of ℓ_1 and ℓ_2 and nonhuman assets of W_1.[26] The interest rate is i, so that $W_2 = W_1(1 + i)$, and total resources are

$$\mathcal{V} = \ell_1 + \ell_2/(1 + i) + W_1$$

---

[24] W_2 does depend on the future rate of interest, that is, on the rate that will prevail during year two. Throughout this chapter we are assuming no change in the future interest rate; this assumption is necessary if we are to treat the whole future as a single year.

[25] See the discussion of this class of assets in Chapter 4, pp. 59–67.

[26] We assume the household is a net creditor; W_1 is positive.

The total consumption set is represented by $OACDB$.

Points C and D divide the consumption set into three regions. If the household chooses a consumption plan on AC it will be a lender, since its current consumption is less than its current income. A consumption plan on DB requires the household to borrow; current consumption exceeds the sum of current income and nonhuman wealth, so that the household must not only dispose of all its assets but also go into debt. Finally, in the intermediate range CD, current consumption exceeds current income, and the household must sell part but not all of its nonhuman assets. As we will see, the effects of a change in the interest rate will be different in each of these three regions.

In Figure 7.5 we analyze the effects of an increase in the rate of interest and isolate the substitution, capital loss, and property income effects of such a change. Initially we suppose that the rate of interest is i_0 and the feasible consumption set is $OACDB$.[27] Three alternative scenarios are illustrated. In each, the consumption plan chosen in the initial situation is represented by point E. In Panel A, the household's preferences are such that it initially chooses to consume less than its current income in year one and thus to be a lender. In Panel B, current consumption exceeds current income and hence part of the household's stock of nonhuman assets must be sold. Finally, in Panel C current consumption exceeds current income by more than the amount of its nonhuman wealth, and hence the household is forced to borrow in addition to selling all its assets.

Suppose the rate of interest rises from i_0 to i_1. Since each dollar set aside in year one now yields a larger return in year two—$(1 + i_1)$ exceeds $(1 + i_0)$—the effect of this change in the interest rate is to increase the slope of the budget constraint AB.

If nonhuman wealth is held in the form of deposit-type assets, its current value, W_1, is unaffected, but its future value rises from $W_1(1 + i_0)$ to $W_1(1 + i_1)$. Hence the effect of the interest-rate increase in this case is to rotate line AB in a clockwise direction about point D.[28] The resource constraint becomes $OA''DB''$. The current value of total resources declines from OB to OB'', reflecting the fact that the household's ability to borrow against future labor income has been reduced from $\ell_2/(1 + i_0)$ to $\ell_2/(1 + i_1)$.

If, on the other hand, assets are held in the form of bonds, their future value, W_2, is unaffected by the rate of interest. Hence in this case line AB is rotated about point C[29] and the resource constraint becomes $OA'CB'$. The current value of its resources declines to OB' in this case, since not only is

---

[27] In this diagram the regions AC, CD, and DB have the same meaning as in Figure 7.4.

[28] The coordinates of point D are $(\ell_1 + W_1)$ and ℓ_2. If assets are held in the form of deposits, both of these quantities are independent of the interest rate. Hence when the interest rate changes, the new budget line still passes through point D.

[29] The coordinates of point C are ℓ_1 and $(\ell_2 + W_2)$. If assets are held in the form of bonds, both of these quantities are independent of the interest rate. Hence when the interest rate changes, the new budget line still passes through point C.

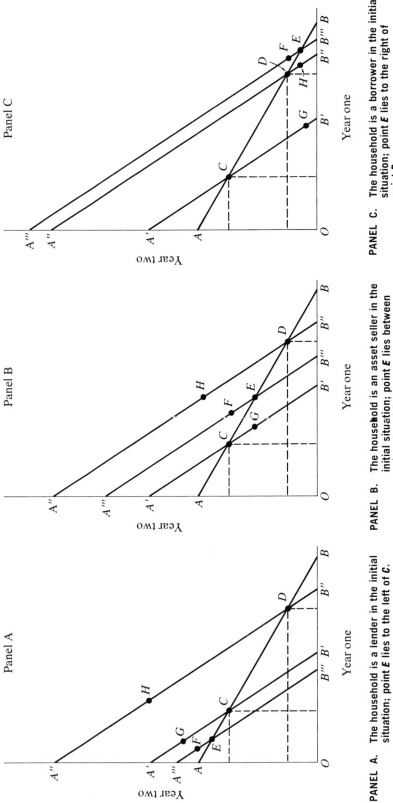

PANEL A. The household is a lender in the initial situation; point E lies to the left of C.

PANEL B. The household is an asset seller in the initial situation; point E lies between points C and D.

PANEL C. The household is a borrower in the initial situation; point E lies to the right of point D.

FIGURE 7.5 The effects of a rise in the interest rate

the household's borrowing power reduced by a higher interest rate, but the current value of its nonhuman wealth is also diminished from $W_2/(1 + i_0)$ to $W_2/(1 + i_1)$.

To isolate the substitution effect[30] of a rise in the interest rate, we suppose that at the same time as the interest rate rises the household's resources are adjusted in such a way that it can still just afford the original consumption plan E despite the interest-rate change. Geometrically, this requires that the resource constraint be rotated about point E. The (hypothetical) consumption set that results is represented by $OA'''EB'''$. In effect, the property income and capital-gains effects are exactly offset by the assumed resource adjustment, so that the consumer is neither worse nor better off than in his original situation. Thus any change that occurs in the consumption plan may be attributed exclusively to the improved terms on which the household can increase future consumption at the expense of present consumption, that is, to the substitution effect.

With a budget constraint $OA'''EB'''$ the household will never choose a consumption plan on EB''' but will always choose one that lies on $A'''E$. This is because plans on EB''' were available to the household in the initial situation but were rejected in favor of E. Since we are assuming that the household's preferences are unchanged, it will never choose a plan that it previously rejected and hence is bound to select a plan on $A'''E$. In the diagram the plan chosen is that represented by point F.[31] The move from E to F represents the substitution effect. Note that F lies above and to the left of E in all three panels of the figure, confirming our earlier statement that the substitution effect of a rise in the rate of interest is to cause current consumption to fall and future consumption to rise.

If the household owns deposit-type assets at the beginning of year one, its constraint after the interest-rate change will be $OA''DB''$ rather than the hypothetical $OA'''EB'''$. If it plans to continue holding some or all these assets during year one, it is made better off by the interest rate increase, since these assets will yield a larger return. This is the situation depicted in Panels A and B. If, on the·other hand, the household plans to sell all its assets and go into debt, a rise in the rate of interest will increase the interest cost of this borrowing and so make it worse off. Panel C shows this situation. In all three panels the distance between B'' and B''' represents the extent to which the household is made better or worse off.[32]

---

[30] The substitution effect described here is known in economic theory as the Slutsky effect, after the Russian economist who first discovered it. It is somewhat different from the Hicks substitution effect discussed in most price theory texts which use indifference curves to analyze household behavior. See Richard A. Bilas, *Microeconomic Theory*, 2nd ed. (New York: McGraw-Hill, 1971), pp. 72–78.

[31] The plans represented by points on $A'''E$ were not available in the original situation but are available in the new (hypothetical) situation. Of these plans one, which we are denoting by F, is preferred to all the others.

[32] Note that in Panels A and B, point B'' lies to the right of B''', indicating that the household is made better off, whereas in Panel C, point B'' lies to the left of B''', showing that it is made worse off.

If the household is made better off by the change in the interest rate, it will choose a consumption plan that involves a higher level of consumption both in the present and in the future than does F. Conversely, if it is made worse off, it will choose lower levels of consumption. In the figure, the plan chosen is represented by point H. The move from F to H represents the property-income effect. For asset holders, this effect acts to raise current consumption (see Panels A and B), whereas for asset issuers (borrowers) it tends to reduce consumption (see Panel C).

If the household owns its wealth in the form of securities, its resource constraint after the interest-rate change will be $OA'CB'$. In all cases this constraint lies inside $OA''DB''$, indicating that if it holds[33] bonds it is worse off after an interest-rate increase than it would have been had it held deposits. The distance between B' and B'' represents the capital loss it sustains on its bond holdings.[34]

This capital loss resulting from the rise in the interest rate will lead to a reduction in consumption both in the present and in the future. The consumption plan chosen is represented by G in Figure 7.5. The shift from H to G represents the capital-loss effect.

Let us now summarize the results of the preceding analysis. For households that plan to sell all their assets and also to borrow, a rise in the rate of interest leads unambiguously to a reduction in current consumption. This group finds that the value of their nonhuman wealth is reduced when they sell it, the cost of borrowing is increased, and the current sacrifice required to increase future consumption has risen. Thus the capital loss, property income, and substitution effects are all negative. This is the case illustrated in Panel C.

From Panel B we see that for households planning to sell some but not all of their assets and that hold those assets exclusively in the form of bonds, current consumption is also reduced. Although the property-income effect is positive in this case, it is more than offset by the capital-loss effect. Essentially, this is because these households will not be adding to their assets, so that, since they hold only bonds, they will not, in fact, receive any additional property income. But they will suffer a capital loss when they sell their assets. Hence they will be made worse off and therefore will consume less. However, households that own deposits will receive additional property income and hence will be made better off by the change. As a result,

---

[33] Throughout this analysis we are assuming that the household is a net creditor at the beginning of year one; that is, it is a holder of assets rather than an issuer. If the household is a net debtor (W_1 is negative) and the interest rate rises, the market value of his liabilities falls if they are in the form of securities but is unchanged if they are in the form of deposits. Thus for net debtors, the capital-loss effect operates in the opposite direction. Although this possibility might be relevant in the analysis of a single household, it is not so for aggregate behavior because the household sector as a whole is a net creditor in the United States.

[34] OB'' represents $\ell_1 + \ell_2/(1 + i_1) + W_1$, whereas OB' represents $\ell_1 + (\ell_2 + W_2)/(1 + i_1)$. Since $W_1 = W_2/(1 + i_0)$, the distance $B''B'$ represents $W_2/(1 + i_0) - W_2/(1 + i_1)$, which is the loss in the current value of bonds that will be worth W_2 in the future.

Table 7.1 Effects of a Rise in the Rate of Interest on Current Consumption*

Type of Effect	Borrowers (Asset issuers)	Asset Sellers	Lenders (Asset purchasers)
A Substitution effect	−	−	−
B Property-income effect	−	+	+
C Capital-loss effect*	−	−	−
B + C	−	−	+
A + B	−	?	?
A + B + C	−	−	?

* Assumes W_1 is not negative.

the effect on the consumption of a deposit-owning household is ambiguous[35] because the substitution and property-income effects operate in opposing directions.

Finally, for households planning to add to their assets, the effect of the interest-rate change is ambiguous regardless of the type of assets owned. These households find that any bonds they own are reduced in value. However, since they do not plan to sell any assets, this paper loss does not affect their behavior. The new assets they acquire yield a higher return and they are made better off. This acts to increase current consumption at the same time as the substitution effect acts to reduce it. Thus the net effect is ambiguous.[36] These results are summarized in tabular form in Table 7.1.

The upshot of the preceding analysis is that the effect of a change in the rate of interest on aggregate consumption cannot be predicted unambiguously on theoretical grounds alone. We should not be surprised at this conclusion; it is analogous to the conclusion in price theory that a rise in the wage rate may or may not induce workers to work harder. A rise in the rate of interest makes current consumption more expensive compared to future consumption and hence tends to cause households to cut down on present consumption in order to enjoy larger future consumption. In addition, it produces capital losses on existing holdings of assets that also tend to lower current consumption. Finally, although the effect via property income is ambiguous (because savers benefit while borrowers suffer from higher interest rates), one would expect that in the aggregate the property income effect will increase current consumption, since households as a group are net savers. Thus the substitution and capital-loss effects tend to reduce total

---

[35] In terms of Panel B of Figure 7.5 we cannot predict unambiguously whether H lies to the left or to the right of E.
[36] In Panel A we know that G and H lie to the right of F. But since F is to the left of E, we cannot predict whether G or H lie to the left or to the right of E.

current consumption, while the property-income effect probably tends to increase it.

Empirical evidence on the effects of interest-rate changes on consumer behavior is mixed. Most (but not all) studies have concluded that consumption and the rate of interest move inversely to one another.[37] In terms of the framework we have developed, this evidence implies that the substitution and capital-loss effects are sufficiently strong in practice to offset the property-income effect. However, we should stress that the volume of empirical work in this area is modest, and this conclusion requires considerably more testing before it can be regarded as firmly established.

The Proportionality Hypothesis

How should one expect consumption plans to be affected by an increase in total resources? In the preceding sections it was taken for granted that an increase in total resources will induce a household to add to its planned consumption both in the current year and in the future. This assumption seems eminently sensible. A household receiving an addition to its spending power will not devote it exclusively either to current consumption or to future consumption.

Several economists have proposed the much stronger hypothesis that the household will allocate any increment to its resources between present and future consumption in the same proportions as it allocated its previous level of resources. Thus if resources were to, say, double, the household would plan to double its consumption in every year. This hypothesis, which is known as the *proportionality hypothesis*, is illustrated in Figure 7.6. When resources rise from $\mathcal{V}_0$ to $\mathcal{V}_1$ the household moves from point C to point D; consumption in the present and in the future both rise in the same proportion.

Under this hypothesis, Eq. (7.3a) becomes[38]

$$C = k(i, u) \cdot \mathcal{V} \qquad (7.5)$$

where $k(\ )$ represents the proportion of total resources that is allocated to current consumption, and depends only on the rate of interest and tastes and not on the amount of total resources.

The proportionality hypothesis is not an essential part of the new theories of consumption. Many of the conclusions of these theories do not depend on the validity of the hypothesis.[39] Moreover, at first sight it does not

---

[37] For an example of a study that reached the opposite conclusions, see Warren E. Weber, "The Effect of Interest Rates on Aggregate Consumption," *American Economic Review*, Vol. LX, Number 4 (September 1970).

[38] From now on we will be concerned exclusively with current consumption, and hence the subscript on C_1 will be dropped.

[39] For example, the conclusions of the previous sections with regard to the effects of permanent and transitory income changes and of changes in the rate of interest do not depend on the proportionality hypothesis.

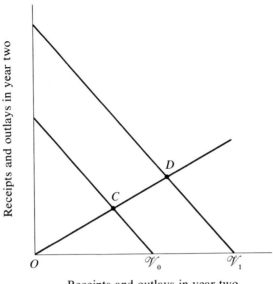

Receipts and outlays in year two

FIGURE 7.6 The proportionality hypothesis

appear to be particularly plausible. Although it may be defended on the ground that any alternative general hypothesis—which would say that any addition to resources will be consumed during some specific period of life (at once, for example)—would be even less acceptable, this is not a very strong defense. The principal virtue of the hypothesis lies in its great simplicity. This makes it a useful working assumption that we can accept as long as it does not conflict with the facts of experience.[40]

In fact, when applied to changes in the aggregate behavior of all households over time, the hypothesis does have considerable empirical support. As we will see in the next section, it can be used to explain the fact that the average propensity to consume has remained fairly constant over long periods of time. The hypothesis does not, however, satisfactorily explain differences in consumption behavior between households. Specifically, households at the lower end of the income and wealth scale tend to consume more relative to their total resources than do those at the upper end of the scale. One explanation of this finding is that consumption behavior is influenced not only by a household's individual situation but also by its position relative to the average situation of the population as a whole. A poor family realizes that its standard of living is below average and thus is

[40] Economists frequently find that they can learn more by beginning with simple (or even simple-minded!) assumptions rather than with ones that, although they may be better descriptions of the real world, are so complicated that no useful conclusions can be drawn from them. As it happens, the proportionality hypothesis is able to explain a number of "real world" facts, particularly with regard to the behavior of all households taken as a group.

encouraged to spend more (relative to its total resources) to enjoy more of the "good things in life" that households further up the scale take for granted. A rich family, on the other hand, has a standard of living that is above average and thus is under no such pressure to spend to "keep up with the Jones." This explanation—which was first proposed by James Duesenberry[41]—is generally described as the *relative income hypothesis* of consumption. Note that if, over time, the resources of all households rise together, the effects stressed by the relative income theory do not operate, since the relative positions of households in the income and wealth scales do not change. The poor remain at the bottom of the heap and the rich remain at the top. Thus we should not be surprised to discover that the proportionality hypothesis works when used to explain aggregrate behavior over time but not as an explanation of interhousehold differences in behavior at the same time. In the remainder of this chapter, we will be concerned primarily with aggregate consumption and hence will accept the proportionality hypothesis.

The Wealth Hypothesis and the Average Propensity to Consume

We are now in a position to explain the empirical finding that the average propensity to consume out of current income has remained approximately constant when the long sweep of history is considered, but frequently declines as income advances over shorter periods of time.

By dividing both sides of Eq. (7.5) by Y, we obtain the following expression for the average propensity to consume, C/Y:

$$\frac{C}{Y} = \frac{k(i, u)}{Y/\mathcal{V}} \tag{7.6}$$

The average propensity to consume depends on two variables: the proportion of total resources devoted to current consumption, $k(\ )$, and the ratio of income to resources, $Y/\mathcal{V}$. Since $k(\ )$ and $\mathcal{V}$ are in turn affected by the interest rate,[42] any explanation of the historical behavior of the APC in terms of the new theories of the consumption function must focus on the behavior of i as well as of $k(\ )$ and $Y/\mathcal{V}$.

We argued earlier that a rise in the interest rate will lead to a decline in current consumption C. However, it also produces a decrease in total resources $\mathcal{V}$ and hence it is theoretically possible[43] for k to increase or

---

[41] See James S. Duesenberry, *Income, Saving and the Theory of Consumer Behavior* (Cambridge, Mass.: Harvard University Press, 1949). Strictly speaking Duesenberry's theory attempted to explain differences in consumption behavior between households in different ranges of the *income* scale. However, his arguments may also be used to explain variations in behavior at different levels of *total resources*.
[42] The variable representing tastes is ignored.
[43] Suppose that when the interest rate is i_0, the household chooses a consumption program (C_1^0, C_2^0). Then

decrease. It seems more likely, however, that a higher interest rate will lead households to devote a smaller proportion of their resources to current consumption and a larger proportion to future consumption. That is,

$$\Delta k/\Delta i < 0$$

There are good reasons for expecting that the *APC* will remain relatively constant over very long periods of time. In the first place, although the rate of interest has fluctuated over the course of the business cycle, it has shown no clear tendency either to rise or to fall over the last 100 years. As a result, $k(\ )$ has probably not changed much over the long haul.

Second, recall that total resources may be written

$$\mathcal{V} = Y_1 + Y_2^E/(1 + i) + Y_3^E/(1 + i)^2 + \ldots$$

where Y_1 represents current income and Y_2^E, Y_3^E, etc. represent expected future income. If the rate of interest is expected to remain constant, the ratio of current income to total resources will increase (decrease) only if expected future incomes rise more slowly (rapidly) than current incomes. However, it is very unlikely that households will expect their future incomes to rise more rapidly or more slowly than their current incomes over long periods of time. This is simply because expectations of the future are strongly influenced by experience in the present and generally will be re- if they are found to be overly optimistic or pessimistic. Households are unlikely, for example, to persist in a belief that their future incomes will

---

$$C_1^0 + C_2^0/(i + i_0) = \mathcal{V}_0$$

$$C_1^0 = k_0\mathcal{V}_0$$

where $\mathcal{V}_0$ is the value of resources at interest rate i_0, and k_0 is the proportion of those resources devoted to present consumption.

If the interest rate increases to i_1, the value of this program becomes

$$C_1^0 + C_2^0/(i + i_1) - \mathcal{V}_2$$

If total resources were reduced to $\mathcal{V}_2$ at the same time as the interest rate rises to i_1, the household would experience only a substitution effect. Its current consumption would become:

$$C_1^S = k_1\mathcal{V}_2$$

Since the substitution effect is negative, we know that $C_1^S < C_1^0$. So we can write

$$k_1\mathcal{V}_2 < k_0\mathcal{V}_0$$

which means that

$$k_1 < k_0\,\mathcal{V}_0/\mathcal{V}_2$$

Under the proportionality hypothesis, the property-income and capital-loss effects do not alter the share of resources devoted to current consumption. Hence if $\mathcal{V}_1$ represents total resources when the interest rate is i_1, current consumption at that interest rate will be

$$C_1^1 = k_1\mathcal{V}_1$$

The share of resources devoted to consumption has changed from k_0 to k_1 but although $k_1 < k_0\,\mathcal{V}_0/\mathcal{V}_2$, this does not imply that $k_1 < k_0$ because $\mathcal{V}_0/\mathcal{V}_2 > 1$.

rise at 10 percent (or 2 percent) a year if their *actual* current incomes in fact grow at 5 percent.

Thus, over the long haul it is likely that expected future incomes will tend to move upward at about the same rate as current income, and hence that in the long run current income is a reasonably good indicator of expected future income. Since there is no trend in the interest rate, this means that the income-resources ratio will remain relatively constant in the long run.[44]

We conclude from this discussion that both determinants of the average propensity to consume (the interest rate and the income-resources ratio) have probably remained relatively constant over the broad span of historical experience. This provides a theoretical explanation of the empirical finding that the *APC* has shown no long-run tendency either to rise or to fall.

Moreover, there are equally good reasons to expect that the *APC* will fluctuate about its long-run value when shorter periods of time are considered. In the first place, when current incomes rise or fall, most households do not immediately revise their expectations of future income to the same extent. They will have experienced fluctuations in their incomes before and will know that at least part of any change in their current income will probably prove to be of a transitory nature. Hence expected future incomes will rise less rapidly than current income during periods of prosperity and will fall more slowly during recessions. As a result, the income-resources ratio $Y/\mathcal{V}$ will tend to rise in booms and to fall in downswings.

Second, the interest rate tends to rise in prosperous times and to fall in recessions. This effect also causes cyclical swings in the income-resources ratio (because a rise in i implies a fall in $\mathcal{V}$ and hence a rise in $Y/\mathcal{V}$). In addition, these cyclical movements in the interest rate will tend to reduce the proportion of resources devoted to current consumption $k(\quad)$ in booms and to increase it in recessions.

The argument[45] of the last two paragraphs suggests that the average propensity to consume is likely to fluctuate over the course of the business cycle. In periods of business expansion, both the interest rate i and the income-wealth ratio $Y/\mathcal{V}$ will tend to rise. Hence the average propensity to consume will tend to fall. During contractions the opposite effects will be felt, so that the average propensity to consume will tend to rise. Hence if we study the relation between consumption and income over a single business

---

[44] Suppose that, on the average, incomes grow at the rate g. When households' expectations become adjusted to this experience, they will estimate total resources as

$$\mathcal{V} = Y + \frac{(1 + g)Y}{1 + i} + \frac{(1 + g)^2 Y}{(1 + i)^2} + \cdots$$

$$= \left(\frac{1 + i}{i - g} \right) Y$$

so that $Y/\mathcal{V} = (i - g)/(1 + i)$, which is a constant if both i and g are constants.

[45] For an example of a very similar argument applied to a different problem, see Milton Friedman, "The Demand for Money: Some Theoretical and Empirical Results," *Journal of Political Economy,* Vol. LXVII (August 1959).

cycle, we observe that the *APC* tends to be greater at low than at high levels of income.

The upshot of this discussion is that wealth hypotheses of consumption— those that focus on the total resources of the household rather than on current income alone—have two major advantages over the simple Keynesian hypothesis introduced in Chapter 3.

First, they have a stronger theoretical rationale, since they are based on an explicit model of consumer choice. Second, when this theoretical model is combined with some reasonably plausible assumptions about how households form expectations of future income and interest rates, it is able to provide an explanation both of the long-run stability of the average propensity to consume and of its tendency to rise during recession periods and to decline during prosperity.

The Permanent Income and Life-Cycle Hypotheses

The approach to consumption theory described in the preceding sections of this chapter represents a generalization of two theories developed during the fifties and early sixties. The *permanent income hypothesis* was initially put forward by Milton Friedman in 1957[46] and has been the subject of intensive research since that time. The *life-cycle hypothesis* was first advanced by Richard Brumberg and Franco Modigliani in 1954.[47] Originally proposed as an explanation of differences in consumption behavior across households, it was later extended to explain behavior over time by Ando and Modigliani.[48] Both hypotheses—and a number of other variants of the basic wealth hypothesis developed in this chapter—have recently been subjected to rigorous empirical study by Thomas Mayer.[49]

The principal emphasis of the permanent income hypothesis is on the argument that consumption during any period depends on total resources rather than on current income and, in particular, on the fact that a household's income during a single year is a less-than-perfect indicator of its total resources. Hence the consumption-income relationship will not be as close as Keynes suggested simply because the "true" relationship is between consumption and total resources. This was essentially the conclusion of the previous sections of this chapter, which were largely based on Friedman's work.

---

[46] Milton Friedman, *A Theory of the Consumption Function* (Princeton: Princeton University Press, 1957).

[47] Franco Modigliani and Richard Brumberg, "Utility Analysis and the Consumption Function: An Interpretation of Cross Section Data," in *Post-Keynesian Economics,* ed. Kenneth K. Kurihara. (New Brunswick: Rutgers University Press, 1954).

[48] Albert Ando and Franco Modigliani, "The 'Life Cycle' Hypothesis of Saving: Aggregate Implications and Tests," reprinted in R. A. Gordon and L. R. Klein, *Readings in Business Cycles,* (Homewood, Ill.: Richard D. Irwin, 1965).

[49] Thomas Mayer, *Permanent Income, Wealth and Consumption* (Berkeley: University of California Press, 1972).

Friedman argues that a household's current income (or *measured income*, as he calls it) may be regarded as consisting of two components: a *permanent* component and a *transitory* component. Thus

$$Y_M = Y_P + Y_T$$

The permanent component is the level of income the household employs in forming its estimate of total resources. The transitory component captures those variations in current income that the household regards as purely random and as not reflecting its long-run position.

On any date the consumer has a given set of expectations with regard to its future income; that is, it has a certain view of the pattern that its future income will follow. This pattern is illustrated, for the case of a relatively young household,[50] in Figure 7.7. The curve *OA* represents the household's best estimate of the path that its future income will follow. Total resources are estimated by adding (the present value of) these best estimates of future income:

$$\mathcal{V} = Y_1 + Y_2^E/(1 + i) + Y_3^E/(1 + i)^2 + \ldots$$

The household recognizes that these predictions of the future are uncertain: On any given date, actual income may exceed or fall short of the expected income represented by *OA*. This fact is illustrated by the scatter of points around *OA* in Figure 7.7. Each point in this scatter represents one possible level of income on any given date.

This best estimate of the future course of income is one interpretation[51] of what Friedman means by *permanent income*. The divergences between these estimates and what actually materializes represent *transitory income*.[52] On this interpretation, an increase (or decrease) in permanent income implies an upward (or downward) movement in the whole path of expected future income and thus a corresponding increase (or decrease) in the estimate of total resources. A change in transitory income, on the other hand, is a purely random event that has no effect on the expected path of income and hence leaves total resources unchanged.

---

[50] For such a household, income generally will be expected to rise to a peak in late middle age and then to decline as retirement is reached and passed.

[51] Friedman provides several definitions of permanent income. A second definition he suggests is that it is that level of income which, if received in perpetuity, would have a present value equal to the household's total resources. That is,

$$Y_p = i\mathcal{V}$$

On this definition, divergences between current and permanent income are not necessarily purely random. A young household (which expects its income to be rising in the future) will have a permanent income (defined in this second way) above its current income, but it will certainly not regard this difference as a random event.

[52] One problem with this approach is that windfalls do not fall into either category. The approach developed earlier in this chapter—in which the analysis is conducted exclusively in terms of total resources (a *stock* concept)—is superior in this respect, since a windfall is also a stock concept.

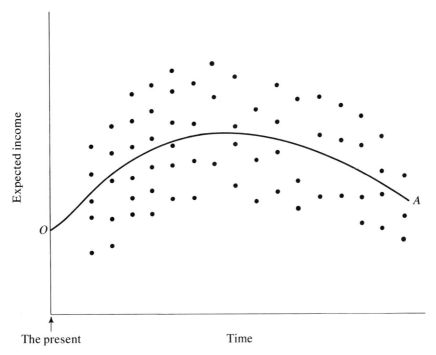

The present   Time

FIGURE 7.7   **A typical income profile**

It follows from this interpretation that permanent income is a perfect indicator of total resources and hence that if consumption is proportional to total resources it will also be proportional to permanent income. Moreover, if the relationship of consumption to resources varies with the interest rate, the same will be true of the relationship between consumption and permanent income. Thus Friedman writes his consumption function in the form

$$C = k(i, u) \cdot Y_P$$

Friedman uses this formulation to explain why the average propensity to consume remains relatively constant over long periods of time but tends to fall in prosperous years and rise in recession years. Over the long haul, current income is a good approximation of permanent income. Since consumption is proportional to permanent income, it is also proportional to current income in the long run. However, in prosperous times current income generally exceeds permanent income, while in recessions current income is less than permanent income. Hence the average propensity to consume, C/Y, falls in booms and rises in slumps. This explanation is essentially the same as that given in the preceding section except that it ignores the role of the interest rate.

The life-cycle hypothesis of Modigliani, Brumberg, and Ando (MBA) is similar to the Friedman approach in that both stress the key role played by the household's total resources in its consumption planning. However, instead of emphasizing the distinction between the permanent and transitory components of current income, MBA stress the fact that the income receipts of a typical household generally follow a particular pattern over its life span. Specifically, income typically rises to a peak and then declines sharply following retirement. In order to maintain a satisfactory level of consumption during old age, the householder must accumulate a stock of assets during his working life that will yield an income (and that he can sell) after he retires.

MBA develop a number of conclusions from this rather simple observation. For example, consumption depends not only on total resources but also on age: Young households will tend to save a larger proportion of their incomes than will older households. This in turn leads to a conclusion about the aggregate economy. Consider two economies that are identical in all respects except that in one economy the population is growing, whereas in the other it is stationary. In the growing economy the proportion of young persons in the population will be larger. Since young persons save more than old persons, the saving ratio, S/Y, will be larger in the growing economy.

As another example of the life-cycle hypothesis, consider two households of the same age earning the same annual income. Household A owns no physical or financial assets and receives its income exclusively in the form of wages. Household B owns a savings account and receives its income in the form of interest on that account. The MBA hypothesis implies that household B will consume at a higher level than will A. The reason for this difference in behavior is that A's wage income will cease when he reaches retirement, whereas B's interest receipts will not. Hence A must set aside part of his current income to prepare for retirement, whereas B need not do this. Note also that the difference in behavior will be least if both households are young and greatest if they are old.[53] This example illustrates that the source of a household's income as well as its dollar amount may be relevant to its decision concerning how much to consume.

Conclusion

In this chapter we have reviewed the new theories of the consumption function. These theories agree that the principal determinant of consumption is not income but total resources. On the other hand, income is a good indicator of total resources in many circumstances. As a result, many economists continue to use the Keynesian consumption function despite the theoretical superiority of the wealth hypothesis. Conclusions derived from the Keynesian function can always be modified in particular circumstances when the assumption that income and resources move together is clearly

---

[53] Why?

inappropriate. The case of an increase in income resulting from a temporary tax reduction is an example of such a circumstance.

One final word on terminology is in order before leaving the subject of consumption. Throughout this chapter we have spoken of consumption rather than consumer expenditures. In the case of nondurable commodities the distinction between these concepts is not important. It is not useful to distinguish between the act of purchasing a hamburger and the act of eating it, since the time lag between the two acts is so short. This is not the case with respect to durable commodities. When I buy an automobile or a home I do so in the expectation of consuming its services over a series of future years: Expenditure and consumption are clearly different activities in this case.

In this chapter we have been concerned with consumption rather than consumer expenditure. Outlays on tangible assets—homes, autos, etc.—that will yield a flow of consumption services in the future are part of investment rather than of consumption. According to the wealth hypotheses, the level of total resources influences my demand for the services of consumer durables. Its effect on my purchases of these durables is an indirect one. The determination of the rate of household fixed investment will be treated in Chapter 8.

References

Ando, Albert, and Franco Modigliani. "The 'Life-Cycle' Hypothesis of Saving: Aggregate Implications and Tests." Reprinted in *Readings in Business Cycles,* eds. R. A. Gordon and L. R. Klein. Homewood, Ill.: Richard D. Irwin, 1965.

Farrell, M. J. "The New Theories of the Consumption Function." *Economic Journal*, Vol. LXIX (December 1959), reprinted in Gordon and Klein.

Friedman, Milton. *A Theory of the Consumption Function*. Princeton: Princeton University Press, 1957.

Mayer, Thomas. *Permanent Income, Wealth and Consumption*. Berkeley: University of California Press, 1972.

Modigliani, Franco, and Richard Brumberg. "Utility Analysis and the Consumption Function: An Interpretation of Cross-Section Data," *Post-Keynesian Economics*, ed. Kenneth K. Kurihara. New Brunswick: Rutgers University Press, 1954.

Questions for Classroom Discussion

1. Suppose I have just learned that I have been named a beneficiary in my rich aunt's will. How will this information affect my current consumption? Does it make any difference whether my aunt has just died or is expected to live for several more years? Explain carefully.

2. Are the following windfalls or transitory income?
   (a) A bequest from a rich aunt.
   (b) A winning streak at roulette in Las Vegas.

3. Carefully explain the distinction between the property-income effect and the capital-loss effect of a rise in the interest rate.

4. Suppose I am currently in debt and am planning to add to my debt this year by consuming in excess of my income. If the interest rate falls, will my consumption rise or fall? *Hint:* In terms of this chapter, the situation is one in which W_1 is negative. Find the directions of the substitution, property-income, and capital-loss effects in this case.

The Theory of Investment

The second major component of aggregate private expenditure on final products is *fixed investment* (or *fixed capital formation* as it is termed in the U.S. income and product accounts). This type of expenditure includes all outlays on long-lived commodities (tangible capital) that will yield streams of services to their owners in the future.

Investment is undertaken both by business firms and by households. Apart from inventory changes, all spending on final products by firms falls into this category since their purchases of short-lived commodities are not part of final expenditures.[1] Investment by households consists of their purchases of homes, automobiles, appliances, and similar commodities that yield a stream of consumption over a number of years. In this chapter we adopt an approach to fixed investment that enables us to treat household and business investment within the same general framework.

Note that a definition of investment that includes purchases of durable commodities by households implies that consumption, the aggregate discussed in Chapter 7, does not include such purchases but does, in principle, include the *services* of durables. Unfortunately, few studies of consumption and tests of the hypotheses advanced in Chapter 7 have made this important distinction, largely because of a lack of data. In the U.S. income and product accounts, home purchases by households are treated as investment, but all other outlays by households are included in personal consumption. The services of owner occupied homes are included in consumption, but no estimates are provided of the services of other durables owned by households.[2]

The analysis of investment demand involves three related but distinct strands of analysis. First, we examine the demand by firms and households for the services of tangible assets. This analysis provides the basis for a theory of the demand by wealth owners (or their representatives, the firms) to hold stocks of tangible assets. Finally, we examine the relation between the demand to own existing assets and the demand to acquire newly produced capital

---

[1] See page 20 of Chapter 2.

[2] In the flow-of-funds accounts, household purchases of durable goods are treated as investment but no estimate is provided of the consumption services yielded by these goods.

goods.[3] Ultimately, it is this flow demand that we wish to explain, but in order to do this we must first treat the earlier strands of the analysis.

Capital Stocks and Capital Services

A *tangible asset* is a commodity that supplies a stream of services to its user over a period of time. Such commodities are frequently described as *capital goods* and the total stock in existence at a given time is termed the society's *capital stock*. We will adopt these terms.

It is important to distinguish the tangible asset itself from the services it yields. Frequently, it is possible to own an asset but not consume its services or, conversely, to use the services of some capital good without owning it. An obvious example is the case of a homeowner who leases his home to another individual. The home is owned by one individual but the services it provides are consumed by another. This distinction is important since the demand for the services of capital may be separated (at least conceptually)[4] from the demand to own the capital goods themselves. A construction company that uses dump trucks in its operations, for example, is interested in the services yielded by the trucks. Its decision on how many truck-hours[5] to employ depends on the cost per truck-hour of these services and not on who owns[6] the trucks.

The Demand for the Services of Capital by Businesses

We begin by considering the demand for the services of capital goods by businesses. The discussion will be brief since it parallels that found in several intermediate texts on price theory.

The total flow of output that a business produces over a given period of time depends on the labor services and capital services it employs.[7] Specifically, if the firm uses either more labor or more capital (or both) it will be able to produce a larger flow of output. This technological relation between the flows of inputs to the production process and the resulting flow of output

---

[3] Several popular treatments of investment also consider the supply of newly produced capital goods. See, for example, the theory of investment presented by Gardner Ackley in *Macroeconomic Theory* and Edward Shapiro in *Macroeconomic Analysis*. In this chapter we ignore the supply side. In effect, we are constructing a theory of the *demand curve* for investment in the same way as Chapter 7 presented a theory of the demand curve for consumption.

[4] Frequently it is not possible to consume the services of an asset without also owning it because there is no rental market. However, this does not alter the fact that the two decisions (how much asset services to use and how many assets to own) are in principle separate.

[5] Note that the services of capital goods are flow variables (having a dimension such as truck-hours per week or machine-days per month), whereas the capital goods themselves are stock variables (with dimensions such as number of trucks on a given date, etc.)

[6] The cost of the services of a capital good is sometimes lower (for technical, tax, or other reasons) if the user is also the owner of the capital. However, this observation does not alter the argument of this paragraph.

[7] For simplicity, we treat the case of a firm that uses only two inputs.

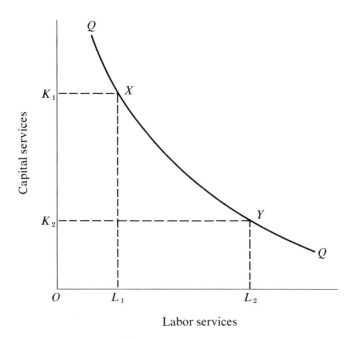

FIGURE 8.1 The production function

is known as the *production function*. Symbolically, we may write this relation as

$$Q = F(K, L) \tag{8.1}$$

where Q represents output and K and L represent inputs of capital and labor services, respectively. If either K or L are increased, then Q will also increase.

We shall assume that businesses are able to vary the proportions in which they employ labor and capital services to produce any given output. Then the production function may be represented diagrammatically as in Figure 8.1.

Any point in this diagram represents a particular combination of labor and capital services and hence is associated with a particular flow of output. Point X, for example, represents a situation in which the firm is employing OK_1 units of capital services and OL_1 units of labor services and is producing a certain level of output (say, Q units). However, this same output may also be produced by other capital-labor combinations. For example, point Y represents a situation in which the firm is producing Q units of output with a production technique that employs less capital (OK_2 units) and more labor (OL_2 units). By connecting all points such as X and Y we generate the curve QQ. This curve is known as an *isoquant*[8] or equal-product curve.

---

[8] The convex shape of QQ reflects the fact that the services of capital and labor are not perfect

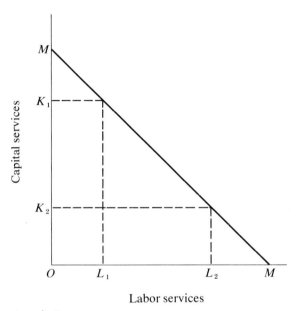

FIGURE 8.2 An isocost line

The cost of using given quantities of labor and capital services depends on their respective prices. If we represent the wage of labor by w and the rental of capital by r,[9] the cost of employing, say, L_1 units of labor and K_1 units of capital is

$$C(L_1, K_1) = wL_1 + rK_1$$

Clearly, however, there are many capital-labor combinations all involving the same dollar outlay. In Figure 8.2, for example, the combinations (L_1, K_1) and (L_2, K_2) both require the same expenditure since

$$wL_1 + rK_1 = wL_2 + rK_2$$

In fact, all other combinations lying on line MM also require the same outlay. Hence lines such as MM are described as *isocost lines*. Factor combinations represented by points northeast of MM will require higher outlays while points southwest of MM involve lower outlays.

Whatever output the firm chooses to produce, it will want to do so at minimum cost. If, for example, it wishes to produce Q units of output, it will select that labor-capital combination that is capable of producing that output (that is, is on the QQ isoquant) and that involves the least dollar outlay. This decision process is shown in Figure 8.3.

---

substitutes. Hence the amount of labor services required to offset the loss of a single unit of capital services increases as the firm adopts more and more labor-intensive methods of production.

[9] We use the term *rental* to emphasize that this is the price of the *services* of labor and capital.

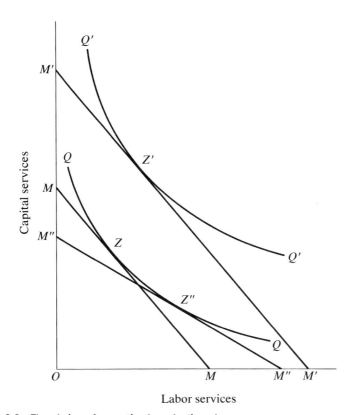

FIGURE 8.3 The choice of an optimal production plan
An increase in output from Q to Q' shifts the production point from Z to Z'.
The firm uses more capital and more labor. A rise in the rental-wage ratio
shifts the production point from Z to Z''. The firm uses less capital and more
labor to produce the same output.

In order to produce Q units of output, the firm must select a labor-capital combination that lies on the isoquant QQ. If the wage of labor and rental of capital are such that MM represents an isocost line, the labor-capital combination represented by point Z involves the smallest dollar outlay. Any other combination on QQ lies northeast of the isocost line MM and hence requires a larger outlay than does Z. Conversely, any other combination on or below MM lies southwest of QQ and hence yields a smaller output than that required.

Inspection of Figure 8.3 shows that the amounts of labor and capital services the firm employs depend on the output it wishes to attain and on the prices of labor and capital services, since these prices determine the slope of the isocost lines. Thus we can write

$$L = \boldsymbol{L}(Q, r, w) \qquad (8.2a)$$

$$K = \boldsymbol{K}(Q, r, w) \qquad (8.2b)$$

In order to produce a larger output, the firm must use more capital services, more labor services, or more of both. We will assume that, as long as neither the wage nor the rental change, an increase in output always leads the firm to employ more of both factors of production. For example, in Figure 8.3, in order to increase its output from Q to Q', the firm moves from point Z on isocost line MM to point Z' on isocost line $M'M'$ and thus increases its usage of both labor services and capital services.

Further inspection of Figure 8.3 shows that if the prices of both inputs were to rise (or fall) in the same proportion, the firm would continue to use the same capital-labor combination to produce any given output. If, for example, both wages and rentals were to double, MM would continue to represent an isocost line and hence Z would still represent the least-cost method of producing output Q.[10] This argument implies that the amount of labor and capital a firm employs to produce a given output depends only on the ratio of the rental of capital services to the wage of labor services. Thus we can modify the above equations and write them as

$$L = l(Q, r/w) \qquad\qquad (8.3a)$$

$$K = k(Q, r/w) \qquad\qquad (8.3b)$$

Finally, we note that an increase in the rental-wage ratio will cause the firm to produce any given output (say, Q units) by a method that employs less capital and more labor. Figure 8.3 also illustrates this point. An increase in the rental-wage ratio may come about either because the rental has risen or the wage has fallen. Hence the firm can obtain either more labor services or less capital services for the same outlay. The isocost lines become "shallower." The optimal production point for an output of Q units shifts from point Z on isocost line MM to point Z'' on isocost line $M''M''$. At this new production point the firm employs less capital and more labor.

Thus at any level of output there is an inverse relationship between the rental-wage ratio and the amount of capital services that the firm will employ. As the rental-wage ratio increases, the amount of capital services demanded by the firm decreases. Since there is a one-to-one relationship between the rental-wage ratio and the quantity of capital services the firm wishes to employ, Eq. (8.3b) may be turned around and written as

$$\frac{r}{w} = r(Q, K) \qquad\qquad (8.4)$$

or

$$r = w \cdot r(Q, K) \qquad\qquad (8.5)$$

In this form, the firm's demand for capital services is illustrated, for a given level of output,[11] Q_0, in Figure 8.4. At any given wage, say w, this

---

[10] The cost of producing the output Q would have doubled but this cost would nevertheless be minimized at point Z.
[11] At a higher level of output, Q_1, all the curves in this figure will be shifted upward and to the right.

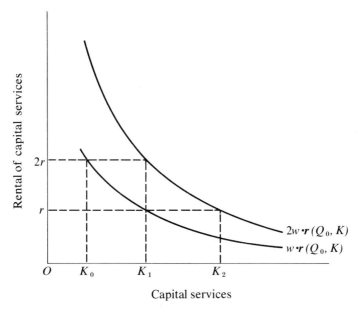

FIGURE 8.4 The demand for capital services

diagram shows that as the rental of capital services increases from, say, r to $2r$, the amount of these services that the firm will employ declines from K_1 to K_0. Similarly, if the wage of labor rises from, say, w to $2w$, the amount of capital services demanded at any given rental, say r, increases from K_1 to K_2.[12]

The Demand for the Services of Capital by Households

The analysis of household behavior with respect to tangible capital will parallel that of business behavior. First, we note that a household's total consumption during any period consists of its purchases of nondurable commodities (food, clothing, vacations, etc.) plus the services of durable goods, such as cars, homes, and appliances, that it consumes. The value of these two categories of consumption during any period, say, the current year, must equal the amount of its total lifetime resources that the household has decided to allocate to consumption during that period. Thus

$$C = rK + p_N N$$

where p_N represents the price and N the quantity of nondurable consumption

---

[12] This statement may be put somewhat differently as follows: If the wage rises and the firm's output remains unchanged, the rental the firm is willing to pay to obtain the same quantity of capital services also rises. In fact, we can be more specific and say that if the wage doubles from w to $2w$, the rental the firm will be willing to pay for a given quantity of capital services, say K_1, will also double from r to $2r$. This fact is embodied in the figure but it is not essential to the argument of this chapter.

goods. The rental of the services of durable goods (capital) is denoted by r and K is the amount of those services that the household consumes. C represents the amount of resources allocated to current consumption by the decision process analyzed in the preceding chapter.

Thus the feasible current consumption set during a given period is represented by the region OAB in Figure 8.5. The household may choose any pattern of current consumption represented by a point in this region. If the amount of resources allocated to current consumption rises (or falls), the line AB, which is usually described as the household's budget constraint, moves outward (or inward). A rise in the price of nondurable goods will cause this constraint to rotate counterclockwise about point B. A rise in the rental of durable services produces a clockwise rotation about point A.

Given its feasible current consumption set, the household will choose that allocation of total consumption as between nondurable commodities and the serivces of durable goods it prefers over all other feasible allocations. In Figure 8.5 this preferred allocation of consumption is represented by point E. Hence, as in the intertemporal decision process analyzed in Chapter 7, the household's choice depends on the interaction between its preferences and its opportunities. Thus

$$N = N(C, r, p_N, u) \qquad (8.6a)$$
$$K = K(C, r, p_N, u) \qquad (8.6b)$$

where C, r, and p_N determine the consumption set and u represents the household's preferences.

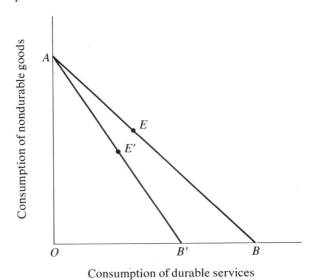

FIGURE 8.5 Household decision making

An increase in the rental of household durables rotates the budget constraint clockwise. The household chooses a consumption "package," which includes fewer durable services and more nondurable consumption goods.

We will assume that an increase in current resources C will lead the household to increase its consumption both of durable services and of nondurable commodities. In the jargon of price theory, both categories of consumption are normal goods. In this case, a rise in the rental of durable services will always lead to a decline in the consumption of those services if current resources and the price of nondurables remain unchanged.[13] In Figure 8.5 a rise in the rental of durable services rotates the budget constraint to AB' and leads to a shift from E to E'. Thus there is a one-to-one relation between the consumption of capital services and their price and hence Eq. (8.6*b*) may be turned around and written as

$$r = r(C, p_N, K) \tag{8.7}$$

This equation, referring to household behavior, is analogous to Eq. (8.5) in the case of firms. For simplicity, we ignore u, the term representing household tastes.

This equation is illustrated in Figure 8.6, which is similar to Figure 8.4. At any given price of nondurables, p_N, and with a given quantity of current resources, there is an inverse relationship between the rental of durable-good services and the amount of those services the household will choose to consume. If the amount of resources available in any period increases, say, from C_0 to C_1, the consumption of the services of durables at any given set of prices, r and p_N, will increase. This is illustrated by the rightward shift of the demand curve from $r(C_0, r, p_N)$ to $r(C_1, r, p_N)$.

The effect of changes in the price of nondurables on the demand for durables services cannot be predicted on theoretical grounds.[14] In the following discussion we will suppose that durables and nondurables are substitutes: that is, that a rise in the price of nondurables leads the typical household to consume more durables services at any given level of current resources and given rental of durables.[15]

The Rental for Capital Services

In the last two sections we have derived demand relationships for capital services by households and businesses. We now turn to the determination of the price or rental of those services. Initially we will assume that capital

---

[13] That is, the demand curve for durables services will always slope downward. A proof of this proposition may be found in any price theory text.

[14] If the price of nondurables increases, then the services of durable goods become more attractive relative to nondurables. On the other hand, the price rise makes the consumer worse off. These substitution and income effects on the demand for durables services work in opposite directions and hence the net effect cannot be predicted.

[15] The substitution effect is assumed to outweigh the income effect so that if the prices of nondurables rise, the household reduces its consumption of these items in order (for example) to live in a larger house or drive a bigger auto. This assumption is not essential to the theory that follows and you should have no difficulty analyzing the converse case in which durables and nondurables are complements.

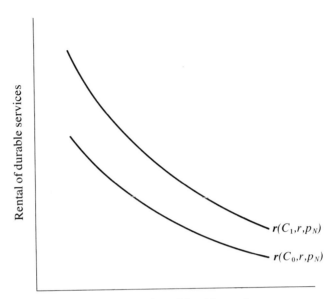

FIGURE 8.6 The demand for the services of durable goods

goods may be freely rented: The owner and the user of a capital good may be different persons. The case in which there is no rental market will be discussed later.

The rental of capital services depends on the available supply of those services and on the demand for them by businesses and households. The market for capital services is illustrated in Figure 8.7. At any given time there is a certain stock of capital in existence that yields a certain flow of services. This flow does not depend on the rental it commands: Hence the supply curve of capital services is a vertical straight line. As we have seen, the demand curve, DD, slopes downward to the right. The rental of capital services must be such that the supply of and demand for these services are equal. Specifically, if the stock of capital in the economy yields a flow of services K^*, the rental of capital services will be r^*. This is the return[16] that an owner of a piece of capital will receive from renting it to a user.

An increase in the level of output implies an increase in the demand for capital services by businesses. This will shift the demand curve to the right and thus lead to a rise in the rental. An increase in the wage of labor will have a similar effect. An increase in output also implies a rise in income. Unless this is viewed by households as purely transitory, the argument of the last chapter implies that total current consumption C will rise. This will in turn imply an increase in the demand for capital services by households

---

[16] It is not the full return since the ownership of capital also involves depreciation and may produce capital gains.

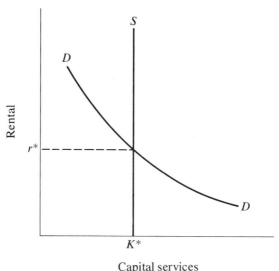

FIGURE 8.7 **The determination of capital rentals**

and thus a rise in their rental. An increase in the price of nondurable consumer goods will have a similar effect.[17]

If there is no rental market for capital goods, owners and users must be the same individuals. That is, in order to use a piece of capital one must also own it. This is the typical situation in much of the United States economy.[18]

This case also may be illustrated by Figure 8.7 if the curves in that figure are interpreted as referring to a single individual rather than to aggregates. On any given date an individual has a certain demand for capital services that may be expressed in terms of the rental he is willing to pay to obtain any given flow of services. He owns a certain stock of capital that yields a particular flow of services, say, K^*. Thus the value to him of these services is r^*. If there were a rental market, he would be prepared to pay a rental of up to r^* in order to obtain the flow of services K^*.

Since firms have different production opportunities and households have different tastes, the value each puts on the services of its capital assets also differs; that is, the value of r^* will differ between individuals. For example, I may feel that the services of my home are worth $250 a month to me while you may value those same services at $350. When there is a market in capital services, such differences will not persist: In this example, a mutu-

---

[17] We have not discussed the effect of the rate of interest on the rental. If the rate of interest declines, total current consumption and hence the demand for the services of consumer durables will increase. This will tend to raise the rental. As we will see, the rate of interest plays another—much more direct—role in the theory of investment and hence this (probably minor) effect via consumption is ignored.

[18] But not all. Factories, vehicles, and homes are frequently rented but machines and most household durables are typically owned by their users.

ally agreeable transaction can be arranged in which I rent my home to you. As a result, the value of capital services is the same for everyone since all can trade in the same market. With no rental market, this mechanism for eliminating differences in the valuation of asset services is not available and hence these differences can persist.

In either case the amount of assets an investor wants to own depends on the rental those assets will yield. If there is a market for asset services, the rental is determined in that market and is the same for all owners. If there is no market for asset services, the rental[19] is the value the owner puts on those asset services; and this value may differ between owners.

The Demand to Hold Capital

Tangible capital is an asset. Hence the demand to hold it depends on the return it yields relative to the returns available on alternative assets and on the income and wealth of the wealth holder.[20]

Thus we can write

$$q_K K^D = K(i_K, i_B, W, Y) \tag{8.8}$$

where i_K and i_B represent the rates of return on capital and bonds, W is total wealth, and Y is income. Total wealth, W, may be written

$$W = q_K K + q_B B + M \tag{8.9}$$

where q_K and q_B represent the prices of capital and bonds and $K, B,$ and M represent the quantities of capital, bonds, and money.

One simple version of Eq. (8.8) occurs when capital and bonds promise perfectly certain and predictable returns so that the average wealth holder treats them as perfect substitutes in his asset portfolio. In this case the wealth owner first allocates his total wealth between money and nonmoney on the basis of wealth, income, and rates of return. If the return to capital exceeds that to bonds, he holds all his nonmonetary wealth in the form of capital and none in the form of bonds. Conversely, if bonds yield a larger return than capital, he holds all bonds and no capital. Hence the demand for capital goods appears as

$$
\begin{aligned}
q_K K^D &= W - M^D(i_K, i_B, W, Y) \qquad \text{if } i_K > i_B \\
&= 0 \qquad \text{if } i_K < i_B
\end{aligned} \tag{8.8a}
$$

where $M^D(\ )$ represents the demand to hold money and hence $W - M^D(\ )$ is the demand to hold nonmoney.

---

[19] In this case economists frequently speak of the *implicit rental*.

[20] This formulation has been discussed and justified previously in Chapters 4 and 6. In previous sections of this chapter the symbol K represented the flow of capital services. However, if the service flow per unit of the capital stock is constant, we can set it to unity so that the flow and stock may be represented by the same symbol.

Being perfect substitutes, bonds and capital must offer the same return if the wealth-holding public is to be willing to hold both; that is,

$$i_K = i_B = i$$

This was the assumption underlying the analysis of Chapters 4 and 5. It is also the assumption that is typically employed in textbook discussions of investment in which it is asserted that firms will undertake investment projects until the rate of return promised by the marginal project is driven down to the market rate of interest.

In the actual world, bonds and capital are not regarded by wealth holders as perfect substitutes. They differ both in the nature and in the extent of the risks involved in holding them. For example, bonds are in most cases more liquid than tangible capital. It is usually easier to dispose of bonds rapidly than it is to sell physical assets. This is because bonds are traded regularly in well-established markets, whereas in most cases physical assets are not.[21]

As a result of considerations such as these, bonds and capital do not generally yield the same rate of return. In this chapter, therefore, we will adopt a more realistic hypothesis regarding investors' behavior. We will assume simply that the demand to hold capital will respond positively to the rate of return it is expected to yield and negatively to the interest rate on bonds.[22] That is, a rise in i_K or a fall in i_B will lead wealth holders to want to hold a larger proportion of their wealth in the form of capital and a smaller proportion in the form of bonds.

Capital yields a return to its owner because it provides capital services that command a rental. However, the rental received from the services of capital does not represent the whole of the return a capital owner receives. In the first place, if the price of capital goods rises, the owners of capital receive a capital gain. Secondly, to the extent that capital depreciates (in the sense that the value of the services it provides declines as time passes), it will be worth less at the end of any period than it was at the beginning. This reduction in value must be deducted from the gross rental to obtain the net return.

As in Chapter 4, we will assume that in each period a constant proportion of the capital stock depreciates. This depreciation rate will be denoted δ. Then if we represent the price of capital goods at date t by q_{Kt}, the values of the stock of capital at dates t and $t + 1$ are $q_{Kt}K_t$ and $(1 - \delta)q_{K\,t+1}K_{t+1}$. During the year, the price of capital goods has gone from q_{Kt} to $q_{K\,t+1}$ and the quantity has fallen from K_t to $(1 - \delta)K_t$. Thus the change in the value of the stock is

---

[21] Of course, some bonds (securities issued by small corporations, for example) are very difficult to sell at short notice. Conversely, some physical assets (for example, used cars) can be sold with very little trouble.

[22] These assumptions were also used in Chapter 6.

$$q_{K\ t+1}(1 - \delta)K_t - q_{Kt}K_t$$

which may also be written as

$$(q_{K\ t+1} - q_{Kt})K_t - \delta q_{K\ t+1}\ K_t$$

The first term in this expression represents the capital gain or loss incurred as a result of the change in the price of capital goods. The second represents the value of the capital that depreciated during the year.[23]

The total return to capital between dates t and $t + 1$ is given by

$$R_{t+1}K_t = r_{t+1}\ K_t + (q_{K\ t+1} - q_{Kt})K_t - \delta q_{K\ t+1}\ K_t$$

The first term represents the rental received from the services of the capital, the second is capital gains, and the last denotes the (negative) return resulting from depreciation.

The annual rate of return on capital i_K represents the yield obtainable in a year from owning one dollar's worth of capital at the beginning of the year:

$$i_{K\ t+1} = \frac{R_{t+1}}{q_{Kt}}$$

$$= \frac{r_{t+1}}{q_{Kt}} + \frac{q_{K\ t+1} - q_{Kt}}{q_{Kt}} - \frac{\delta q_{K\ t+1}}{q_{Kt}} \tag{8.10}$$

Note that when $(q_{K\ t+1} - q_{Kt})/q_{Kt}$, the rate at which the price of capital goods is expected to rise, increases, the rate of return on capital also increases.

In the following discussion we will be concerned with the relation between the rate of return on capital i_K and the current price of capital q_K. Since this rate of return includes the capital gains that are expected to accrue, this relation depends critically on how changes in the current price of capital affect wealth holders' expectations of the future price.

We will assume that the rate at which the price of capital goods is expected to rise (or fall) does not change when the current price of these goods rises or falls. That is, if wealth holders expect the price of these goods to rise by, say, 5 percent, they will persist in this forecast regardless of the current price. Obviously, such an assumption is imperfect and arbitrary. We introduce it not only because it greatly simplifies the analysis but also because our knowledge of how expectations are, in fact, formed is very limited so that any alternative assumption would be equally arbitrary.[24] For short-period analysis, the assumption is probably a fairly accurate one;

---

[23] This result duplicates one reached in Chapter 4. However, at that time we were concerned to demonstrate that capital goods of various vintages must all yield the same rate of return and hence may be aggregated. In this chapter we take this possibility of aggregation for granted.
[24] An alternative, but equally arbitrary, assumption would be that wealth holders always expect prices to return to some normal level. In that case, when prices are high investors expect them to fall and when they are low they are expected to rise. This assumption, applied to the case of bond prices, underlies Keynes's theory of the speculative demand for money that will be discussed in Chapter 9.

obviously it would be much less satisfactory if we wanted to analyze the behavior of an economy over an extended period. This assumption means that the second and third terms in Eq. (8.10) do not change when q_{Kt} changes and hence that the rate of return always moves inversely to the price of capital.

For simplicity, we again adopt the assumption that the wealth elasticity of demand for capital is unity. Thus we can write the demand to hold capital in the form

$$q_K K^D = k[i_K, i_B, Y] \cdot W = k[R/q_K, i_B, Y] \cdot W$$

or

$$q_K K^D / W = k[R/q_K, i_B, Y] \qquad (8.11)$$

The desired ratio of capital to total wealth depends on the dollar return from holding capital, the price of capital, the bond rate, and the level of income. At this point we should perhaps note that the capital-wealth ratio may exceed unity for some wealth holders. A household that owns a home financed by a substantial mortgage debt, for example, may find that the value of its home exceeds its net worth.

At any point in time there is a given stock of capital in existence. This is determined by past decisions to produce capital goods (minus past depreciation). Wealth holders will be willing to hold this existing stock only if the price is right. Equilibrium in the market for capital goods[25] represents a situation in which all existing stocks of these goods are willingly held.

In Figure 8.8 the actual and desired capital-wealth ratios are plotted against the price of capital goods. The curve denoted $k(R^0/q_K, i_B^0, Y^0)$ represents the desired capital-wealth ratio at given levels of income, Y^0, the interest rate, i_B^0, and the dollar return on capital, R^0. It illustrates the relationship represented algebraically in Eq. (8.11). This curve slopes downward to the right since a fall in the price of capital goods makes them a more attractive asset to hold relative to money or bonds, and hence leads to a rise in the desired capital-wealth ratio. The curve labeled $q_K K/W$ represents the actual capital-wealth ratio: This ratio rises as the price of capital goods increases.

The price of capital goods is determined by the requirement that the inherited stocks of assets must be willingly held by the wealth-owning public. In terms of Figure 8.8, if the return on capital is R^0, the bond interest rate is i_B^0, and the level of income is Y^0, wealth owners will be content to hold the existing stock of capital goods if and only if the price of capital is q_K^*. At this price the proportion of its total wealth that the public wants to hold in the form of capital is precisely equal to the proportion that actually prevails.

---

[25] In this chapter we are concerned only with the market for capital goods and ignore the fact—stressed in Chapter 6—that full equilibrium requires that the markets for other assets in the economy must also be in equilibrium.

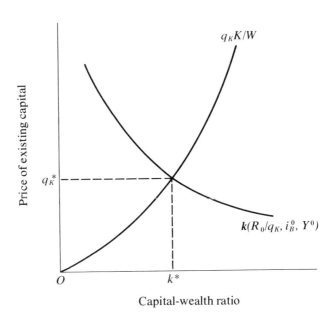

FIGURE 8.8 **The market for capital goods**

The Demand for New Capital Goods

In the previous section we were concerned with the demand to hold the existing stock of capital goods. We turn now to the demand over some period for newly produced capital goods. This is the demand for investment. Note that it is a *flow* demand rather than a *stock* demand.

On any date an individual has a certain total wealth of which a proportion is held in the form of capital goods. Over the ensuing period, say, a year, he will expect a certain increase or decrease in his wealth. If asset prices remain constant, this expected change in wealth will be equal to his planned net saving over the year. In the case of a household this planned addition to its wealth is equal to its expected income less its planned consumption, while for a corporation it is equal to its expected net retained earnings.[26]

The wealth owner will wish to use a certain proportion of this increase in his wealth to accumulate additional stocks of capital goods. In fact, if there is no change in the proportion of his wealth that he wishes to hold in the form of capital goods,[27] he will want to invest that *same* proportion of his net savings in tangible capital. Thus his demand to add to his stock of capital[28] may be written

$$q_K \Delta K^D = k(R/q_K, i_B, Y) \cdot S \qquad (8.13)$$

---

[26] For more details you should refer to Chapter 2.
[27] That is, no change in the desired capital-wealth ratio.
[28] This formulation assumes that actual capital holdings at the beginning of the year were equal to desired holdings. Asset markets were in equilibrium at the beginning of the year.

where $k(\ )$ represents the desired capital-wealth ratio and S represents planned saving.

Equation (8.13) represents the demand for additions to their stocks of capital by wealth holders. Although this demand is clearly related to their demand for newly produced capital goods, these demands are not identical either for the individual or in the aggregate. In this regard it is important to realize that we are discussing wealth holders' plans. In the aggregate, of course, the actual addition to the stock of capital over any period must be equal to *actual* purchases of new capital goods (net of depreciation). But this ex post accounting identity does not imply that the addition to the capital stock which is planned by wealth owners—either individually or in the aggregate—must also be equal to their *planned* purchases of new capital.

The reason that planned additions to the capital stock may differ from planned purchases of new capital is simply that an individual wealth owner may add to his stock of capital assets by purchasing used items, as when a household buys an existing home or a used car. In this case, there is a demand for additions to the capital stock but no demand for new capital. Conversely, a wealth owner may purchase a new capital good to replace an existing one of equal or lesser value. Most new cars, for example, are bought by individuals who already own used cars that they trade in. In this case, their demand for new capital exceeds the planned addition to their capital stock. Thus an individual wealth owner's planned purchases of new capital may exceed or fall short of the addition to his capital stock that he plans to make. Hence the same may also be true of aggregate planned purchases by all wealth holders.[29]

Since wealth owners may add to their capital stocks by purchasing either new or used capital goods, the demand for newly produced physical capital, that is, investment, depends not only on the net addition to their capital stock that investors plan to make but also on the relative prices of new and used capital goods.

If the prices of new capital goods are below those of equivalent used goods, wealth holders who are planning to add to their stocks of capital generally will prefer to acquire new rather than used items. In addition, some wealth owners may wish to exchange their used assets for (cheaper) new ones even though they are not on balance adding to their stocks. As a result, the aggregate demand for new capital goods will exceed planned additions to the capital stock.

Conversely, if new capital is more expensive than existing capital, investors planning to add to their stocks will prefer to buy used goods rather than newly produced ones. Hence the aggregate demand for new

---

[29] You may object that although individuals can add to their capital stocks by acquiring used items, wealth holders in the aggregate cannot do this. This is true. Again, however, we emphasize that we are discussing purchase plans rather than actual purchases. The fact that actual net purchases of used capital must sum to zero in the aggregate because purchases and sales are necessarily equal does not imply that the same is true of planned purchases.

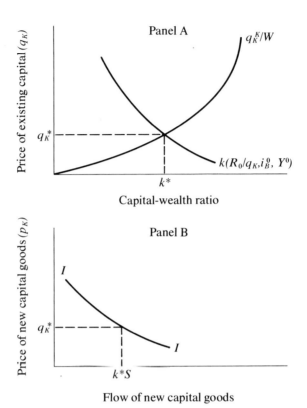

Panel A

q_K^K/W

Price of existing capital (q_K)

q_K^*

$k(R_0/q_K, i_B^0, Y^0)$

k^*

Capital-wealth ratio

Panel B

Price of new capital goods (p_K)

I

q_K^*

I

k^*S

Flow of new capital goods

FIGURE 8.9 The demand for investment

capital goods will be less than the total planned addition to the capital stock.

Finally, if new and used asset prices are equal,[30] investors will be indifferent between purchasing new and used capital. Although some individuals may use their savings to demand used items, these demands will be met by the supply from other individuals who are replacing used items with new ones. Thus, in the aggregate, the demand for new capital goods will be equal to the demand for additions to the capital stock.

These conclusions are illustrated in Figure 8.9. In this figure Panel A reproduces Figure 8.8. Thus q_K^* and k^* represent the price of used capital and the equilibrium capital-wealth ratio determined in the market for existing assets.[31] Panel B represents the demand for new capital. If the price of new capital goods p_K is equal to the price of used capital q_K^*, the flow demand for newly produced capital goods is k^*S, where S represents planned saving during the period. At new capital prices above q_K^* the

---

[30] This does not, of course, mean that one can buy a new car for the same price as a used one. However, it does mean that the reason new cars cost more is that they incorporate "more car" and not that their price—adjusted for quality—is higher.

[31] See the discussion accompanying Figure 8.8.

demand for investment is less than $k*S$, while it is greater than that when p_K is less than q_K^*.[32]

The Determinants of Investment

We have now developed a theory of the demand for new capital (investment) and are in a position to investigate how this demand will respond to changes in other variables. Since the model involves several distinct strands of analysis, we will not be surprised to find that external changes may affect investment via a number of different routes.

Consider first a rise in the level of income. This will influence investment both by producing an increase in the rental of capital services and by enlarging the flow of savings available for investment spending.

An increase in income implies (by the accounting identity between income and output) a corresponding rise in the output of business firms. As we saw earlier, a larger output implies an increased demand for the services of capital by businesses. At the same time an increase in income tends to raise current consumption, especially if the increase is expected to be a permanent one. As a result, the demand for the services of durable goods by consumers also increases. Thus an increase in income leads to a rise in the demand for capital services by both businesses and households. Given the existing supply of those services, this increase in demand will lead to a rise in the rental[33] of capital services.

A rise in the rental of capital *services* implies an increase in the rate of return on capital *goods*. The proportion of wealth that wealth holders will wish to hold in the form of capital will, therefore, rise.[34] As a result, the prices of existing capital goods will increase. In terms of Panel A of Figure 8.10 the curve labeled $k[R^0/q_K, i_B^0, Y^0]$ shifts rightward to $k[R^1/q_K, i_B^0, Y^1]$ and the price of existing capital rises from q_K^0 to q_K^1. Note that the equilibrium capital-wealth ratio also rises from k_0 to k_1. Hence the demand for new capital goods will increase both because savers will wish to invest a larger proportion of their new savings in capital goods (the capital-wealth ratio has risen from k_0 to k_1) and because new capital is now cheaper relative to existing capital.

Moreover, an increase in income also influences investment via a second

---

[32] A special case of this demand curve occurs when investors view new and used capital as perfect substitutes. In this case, demand is zero when p_K exceeds q_K^* and is very large when p_K is less q_K^* since all existing capital holders will wish to sell their used capital and purchase new capital. The demand curve is a horizontal line at $p_K = q_K^*$. In this case, the amount of investment that takes place depends only on the amount that producers of capital goods are willing to supply at that price. This is the assumption that apparently underlies the treatment of investment by Ackley and Shapiro.

[33] Or, in the case of capital services for which no rental market exists, in the *implicit rental*.

[34] An increase in income also leads to a rise in the demand for money and hence to a corresponding decline in the demand for nonmoney assets including capital. As in Chapter 6 (p. 113) we assume that this transactions effect is more than offset by the rate of return effect described in the text.

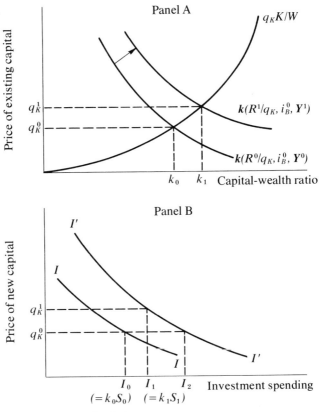

FIGURE 8.10 The effect of a rise in income

route. Such an increase leads not only to a rise in consumption but also to a rise in savings. Part of any income increase will accrue to households that will spend only a portion of it on current consumption. Part will accrue to firms in the form of additional retained earnings. Thus the flow of funds available for investment spending by both households and firms will increase.[35]

We conclude from the above discussion that an increase in income tends to stimulate new capital formation. It increases the flow of savings available for investment. Also, it causes individual savers to wish to invest a larger proportion of that savings flow in capital goods rather than financial assets. Finally, by raising the price of existing capital relative to new capital, it leads investors to add to their capital-good holdings by the purchase of newly produced items rather than of used capital goods.

Panel B of Figure 8.10 illustrates these three sources of additional invest-

---

[35] An increase in income will also raise the tax revenue of state and local governments and reduce certain of their expenses (for example, welfare payments). These governments find they have additional funds available and frequently will use them for capital projects.

ment demand. Before the increase in income the capital-wealth ratio was k_0, the rate of planned savings was S_0, and the price of existing capital was q_K^0. At a price of *new* capital of q_K^0 the demand for new capital was $I_0 (= k_0 S_0)$. The demand curve for investment goods was *I-I*. From Panel A we see that the rise in income causes the capital-wealth ratio to rise to k_1 and the price of existing capital to rise to q_K^1. In addition, the flow of saving increases from S_0 to S_1. Hence the demand for new capital at a price of q_K^1 would be $I_1 (= k_1 S_1)$: The demand curve shifts rightward from *I-I* to *I'-I'*. Note that if the price of new capital remained constant at, say, q_K^0, the demand for investment would rise from I_0 to I_2.

The difference between I_0 and I_1 represents the effects of the larger flow of savings $(S_1 > S_0)$ and the increased proportion of those savings $(k_1 > k_0)$ that are directed toward capital goods. The further rise from I_1 to I_2 represents the additional investment spending that results from the fact that existing capital is now more expensive $(q_K^1 > q_K^0)$.

By similar reasoning, we can readily show that an increase in the wage of labor or in the price of nondurable consumer goods will each tend to stimulate fixed investment. A rise in the wage increases the demand for capital services by businesses. An increase in the price of nondurable consumer items leads to a greater demand for the services of durables by households. As a result, the rental of capital services, and hence the rate of return on capital goods, will rise. Capital goods become a more attractive asset to hold, the desired capital-wealth ratio increases, and the prices of existing capital goods rise. New capital formation increases both because wealth holders wish to invest a larger proportion of their new savings in capital (the capital-wealth ratio has risen) and because new capital is cheaper relative to used capital.[36] In this case, however, there is no further effect via an increased flow of savings as there is when incomes rise.

We turn now to the effects on investment spending of an increase in the rate of interest on bonds.[37] Such as increase will reduce the demand for new capital goods.

An increase in the bond rate from i_B^0 to i_B^1 implies a corresponding decline in bond prices and hence a lower value of total wealth. It also makes bonds a more attractive asset relative to capital. As a result, the demand to hold capital declines both because wealth owners have less wealth and because they want to hold a smaller proportion of it in capital. As a result, the price of existing capital goods falls. In different terms, the reduction in bond prices causes the actual capital-wealth ratio to rise and the desired ratio to decline. As Panel A of Figure 8.11 demonstrates, this causes the price of existing capital to fall from q_K^1 to q_K^0. In this new equilibrium the capital-

---

[36] If wealth holders come to expect that the prices of capital goods will rise more rapidly in the future, the rate of return on capital increases and hence both the price of existing capital and the desired capital-wealth ratio increase. This also stimulates investment spending.

[37] Of course, this rate of interest is not a true independent variable but is determined simultaneously with the price of capital (see Chapter 6). In the present analysis, however, we are focusing our attention on the markets for capital goods only.

wealth ratio may be either higher or lower than in the original equilibrium: In the figure we illustrate the special case in which this ratio remains unchanged at k^*.

This decrease in the price of existing capital relative to that of new capital will lead to a decline in the demand for new capital, that is, for investment. At any given price of new capital, say q_K^1, wealth owners wishing to add to their stocks of capital out of current savings will prefer to purchase existing capital goods rather than newly produced ones that are now relatively more expensive. Put differently, investors will continue to purchase the same quantity of new capital goods only if their prices decline in line with the reduction in the prices of existing capital. In terms of Panel B of Figure 8.11 the demand curve for new capital shifts downward. In particular, if there were no change either in the desired capital-wealth ratio[38] or in the flow of savings, investment spending would continue at the original rate of k^*S only if the price of new capital also declined from q_K^1 to q_K^0.[39] This implies that the demand curve for new capital shifts downward from D_2D_2 to D_0D_0 in Panel B. If the price of new capital actually remains at q_K^1, purchases will decline from I_2 to I_0.

Generally, however, the capital-wealth ratio and the flow of savings will not remain unchanged. As we have already seen, the desired capital-wealth ratio may rise or fall. In addition, the increased rates of return available on both bonds and capital[40] may tend to increase the flow of savings. For example, lower prices of plant and equipment may induce corporations to withhold a larger proportion of their profits for capital investment.

To the extent that higher rates of return do stimulate savings and that the desired capital-wealth ratio rises, the cutback in investment demand will be smaller. The demand curve in Panel B shifts leftward only to D_1D_1 rather than to D_0D_0 so that the demand of new capital at a price of q_K^0 will exceed k^*S. Nonetheless, at any given price of new capital,[41] the flow of investment spending declines as a result of the rise in the bond rate. In Panel B, for example, the demand for investment when the price of new capital is, say, q_K^1, declines from $I_2(= k^*S)$ to I_1.

We have now provided a theoretical rationale for two important hypotheses that were used in the analysis of Part 2. A decrease in the rate of

---

[38] As noted above, Panel A depicts this special case in which the capital-wealth ratio remains unchanged at k^*.

[39] The demand for additions to the capital stock depends on the flow of new savings S and on the proportion of this flow k^* that is used to acquire tangible capital. Since we are supposing that both k^* and S are unchanged in the new equilibrium, this demand for adding to the stock of capital also will be unchanged. Further, the demand for new capital is equal to the demand for additions to the stock when the prices of new and used capital are equal. The price of used capital has declined from q_K^1 to q_K^0. Hence the demand for new capital will remain at k^*S only if its price also declines to q_K^0. This is the conclusion stated above.

[40] The increased rate of return on capital is, of course, the result of the decline in capital-good prices.

[41] In this part of the book we are assuming that the prices of all flows in the economy (and this includes the flow of newly produced capital goods) remain constant.

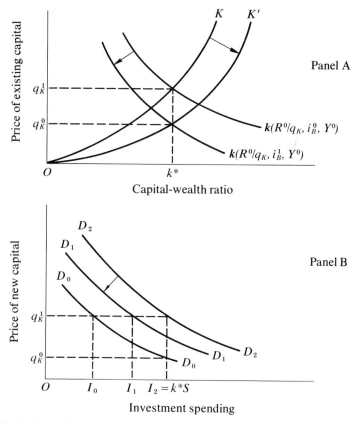

FIGURE 8.11 The effect of a rise in the bond rate

interest on bonds or an increase in the level of income each tend to stimulate investment demand. Specifically, they each lead to an increased demand to hold stocks of capital. As a result, the prices of existing capital goods rise and hence part of this added demand for capital spills over into the market for newly produced capital goods.

The argument may be illustrated by reference to a market with which you are probably familiar: the automobile market. When this market is in full equilibrium, the prices of equivalent new and used autos will be equal. An increased desire to own cars (resulting from rising incomes, for example) is usually reflected in a rise in used-car prices. This encourages some individuals to purchase a new car rather than a used car. As a result, the demand for new cars increases and auto manufacturers are induced to expand their output.

However, even if all other variables[42] remain unchanged, investment

---

[42] Such as the prices of nondurables, the wages of labor, and the productivity of capital services.

spending does not depend uniquely on the levels of income and the rate of interest. The demand to hold stocks of capital goods depends on these variables, but the flow of new investment is determined by the interaction between this demand and the inherited stock. As time passes, the inherited stock of capital will change as long as net investment is not zero. As this stock changes, the flow of investment will also change.

Suppose, for example, that net investment in the current period is positive. Then the stocks of capital with which wealth holders will enter the next period will be larger. In fact, if the government budget is in balance (so that the stocks of money and bonds do not change) the capital stock will increase by the same amount as does total wealth.[43] As a result, the actual capital-wealth ratio will rise. At the same time, the increased stock of capital will—if there is no rise in income and output—cause the rental of capital services to decline. Hence the desired capital-wealth ratio will fall. The price of existing capital goods will decrease and, as a result, the flow of new investment spending will be lower next period than this period.

In terms of the *IS–LM* framework this argument implies that as investment proceeds and the capital stock rises, the *IS* curve will tend to move to the left. This is because a rising capital stock causes the amount of investment spending undertaken at any given interest rate to decline. Once again, therefore,[44] we conclude that the *IS–LM* framework should be used only for short-period analysis in which the available stocks of the various assets may (for practical purposes) be regarded as constant.

References

The approach to investment in this chapter is somewhat unique, though elements of it may be found in the work of Gardner Ackley, James Tobin, and Dale Jorgenson.

Ackley, Gardner. *Macroeconomic Theory.* New York: Macmillan, 1961. Chapter 17 and especially pp. 477–485.

Ackley stresses the role of the supply curve of capital goods in determining the amount of investment that takes place. He implicitly assumes that new and used capital goods are perfect substitutes. See footnote 32.

Jorgenson, Dale W. "Capital Theory and Investment Behavior." *American Economic Review,* Vol. LIII (May 1963).

Jorgenson emphasizes the fact that the demand for capital *services* can be derived from the standard theory of the competitive firm. He implicitly assumes that investors view bonds and capital as perfect substitutes so that $i_K = i_B$.

---

[43] You may find this assertion difficult to swallow in view of our earlier assumption that wealth holders plan to invest a proportion k of their savings in capital goods. However, this assumption referred to planned investment out of planned saving, which may differ from the actual ex post amounts. If no new money or bonds are issued, all income not spent on consumption must be spent (by someone, not necessarily the original income receivers) on newly produced capital goods. See Chapter 2.

[44] Compare, for example, the discussion on page 88 of Chapter 5.

Tobin, James. "A General Equilibrium Approach to Monetary Theory." *Journal of Money, Credit and Banking,* Vol. I, Number 1 (February 1969).
Though not primarily concerned with investment, this article is an example of Tobin's view that the demand for capital should be treated as part of portfolio theory and that the demand for new capital goods is strongly influenced by the prices of existing goods.

Shapiro, Edward. *Macroeconomic Analysis,* 3rd ed. New York: Harcourt, Brace, Jovanovich, 1974. Chapters 11–13.

Questions for Classroom Discussion

1. How would you expect apartment rents to be affected by an increase in the supply of single-family homes?
2. In many cities rents are controlled below the level they would reach in the absence of control. How does this policy affect new construction? Explain.
3. How would you expect investment to be affected by
   (a) A new discovery that substantially increases the life expectancy of the existing stock of capital (reduces δ, the depreciation rate).
   (b) A reduction in the wage of labor?
   (c) An increase in the stock of money?
   Provide a brief explanation in each case.
4. Consider the three-asset model developed in Chapter 6. In that model, stock equilibrium required that all asset markets be simultaneously in equilibrium. Answer Question 3 in the context of this broader model.

The Demand for Money

In the last two chapters we were concerned with the determination of two important flow variables: consumption and fixed capital investment. In this chapter we return to the activities of wealth holders and specifically to their demand to hold money. In Chapter 4 we presented a number of hypotheses concerning this demand; in this chapter we will examine those hypotheses in more detail. However, before turning to a detailed examination of the various theories of the demand for money, let us briefly examine the role that money plays in capitalist economies.

Money in the Economy

Money is an asset; that is, it is one out of many available *stores of value* in which individuals may hold their accumulated savings. The services that it provides in this role are essentially the same as those provided by other financial assets. The existence of these assets makes it possible for individuals, businesses, and governments to separate the act of receiving income from that of spending it. As a result, they have greater flexibility in choosing the time patterns of their receipts and payments, since they can determine their spending plans without regard to the pattern of their receipts (and conversely).

The implications of this greater flexibility that the existence of financial assets makes possible will be explored in more detail in Chapter 10. In the meantime, however, there is the question of which characteristics of money distinguish it from other stores of value. We saw in Part 2 that one important feature of money that makes it (more or less) unique is that the rate of return that it yields is fixed either by law or by custom and that this feature plays an important role in the theory of a monetary economy. Later in this chapter we will see that this characteristic is also an important element in several theories of the demand for money. Most economists agree, however, that the principal characteristic that separates money from other assets is that it is not only used as a store of value but also functions as a *medium of exchange*.

In its role as a medium of exchange, money is anything

that is generally acceptable in payment of debts. In the United States, for example, dollar bills are used as money. When you sell something (such as your own labor services), you may receive payment in dollar bills. Why are you willing to accept these pieces of paper, which have no intrinsic value of their own, in return for your time and effort? Obviously it is because you know that when you want to buy the goods and services you need, the sellers of those commodities also will be willing to accept those pieces of paper just as you were when you were a seller.

In many countries, including the United States, this general acceptability is backed up by legal sanctions. Certain forms of money are established as *legal tender*. In the United States both coin and Federal Reserve notes are legal tender. If a debtor offers legal tender notes or coin in payment of his debt, his creditor cannot insist on being paid in terms of some other asset unless this was part of the original contract that gave rise to the debt. However, such legal sanctions are no substitute for general acceptability, though they may help to promote it. If, for example, a seller is unwilling to accept payment in legal tender money, he can refuse to sell unless the buyer agrees to pay his debt in some other form.

The existence of a generally acceptable medium of exchange makes it much easier for the members of a society to trade with one another. Hence the invention of money is virtually essential to economic development. Consider, for example, the problem faced by a wheat producer who wishes to acquire a tractor. He can obtain one only by engaging in exchange with some other individual. If he is lucky enough to find someone who not only has a tractor he wishes to sell but who also is prepared to accept several bushels of wheat in exchange, a direct barter of wheat for the tractor can be arranged. However, the likelihood of such a double coincidence of wants is fairly remote. Moreover, even if such a double coincidence did exist, the two parties might not know about it; that is, there may be a problem of lack of information.

If no such double coincidence can be found, an alternative possibility is that the wheat producer can arrange to exchange his wheat for a tractor indirectly through engaging in a sequence of transactions, each of which involves a direct exchange. For example, he might exchange his wheat for a horse and the horse, in turn, for a tractor. Obviously longer sequences involving larger numbers of transactions are theoretically conceivable.

Arranging sequences of transactions might cause no great difficulty if each individual in the economy had complete knowledge of all the trades that other persons were prepared to undertake. In all but the most primitive societies, people do not have this knowledge. Hence in order to successfully conclude a sequence of transactions, an individual would have to accumulate a vast amount of information (who wants to exchange a horse for wheat, who will accept a horse in payment for a tractor, etc.). The time and other resources required to gather and analyze this information would presumably be better employed growing more wheat, making more tractors, or in leisure. Moreover, there will generally be many possible sequences of transactions through which wheat can be (indirectly) exchanged for a tractor. Even with full knowledge the computations required to discover which sequence would give the best deal (that is, which sequence would involve the smallest outlay of wheat for a tractor) would also take time and resources better employed elsewhere.

Finally, the wheat producer may be uncertain about his future wants. Nonetheless, it may not be in his best interests to hold on to his store of wheat until his needs are known for sure. When his wants are known, he may find that it is difficult to obtain them in exchange for wheat, either directly or indirectly. It may be preferable to exchange wheat for corn now if the latter will be more easily exchangeable for his real needs when they become known. However, in order to make a judgment on whether to hold on to his wheat or exchange it for corn, the wheat grower requires information on the trades that other persons are prepared to undertake both now and in the future. However, if other individuals also do not know precisely what their future needs will be, they will be unable to supply this information. As a result, the wheat producer cannot know which strategy is the best one to follow, and hence his future living standards cannot be predicted with any degree of certainty.

The invention of money removes or reduces many of these difficulties. The wheat producer can sell his wheat (probably to many buyers rather than to just one) in return for money and can use that money to pay for the tractor. All exchanges come to be made via the same short sequence of transactions in which one commodity is exchanged for money and then money is exchanged for another commodity. Since money is generally acceptable, no lengthy sequences of transactions are required. As a result, the amount of information that each individual must accumulate is greatly reduced, and the need for complex computations is removed. The resources formerly devoted to these tasks can be used in other ways, including leisure. Moreover, since the individual knows that exchanges can always be accomplished through the intermediation of money, uncertainty about the future is reduced.

Probably the most important idea in economics is the concept of *price*. What do prices tell us? Ultimately, they tell us the *terms of exchange* between pairs of commodities. For example, if the wage of a certain type of worker is six dollars an hour and the price of a T-bone steak is two dollars a pound, then we know that one hour of labor services exchanges for three pounds of T-bone steak. Moreover, it is this ratio that is really of interest to us. If the dollar prices of all commodities (including goods, services, labor, paper assets, etc.) were exactly doubled, the rates of exchange between all pairs of commodities would remain unchanged, and we would expect that no one's behavior would be influenced by the change. Nonetheless, although it is these commodity rates of exchange that are of interest to us, it is more convenient to express all prices in terms of a single unit, called the *unit of account*. Individuals can then calculate the rates of exchange between commodities themselves. This convention is useful because it again reduces the amount of information an individual must accumulate in order to carry on exchange. Instead of requiring knowledge of the exchange rates between every pair of commodities, the individual needs only to know the rates between each commodity and the unit of account.

In the United States the unit of account is called the *dollar;* that is, money functions as the unit of account in addition to serving as a store of value and as a medium of exchange. The price, in terms of the unit of account, of the asset we use as our medium of exchange is fixed at unity: the price of a one-dollar bill is one dollar! Such a convention is obviously very convenient. Although we are ultimately interested only in commodity rates of exchange, our calculations are simplified and our transactions facilitated if we not only express all prices in terms of a single unit of account but also agree to use as that unit the same object we use as the medium of exchange.

The function of money as a unit of account is much less critical than its use as a medium of exchange. Transactions would not be unduly complicated if something other than the medium of exchange were used as the unit of account. Individuals would need to know only one additional piece of information, the price of money in terms of the unit of account, in order to conduct business. In Britain, for example, some prices were for many years quoted in terms of guineas rather than pounds, but this appeared to cause little difficulty.

The advantages that accrue from the use of money are worth a great deal. This is indicated by the fact that people continue to use money as a medium of exchange even when the costs of holding it become very large. In periods of rapid inflation, for example, it becomes very costly to use money since its value (in terms of goods) depreciates so fast. Nonetheless, advanced economies almost never retreat to barter, even in such extreme circumstances. It appears that countries that have become accustomed to using money find it virtually impossible to dispense with its services.

Although most economists would probably agree with the main thrust of this discussion, the "correct" definition of money remains a source of some controversy, with some economists emphasizing the store-of-value aspect of money and others arguing that only assets that can be used as mediums of exchange should be classified as money. Milton Friedman, for example, defines money as a "temporary abode of purchasing power," thus stressing the store of value aspect. In terms of this definition Friedman argues that time deposits at commercial banks should be classified as money, since they can be converted into a medium of exchange almost instantaneously and with no risk of loss. Other economists would go further and include deposits at other financial intermediaries (savings and loan associations, mutual saving banks, etc.) in their definition of money. In this book, however, we adopt what has come to be known as the "narrow" definition of money—to include only coin, notes, and demand deposits transferable by checks. These assets are not only stores of value ("temporary abodes of purchasing power") but also function as means of exchange. In addition these assets have the characteristic that the interest rate they yield is fixed (at zero). As we saw in Part 2, this constancy of the rate of return on money plays a key role in our theories of the functioning of a monetary economy.

Alternative Approaches to the Demand for Money

In their studies of the demand for money, economists have adopted three principal lines of approach.[1] First, some economists have stressed the need to have money in order to make payments. These theorists emphasize the medium-of-exchange aspects of money; the services that money provides are closely related to the fact that it is needed in order to carry out transactions. This approach leads to the transactions demand for money and the precautionary demand for money. A second set of theories stresses the fact that money serves as a store of value; that is, it is an asset in which individuals and firms may hold their accumulated savings. Economists associated with this approach argue that the crucial characteristic of money that distinguishes it from other types of assets is that its price (the terms on which it can be exchanged for goods and services) and its rate of return remain more stable and can be predicted with greater certainty than the prices of and rates of return on other assets. This approach leads to the asset demand for money and the speculative demand for money. The third approach to the demand for money also emphasizes that money is an asset. However, it is more general than the other two approaches in that it merely suggests that money yields a number of unspecified services to its holder and is, therefore, a useful asset to hold. Exponents of this approach argue that the demand for money should be treated in the same way as the demand for any other durable commodity. The leading exponent of this approach is Milton Friedman of the University of Chicago; and it has come to be described as the modern quantity theory of money.

The Transactions Demand for Money

An early exponent of the transactions approach to the demand for money was the American economist Irving Fisher. Fisher began his analysis with the following identity, which is known as the *equation of exchange*:

$$p_T T \equiv M V_T \tag{9.1}$$

In any economy using money as a medium of exchange, all transactions involve a buyer, who gives up money in exchange for goods and services, and a seller, who disposes of goods and services and receives money. The

---

[1] A number of economists have used more than one approach. John Maynard Keynes, for example, argued that persons hold money for both transactions motives and asset motives.

value of the goods and services changing hands is necessarily equal to the value of the money changing hands. Moreover, since this is true for any individual transaction, it must also be true for the total of all transactions taking place in the economy over some interval of time. The equation of exchange formalizes this simple accounting fact.

Specifically, T represents the total volume of transactions taking place over a given period of time, and p_T is the average price of the goods and services changing hands in those transactions. Hence $p_T T$, the left side of the equation of exchange, represents *the value of all goods and services changing hands* during the period.

M represents the stock of money. Over any period some dollars in this stock will not have changed hands at all while others will have been involved in one, two, three, or more transactions. The average number of times that each dollar changes hands over any given period is described as the *transactions velocity of circulation* and is denoted by V_T. Thus the right side of the equation of exchange is the product of the number of dollars in existence, M, and the average number of times that each dollar in this total changes hands, V_T. This product, MV_T, is therefore equal to *the total value of all dollars changing hands* during the period. This must equal the value of all goods and services changing hands, $p_T T$.

Fisher argued that V_T, the transactions velocity of money, is largely determined by institutional and technological considerations that change only slowly. For example, it will depend on the type of money that is in use in the economy: If all money takes the form of gold coins that must be physically transported from the buyer to the seller, an average dollar will probably change hands less frequently than if money consists of demand deposits that can be transferred instantly (even between persons who are geographically separated) by the stroke of a pen or the whir of a computer.

The average period between receipts and payments will be particularly important in determining the speed with which dollars turn over, and any development that shortens this period will tend to increase the number of times an average dollar changes hands and thus will increase velocity. For example, if a worker is paid $700 biweekly and spends his wages steadily, the average lag between receipts and payments will be one week, and his average money holding will be $350. If he is paid daily (at the rate of $50 a day), the average lag will be only half a day, and his average money holding will be only $25. Thus a smaller number of dollars can finance the same rate of spending: Velocity has increased. The introduction of credit cards also increases velocity, since individuals can pay many of their bills at the same time they receive their wages, and hence the average lag between receipts and payments is shortened.[2] Again, a smaller amount of money is required to finance a given amount of purchases.

---

[2] This ignores the demand for money by credit-card companies. However, this demand is almost certainly smaller than the aggregate demand for money by their customers which it replaces.

The hypothesis that the transactions velocity of money is a constant transforms Eq. (9.1) from an identity into a theory of the demand for money. Writing the equation in the form

$$M^D = \frac{1}{V_T} \cdot p_T T \tag{9.2}$$

we see that the amount of money individuals wish to hold depends on the value of transactions they carry on, $p_T T$, and on the average number of times they use each dollar. The more rapidly dollars are turned over (the larger is V_T) the fewer dollars are required to carry on a given value of transactions. If velocity is a constant, then the demand for money is proportional to the value of transactions.

In the Fisherian analysis the total value of transactions, $p_T T$, includes not only purchases of newly produced final products but also expenditures on existing commodities and on intermediate goods. Money is required to finance not only transactions that generate income but also those involving the exchange of existing assets between wealth holders and those in raw materials and semifinished goods between businesses at different stages of the production process.

If transactions that represent spending on final products are a certain proportion of the total of all transactions, the value of all transactions, $p_T T$, will be proportional to gross national expenditure at market prices and hence to the gross national product:

$$Y = \lambda p_T T$$

where λ is the factor of proportionality.

By multiplying both sides of the equation of exchange by λ and by dividing the GNP into its price and quantity components, we obtain

$$M\lambda V_T = \lambda p_T T = Y = p_Y Q$$

where Q is GNP at constant prices and p_Y is the implicit price deflator.[3] Finally, by defining $V_Y = \lambda V_T$, we reach the income version of the equation of exchange:

$$MV_Y = p_Y Q \tag{9.3}$$

In this form V_Y is the average number of times a dollar changes hands in the course of a transaction involving final products. This quantity is known as the *income velocity of circulation of money*.

Fisher, as we have seen, suggested that the transactions velocity is determined by institutional and technological factors that do not change much in the short run. Hence he argued that we can take V_T to represent an institutional constant. It has also been suggested that the proportion of all transactions that represents spending on final products may also be approx-

---

[3] See Chapter 2, p. 24.

imately constant. If this assumption[4] is accepted, the income velocity will also be constant.

In this case we have a theory that asserts that the demand for money is proportional to the level of income:

$$M^D = \frac{1}{V_Y} \cdot Y = \frac{1}{V_Y} \cdot p_Y Q$$

Thus the amount of money that people want to hold is a constant proportion of their nominal income.

All money in existence must be held by someone and hence

$$M = M^D$$

As a result, we find

$$M = \frac{1}{V_Y} \cdot Y$$

or

$$Y = V_Y \cdot M \tag{9.4}$$

which states that the level of income depends on the stock of money. An increase in the stock will produce either an increase in output or an increase in the general level of prices. Fisher and his contemporaries believed that (at least in the long run) the economy would tend to operate at full employment; thus total output could be regarded as a constant. Hence they concluded that an increase in the stock of money would produce a proportionate rise in the level of prices.

Equation (9.4) is the equation of the *LM* curve under Fisherian assumptions. This equation is a special case of Eq. (4A.1). It does not involve either the level of wealth or the rate of interest because neither of these variables affects the demand to hold money. When plotted within the usual axes, the equation is represented by a vertical straight line, reflecting the fact that if the stock of money is M, wealth holders are willing to hold that stock if and only if the level of income is $V_Y M$ regardless of the rate of interest or the level of total wealth. This is shown in Figure 9.1. Increases in the stock of money lead to proportional increases in the level of nominal income regardless of the slope of the *IS* curve. Conversely, shifts in the *IS* curve have no effect on nominal income, which depends exclusively on the stock of money.

The Fisherian analysis, originally developed in 1911, remained an accepted part of monetary theory until early in the postwar period. It was adopted, for example, by John Maynard Keynes in his treatment of the transactions demand for money, although Keynes extended Fisher's analy-

---

[4] It is not difficult to think of reasons why this assumption may be false. For example, the volume of transactions in financial markets (which are included in $P_T T$ but not in $P_Y Y$) tends to fluctuate more violently than the level of income. Unfortunately, the assumption is difficult to test since independent data on the value of $P_T T$ are not available.

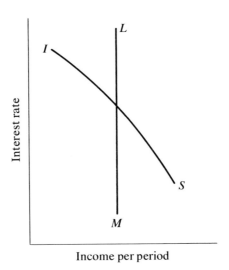

FIGURE 9.1 **The Fisher model**

sis by arguing that money is held for other reasons besides that of its use in making payments. Thus for Keynes and his followers, the transactions demand was only a part of the total demand for money.

More recently, a number of monetary economists have sought to show that under certain conditions the demand for money for transactions purposes may be sensitive to the rate of interest. In terms of the equation of exchange, these economists argue that velocity is not a constant depending only on institutional considerations but a variable that depends, among other things, on the rate of interest. An example of this type of analysis is the model constructed by William Baumol; although very simple, this model conveys the spirit of the modern approach.

Baumol considers a householder who receives a monthly income of Y dollars, which he spends steadily over the month. If he were to hold his entire income in the form of money, his average money stock over the month as a whole would be $Y/2$ dollars. Any increase in income would produce an equiproportionate increase in the demand for money; this is the Fisherian conclusion.

In addition to holding money, Baumol assumes that the household has the opportunity to invest part of its income in some earning asset for the period between the receipt of income and its expenditure on goods and services. For example, a household might invest half its income ($Y/2$ dollars) in bonds at the beginning of the month and then sell them midway through the month. In this case its average holding of money over the month as a whole would be only $Y/4$ dollars. It holds $Y/2$ dollars worth of bonds during the first half of the month and none during the second half, so its average holding of bonds is also $Y/4$ dollars. If the interest rate on bonds is i per month, it earns an income of $iY/4$ dollars by this procedure.

By investing a larger proportion of his income in bonds, the householder can increase his average bond holding and hence his interest income. In fact, by investing all his income in bonds and selling them only when he wishes to make a purchase, the householder could increase his average bond holding to $Y/2$. In this limiting case he would hold no money and would obtain an interest income of $iY/2$. This is illustrated in Figure 9.2.

Although this last strategy gives maximum interest income, few individuals will pursue it. The reason, explains Baumol, is that there are costs incurred when earning assets are sold; these costs may be monetary or nonmonetary. For example, bonds must usually be sold through a broker, who will charge a fee. A strategy that requires the householder to make a large number of small bond sales during the month will produce a high interest income but will also involve heavy brokerage costs. For some types of earning assets (such as bank savings accounts) there is no explicit fee involved, but frequent small transactions are inconvenient and bothersome.

If the householder holds all money and no earning assets, he earns no income and incurs no brokerage costs. Conversely, if he holds no money, he earns maximum interest income but also incurs maximum costs, since he must liquidate earning assets very frequently. In general the optimal strategy is neither of these extreme cases.

Baumol calculates this optimal strategy as follows. Suppose the household divides the month into n subperiods. Total outlays in the month will be Y dollars, of which s dollars will be spent during each subperiod. Hence $ns = Y$. At the beginning of the month the household invests $Y - s$ dollars in earning assets and retains s dollars in cash. At the beginning of each subsequent subperiod it sells s dollars of earning assets in order to finance expenditures during that subperiod. Hence the average money holding is $s/2$ dollars. By the end of the month the stock of earning assets will be zero, so that the average stock of earning assets is $(Y - s)/2$, and the total monthly income from interest on earning assets is

$$R = i \left(\frac{Y - s}{2} \right)$$

During the month the household makes $n - 1$ separate sales of earning assets and one purchase. If there is a fixed brokerage fee of b dollars for each of these n transactions, these transaction costs amount[5] to

$$C = bn = bY/s$$

where we have used the fact that $ns = Y$.

In Figure 9.3 costs and revenues are plotted for various values of s. When $s = Y$ (the household holds no bonds), both R and C are zero. As s becomes small (the household holds little money and makes many small bond sales) R approaches $iY/2$ and C becomes very large.

---

[5] This equation gives the wrong result for the case in which the household buys no bonds. In that case $Y = s$ but C is, of course, not b but zero.

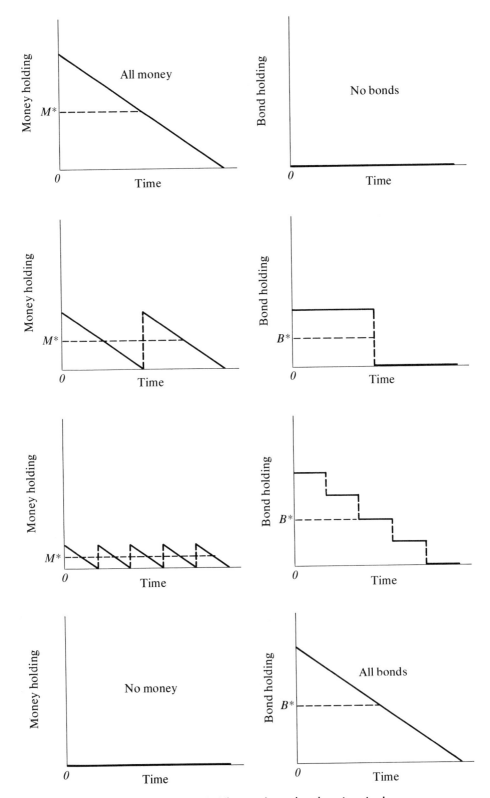

FIGURE 9.2 Bond holdings and money holdings under various investment rules

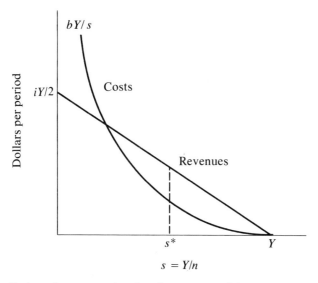

FIGURE 9.3 Costs and revenues of various investment policies

The individual will choose s (or n) to maximize the difference between revenues and costs. This choice will in turn determine his average holdings of money and of bonds over the month. In Figure 9.3 the optimal value is given by s^*, where the slopes of the revenue and cost curves are equal.[6] His average money holding will be $s^*/2$.

An increase in the rate of interest will cause the revenue curve to rotate in a clockwise direction, leaving the cost curve unaffected. The critical value of s will move to the left; that is, an increase in the rate of interest will make it profitable for the individual to increase his average holding of bonds and to sell them in smaller lots so that his average holding of money is reduced.

Similarly, an increase in the brokerage charge will cause the cost curve to rotate in a clockwise direction (since the cost associated with any value of s increases). The revenue curve is not affected. Hence the optimal value of s

---

[6] By use of calculus we can show the relation between s and its determinants more precisely. We wish to maximize the difference between revenues and costs:

$$R - C = i(Y - s)/2 - bY/s$$

To accomplish this, differentiate with respect to s and equate the result to zero. This yields

$$-i/2 + bY/s^2 = 0$$

which may be arranged as

$$s = \sqrt{\frac{2bY}{i}}$$

Average money holdings are equal to $s/2$, and hence we can write the demand for money as

$$M^D = \frac{s}{2} = \frac{1}{2}\sqrt{\frac{2bY}{i}} \tag{9.5}$$

moves to the right: An increase in the brokerage fee induces the individual to make fewer bond sales and so to hold more cash. Thus the demand for money is increased.[7]

A number of economists have elaborated Baumol's basic model. One of the undesirable features of the model is the assumption that the pattern of the household's expenditures is fixed. In general the household can change the pattern of its outlays as well as the structure of its asset portfolio.

As an extreme example, suppose the household purchases all its needs on payday and stores them for use during the ensuing month. On the average it will hold no money and will have holdings of consumer goods equal in value to one-half of its monthly income. A strategy of this type might be adopted by a household living in an isolated area because trips to the store involve costs in both money and time. By visiting the store infrequently these costs are reduced.

On the other hand, the result of a policy of this type is that the household finds itself with a large stock of consumer goods that it uses steadily over the month. Ownership of this stock involves storage costs that must be balanced against the savings that result from reducing the number of trips to the store.

Normally households do not adopt the extreme policies of either making all their monthly purchases at one time or spending in a perfectly steady stream. Nor do they hold the unspent portion of their incomes exclusively in the form of money or of earning assets. In general there will be some pattern of money holdings, of bond purchases and sales, and of consumer-good purchases and storage that will minimize the cost of attaining a certain consumption program. This pattern will not only depend on the interest rate on earning assets and the brokerage costs of buying and selling such assets, but it will also be affected by the costs of making purchases of and storing consumer goods. Developments that increase the cost of making purchases or that reduce storage costs (for example, the disappearance of the small neighborhood store, and the invention of the refrigerator) will reduce the frequency of consumer-good purchases and so tend to lower the demand for money.

The Precautionary Demand for Money

In the last section it was taken for granted that the timing of future receipts and expenditures was known for certain by the household or business firm.

---

[7] The conclusions of these two paragraphs can be reached immediately from Eq. (9.5) in the preceding footnote. If the brokerage fee b rises, the demand for money also rises. If the rate of interest i rises, the demand for money falls. Equation (9.5) also illustrates another implication of the Baumol model, which is less obvious from the diagram, namely, that an increase in income leads to a *less than proportionate* rise in the demand for money. This implication differs from the Fisherian hypothesis of constant velocity. In fact, it means that velocity will *decline* as incomes rise.

In the Baumol model, for example, revenues accrued once a month on a known date (payday), and outlays occurred in a steady stream.

Frequently the precise dates on which expenditures and/or receipts will occur are not known for certain. Unforeseen contingencies may require expenditures that were not anticipated; and opportunities to make advantageous purchases may present themselves unexpectedly. Finally, revenues may not materialize on the dates expected.

As a result of this kind of uncertainty, the household or firm runs the risk that its expenditures over some period may exceed its receipts. If this occurs, it may cause inconvenience, embarrassment, or even actual monetary loss. As a result, most businesses and households find it desirable to hold a reserve of assets as a precaution against this possibility.

If earning assets could be converted instantaneously into money at no cost, persons would presumably hold their precautionary reserve in the form of assets that would yield them an income. If revenues unexpectedly fell short of expenditures over some period, they would convert part of their reserve assets into money to meet the shortfall. In fact, as we have seen in connection with the Baumol model, earning assets frequently cannot be liquidated at once and at no cost. As a result, households and businesses normally hold part of their precautionary reserve in the form of money. We call the demand for money for this purpose the *precautionary demand for money*.

A transactor will likely hold larger precautionary reserves when the future is highly uncertain than when it is reasonably secure. He will also hold a larger reserve if there are greater costs[8] incurred in the event that he is unable, because of a lack of ready cash, to make necessary or desired purchases. A trivial example of these considerations is the observation that an individual making a cross-country trip typically will carry a larger reserve of cash than when he is at home. This is because it is more difficult to predict one's exact needs when away from home and because the costs involved in being temporarily unable to make required purchases (because of a lack of cash) are likely to be much greater.

At the aggregate level increased uncertainty about the business outlook will often add to the demand for precautionary balances. For example, when unemployment is rising, workers will frequently reduce their consumption in order to accumulate reserves against the possibility that they will be laid off. Similarly, in the early stages of an inflation, saving often increases because households are unsure of the prices they will be required to pay for future purchases; hence they wish to hold additional reserves in case those prices rise more rapidly than their incomes.

The demand for precautionary balances is also likely to depend on the level of income (or of total transactions). At high levels of income any unexpected deficiency of receipts below outlays is likely to be larger than it

---

[8] This "cost" may, of course, be in the form of an inconvenience or embarrassment rather than an actual monetary expense.

is at low income levels. Since precautionary reserves are held to meet such deficiencies, households and firms are likely to want larger reserves when their spending rates are greater.

These factors influence the demand for all types of precautionary assets. Other considerations will determine the share of this total that will be held in the form of money. The most important considerations are the rates of return yielded by earning assets and the costs of liquidating those assets. As already mentioned, the precautionary demand for money would presumably not exist if the latter cost were zero; that is, if earning assets could be instantaneously and costlessly converted into money. If, on the other hand, the yield on earning assets is low and the cost of selling them is high, the precautionary demand for money will be large, since the benefits from holding other assets will be small and the cost of liquidating them if the need arises will be large. These arguments are, of course, analogous to those regarding the rate of interest and the brokerage fee in the Baumol model.[9]

Uncertainty and the Asset Demand for Money

The uncertainties emphasized in the previous section relate to the timing of the individual's receipts and payments; that is, the individual was assumed to be uncertain of the precise transactions in which he would be involved in the future. Many economists who stress the role of money as a store of value emphasize a different type of uncertainty. Wealth holders may be uncertain about the *market value of their assets* in the future. This type of uncertainty arises because both the prices of, and the yields on, most physical and financial assets vary from one time to another and cannot be predicted with certainty. Hence the market value of a wealth holder's stock of nonmoney assets on any given future date is uncertain. The price of money, on the other hand, is always fixed, since money functions as the unit of account and its rate of return is fixed at zero by government fiat. As a result, uncertainty regarding the future market value of one's asset portfolio may be reduced by holding part of it in the form of money.[10] However, when the investor holds his wealth in the form of money, he sacrifices the income that earning assets provide. Hence in allocating his wealth between money and earning assets, the individual must balance the yield from the latter against the risks associated with them.

A number of economists have addressed themselves to this problem. As in the case of the transactions demand, we will look at one contribution to this literature that has proven particularly helpful in understanding the issues

---

[9] For an example of a formal model of the precautionary demand for money that emphasizes these analogies with the Baumol approach, see Edward L. Whalen, "A Rationalization of the Precautionary Demand for Cash," *Quarterly Journal of Economics*, Vol. LXXX, No. 2 (May 1966).

[10] However, the purchasing power of money over goods and services cannot be predicted with certainty. Hence, if prices are expected to fluctuate, money will not be a riskless asset. This problem is ignored in the analysis that follows.

involved. In this case the model we will describe was devised by James Tobin of Yale as an application of a more general approach to portfolio selection originated by Harry Markowitz.

Tobin analyzes the behavior of an individual who has a given stock of wealth that he may hold either in the form of money or in the form of securities.[11] Money yields no income; securities yield a coupon and may also produce capital gains or losses. Hence the rate of return on securities during any period may be written

$$i_{t+1} = \frac{c}{q_t} + \frac{g_{t+1}}{q_t} \tag{9.6}$$

where c represents the coupon on securities, q_t is the price of securities at date t, and g_{t+1} is the capital gain (or loss if negative) that accrues between date t and date $t + 1$.

The future price of securities—and hence the capital gains (or losses) on holdings of securities—cannot be predicted with certainty.[12] The wealth holder does, however, have *expectations* regarding the future course of security prices and does estimate the *probabilities* of realizing gains (or losses) of various amounts.

For simplicity Tobin assumes that the wealth owner's mean expectation is that there will be no capital gains or losses on securities. Symbolically,

$$E(g_{t+1}/q_t) = 0$$

This means, roughly speaking, that although the wealth owner is not certain that capital gains will be zero, he regards it as equally probable that they will be positive or negative. We will adopt this assumption while noting that it is not essential to the argument. Tobin also assumes that the wealth holder's expectations about the rate at which capital gains or losses will accrue do not change when either the coupon or the present price of bonds changes. If, for example, the investor believes that there is a 20 percent chance that bond prices will double, so that he will make a 100 percent capital gain, Tobin's assumption is that he will continue in this belief regardless of the present price of bonds.[13] In the next section we will examine a model in which this assumption is replaced by an alternative one.

If total wealth at date t is W_t and the wealth holder decides to hold a

---

[11] The single asset, securities, could represent a whole portfolio of assets, including tangible capital. The important distinction is between money, which is a riskless asset, and other assets, which are not.

[12] Tobin assumes for simplicity that the coupon is known with certainty. However, his analysis may be applied with only minor changes to the case of assets, such as savings accounts, that yield a varying coupon but have a fixed price as well as to those for which both the coupon and the price are uncertain (e.g., common stocks).

[13] The capital gains portion of the total return to securities may be written as

$$\frac{g_{t+1}}{q_t} = \frac{q_{t+1} - q_t}{q_t}$$

Tobin's assumption is that the wealth owner's forecast of g_{t+1}/q_t does not change when q_t changes. This means that if q_t rises (or falls), his estimate of q_{t+1} rises (or falls) in the same proportion.

proportion α of this total in the form of securities and the remainder in the form of money, his wealth at date $t + 1$ will be

$$W_{t+1} = \alpha W_t(1 + i_{t+1}) + (1 - \alpha)W_t \tag{9.7}$$

In this expression the first term represents the value of his securities at the end of period t, which is equal to their value at the beginning of period t plus the return (including both the coupon and the uncertain capital gain) that they are expected to yield. The second term represents the value of his money holding, which is the same at the end as it was at the beginning of period t.

Since the rate of return on securities is uncertain, the value of his wealth at date $t + 1$ is uncertain. His mean expectation of the value of his wealth at $t + 1$ is

$$E(W_{t+1}) = \alpha W_t(1 + c/q_t) + (1 - \alpha)W_t$$

since he expects that (on the average) capital gains will be zero,[14] so that i_{t+1} will be equal to c/q_t. He regards it as equally likely that his wealth at date $t + 1$ will be above or below $E(W_{t+1})$.

If the wealth holder chooses to hold no securities ($\alpha = 0$), then

$$E(W_{t+1}) = W_t$$

Conversely, if he chooses to hold no money ($\alpha = 1$), then

$$E(W_{t+1}) = W_t(1 + c/q_t)$$

As he increases the proportion of wealth that he holds in the form of securities, his mean expectation of his future wealth will rise[15] from W_t to $W_t(1 + c/q_t)$. Hence if the wealth owner were concerned only with the mean expectation of his future wealth, he would set α equal to one; that is, he would hold all his wealth in the form of securities and none in the form of money.

However, when the investor holds more bonds in his portfolio, he not only adds to the expected value of his future wealth but also increases the uncertainty associated with it. Suppose, for example, that the investor knows that he will receive a coupon of 10 percent on his bondholding but believes that there is a 50 percent chance of a 15-percent capital gain and an equal chance of a 15-percent capital loss. If his total wealth is $100, the mean expectation of his future wealth will be

$$E(W_{t+1}) = 100\alpha(1 + .10) + 100(1 - \alpha)$$

If he were concerned only with his mean expectation, he would hold no money, since the value of $E(W_{t+1})$ is at a maximum when α is equal to one.

However, his actual future wealth will not be equal to $E(W_{t+1})$, but it will

---

[14] This does not necessarily mean that he believes that a zero capital gain is the most likely outcome.

[15] As long as c/q_t is positive, which it normally is.

be greater or less than this amount according to whether he reaps a capital gain or a capital loss. Specifically,

$$W_{t+1} = 100\alpha(1 + .10 - .15) + 100(1 - \alpha)$$

if there is a capital loss and

$$W_{t+1} = 100\alpha(1 + .10 + .15) + 100(1 - \alpha)$$

if there is a capital gain. Note that if there is a capital loss and he holds any securities he will end up with wealth of *less* than $100. Thus there is a 50 percent chance that he will actually be worse off if he holds some securities than if he holds only money. If, like most investors, the individual does not like risk,[16] we would not be surprised if in this situation he held at least some of his portfolio in the form of money.

Increasing the proportion of wealth that he holds in the form of securities increases the mean expected value of his future wealth but also increases the uncertainty.[18] Since the wealth holder regards increased wealth as something to be sought but increased risk as something to be avoided, he must strike a balance between these two conflicting tendencies.

In order to make this theory operational, some measure of uncertainty must be selected. Tobin chooses to measure uncertainty by the standard deviation of future wealth. The standard deviation, which is usually denoted by the Greek letter σ, is a statistical measure of the dispersion of the wealth holder's estimates of his future wealth about his mean estimate. If he believes that capital gains or losses are not likely to occur or that, if they do occur, they will be small, the standard deviation will be low. Conversely, if he thinks that the probability of gains or losses is considerable or that, if they occur, they will be large, the standard deviation will be high. Thus when σ is large, the future is more uncertain than when σ is small.

As the proportion of wealth held in the form of securities rises, the dispersion of the estimates of future wealth will widen.[19] Put differently, as α increases, the standard deviation of future wealth, $\sigma(W_{t-1})$, also increases. An attractive geometric feature of the use of the standard deviation of future wealth as a measure of risk is that the relation between σ and α is a straight line.[20]

---

[16] An individual who does not like uncertainty is usually described as a *risk averter*. Some people do, of course, gamble; that is, they pay a price to give up certainty for uncertainty. However, gambling is less widespread than its opposite, insurance, in which people pay a price in order to avoid risks. This suggests that most wealth owners are averse to risk.

[17] We will assume that individuals are not absolutely averse to risk. If the wealth holder always preferred certainty to uncertainty, regardless of the yield offered by the uncertain asset, he would always invest his entire portfolio in money.

[18] Consider the example of the last paragraph. If he holds all money, there is no risk and his future wealth will be $100. If he holds all securities, the mean value of his future wealth will be $110 but its actual value may be as high as $125 or as low as $95.

[19] See footnote 18 for an example of this effect.

[20] This will not be proved here. If you have some knowledge of elementary statistics you should be able to prove it for yourself.

The relation between the mean value and the standard deviation of future wealth is illustrated in Figure 9.4. Panels A and B of this figure show the relation between α, the proportion of wealth held in the form of securities, and the expected value, $E(W_{t+1})$, and the standard deviation, $\sigma(W_{t+1})$, of future wealth. Since both $E(W_{t+1})$ and $\sigma(W_{t+1})$ are related to α, they are related to one another and in Panel C the implied relation between $E(W_{t+1})$ and $\sigma(W_{t+1})$ is displayed. Each point on the line WW' corresponds to a certain value of α.

The line WW' in Panel C is analogous to the consumer budget constraint introduced in Chapter 7. It slopes upward because the investor cannot increase the expected value of his future wealth without also increasing its standard deviation. The wealth holder, in selecting a given allocation of wealth,[21] is choosing a point on this constraint.[22]

Given this constraint on the portfolios available to him, the wealth holder will choose a value for α (an allocation of his wealth between securities and money) that he prefers over all other values. This choice determines the amounts of bonds and money that he will hold and hence determines the mean expected value and the standard deviation of his future wealth. If, for example, he chooses to hold a proportion α^* of his wealth in the form of securities (and hence $1 - \alpha^*$ in the form of money), the expected value of his future wealth will be W^* (see Panel A) with a standard deviation of σ^* (see Panel B). Thus this choice is represented by the point X on the portfolio constraint WW' in Panel C.

The portfolio chosen by the wealth holder depends on his total wealth, the mean expected rate of return on bonds (c/q_t), and his estimate of the uncertainties attached to holding bonds. If any of these change, the budget constraint will shift, and he will change his holdings of money and/or securities.

How will the wealth holder respond to an increase in his initial wealth or in the mean rate of return on securities? This question is investigated in Figure 9.5.

In Panel A of this figure we show the response to an increase in initial wealth. This causes the wealth constraint to shift vertically upward by the amount of the wealth increase.[23] Without further information about the individual's tastes we cannot predict whether the wealth owner will want to hold more or less securities when the size of his portfolio increases.

---

[21] The choice of an allocation of wealth as between securities and money corresponds to a choice of the proportion α. This choice determines the values of $E(W_{t+1})$ and $\sigma(W_{t+1})$ and hence is represented by a point on the line WW'.

[22] Why will the wealth holder never choose a portfolio that is represented by a point that lies below WW'?

[23] Suppose current wealth increases by one dollar. Then by holding this dollar in money, the wealth owner can increase future wealth (by a dollar) with no change in its standard deviation. This implies an upward shift in the constraint.

In addition, any given value of α implies a larger stock of risky assets and hence a larger standard deviation. Hence the maximum standard deviation (that associated with $\alpha = 1$) rises when wealth increases: the constraint extends further to the right.

Panel A

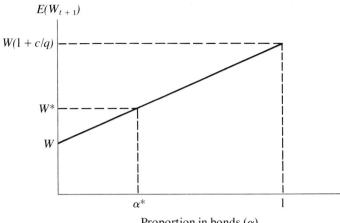

Proportion in bonds (α)

Panel B

Proportion in bonds (α)

Panel C

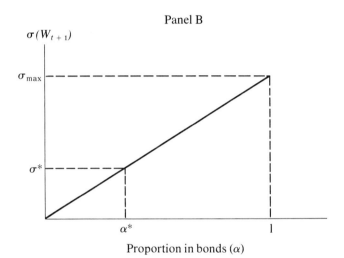

FIGURE 9.4 The mean and standard deviation of various portfolios

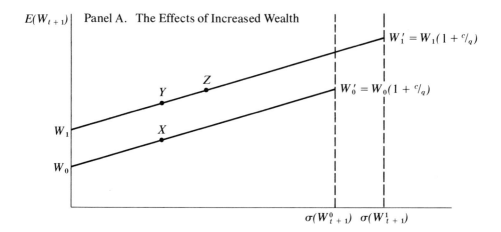

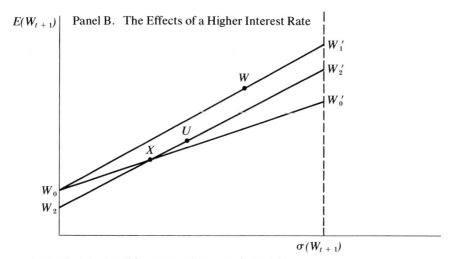

FIGURE 9.5 Portfolio changes in the Tobin Model

Suppose he chooses to hold all his additional wealth in the form of money. Then the mean expected value of his future wealth will increase by the same amount as his initial wealth, and he will undertake no added risk. In terms of the diagram, his preferred portfolio will shift vertically upward from X to Y. Though theoretically possible, this result does not seem very likely.[24] Casual observation suggests that when their wealth increases, individuals usually invest at least part of the increase in risky assets. Thus a rise in the

---

[24] It is, of course, possible (but unlikely) that the wealth holder will choose to hold fewer risky assets when his portfolio becomes larger. This corresponds to the case in which Y lies to the left of X. For a rigorous (but difficult) discussion of the conditions under which an increase in wealth will always induce a wealth owner to undertake more risk and so hold more earning assets, see D. Cass and J. E. Stiglitz, "Risk Aversion and Wealth Effects on Portfolios with Many Assets," *The Review of Economic Studies,* Vol. XXXIX, No. 3 (July 1972).

total size of the portfolio will generally lead the wealth holder to increase his holding of both money and bonds. In this case the new portfolio will be represented by a point such as Z in Panel A of Figure 9.5.

Panel B of Figure 9.5 illustrates the effect of a rise in the mean rate of return on securities, c/q. Such an increase enables the wealth holder to add to his expected future wealth with no more risk, since by holding the same quantity of bonds he can obtain a larger return. In terms of the diagram, $E(W_{t+1})$ rises at every value of $\sigma(W_{t+1})$, so the wealth constraint rotates counterclockwise from W_0W_0' to W_0W_1'.[25] If we accept the previous assertion that an increase in wealth will always lead the wealth owner to undertake more risk and thus to hold more securities, we can easily show that a rise in c/q will cause him to hold a larger share of his portfolio in the form of securities and a smaller share in the form of money.

To demonstrate this proposition we proceed as follows.[26] Suppose that at the same time the rate of return is raised, initial wealth is decreased in such a way that the previous portfolio choice, represented by point X, is just attainable by the wealth holder. This means that the budget constraint will be represented by W_2W_2', which passes through point X and has the same slope as W_0W_1'. With such a constraint he will choose a portfolio such as that represented by U. We know this because portfolios to the left of X on W_2W_2' were available to him when he chose X but were rejected, which means that he regards them as inferior to X. Hence he will choose a portfolio represented by a point to the right of X: U is such a portfolio. Now suppose that initial wealth is restored to its previous level so that the wealth constraint becomes W_0W_1'. Given our assumption that an increase in wealth leads to an increase in bond holding, the wealth holder will now choose a portfolio on W_0W_1' that lies to the right of U: Point V represents such a portfolio. Clearly, V must lie to the right of X. Hence we have shown that an increase in the interest rate will induce the wealth holder to accept more risk; that is, it will lead him to hold more securities and less money in his portfolio.

The response to an increase in risk may be analyzed in a similar manner. If bonds become more risky, the wealth holder can obtain the same expected return only by accepting the added risk. In terms of the diagram used earlier, the budget constraint rotates clockwise. Thus the effects of an increase in riskiness are analogous to those of a decrease in the mean rate of interest. Each will lead the wealth owner to hold less securities and more money.[27]

This concludes our discussion of Tobin's approach to the demand for

---

[25] An increase in c/q may come about either as a result of an increase in the coupon c or a decrease in the price of bonds q. If the wealth owner holds any bonds at the beginning of the period, the latter effect will also reduce initial wealth. This factor is ignored in the following analysis.

[26] The argument that follows is analogous to that used in discussing the effects of a change in the rate of interest on consumption and saving. See Chapter 7, pp. 146–154.

[27] Work through the analysis of this case, which is the exact opposite of that discussed in the previous paragraph.

money. The importance of this analysis is that it emphasizes the fact that money is only one asset in a portfolio of wealth. Thus the wealth holder's demand for money depends on the total size of that portfolio and on the relative attractiveness of the various assets available. The characteristic of money that is crucial to the analysis is not that it functions as a medium of exchange but rather that the return on money[28] is certain, while the return on competing assets is uncertain.

The Speculative Demand for Money

The notion that investors may hold stocks of money for essentially *speculative* reasons was suggested by John Maynard Keynes. Whereas in the Tobin analysis the demand for money exists because wealth owners are uncertain about the future price of bonds, the Keynesian speculative demand exists because investors believe that bond prices will *fall*. Thus Keynes emphasizes the fact that the future price of bonds will be *different* from the present price rather than the fact that the future price is uncertain.

Suppose the present price of bonds is q and each bond yields a coupon of c dollars. Suppose an individual wealth holder expects[29] that the future price of bonds will be q^e. If the wealth holder has initial wealth of W, he can buy W/q bonds, and if he does so his future wealth will be

$$W^e = \frac{W}{q} (c + q^e)$$

If, on the other hand, he holds only money, his future wealth will be the same as his present wealth, namely, W. Then if W is greater than W^e, he will hold exclusively money; whereas if W is less than W^e, he will hold only bonds.

It is easy to see that if $W > W^e$, then $q - q^e > c > 0$; that is, bond prices are expected to fall, and the expected capital loss exceeds the coupon. Hence the investor will hold no bonds; he is a "bear." Conversely, if $W < W^e$ then $q - q^e < c$; that is, bond prices are expected to rise (or to fall by less than the amount of the coupon). Hence the investor will hold bonds exclusively; he is a "bull."[30]

Thus the demand for bonds by an individual wealth holder will appear as shown in Figure 9.6. In this figure OW represents the total portfolio;[31] if the current price of bonds is above $q^e + c$, the wealth holder will hold only money, while if it is below $q^e + c$, he will hold only bonds. At $q^* = q^e + c$ he is indifferent between bonds and money.

---

[28] The fact that the rate of return on money is zero is less important than the fact that it is fixed.

[29] The argument of the next few paragraphs assumes that expectations are held with absolute conviction.

[30] A "bull" is an investor who expects bond prices to rise while a "bear" is one who expects them to fall.

[31] This figure shows the relation between the demand for bonds and the price of bonds for a fixed initial wealth. However, as the price of bonds changes, the value of initial wealth will change. As in the preceding section, this consideration is ignored.

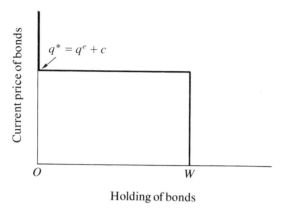

FIGURE 9.6 The speculative demand for bonds

This analysis implies a similar relation between the rate of interest (or, more accurately, the running yield) and the demand for money. If the rate of interest is expected to fall (or bond prices to rise), the investor will hold all his wealth in the form of bonds. If it is expected to rise (or bond prices to fall), he will hold only money.[32] This yields the relation shown in Figure 9.7, where i^* is the so-called critical rate of interest[33] at which the investor is just indifferent between holding money and holding bonds.

Generally wealth holders will not agree in their predictions of future bond prices; that is, the value of q^e and hence of i^* will differ between investors. Presumably, however, there is some (possibly very high) level of the rate of interest such that, if it were reached, all wealth holders would agree that the future interest rate would be lower than the present rate. At this high rate of interest *all* wealth holders would want to hold bonds exclusively in their portfolios, since all would be expecting bond prices to rise. Similarly, there is some low level of the rate of interest at which opinion would be unanimous that interest rates were bound to rise (or bond prices to fall), so that all investors would wish to hold money exclusively.

When the interest rate is so high that everyone agrees that it will be lower in the future, the speculative demand for money will be zero. As the rate falls from this level, more and more investors will find that the current rate is

---

[32] This statement is not quite accurate. If the expected fall in bond prices is small, wealth holders may continue to hold bonds because the coupon exceeds the expected capital loss.
[33] The critical point is that at which

$$q^* = c + q^e$$

Dividing both sides of this condition by q^* and rearranging it gives

$$i^* = \frac{c}{q^*} = \frac{q^* - q^e}{q^*}$$

If the running yield exceeds the capital loss or if a capital gain is expected, the wealth holder will hold bonds; if not he will hold money.

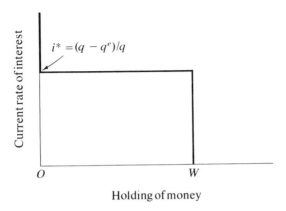

FIGURE 9.7 **The speculative demand for money**

now *less* than their forecast of the future rate. When this happens they will be induced to sell their bonds and hold their wealth in the form of money, since they expect bond prices to fall. As Keynes put it,[34] each rise in the price of bonds (or fall in the rate of interest) will cause the current price "to exceed the expectations of some 'bull' and so influence him to sell his bond for cash and join the 'bear brigade.' "

Thus as the interest rate declines (or bond prices rise) the aggregate demand for money increases, since an increasing number of wealth owners move out of bonds into money (that is, "join the 'bear brigade' ") because they expect the future price of bonds to be below the current price and thus they will incur a capital loss if they continue to hold bonds. Finally, the interest rate falls to the point at which everyone is a bear (believes interest rates will rise) and so holds all his wealth in the form of money. At this point the economy is in the "liquidity trap" discussed in Chapter 5 (pp. 108–109).

Figure 9.8 illustrates the aggregate demand for money implied by this argument. In this figure i_H and i_L represent the extreme values of the interest rate at which all investors are respectively either bulls or bears.

The preceding analysis was first presented by Maynard Keynes in 1936. In the postwar period, however, most monetary economists who regarded themselves as followers of Keynes discarded this particular element in his theory, considering the arguments advanced by Tobin and Baumol for expecting an inverse relation between the demand for money and the rate of interest to be more sound than those advanced by Keynes himself.

The problem with the Keynesian analysis is that each individual wealth owner is assumed to be either a bull or a bear; that is, he holds his wealth either in the form of earning assets or in the form of money. Thus, as illustrated in Figures 9.6 and 9.7, there is no smooth relation between the rate of interest (or price of bonds) and the demand for money by an indi-

[34] J. M. Keynes, *The General Theory of Employment, Interest and Money* (London: Macmillan, 1936), p. 171.

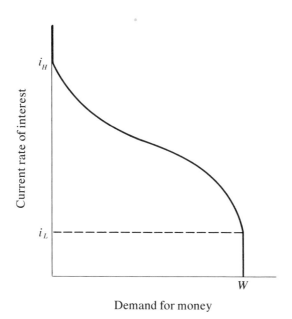

FIGURE 9.8 The aggregate speculative demand for money

vidual investor. The smooth aggregate relation depicted in Figure 9.8 results from the assumed differences of opinion among individuals.

In practice, however, wealth holders hold *diversified* portfolios. They do not hold either bonds or money exclusively, but instead hold some of each type of asset. The Tobin approach to asset selection under uncertainty provides an explanation of this type of behavior.

Nonetheless, it is clear that Keynes's argument contains more than a grain of truth. Wealth holders do make forecasts of the future price of bonds and they do attempt to add to their bond holdings if they expect bond prices to rise. However, this simple idea may be incorporated into Tobin's formal theory with no difficulty.

In our discussion of the Tobin model we wrote the total rate of return on securities during any period as

$$i_{t+1} = \frac{c}{q_t} + \frac{g_{t+1}}{q_t}$$

In this expression g_{t+1} represents the capital gain (or loss) that the investor will receive from holding the security during the period from date t to date $t + 1$. This capital gain is equal to the difference between the future and the present price of securities. Hence we can write

$$i_{t+1} = \frac{c}{q_t} + \frac{q_{t+1} - q_t}{q_t}$$

As we saw in the last section, wealth at date $t + 1$ may be expressed as

$$W_{t+1} = \alpha W_t(1 + i_{t+1}) + (1 - \alpha)W_t$$

where α is the proportion of the portfolio that is held in the form of bonds. If we substitute the expression given above for i_{t+1} into this equation, we obtain

$$W_{t+1} = \alpha W_t\left(\frac{c}{q_t} + \frac{q_{t+1}}{q_t}\right) + (1 - \alpha)W_t \qquad (9.8)$$

In discussing Tobin's theory we assumed that a wealth holder's expectations regarding capital gains or losses do not change when the present price of bonds rises or falls. Thus if the present price of bonds rises (or falls), the expected future price also rises (or falls) in the same proportion. In terms of Eq. (9.8), if q_t rises, the predicted value of q_{t+1} also rises, so that q_{t+1}/q_t remains unchanged.[35]   Under this assumption about expectations, the investor's mean expectation of the future value of his wealth is

$$E(W_{t+1}) = \alpha W_t\left[\frac{c}{q_t} + E\left(\frac{q_{t+1}}{q_t}\right)\right] + (1 - \alpha)W_t$$

where $E(q_{t+1}/q_t)$ does not change when q_t changes. This assumption is the exact opposite of the one that underlies Keynes's discussion of the speculative demand for money. In that analysis the expected future price of bonds was assumed to remain constant when the present price of bonds changed. If this Keynesian assumption about expectations is made, the wealth owner's mean expectation of the value of his wealth is

$$E(W_{t+1}) = \alpha W_t\left(\frac{c}{q_t} + \frac{E(q_{t+1})}{q_t}\right) + (1 - \alpha)W_t$$

where $E(q_{t+1})$ represents his mean forecast of the future price of bonds and does not change when q_t changes. This implies that $E(q_{t+1})/q_t$ *does* change when q_t changes. If $E(q_{t+1})$ is greater than q_t, he is a bull; if it is less, he is a bear. However, bulls may hold some money, and bears may hold some bonds because they do not hold their beliefs about future bond prices with complete conviction.

This change in assumptions about the way in which people form their expectations does not alter the main outline of the Tobin analysis. As before, an increase in α (the proportion of the portfolio held in bonds) implies an increase both in the expected value and in the standard deviation of future wealth. Again, both $E(W_{t+1})$ and $\sigma(W_{t+1})$ increase linearly as α increases. Hence we can construct a constraint (like that illustrated in Panel C of Figure 9.4) that represents the trade-off between risk, represented by $\sigma(W_{t+1})$, and return, represented by $E(W_{t+1})$. The wealth owner will choose

---

[35] In particular, we assumed that the wealth holder's mean expectation was that capital gains would be zero; that is, his mean expectation was that the future price of bonds would be the same as the present price. In algebraic terms, $E(q_{t+1}/q_t) = 1$ irrespective of q_t. However, the assumed value of $E(q_{t+1}/q_t)$ was not important to the argument (though it simplified the algebra). All that mattered was that $E(q_{t+1}/q_t)$ did not depend on q_t.

an allocation of his total portfolio between money and earning assets subject to this constraint.

However, the change in assumptions about expectations does alter the analysis of the effects of a change in the price of bonds. Such a change has a different effect on the investor's portfolio constraint (Panel C of Figure 9.4) under Keynes's assumption than it has under Tobin's assumption. As a result, the optimal portfolio is affected differently in the two cases.

Under the Tobin assumption about expectations, a decrease in the current price of bonds q_t leads to a rise in c/q_t, but to *no change* in $E(q_{t+1}/q_t)$. This is because Tobin assumes that when the current price of bonds falls, the expected future price of bonds also falls. Keynes, on the other hand, assumed that the expected future price of bonds remains the same when the current price falls, and hence a decrease in q_t causes both c/q_t and $E(q_{t+1})/q_t$ to rise. As a result, a fall in the current price of bonds causes a larger increase in $E(W_{t+1})$ for any given choice of α under the Keynes assumption than it causes under the Tobin assumption. In terms of Panel A of Figure 9.4, when q_t falls, there is a larger counterclockwise rotation of the relation between $E(W_{t+1})$ and α under the Keynes assumption than there is under the Tobin assumption.

Under the Tobin assumption a reduction in q_t has no effect on the riskiness of the portfolio for any given choice of α. Panel B of Figure 9.4 is unaffected. By contrast, under the Keynes assumption a reduction in the current price of bonds increases the riskiness of the portfolio for any given choice of α. In terms of Panel B of Figure 9.4, a reduction in the price of bonds produces a counterclockwise rotation of the relation between σ and α. This is because a reduction in current bond prices means that the same choice of α implies a portfolio that contains more bonds and, because expectations of future bond prices are unaffected by a change in current prices in the Keynes model, a portfolio containing more bonds will involve greater risk.[36]

We conclude that, following a reduction in q_t, the values of *both* $E(W_{t+1})$ and $\sigma(W_{t+1})$ associated with any given choice of α will be higher under Keynes's assumptions than under Tobin's assumptions. Hence it is not immediately obvious how the difference in assumptions affects the relation between $E(W_{t+1})$ and $\sigma(W_{t+1})$. It can be shown, however, that for any given risk level the increase in expected future wealth resulting from a reduction in current bond prices will be greater under Keynes's assumption; the constraint in Panel C rotates farther in the counterclockwise direction.[37]

As we saw earlier in Figure 9.5, a counterclockwise rotation of the constraint leads the investor to choose a portfolio promising more risk and a larger expected return. Hence an investor faced with a reduction in the price of bonds will select a portfolio promising a larger return and more risk

---

[36] That is, its future value will be subject to greater uncertainty because it will contain a larger proportion of the asset (bonds) with an uncertain price.
[37] See the appendix to this chapter.

in the Keynes model than in the Tobin model. However, this conclusion does not guarantee that a decrease in the price of bonds will cause a bigger shift into bonds in the Keynes case. The reason is that any given choice of α is associated with a higher return and greater risk in that case. Hence it is possible that in the Keynes case the investor may select a portfolio that yields more return and more risk than he would have chosen in the Tobin case but that contains fewer bonds and more money. This seems an unlikely result in the real world, but it cannot be ruled out a priori.[38]

Money as a Durable Commodity

Each of the theories discussed so far focuses on a particular characteristic of money to the exclusion of other characteristics. The analysis of Fisher and Baumol stresses the need to hold money in order to make payments, while the work of Tobin and Keynes emphasizes the role of money as a store of value.

The third approach to money-demand theory argues that this emphasis on the various "motives" for holding money, while it enables us to tell a number of intuitively appealing stories about the behavior of individuals or firms, does not lead us to a theory of the *aggregate demand* for money that is suitable for testing against the available empirical evidence. Exponents of this view argue that just as the ice cube and cold milk motives for owning a refrigerator cannot be separately observed,[39] neither can the demands for money as a store of value and as a medium of exchange.

The leading proponent of this approach is Milton Friedman of the University of Chicago. However, Friedman's work in a sense represents the culmination of a tradition that began with the famous Cambridge economist, A. C. Pigou.[40]

Pigou, writing in 1917, already recognized that money is only one asset in a portfolio of assets. He argued that the primary influence on the amount of money an individual will want to hold is his wealth or, as Pigou called it, his *resources*.[41] Thus he wrote the demand for money as

$$M^D = k^* \mathcal{V}$$

where $\mathcal{V}$ represents total resources and k^* is the proportion of resources the individual will want to hold in the form of money.

The latter proportion depends, Pigou argued, on the advantages and

---

[38] The results of this paragraph are derived rigorously in the appendix.

[39] This example is due to David Laidler. See David E. W. Laidler, *The Demand for Money: Theories and Evidence* (Scranton, Pa.: International Textbook, 1969), p. 57.

[40] Friedman argues that his approach continues the "oral tradition" of the University of Chicago. However, another Chicago-trained economist, Don Patinkin, has emphatically denied this. See Don Patinkin, "The Chicago Tradition, the Quantity Theory, and Friedman," *Journal of Money, Credit and Banking*, Vol. I, No. 1 (February 1969).

[41] A. C. Pigou, "The Value of Money," *Quarterly Journal of Economics*, Vol. XXXII (November 1917). Pigou is unclear as to the precise definition of *resources*.

disadvantages of holding money compared with those of other uses to which resources might be put. In discussing the attractions of holding money, Pigou mentioned, specifically, the facts that money is needed to make payments and that the timing of future transactions is not completely predictable. These are, of course, the considerations emphasized in the transactions approaches to money demand. However, Pigou also dwelt at length on the returns available on alternative assets and particularly on the return to investing in tangible capital. These considerations were largely ignored by Fisher and other "transactions" theorists before Baumol.

At a first approximation, Pigou suggested that the ratio of total resources to current income might be treated as a constant. In this case the demand for money may also be written

$$M^D = k^* \frac{\mathcal{V}}{Y} \cdot Y = kY \tag{9.9}$$

where $k = k^*\mathcal{V}/Y$. The variable k came to be known in the literature of monetary theory as the "Cambridge k."

When expressed in this form, Pigou's approach to the demand for money is algebraically identical to that of Fisher. While Fisher wrote

$$M^D = \frac{1}{V_Y} \cdot Y$$

Pigou wrote

$$M^D = kY$$

Both theorists expressed the demand for money as some proportion of income. However, despite their apparent similarity, the Fisherian and Pigovian approaches are radically different.

As we have seen, Fisher emphasizes the role of money as a medium of exchange. The institutional and technical setup of the economy determines how much money is needed to carry on a given level of transactions; and the level of income serves as a proxy for the volume of transations going on in the economy. For Pigou, money is an asset; the amount of money that wealth holders want to hold depends on their total wealth and on the relative attractiveness of money and nonmoney assets. In this approach income serves as a proxy for the wealth of the investor, not for the volume of transactions. Moreover, the variable k is not really a constant in the Pigovian scheme; it is a variable that depends not only on the factors emphasized by Fisher but also on the rates of return available on all other assets.

The Pigovian approach was later formalized by John Hicks.[42] Writing in 1935, Hicks argued strongly that the demand for money should be treated in the same way as the demand for any other commodity; namely, in terms of the budget constraint on the investor and the relative prices of the various

---

[42] This is the same Hicks who developed the *IS* and *LM* curves. See J. R. Hicks, "A Suggestion for Simplifying the Theory of Money," *Economica*, Vol. II (June 1935).

nonmoney assets available. However, Hicks's argument received little support from other theorists until it was revived in 1956 by Milton Friedman.

Friedman's purpose was to provide a more precise specification of the factors determining the demand for money as an asset than had been given by earlier monetary theorists. This involved him in a more rigorous and careful examination of the budget constraint under which the average wealth holder operates and of the returns available on the various types of asset available.

For theorists in the Tobin tradition, wealth is the aggregate of all financial and tangible assets that yield income either in cash or in kind. Friedman views wealth more broadly to include all sources of income. He points out that individuals not only receive property income (interest, rents, profits, etc.) from their holdings of physical and financial assets but also obtain labor income (wages and salaries) by selling their own personal services. Hence he includes in aggregate wealth not only nonhuman wealth (financial and tangible assets) but also *human wealth,* which represents the present market value of future labor income.[43]

In a slave economy human wealth can be bought and sold in the same way as any other form of wealth. In a nonslave economy there is no market in human wealth and hence its value cannot be directly observed in the same way as the values of bonds or machines can be observed. However, for any individual, the value of his human wealth is equal to the maximum amount he can borrow on the security of future labor income, and this quantity *can* be observed. Hence the value of both human and nonhuman assets can, in principle at least, be measured and both, according to Friedman, will influence the demand for money.

In addition to total resources (or wealth as he calls it), Friedman argues that the demand for money depends on the rates of return available on the various types of assets available in the economy. He chooses to consider an economy in which there are five types of assets: money, human assets, goods, equities, and bonds.

In a slave economy, human assets are strictly analogous to tangible assets. At any date a slave can be bought or sold at a given price. Slaves yield a "coupon" in the form of the services they provide and produce a capital gain (or loss) if slave prices rise (or fall). Thus the rate of return on human assets may be computed and compared with the rates of return on other assets. In a slave society, the demand for money will depend on the rate of return on slaves since they are one of the forms in which wealth can be held.

In a nonslave economy, the rate of return on human assets is not directly observable. Hence Friedman omits this rate of return from his demand-for-money function. However, he includes a closely related variable. He

---

[43] This broader concept of wealth corresponds to the aggregate we termed *total resources* in the discussion of consumption theory in Chapter 7. In fact, as we saw in that chapter, Friedman was an important contributor to the modern theory of consumption.

hazards the view that the demand for money will be affected by the proportion of total resources that is held in the form of human wealth. He points out that it is generally more difficult to borrow against human wealth than it is to sell or to borrow against nonhuman wealth.[44] Hence the risk that he will be unable to meet a given debt when it falls due will be greater for a wealth holder who holds a high proportion of his resources in human form (that is, who is heavily dependent on labor as opposed to property income) than for one who has a large stock of readily marketable financial or tangible assets. Hence, argues Friedman, such an individual will tend to hold more money to offset the added uncertainty.

The rates of return on other types of nonmoney assets — goods, equities, and bonds — are directly observable and hence cause no special difficulties.

Goods yield two types of return. They provide a stream of services (income in kind) and they may also appreciate in value. Friedman chooses to ignore the in-kind return and hence writes the return on goods as equal to the capital gains they produce:[45]

$$i^g_{t+1} = \frac{p_{t+1} - p_t}{p_t} \tag{9.10}$$

where p_t represents the price of goods at date t.

Equities are claims to a share in the profits of business. They yield a dividend and may also produce capital gains (or losses) if their prices rise (or fall). Thus the rate of return on equities may be written

$$i^e_{t+1} = r^e_{t+1} + \frac{q^e_{t+1} - q^e_t}{q^e_t} \tag{9.11}$$

where the r^e_{t+1} represents the dividend or "running" yield and q^e_t is the price of equities so that the second term represents the capital gain or loss.

Friedman assumes that the dividend on equities remains constant in real terms. Thus if the general level of commodity prices rises, businesses increase their nominal dividends in the same proportion. Hence the dividend yield may be written

$$r^e_{t+1} = \frac{p_t d^e}{q^e_t} \tag{9.12}$$

where d^e represents the real dividend on equities so that $p_t d^e$ is the nominal dividend.

---

[44] This reflects the absence of a market in human beings. If I have a bank loan secured by my car, the bank can sell the car if I fail to meet my obligations. If the loan is secured only by my labor income, the bank cannot sell me into slavery if I fail to pay. Hence the bank is more willing to make the former type of loan than the latter.

[45] The reader may object that people rarely sell their possessions and hence do not realize these gains. This is not a valid objection. Suppose an individual expects car prices to rise and hence buys his car at the beginning of the year rather than at the end. The saving that results represents a capital gain in the sense that if he had not bought the car he would have had to pay more for it.

This expression may be turned around and written

$$q_t^e = \frac{p_t d^e}{r_{t+1}^e}$$

Hence the capital gains term in Eq. (9.11) may be written

$$\frac{q_{t+1}^e - q_t^e}{q_t^e} = \frac{(p_{t+1} \, d^e/r_{t+2}^e) - (p_t \, d^e/r_{t+1}^e)}{p_t \, d^e/r_{t+1}^e} = \frac{(p_{t+1}/r_{t+2}^e) - (p_t/r_{t+1}^e)}{p_t/r_{t+1}^e}$$

After some manipulation[46] this may be written as

$$\frac{q_{t+1}^e - q_t^e}{q_t^e} = \frac{r_{t+1}^e}{r_{t+2}^e} \cdot \frac{p_{t+1} - p_t}{p_t} - \frac{r_{t+2}^e - r_{t+1}^e}{r_{t+2}^e} \qquad (9.13)$$

This expression shows that the price of a common stock may rise for two reasons. First, the nominal dividend may rise as a result of an increase in the prices of goods and services. This effect is captured in the first term of the above expression. If the dividend yield r^e remains unchanged, the price of equities will rise in the same proportion as the general level of prices. Second, investors may become willing to pay a higher price for a claim to the same dividend or (what is the same thing) to pay the same price for a claim to a *smaller* dividend. This implies that the dividend yield has fallen; This effect is captured in the second term of Eq. (9.13). Note that when the dividend yield rises (r_{t+2}^e exceeds r_{t+1}^e) the price of equities falls.

Bonds, like equities, yield a return both in the form of an income payment (or coupon) from the bond issuer and in the form of capital gains or losses. However, a bond is a claim to a coupon that is fixed in nominal terms. Unlike equities, the dollar return on bonds does not rise when the general level of prices rises.

The rate of return on bonds may be written

$$i_{t+1}^b = r_{t+1}^b + \frac{q_{t+1}^b - q_t^b}{q_t^b} \qquad (9.14)$$

where

$$r_{t+1}^b = \frac{c^b}{q_t^b}$$

---

[46] Multiply both the numerator and the denominator by r_{t+1}^e. This gives

$$\frac{(r_{t+1}^e/r_{t+2}^e) \, p_{t+1} - p_t}{p_t}$$

Adding and subtracting $(r_{t+1}^e/r_{t+2}^e) \, p_t$ and writing p_t as $(r_{t+2}^e/r_{t+2}^e) \cdot p_t$, we obtain

$$\frac{(r_{t+1}^e/r_{t+2}^e) \, p_{t+1} - (r_{t+1}^e/r_{t+2}^e) \, p_t + (r_{t+1}^e/r_{t+2}^e) \, p_t - (r_{t+2}^e/r_{t+2}^e) \, p_t}{p_t}$$

or

$$\frac{r_{t+1}^e}{r_{t+2}^e} \frac{p_{t+1} - p_t}{p_t} - \frac{r_{t+2}^e - r_{t+1}^e}{r_{t+2}^e}$$

This is the expression in the text.

The coupon c^b is assumed to be constant. By an argument similar to that used in the case of equities,[47] the second (capital gains) term of Eq. (9.14) may be written

$$\frac{q^b_{t+1} - q^b_t}{q^b_t} = -\frac{r^b_{t+2} - r^b_{t+1}}{r^b_{t+2}} \tag{9.15}$$

The final asset that Friedman considers is money itself and for simplicity he assumes that it yields no return apart from a convenience yield. This yield may come about because money is a riskless asset, because it is a medium of exchange, or for some other reason (for example, miserliness). Thus Friedman would not argue that the analysis of other theorists who focus on particular characteristics of money is wrong but rather that it is unnecessary. For his approach all that is required is that money has some characteristics that make it a desirable asset to hold.

Friedman assumes that the convenience yield on money depends on its purchasing power over goods and services. The wealth holder is concerned not with the nominal number of dollars he owns but with their real value. Thus he assumes that if commodity prices double, the amount of money that wealth owners will want to hold will also double.

The upshot of the above discussion is the Friedmanian expression for the demand for money, which may be written[48]

$$M^D = f[\mathcal{V}, \Delta p/p, r^e + \Delta p/p - \Delta r^e/r^e, r^b - \Delta r^b/r^b, p, h, u] \tag{9.16}$$
$$\quad + \quad - \qquad\qquad - \qquad\qquad\qquad - \quad + +$$

where $\mathcal{V}$ represents total resources, h is the ratio of human wealth to nonhuman wealth, and u represents the wealth owner's tastes. Friedman's argument implies that when the rate of price inflation[49] (which represents the implicit rate of return on goods) or the rates of return on bonds or equities rise, the demand for money is expected to fall, and when $\mathcal{V}, h$, or p rise, the demand for money is expected to rise. In particular, if p rises, the demand for money rises in the same proportion and hence Eq. (9.16) may also be written

---

[47] Since $r^b_{t+1} = c^b/q^b_t$, $q^b_t = c^b/r^b_{t+1}$.
Hence the capital gains term may be written

$$\frac{q^b_{t+1} - q^b_t}{q^b_t} = \frac{c^b/r^b_{t+2} - c^b/r^b_{t+1}}{c^b/r^b_{t+1}}$$

Multiplying numerator and denominator by r^b_{t+1}/c^b gives

$$r^b_{t+1}/r^b_{t+2} - 1$$

$$= \frac{r^b_{t+1} - r^b_{t+2}}{r^b_{t+2}}$$

which is equal to the expression in the text.

[48] In this expression a more compact notation for rates of change has been employed. Δp, for example, represents $p_{t+1} - p_t$.

[49] It is important not to confuse the level of prices with the rate of change of prices. When prices are high, the demand for money is larger than when prices are low. When prices are rising, the demand for money is less than when prices are falling.

$$M^D = p \cdot F[\mathcal{V}, \Delta p/p, r^e + \Delta p/p - \Delta r^e/r^e, r^b - \Delta r^b/r^b, h, u]$$

or

$$\frac{M^D}{p} = F[\mathcal{V}, \Delta p/p, r^e + \Delta p/p - \Delta r^e/r^e, r^b - \Delta r^b/r, h, u]$$

A notable feature of Friedman's demand for money function is that income does not feature as an independent variable.[50] In this respect his approach to the demand for money is similar to his analysis of the determinants of consumption. As in the theory of consumption,[51] however, a link between income and the demand for money can be forged if we can establish a connection between income and total resources.

Over the long sweep of U.S. history, increasing levels of income have been accompanied by a steady rise in the demand for money.[52] However, increases (and decreases) in income have generally been associated with smaller (proportionate) changes in the demand for money in the short run than in the long run. In Fisher's terminology, the income velocity of money, Y/M, has tended to rise in booms and to fall in slumps. This finding is analogous to the observation that the average propensity to consume has remained relatively stable over the long haul but tends to rise in recessions and to fall in expansions. Moreover it can be explained by a similar line of argument to that used in the analysis of consumption.[53]

Over the long haul current income is a fairly good indicator of expected future income and therefore of total resources. In addition, in the long run, rates of return have not shown any definite trend. As a result, income and the demand for money would be expected to move together in the long run.

In the upswing of a business cycle, however, current income rises more rapidly than expected future income and hence more rapidly than total resources. At the same time rates of return on nonmoney assets tend to rise. Hence the demand for money rises less rapidly than income and velocity increases. Conversely, in business-cycle downswings incomes tend to fall more rapidly than total resources while interest rates tend to decline. Hence

---

[50] The convenience yield on money was omitted in Eq. (9.16). Exponents of transactions theories of money demand (such as Baumol and Fisher) might argue that this yield depends on the volume of transactions or income. Such an approach would bring income into the equation via the convenience yield on money. Friedman himself does not make this argument, but primitive versions of it may be found in the work of Pigou and Hicks.

[51] See Chapter 7, pages 157–159.

[52] It appears that the long-run relation between income and the stock of money changed sometime during the decade of the forties. During the preceding seventy years the stock of money had tended to rise more rapidly than income: velocity tended to fall. Since about 1950 the reverse has been true and velocity has been on the rise.

[53] The argument will be presented quite briefly since it is very similar to that presented to explain the different behavior of the average propensity to consume over the long and short runs. Friedman himself has made an argument that is very similar to that presented here though it is couched in terms of permanent income rather than total resources. See Milton Friedman, "The Demand for Money: Some Theoretical and Empirical Results," *Journal of Political Economy*, Vol. LXVII, Number 4 (August 1959).

the demand for money decreases less rapidly than does total income, and velocity declines.

Friedman lays considerable stress in his writings on the fact that his definition of wealth (which we have called *total resources*) is superior to that employed by other theorists who do not include wealth held in human form. Few economists would deny that Friedman is correct in principle but many would argue that, in fact, the amount of money wealth holders wish to hold is little (if at all) affected by the amount of their human wealth.

Tobin, for example, makes this point explicitly. He assumes that individuals make decisions by a two-stage process. In the first stage, they determine how much saving to do and hence how much to add to their nonhuman assets. As a result, nonhuman wealth is determined. They then go on to the second stage in which they decide how to allocate this total among the various nonhuman assets (including money) available. Friedman denies that such a decision process makes sense; he argues that decisions about consumption and about money holding are made simultaneously[54] rather than sequentially. This implies that one alternative to holding money is spending it on consumption. Hence in discussing how wealth holders respond to an increase in their money holding, he argues that part of such an increase will be devoted to consumption and he chides other theorists (Keynesians) for ignoring this link between the stock of money and aggregate demand.

The participants in this controversy unfortunately do not distinguish between increases in money holdings that represent net additions to wealth (that is, those which result from the financing of government deficits by money creation) and those that do not. Tobin would probably agree that the former type of increase would lead to more consumption but would argue that this was because households are *wealthier* rather than because they have *more money*.

Friedman's notion that decisions are made simultaneously rather than sequentially — which in turn implies that his definition of wealth is the more appropriate one — is undoubtedly correct in principle. However, his approach leads to a more complicated theory of money demand and one that is more difficult to subject to empirical testing. If the Tobin assumption is an adequate approximation to the true situation, we may be justified in retaining it. On this point it is worth noting that Friedman recognizes that in a nonslave society the ratio of nonhuman wealth to total resources cannot be changed rapidly. Hence, for practical purposes, he might be prepared to agree that the nonhuman portion of total resources is an adequate proxy for that total.

---

[54] Pigou and Hicks both viewed the decision process in the same way as Friedman. Thus, for Friedman, Pigou, and Hicks, *consumption* is one alternative to holding money. For Tobin, the consumption decision is made first; the only alternatives to holding money are holding other assets.

Conclusion

We have now reviewed the work of the principal contributors to the theory of the demand for money. This review suggests that although the simple demand-for-money function introduced in Chapter 4 is not wildly in error, it could be improved in a number of ways.

Baumol's work, for example, suggests that the cost of exchanging money for nonmoney assets may have an important effect on the demand to hold money. The development of the credit card and of a set of financial intermediaries that issue assets which are very close to money (saving and loan shares, for example) may explain the slower growth in the demand for money and the corresponding increase in velocity during the post-World War II period.

Similarly, the Keynes and Tobin analyses emphasize the importance of investors' views about the expected gains and risks involved in holding nonmoney as opposed to money assets. If these views change sharply, the demand for money — and hence the *LM* curve — will shift. Finally, both Friedman and Tobin draw attention to the fact that money is only one asset among many, each of which has its own peculiar characteristics. This point suggests that the *IS–LM* analysis, which distinguished only two assets, may be seriously incomplete. In Chapter 6 we attempted to make a modest improvement to the *IS–LM* model by developing a theory of asset markets that distinguished three assets. Such a model provides a much richer picture of the way in which actual economies behave. Interestingly, however, it did not lead us to alter any of our previous conclusions.

References

Baumol, W. J. "The Transactions Demand for Cash; An Inventory-Theoretic Approach." *Quarterly Journal of Economics,* Vol. LXVI (November 1952).

Brunner, Karl, and Alan H. Meltzer. "The Uses of Money: Money in the Theory of an Exchange Economy." *American Economic Review,* Vol. LXI, Number 5 (December 1971).

Fisher, Irving. *The Purchasing Power of Money.* New York (1911).

Friedman, Milton. "The Quantity Theory of Money — A Restatement," *Studies in the Quantity Theory of Money,* ed. Milton Friedman. Chicago: The University of Chicago Press, 1956.

————. "The Demand for Money: Some Theoretical and Empirical Results." *Journal of Political Economy,* Vol. LXVII (June 1959).

Laidler, David E. W. *The Demand for Money: Theories and Evidence.* Scranton, Pa.: International Textbook, 1969.
A comprehensive discussion of the principal theories relating to the demand for money, together with a description of the various attempts that have been made to validate them. Also contains an extensive bibliography.

Pigou, A. C. "The Value of Money." *Quarterly Journal of Economics,* Vol. XXXII (1917).

Tobin, James. "Liquidity Preference as Behavior Toward Risk," *Review of Economic Studies,* Vol. XXV (February 1958).

———. "A General Equilibrium Approach to Monetary Theory." *Journal of Money, Credit and Banking,* Vol. 1, Number 1 (February 1969).

Whalen, Edward L. "A Rationalization of the Precautionary Demand for Cash." *Quarterly Journal of Economics,* Vol. LXXX (May 1966).

Questions for Classroom Discussion

1. How would you expect each of the following factors to influence the amount of money people want to hold for transactions purposes?
   (a) A rise in the rate of interest that banks pay on savings deposits.
   (b) The widespread adoption of credit cards such as BankAmericard, etc.
   (c) The invention of the freezer.
   (d) A decision on the part of banks to supply "free checking" to customers who maintain a minimum balance of at least $300.

2. For an individual, the Keynesian theory of the speculative demand for money implies that he will hold either all money or all bonds. But the relation between the interest rate and the demand for money by all individuals taken together is a smooth downward-sloping one. How can this be?

3. If the interest rate rises, the Tobin theory predicts that the demand for money will decline. Is this statement *true, false,* or *uncertain*? Explain your answer.

4. If a rise in the interest rate leads to a drop in the demand for money, then an increase in risk will lead to rise in the demand for money. Explain.

5. If the rate of inflation increases from 2 percent to 5 percent, what will happen to
   (a) The nominal rate of return on bonds?
   (b) The nominal rate of return on equities?
   (c) The demand for money?

Appendix   The Role of Expectations in the Tobin Model

Wealth in the future, W_{t+1}, depends on current wealth, W_t, the prices of securities now and in the future, q_t and q_{t+1}, the coupon on securities, c, and the share of wealth held in securities, α:

$$W_{t+1} = \alpha W_t \left[\frac{c}{q_t} + \frac{q_{t+1}}{q_t} \right] + (1 - \alpha)W_t$$

The expected value and the standard deviation of future wealth may be written

$$E(W_{t+1}) = \alpha W_t \left[\frac{c}{q_t} + E\left(\frac{q_{t+1}}{q_t} \right) \right] + (1 - \alpha)W_t \qquad (9A.1)$$

$$\sigma(W_{t+1}) = \alpha W_t \sigma\left(\frac{q_{t+1}}{q_t} \right) \qquad (9A.2)$$

In the text two alternative assumptions were presented with regard to investors' expectations of future security prices.

(i) Tobin assumption

$$E\left(\frac{q_{t+1}}{q_t} \right) \quad \text{and} \quad \sigma\left(\frac{q_{t+1}}{q_t} \right)$$

are independent of q_t.

(ii) Keynes assumption

$$E(q_{t+1}) \text{ and } \sigma(q_{t+1})$$

are independent of q_t.

To construct the portfolio constraint connecting $E(W_{t+1})$ and $\sigma(W_{t+1})$ we first solve Eq. (9A.2) for α:

$$\alpha = \frac{\sigma(W_{t+1})}{W_t \cdot \sigma(q_{t+1}/q_t)} \qquad (9A.3)$$

Note that this expression may also be written

$$\alpha = \frac{q_t \sigma(W_{t+1})}{W_t \sigma(q_{t+1})} \qquad (9A.3a)$$

Substituting Eq. (9A.3) into Eq. (9A.1) gives

$$E(W_{t+1}) = \frac{\sigma(W_{t+1})}{\sigma(q_{t+1}/q_t)} \left[\frac{c}{q_t} + E\left(\frac{q_{t+1}}{q_t} \right) \right]$$

$$+ \left[1 - \frac{\sigma(W_{t+1})}{W_t \cdot \sigma(q_{t+1}/q_t)} \right] \cdot W_t$$

$$= W_t + \frac{\sigma(W_{t+1})}{\sigma(q_{t+1}/q_t)} \left[\frac{c}{q_t} + E\left(\frac{q_{t+1}}{q_t} \right) - 1 \right] \qquad (9A.4)$$

This is the portfolio constraint linking $E(W_{t+1})$ and $\sigma(W_{t+1})$. Note that, as shown in Panel C of Figure 9.4, it is a *linear* relationship.

The slope of this constraint may be written in two alternative ways:

$$\frac{\partial E(W_{t+1})}{\partial \sigma(W_{t+1})} = \frac{\dfrac{c}{q_t} + E\left(\dfrac{q_{t+1}}{q_t}\right) - 1}{\sigma\left(\dfrac{q_{t+1}}{q_t}\right)} \tag{9A.5}$$

$$= \frac{c + E(q_{t+1}) - q_t}{\sigma(q_{t+1})} \tag{9A.5a}$$

To determine how this slope is affected by a change in q_t we differentiate either Eq. (9A.5) or (9A.5a).

Under the Tobin assumption, we use Eq. (9A.5):

$$\frac{d}{dq_t}\left[\frac{\partial E(W_{t+1})}{\partial \sigma(W_{t+1})}\right]\bigg|_T = \frac{-c/q_t^2}{\sigma(q_{t+1}/q_t)} = \frac{-c}{q_t\sigma(q_{t+1})} < 0$$

Under the Keynes assumption, we use Eq. (9A.5a):

$$\frac{d}{dq_t}\left[\frac{\partial E(W_{t+1})}{\partial \sigma(W_{t+1})}\right]\bigg|_K = \frac{-1}{\sigma(q_{t+1})} < \frac{-c}{q_t\sigma(q_{t+1})} < 0$$

Thus we conclude that an increase (decrease) in q_t produces a clockwise (counterclockwise) rotation of the constraint and that, so long as $c/q_t < 1$, this rotation is greater in the Keynesian case.

In the text (see page 211) we saw that a clockwise (counterclockwise) rotation of the constraint will lead the investor to choose a portfolio involving less (more) risk. That is, $\partial\sigma(W_{t+1})/\partial q_t < 0$. Since this rotation is greater in the Keynesian case, its effect on the amount of risk undertaken will also be greater. That is,

$$\frac{\partial\sigma(W_{t+1})}{\partial q_t}\bigg|_K < \frac{\partial\sigma(W_{t+1})}{\partial q_t}\bigg|_T < 0$$

To determine the effect of a change in q_t on α, we differentiate Eq. (9A.3) or (9A.3a) and use the preceding result.

Under the Tobin assumption, we use Eq. (9A.3) to obtain

$$\frac{\partial\alpha}{\partial q_t}\bigg|_T = \frac{q_t}{W_t\sigma(q_{t+1})} \cdot \frac{\partial\sigma(W_{t+1})}{\partial q_t}\bigg|_T < 0 \tag{9A.6}$$

An increase in security prices will lead the investor to hold fewer securities and more money.

Under the Keynes assumption we use Eq. (9A.3a) to obtain

$$\left.\frac{\partial \alpha}{\partial q_t}\right|_K = \frac{q_t}{W_t \sigma(q_{t+1})} \cdot \left.\frac{\partial \sigma(W_{t+1})}{\partial q_t}\right|_K + \frac{\sigma(W_{t+1})}{W_t \sigma(q_{t+1})} \tag{9A.7}$$

The first term in this expression is negative. In fact, it is *more* negative than the expression in Eq. (9A.6) since the investor chooses a *less* risky portfolio in the Keynes case than in the Tobin case.[1] However, the second term in Eq. (9A.7) is *positive*. Hence we cannot compare the sizes of the derivatives in these two equations. The shift from bonds into money, which results from an increase in the price of bonds, may be greater or smaller in the Keynes case as compared with the Tobin case. Indeed, since the sign of the derivative in Eq. (9A.7) is ambiguous, it is possible that a "Keynesian" investor might hold more bonds[2] when their price rises rather than less.

The explanation of this result is that a rise in q_t has three distinct effects.

   (i)   It reduces the running yield on bonds.

  (ii)   In the Keynesian case, it reduces the expected rate of capital gain.

 (iii)   In the Keynesian case it *reduces* the risk associated with a given choice of α.

The first two effects will cause investors to hold fewer bonds. However, the third effect will cause Keynesian investors to hold more bonds[2] since they can do so without accepting more risk. It is theoretically possible, therefore, that an increase in security prices will cause investors to hold a larger proportion of their wealth in securities and a smaller proportion in money.

---

[1] That is,

$$\left.\frac{\partial \sigma(W_{t+1})}{\partial q_t}\right|_K < \left.\frac{\partial \sigma(W_{t+1})}{\partial q_t}\right|_T$$

[2] In the sense of investing more funds in bonds and hence holding less money.

Part Four

Money and Banking

In Parts 2 and 3 we assumed that all money is issued by the central government. Money was treated as a part of the government debt that yields no interest and is used by the public as a medium of exchange. As a result, the nominal stock of money was assumed to be wholly under the control of the central authorities.

In the United States and other advanced economies only a relatively small proportion of the total money supply—that consisting of coin and paper notes—is issued and directly controlled by government agencies. Most money takes the form of demand deposits (checking accounts) at commercial banks and most payments are made by check rather than in currency. The authorities do not directly control the volume of checking accounts outstanding; this is determined by the private decisions of individual commercial banks and their customers. Federal agencies (principally the Federal Reserve System and the Treasury) do, however, have considerable influence over these private decisions.

In this part the role of the banking system in an advanced economy will be studied. We begin by discussing the functions of financial intermediaries in general and of commercial banks in particular. Later, we examine the factors that determine the quantity of bank deposits that are outstanding. The framework for this examination is the so-called new view of commercial banking, which represents an extension of the portfolio models developed in Part 2. Finally, we turn to an examination of the activities of the Federal Reserve System and of monetary policy.

Financial Systems

Most people find that they wish to consume less than they earn over some portions of their lifetimes in order to be able to consume in excess of their incomes at other times. For example, they make provision for retirement during the years in which they are working. Businesses and governments similarly find that sometimes their expenditures exceed their receipts while at other times the reverse is true. For this type of activity to be possible, there must be some long-lived commodity or commodities available in which persons can hold their accumulated savings. One of the outstanding characteristics of economically advanced countries is that the menu of these commodities is both large and varied. It includes both material assets, such as machines, homes, and automobiles, and financial assets such as bank deposits and government securities. Moreover financial assets include not only *primary securities,* which are issued by the ultimate borrowers, but also *secondary securities,* which are issued by financial institutions to obtain funds that are then relent to the ultimate borrowers.

Up to now the existence of these secondary securities and of the institutions that issue them has been largely ignored. In this chapter we examine the role played by financial institutions in advanced economies. This discussion will provide the background for our later study of a particular class of institution—the commercial bank—and a particular type of asset, namely, the bank deposit. Before discussing the asset structure of a complex modern economy, however, it is helpful to examine a much simpler situation: that of Robinson Crusoe alone on his island.

Saving and Investment
in a Crusoe Economy

To keep the argument simple, let us suppose that there is only one consumption good on the island and that Robinson has available to him a given amount of this commodity. We refer to this quantity as his *endowment* of the consumer good. To be specific we will suppose that the single commodity is yams which grow wild on the island. Robinson's annual endowment is the quantity of wild yams that he can gather in a year.[1]

Robinson may decide to consume less than his endowment in some years in order to increase his consumption in other years. He can accomplish such a reallocation of his endowment stream by, for example, planting those yams he does not eat in one year and so obtaining a crop of cultivated yams in the following year in addition to his endowment.

Suppose Robinson Crusoe expects to remain on his island for two years. Then the relation between present and future consumption may be analyzed by a diagram[2] such as that shown in Figure 10.1. In this figure *OA* and *OC* represent Robinson's endowments of yams. The line *BD* represents the amounts of yams he can obtain in the second year by planting those he does not eat in the first year. In the terminology of Chapter 7, the possibility of production[3] extends his feasible consumption set from *OABC* to *OABD* and thus makes him better off.[4]

The planting or storage of the yams he does not eat is one possible method by which sacrifices of present consumption may be "transformed" into future consumption. In this simple technique, the commodity in which Robinson holds his savings—yams—is the same as that which he consumes. In technical language, there is no difference between his *capital goods* and his *consumption goods*.

A somewhat more complicated strategy, which Robinson might adopt, would be to devote part of his time to the construction of a plow. As a result, he will have less time available to gather wild yams and hence must reduce his consumption of yams in year one.[5] On the other hand, possession of the plow will enable him to cultivate his land more effectively and hence to obtain a larger crop in year two from planting any given number of yams in year one.

The construction and use of a plow is a more indirect, or roundabout, method of increasing future consumption since it involves, as an intermediate step, the production of a commodity (the plow), which itself cannot

---

[1] Other interpretations of the endowment are possible. Robinson might have rescued a stock of food when his ship was sunk. His endowment is equal to this stock in the first year and is zero thereafter. The important point is that the endowment is independent of Robinson's current actions. Presumably, under the wild yam interpretation, if Robinson ate *every* yam on the island, none would remain to propagate next year's crop. This botanical problem is ignored.

[2] Note the similarity between Figure 10.1 and those used in Chapter 7 to illustrate the household's consumption opportunities.

[3] Storage may be regarded as a particular type of production. If Robinson chooses to store rather than plant the yams he saves and no spoilage occurs, *BD* will be a straight line with a slope of 45°. The present argument does not depend on the particular shape of *BD* as long as it slopes upward.

[4] This conclusion does not depend on there being more yams available in the two years taken together. If yams are stored and some spoil (so that *BD* is a straight line with slope less than 45°), the two-year supply is reduced but the conclusion of the text still holds.

[5] Thus Robinson, in effect, "uses" his endowment to produce a plow. Of course, he does not literally transform his yam endowment into a plow, but he does sacrifice yams in order to build the plow.

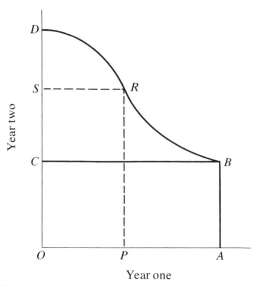

Year one

FIGURE 10.1   Robinson Crusoe: Production and consumption

be consumed. Such commodities, which are wanted not for their own sakes but because they make possible a flow of other commodities in the future, are known as *capital goods*. Typically, methods of providing for future consumption that involve the accumulation of stocks of capital goods are more productive[6] than are simpler methods, but they also involve a larger initial sacrifice.[7] Hence they can be adopted only if individuals—either singly or collectively—are willing to make that sacrifice. We will see in the next section that in advanced economies the financial system plays an important role in making it possible for a society to adopt more roundabout and capital-intensive methods of production.

Before proceeding with that discussion, one final point must be made. We will take it for granted that the accumulation of more capital goods always leads to higher levels of consumption in the future. However, although additions to the stock of capital this year will almost always make it possible for society to consume more next year,[8] this does not necessarily mean that such additions will raise consumption in a *whole series* of future years. It is

---

[6] In the present example, the possession of a plow enables Robinson Crusoe to obtain a larger crop from a given number of yams planted. The high living standards enjoyed in advanced economies are largely the result of their stocks of capital equipment accumulated through the saving of earlier generations.

[7] Some production methods require a larger sacrifice in a somewhat different sense. They require the saver to wait for a longer period before the additional consumption goods become available. The classic example of this situation is forestry, in which the output of timber may be increased simply by waiting for the trees to grow. In such cases future consumption may be increased by making sacrifices over a longer period rather than larger sacrifices in any single period. Although we will not explore this case in detail, the conclusions of this chapter may readily be extended to cover it.

[8] That is, in price theory terms, the marginal product of capital is normally positive.

quite possible for a society to have too much capital in the sense that the replacement of the machines that wear out each year uses up such a large share of total output that consumption could be increased in every year by reducing the stock of capital goods.[9] Despite this theoretical caveat, it is clear that, in fact, the high living standards enjoyed in economically advanced economies could not have been attained without the accumulation of their present large stocks of capital goods and that the financial system played, and continues to play, a vital role in making that accumulation possible.

The Role of Financial Assets

In the preceding section we suggested that methods of production that involve the accumulation of capital goods are typically more productive than more direct methods (in the sense that they provide a larger future output for a given present input) but that they also require larger sacrifices of present consumption. This situation is illustrated in Figure 10.2.

---

[9] For a discussion of this issue within the framework of neoclassical growth theory, see Edmund S. Phelps, "The Golden Rule of Accumulation: A Fable for Growthmen," *American Economic Review* (September 1961).

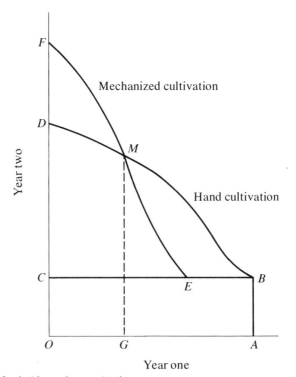

FIGURE 10.2 Capital-intensive production

In this figure the consumption options made available by "mechanized cultivation" are represented by the kinked line *BEF*. *BE* represents the cost (in terms of yams foregone in year one[10]) of producing a plow and *EF* shows the crop obtainable from planting various quantities of yams and cultivating them with the aid of the plow. The line *BD* again represents the production possibilities of "hand cultivation." The fact that *EF* is steeper than *BD* shows that mechanized cultivation yields a larger crop from planting any given number of yams than does hand cultivation. Nonetheless, despite the greater productiveness of the more capital-intensive technique, the construction and use of a plow is a sensible strategy only if Robinson is prepared to sacrifice more than *AG* yams in the first year. If he is unwilling (or unable) to sacrifice this amount, hand cultivation provides a larger return in year two and is preferred.[11]

So far we have assumed that Robinson is alone on the island. In that case, Robinson may find that the current sacrifice required to obtain a plow is so high that hand cultivation is preferable to mechanization despite the latter's technical superiority. However, suppose he is joined by a number of other families. Then, by cooperating with his new neighbors, the sacrifice involved in obtaining the plow can be reduced and his consumption options extended. For example, if a group of neighbors can get together and agree to each contribute a share of the yams required to acquire a plow[12] in return for an equivalent share in the additional output that its use makes possible, each can secure a consumption program that is better than any single individual could obtain by his own unaided efforts. Figure 10.3 illustrates the situation.

In this figure we assume there are two persons on the island. Each has at his disposal the same pair of productive techniques (hand cultivation and mechanized cultivation). Each would use hand cultivation for small sacrifices of present consumption and mechanized cultivation for larger sacrifices. Hence the terms on which each is able to transform present savings into additional future consumption are represented by the curve *BMF*. Given these terms, suppose that each individual chooses to set aside *BH* yams in year one and to use hand cultivation to produce *HK* yams in year two. Neither finds it economic to acquire a plow since hand cultivation is more productive at low levels of output.

However, if the individuals collaborate, mechanization becomes economic, and both benefit from the larger output that use of a plow makes possible. Since each is setting aside *BH* yams in year one; their combined saving totals *BJ* (where *BH* = *HJ*). Working independently, each obtains a

---

[10] On our earlier interpretation of the endowment, this means that in the time it takes Robinson to construct the plow, he could have gathered *BE* yams.

[11] Remember our assumption that Robinson will be rescued after two years. Of course, if the plow could be used for several years, the statement in the text would require modification.

[12] This could be done by the neighbors' agreeing to supply food to one of their number while he devotes all his time to constructing the plow. This might be considered the beginnings of the distinction between consumer-good industries and capital-good industries.

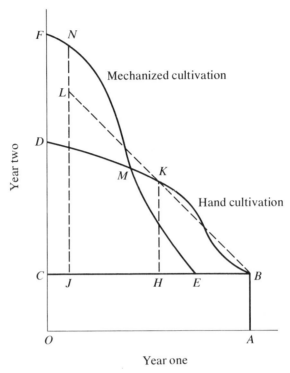

FIGURE 10.3 **The benefits of cooperation**

crop of *HK* so that their combined return is twice that amount, namely, *JL*. From the figure we see that by pooling their savings, the two individuals are able to acquire the plow and produce *JN* yams in the second year. Since the total supply of yams in year two is enlarged by this cooperative arrangement (*JN* exceeds *JL*), with no increase in the sacrifices required in year one, both individuals can benefit.

This example illustrates the fact that if individuals collaborate they can make use of more capital-intensive methods of production and, because such methods are generally more productive than those that use less capital, all parties to such cooperative endeavors can obtain preferred consumption programs.

In modern capitalist economies the principal institution, through which this type of cooperation is achieved, is the *corporation*. Like Robinson Crusoe and his neighbor, stockholders in a modern corporation turn over their savings to the corporation in return for a share in its net return. As a result, they become (indirect) owners of large pieces of capital equipment, which otherwise they could not afford. The corporation also makes possible the employment of the large force of specialized labor that is needed to operate the equipment in the most effective way. Because of the advantages of large-scale production, each individual's share in the corporation's net return is larger than he could obtain by engaging in production on his own.

When wealth holders turn over their resources to a corporation, they become holders of claims on the assets[13] of the corporation. These claims are financial assets: They are *common stocks*. Thus the development of the corporation leads to a change in the portfolios of wealth holders in which *tangible assets* (yams, plows, etc.) are replaced by *financial assets*.

In addition to making it possible for society to enjoy the advantages of large-scale and capital-intensive methods of production, the corporation also provides important benefits through its role in reducing uncertainty. Suppose, for example, that Robinson Crusoe grows only yams and his neighbor (Man Friday) grows only corn. If a crop fails, its producer will starve. This risk of starvation will be reduced[14] if two corporations are formed in which Crusoe and Friday each own a half-share. In that case neither will starve unless both crops fail simultaneously. The investor in a modern economy has a similar opportunity to reduce the risk of loss by spreading his savings over a wide range of common stocks. Thus a second advantage, which arises from the invention of the corporation and of the common stock as a claim to the tangible assets of the corporation, is that such claims can be divided into arbitrarily small units so that individual wealth owners are able to own shares in a number of different enterprises. If a single enterprise fails, the impact on any individual's consumption is less severe than it would have been had he invested the whole of his accumulated wealth in the failing enterprise. This advantage—which applies to all financial assets in some degree—is usually described as being the result of *diversification*,[15] or "risk spreading."

The invention of the corporation, which permits the individual saver to hold his accumulated wealth in the form of financial rather than material assets, sets the stage for the development of a financial system. Some savers, for example, may feel that owning common stock or engaging in production on their own account are too risky for their tastes since the return (in future consumption) is uncertain and depends on the success of the enterprise. On the other hand, storage of consumer goods (which is a relatively riskless strategy) usually is costly and inconvenient. Hence they may prefer to put their resources at the disposal of a corporation (or of a single producer) in return for a fixed but guaranteed payment: Thus the

---

[13] In general, these assets will consist of the corporation's stocks of physical capital (plows, etc.) plus its current output. Normally, the former will greatly exceed the latter. In our special two-period example, however, the assets (in year two, which is when Robinson and his neighbor will exercise their claims) consist only of the corporation's output (JN in Figure 10.3) since the plow is worthless after the end of year two.

[14] This will not be true if corn-crop failure and yam-crop failure are perfectly and positively correlated; that is, whenever one crop fails so does the other.

[15] We have already seen another example of the advantages of diversification in our discussion of Tobin's theory of the asset demand for money in Chapter 9.

corporate bond, which is a claim on the assets of the owners of the corporation, is invented.

The issue of bonds by a corporation enables it to add to its stocks of capital and so to increase its future output without any additional sacrifice by its owners. Part of the returns that accrue from selling this output is, of course, required to pay principal and interest on the bonds. However, any surplus accrues to the owners of the corporation. Thus corporate borrowing makes it possible for stockholders to obtain a higher level of consumption in the future with no additional sacrifice in the present.[16] At the same time the bond purchasers (lenders) are able to obtain a time pattern of consumption—one involving less present consumption and more future consumption—which they prefer over the pattern of their endowment stream.[17] Thus both the issuers and the holders of bonds stand to gain.

Producers are willing to borrow because the return they obtain in the future from the use of the lenders' resources exceeds the interest payment demanded by the lenders. However, the opportunity to borrow and lend may improve well-being even if *no* additional production results. This can occur when individuals' endowments or their preferences as between present and future consumption (or both) are different. Individuals who expect their incomes to rise in the future may be able to borrow from others whose expectations are for a decline in income. Similarly, a person with a strong preference for present consumption may be able to negotiate a mutually advantageous loan from an individual who prefers to reduce his consumption now in order to be able to consume more in the future. An example of both these possibilities is the fact that young families with large current needs but meager incomes borrow from older households whose needs are less and who wish to save part of their current income against the time when retirement will produce a sharp drop in their wage incomes. This notion that borrowing and lending add to consumer welfare was, of course, central to the discussion of consumption theory in Chapter 7.

Financial Markets and Financial Intermediaries

The discussion of the past several pages shows that society benefits from intertemporal exchange; that is, from trades in which present goods are

---

[16] Obviously, this higher level of consumption depends on there being an actual surplus available over and above the payment due on the bonds. Our purpose here is simply to demonstrate that the existence of corporate bonds offers the possibility that stockholders can benefit from their issue.

[17] The argument does not require that the amount repaid be greater than the amount borrowed; that is, it does not depend on the rate of interest being positive. Ordinarily, of course, interest rates are positive. This is because the return to capital is positive, so that borrowers are able to pay positive interest, and because most individuals are impatient (that is, prefer present consumption over future consumption) and hence are unwilling to sacrifice present consumption (lend) unless they are promised a positive rate of return. For a classic discussion of the roles of productivity and impatience in the determination of the rate of interest, see Irving Fisher, *The Theory of Interest* (New York: Macmillan, 1930).

exchanged for claims to future goods. The invention of *common stock,* which is a claim on the assets of a corporation, enables individual wealth owners to hold shares in large items of capital equipment. As a result, more productive techniques may be used for transforming current savings into future output, thus making it possible to increase the supply of consumption goods both in the present and in the future. The *production loan*[18] similarly assists in channeling household savings into productive uses and also permits individuals to choose a different (and hence preferred) pattern of consumption by enabling them to hold their savings in a form that better suits their tastes and circumstances. Finally, the *consumption loan* makes it possible for households with different tastes or different endowments to enter into transactions in which both the borrower and the lender obtain a pattern of consumption, over time, that they prefer.

The scope for intertemporal exchange is not exhausted with the invention of the common stock and the bond.[19] Further development of the financial structure and the introduction of additional new assets increases still further the number of trades that can be negotiated.

Some wealth owners, for example, may find neither the common stock nor the bond suitable to their tastes because they wish to hold their wealth in the form of an asset that can be exchanged for goods rapidly and at a known price. Such an asset is described as a *liquid asset.* Asset issuers, on the other hand, may be unwilling to supply such an asset, fearing that if large numbers of their creditors were all to demand repayment at the same time they would find themselves in difficulty. A corporation, for example, might be unwilling to use borrowed funds to purchase plant and equipment if there were a danger that the loan would be recalled at short notice. Similarly, few households would be willing to borrow at short term to finance the purchase of a home or an automobile.

This problem has been dealt with in two ways. First, markets in existing financial assets develop in which individuals may buy or sell their claims on corporations or households. Examples are the stock exchange and the bond and mortgage markets. Individuals enter, and become experts in, the business of dealing in these markets and of bringing buyers and sellers together. Stock brokers, bond dealers, and mortgage brokers are examples of businesses that perform this function. The existence of these markets makes it possible for a single individual to liquidate his claim on a borrower by simply selling that claim to another individual. In a large and well-developed market, the price at which a security can be sold will be known within quite

---

[18] Producers borrow in other ways than by issuing corporate bonds. Clearly, the preceding argument concerning the benefits that result from borrowing by businesses does not depend on the legal characteristics of the loan transaction but holds for any form of borrowing.

[19] Households do not normally borrow by issuing financial instruments known as *bonds.* Businesses issue bonds but also borrow in other ways. To economize on terminology, however, all financial claims that promise a fixed future stream of payments will be described as bonds regardless of whether they are issued by households, businesses, or governments.

narrow limits and hence such a sale can be negotiated rapidly and on fairly predictable terms.

Thus the development of financial markets increases the liquidity of individual financial assets. As a result, wealth owners are more willing to hold financial claims, corporations and households are more able to borrow by issuing such claims, and society as a whole benefits from the additional intertemporal trades that become possible as a result.

Of course, not all securities that are traded in an established market (the New York Stock Exchange, for example) are equally liquid. In the case of a security that is not widely known, an investor may find either that it takes some time to find a buyer or that he must accept a lower price in order to make a quick sale.[20] Nonetheless, the existence of some type of market, however narrow, will normally make a financial asset significantly more attractive to investors than one that cannot be traded but must be held to maturity.

In addition to the establishment of markets in financial assets, the unwillingness of investors to hold illiquid assets may also be overcome by the development of new types of institutions, which hold claims on businesses and households as assets and which issue as liabilities more liquid financial instruments that better satisfy the tastes of wealth owners.

A familiar example of such an institution is the saving and loan association. These institutions issue deposits[21] that may be liquidated virtually on demand. With the funds received, they purchase assets in the form (mainly) of mortgage loans that are claims on home owners. Thus a wealth owner, who would be unwilling to tie up his assets in a long-term mortgage loan, and a home purchaser, who would be unwilling to finance his purchase by a loan that was repayable on demand, can in effect do business with one another through the intermediation of the saving and loan association.

The saving and loan association is an example of a type of institution known as a *financial intermediary*. By accepting the assets borrowers are prepared to issue and by issuing the assets wealth owners are prepared to hold, these institutions enable potential borrowers and lenders to do business with one another indirectly. In the case of the saving and loan association, the crucial difference between the assets that the ultimate lenders are willing to hold and those that the ultimate borrowers will supply lies in their relative liquidity. Similar considerations explain the existence of commercial banks, mutual saving banks, and credit unions. Each of these institutions accepts highly liquid deposits from one group of households and businesses and uses these resources to acquire claims on other groups that wish to borrow. They may acquire these claims either directly from the

---

[20] Hence stocks and bonds issued by large and well-known institutions will be more liquid and will tend to command a higher price than those that are less widely known. Evidence of this effect is presented in Ray Fair and Burton Malkiel, "The Determination of Yield Differentials between Debt Instrument of the Same Maturity," *Journal of Money, Credit and Banking*, Vol. III, Number 4 (November 1971).

[21] In the case of saving and loan associations, these deposits are actually called *shares*.

issuer or by purchasing them in the financial markets. In most cases the deposits issued by these institutions are not marketable.[22]

The deposit-issuing intermediaries described above develop in situations in which wealth owners wish to hold, but borrowers are unwilling to supply, claims that are highly liquid: that is, assets that can be rapidly and with a high degree of certainty converted into goods. Other types of intermediaries operate in situations in which the differences in tastes between potential borrowers and lenders take other forms.

Consider, for example, an individual who wishes to save for his retirement. He will want to put aside a part of his current income each year during his working life and accumulate assets that will yield him an income after he ceases work. He may plan to sell off those assets and consume the proceeds before he dies.

One option open to such a person is to purchase corporate stocks and bonds. However, such securities, even those issued by reputable and well-known businesses and traded in established markets, may not be suitable assets for his purposes, since both their market values and (in the case of common stocks) the incomes they will yield in the future are uncertain and difficult to predict. Since these assets will be his principal source of support during his retirement, he may be unwilling to accept this uncertainty unless they promise a substantially larger return than alternative assets. It is true, of course, that an individual may be able to reduce the uncertainty or add to the probable return from a portfolio of this kind by careful choice of the securities he purchases. However, most people lack both the time and the talent required to make correct decisions in this area.

Alternatively, a saver may accumulate various types of deposits (in banks, savings associations, and the like). These assets promise a sure return and hence are not subject to the uncertainties associated with stocks and bonds. On the other hand, deposits have a feature, namely, high liquidity, which he does not require. It is not important to him[23] that his assets can be liquidated rapidly: He is concerned with the more distant future. However, assets that do have this liquidity feature are likely to provide a lower return than other assets, which promise an equally certain income but which cannot be liquidated on demand.

Thus neither deposits nor marketable securities provide the precise package of characteristics that retirement savers require. On the other hand, borrowers, such as corporations wishing to build new plants and households wanting to purchase homes, are not likely to be willing to issue claims that do have these characteristics. Savers wish to set aside a small sum each month and receive repayment in the form of a regular income, beginning at

---

[22] However, since the mid-sixties commercial banks have been issuing marketable deposits known as negotiable certificates of deposit (C.D.s).

[23] Liquidity may even be an undesirable characteristic for him. For example, he may be afraid that he may be tempted to spend his accumulated savings before retirement and hence he may want to hold an asset that cannot be liquidated.

some specified future date (retirement). On the other hand, most borrowers wish to obtain control of a large fund of resources all at the same time to make a major purchase. They also find it convenient to repay the loan on a single date. Finally, borrowers prefer to deal with a single lender who can supply all the funds they require rather than deal with a large number of small savers.

The problem posed above is solved by the development of a financial intermediary, the *private pension fund*. The assets these institutions issue to savers are claims to a particular income during retirement; and the saver is able to purchase such claims by means of a small monthly payment. By purchasing corporate bonds and stock, pension funds channel savings into corporations that use these resources to acquire material assets. In this way, a worker saving for his retirement, who would be unwilling to hold common stock or corporate bonds directly (and *a fortiori* unwilling to hold his savings in the form of a piece of physical capital, such as a machine or a truck), becomes—through the intermediation of the pension fund and the corporation—the indirect owner of productive equipment. Conversely, corporations and other producers are able to obtain the funds they require to purchase that equipment through the intermediation of the pension fund. As a result, both sides to this indirect transaction benefit. Moreover, society at large also benefits since it becomes possible to use more capital-intensive (and hence more productive) methods for converting current savings into future output.

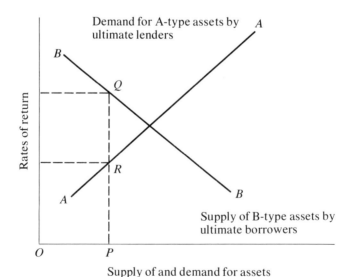

FIGURE 10.4 Financial intermediation
Borrowers are willing to issue OP of B-type assets yielding a rate of return PQ, while lenders are willing to hold the same quantity of A-type assets yielding a lower return, PR. Thus an intermediary that issues A-type assets and holds B-type assets can obtain a net rate of return of RQ.

Figure 10.4 illustrates the activities of a financial intermediary graphically. For simplicity, assume that there are two types of financial assets, type A and type B. Suppose further that lenders are willing to hold only type-A assets but borrowers are willing to issue only type-B assets. In the diagram, *AA* represents the terms on which lenders are prepared to hold varying quantities of A-type assets. Similarly, *BB* represents the terms on which borrowers are prepared to issue B-type assets.

In these circumstances, no mutually advantageous trade can be negotiated between the parties. The terms on which lenders are prepared to lend are inconsistent with the terms that borrowers are willing to offer. However, an *indirect trade* can be arranged through a financial intermediary. For example, wealth holders are prepared to lend an amount *OP* at a rate of return of *PR* if this comes in the form of income from type-A assets. Borrowers are willing to pay *PQ* for the use of these resources if they can obtain them through the issue of type-B assets. Thus a financial intermediary that issues an amount *OP* of type-A assets bearing a return of *PR* and purchases an equal amount of type-B assets yielding *PQ* will find lenders willing to hold its liabilities and borrowers willing to supply its assets. Such an activity will yield a surplus to the intermediary of *RQ*. This surplus provides the incomes of the persons who own and operate the intermediary and represents society's payment for the intermediation services that it provides.[24]

This section has not discussed the activities of all financial intermediaries. Among those not mentioned are life insurance companies, mutual funds, and investment companies. On the basis of the general considerations treated so far, you should be able to explain the nature of the intermediation services supplied by each of these types of institutions.

Commercial Banks

Banks[25] are financial intermediaries. Like all such institutions they perform the function of facilitating the flow of resources from those who wish to lend to those who wish to borrow. They do this by making available assets that are better suited to the tastes and circumstances of the ultimate lenders than are those which the ultimate borrowers are able or willing to provide. The assets banks *issue* include demand deposits, saving accounts, and various forms of time deposits. The assets they *hold* include various claims on other

---

[24] An example may clarify the argument. Suppose type-A assets are deposits and type-B assets are 30-year mortgages. Individuals with resources to lend may be unwilling to tie up their funds for as long as thirty years; hence they are prepared to hold only deposits. Home buyers wishing to finance their purchases may be unwilling to borrow by issuing liabilities that are repayable on demand; hence they are prepared to issue only mortgages. Savings and loan associations make it possible for these groups to negotiate a mutually acceptable deal indirectly. These institutions issue deposits to lenders and use the funds to purchase mortgages issued by home buyers.

[25] In the United States the word *bank* is applied to several other types of financial institutions besides commercial banks (for example, mutual savings banks, investment banks, Federal Land Banks, etc.). In this book the unmodified word *bank* always refers to commercial banks; that is, to institutions that issue liabilities that are used by the public as a medium of exchange.

businesses, governments, and households: promises to repay loans, corporate and government securities, mortgages, etc.

A distinguishing feature of banks is that one class of assets they issue—namely, demand deposits—is used as a medium of exchange: That is, it functions as *money*. As we will see in succeeding chapters, however, this is not the only feature of banks that makes them unique. Indeed, some economists would argue that their role as money producers is not even the most important characteristic of banks. Other characteristics include the facts that the aggregate stock of one of the assets banks hold—namely, bank reserves—is under the control of the monetary authorities and that the latter also regulate the rate of return banks are permitted to offer on the assets they issue.[26] As we will see, it is because of these characteristics that the behavior of banks can be influenced by the authorities to a much greater extent than can that of other intermediaries. Moreover, it is these characteristics, as well as the fact that banks supply our medium of exchange, that explain why the activities of banks have a greater impact on the functioning of our economy than does the behavior of other financial intermediaries.[27] With this in mind we turn now to a discussion of the commercial banking system.

References

Fisher, Irving. *The Theory of Interest.* New York: Macmillan, 1930; reprinted by Kelley and Millman, Inc., 1954.
The graphical device used to illustrate the activities of Robinson Crusoe was originally developed by Fisher.

Gurley, John G., and Edward S. Shaw. *Money in a Theory of Finance.* Washington, D.C.: The Brookings Institution, 1960.
A theoretical study of the role of money and financial institutions in the process of economic growth.

Nichols, Donald A., and Clark W. Reynolds. *Principles of Economics.* New York: Holt, Rinehart & Winston, 1971.
Chapter 34 contains an excellent discussion of the role of financial institutions in our economy.

Questions for Classroom Discussion

1. Explain how the possibility of borrowing and lending can make everyone better off even if no additional production takes place.

---

[26] This is a characteristic that is shared by other deposit-issuing institutions, such as saving and loan associations and mutual saving banks.

[27] Indeed, some economists might argue that if demand deposits yielded interest at a market-determined rate, the activities of their producers (namely, banks) would be no more significant than those of any other intermediary. See the quotation from James Tobin in Question 1 on page 135 of Chapter 6.

2. What is a financial intermediary? Give two examples of intermediaries and describe their principal activities. What social function do intermediaries perform?

3. Does the stock market perform a useful social function? If you believe that it does, explain what that function is.

4. Describe the similarities and differences between the social security system and private pension funds.

Commercial Banks
and the Creation of Money

11

In the United States, about one-fourth of the total money supply is in the form of notes and coin.[1] The remainder consists of checking accounts (or demand deposits, as they are properly called) at commercial banks.[2]

Commercial banks are financial intermediaries. As such, they issue financial assets that are held by members of the public as part of their portfolios of wealth. These assets include demand deposits, saving accounts, and time deposits. A distinguishing feature of banks is that one of the assets they issue—demand deposits—is used by the public as a medium of exchange. The owner of a demand deposit may make a payment by instructing his bank—normally by means of a check—to transfer ownership of a portion of his deposit to his creditor. The bank then reduces the amount of its deposit liability to the debtor and adds an equal amount to the deposit of the creditor.[3]

Bank Deposits and Reserves

How do demand deposits come into existence? Banks *create* new demand deposits by purchasing assets from members of the public and paying for them by issuing new claims on themselves. They are able to do this because these claims (demand deposits) are a medium of exchange. Some examples will show how this process works.

Suppose Mr. X makes a deposit of $100 in currency into the First National Bank. He will receive a checking account (demand deposit) at the bank for that amount. In effect, the bank has "bought" the currency from Mr. X and has "paid" for it with the new demand deposit. In the converse transaction, Mr. X "sells" the demand deposit back to the bank and receives payment in the form of currency; this transaction is usually described as "cashing a

---

[1] Since notes and coin are both issued by the central authorities and are totally under their control, they need not be treated separately. From now on this portion of the money supply will be described simply as currency.

[2] You may find the exact details by consulting a recent issue of the *Federal Reserve Bulletin*.

[3] The situation is slightly more complicated when debtors and creditors have different banks.

check.'' Note that these transactions alter the form in which the nonbank public[4] holds its money (more or less demand deposits relative to currency), but do not affect the total amount of money that it owns.

As a second example, suppose Mr. X sells $1000 worth of government securities to the First National Bank. He will receive payment in the form of a check drawn by the bank on itself. When he pays this check into his account, the bank will add $1000 to his demand deposit. Thus the bank has bought securities from Mr. X and has paid for them with newly created demand deposits. Since demand deposits are money and securities are not, this transaction does increase the stock of money in the hands of the nonbank public.[5]

When Mr. X borrows $1000 from the First National Bank the situation is analogous. He receives his loan in the form of a checking account at the bank. Thus the bank in effect ''purchases'' an asset from Mr. X and pays for it with a new demand deposit. In this case, however, the asset takes the form of Mr. X's promise to repay the loan rather than of a marketable security. Once again, the transaction increases the stock of money outstanding but not the wealth of the public.[6]

Several other types of financial intermediary also issue deposits. Examples include saving and loan associations, mutual saving banks, and credit unions. These institutions ''sell'' their own deposit liabilities in exchange for money in the same way as commercial banks sell demand deposits for currency. However, unlike banks, this is the only way in which these other types of intermediary can (or at least normally do) add to their deposits. They cannot add to their deposit liabilities by purchasing *nonmoney* assets and paying for them with new deposits in the way banks can. This is because deposits issued by nonbank intermediaries are not money:[7] They do not function as a medium of exchange.[8] When Mr. X borrows from the First Savings and Loan Association, he does not receive his loan in the form of a saving and loan share; he receives it in the form of *money*. First Saving and Loan writes a check in favor of Mr. X on its account at the First National Bank. When this check clears, Mr. X's demand deposit is greater and that of First Saving and Loan is smaller. However, there is no change

---

[4] Up to now we have considered an economy that has only two sectors: a private sector and a government sector. In this part of the book, three sectors are distinguished: the government, the bank sector, and the nonbank public. The latter comprises both households and nonbank businesses.

[5] The total wealth of the public is unaffected, however, since this transaction represents an exchange of one type of asset (securities) for another type (money).

[6] In this case the public gains an additional asset (money) but also incurs an additional liability (a bank loan).

[7] This is not quite true. A few nonbanks in New England offer so-called NOW accounts, which, although they are legally saving accounts, also have checking privileges. There are various proposals for extending these accounts nationwide. If this occurs, the distinction between banks and nonbanks will be blurred: Indeed, this is the objective of these proposals.

[8] The same is true of savings and time deposits issued by banks. So far as these types of deposits are concerned, banks are in the same position as other intermediaries.

either in the total stock of money outstanding[9] or in the stock of saving and loan shares.

There is some difference of opinion among economists as to whether this difference in operating procedures is a key factor in differentiating banks from other types of intermediary. Several monetary economists have argued that this difference is one of form only and is not of crucial significance in understanding the special roles played in the economy by money and by commercial banks.

Members of the public are willing to hold checking accounts rather than rely exclusively on currency because the use of checks is more convenient for many types of transactions. Currency can be lost or stolen but demand deposits cannot. Bank statements provide customers with a record of their receipts and payments. Since checks can be written for the exact amount of a payment, they eliminate the need to make change. On the other hand, the clearing of checks involves costs to the bank for which it usually makes a service charge. Hence small payments are normally made in currency and most businesses and households keep some small amount of currency on hand for these purposes.

The willingness of the public to hold demand deposits is enhanced by the fact that banks are required to supply notes and coin to any customer who wishes to exchange his holdings of demand deposits for currency (that is, who wishes to cash a check). Banks are not only prepared to sell new demand deposits in exchange for currency and other assets but are also required to buy them back for currency to any customer who no longer wishes to hold them. In order to be able to meet this commitment, banks must hold a reserve of currency on hand. However, it is not necessary for banks to hold reserves equal to the total amount of their deposit liabilities, since they know from experience that on any given day only a small proportion of their customers will require them to exchange deposits for cash.

Banks do not hold all their reserves in the form of notes and coin. They also maintain checking accounts with their regional Federal Reserve banks.[10] These accounts are analogous to the demand deposits that members of the public hold at commercial banks. The role of the Federal Reserve System will be discussed in detail later. For present purposes it suffices to note that the Federal Reserve banks act as bankers to the commercial banks; they provide checking account facilities and, on occasion, also supply loans.

Member banks hold part of their reserves in the form of checking accounts at the Fed for essentially the same reasons as those which lead households and businesses to use demand deposits rather than to rely on currency. The

---

[9] Note that saving and loan associations are part of the "nonbank public" and hence money held by them is "outstanding."

[10] This statement is true only of banks that are members of the Federal Reserve System. Although only a minority of all banks are members, they represent four-fifths of the total demand deposits outstanding.

central bank provides a "safekeeping" service for commercial banks, which is similar to that which they themselves provide for their customers. By reducing the amount of currency that banks must hold in their vaults, the availability of central bank checking accounts reduces storage costs and eliminates the risk of loss.

This reduction in storage costs is not the main advantage of holding central bank reserve deposits. A more important advantage is that these deposits reduce the cost of settling debts between banks in the same way as demand deposits lower the cost of making payments between businesses and households. To see how such interbank debts arise and how they are settled, let us consider a hypothetical transaction.

Suppose Mr. X banks with Bank A and Mr. Y banks with Bank B. Both banks are members of the Federal Reserve System. Mr. X makes a payment to Mr. Y by drawing a check against his account in Bank A and sending it to Mr. Y. On receiving this check, Mr. Y deposits it at Bank B, which credits his checking account accordingly. Bank B now holds a claim on Bank A in the form of Mr. X's check.[11]

The Federal Reserve System provides a cheap and convenient mechanism by which Bank B may obtain settlement of its claim on Bank A.[12] Bank B sends Mr. X's check to the Federal Reserve Bank, which will add $1000 to B's reserve account. The Fed then passes the check to Bank A and debits the latter's reserve account. Finally, Bank A reduces Mr. X's demand deposit by $1000. Table 11.1 shows how the banks' balance sheets are altered by these transactions.

Table 11.1 The Effects of Check Clearing

Assets		*Liabilities*	
	BANK A		
Reserve deposit at Fed	−1000	Mr. X's checking account	−1000
	BANK B		
Reserve deposit at Fed	+1000	Mr. Y's checking account	+1000

---

[11] This claim appears as an asset in B's balance sheet under the title "Cash Items in Course of Collection."

[12] This mechanism is not the only one by which interbank debts may be settled. First, Bank A may have offsetting claims on Bank B as a result of payments to its customers by customers of Bank B. Second, Bank A may own a checking account at Bank B; in this case, Bank B will simply debit this account before returning the check to Bank A. Conversely, Bank B may own a checking account at Bank A; when Bank B delivers the check to Bank A, the latter will credit this account. Finally, both A and B may own checking accounts at some third bank, Bank C. In this case, after the check has been delivered to Bank A, the latter will draw a check on its account in Bank C in favor of Bank B. In the United States all three methods are used in addition to the Federal Reserve facilities. This is why small banks can carry on business without becoming members of the Federal Reserve System.

This method of settling debts between banks is, in general, less costly than the shipment of currency from Bank A to Bank B.[13] This cost saving affects not only the banks themselves but also society at large, which does not need to use its scarce resources to provide armor-plated trucks, guard services, and the like.

In this example Bank A suffered a $1000 reduction in its reserves. Thus an individual bank may lose reserves not only through its customers' requiring it to exchange demand deposits for currency but also as a result of their making payments to customers of other banks. Hence the amount of reserves a bank will want to hold will depend on its forecasts of reserve losses from both of these causes in the days and weeks ahead. In the United States total bank reserves[14] in recent years have varied between 10 and 15 percent of the banking system's deposit liabilities. Of these reserves, about one-fourth are held in the form of notes and coin[15] and the remainder are deposits at Federal Reserve banks. The Fed makes no attempt to control the proportion of total reserves that are held in cash. It stands ready at all times to exchange reserve deposits for currency or vice versa without restriction.[16]

The Creation of Money by the Banking System

We are now in a position to describe how commercial banks create money. We will consider a very simple case: that of a system which consists of ten identical banks, each of which issues only demand deposits and holds only one class of earning assets, namely, bank loans. To provide against reserve losses, each bank holds a certain proportion of its deposit liabilities in the form of reserves.[17] We denote this proportion by r and assume that it remains constant. The nonbank public holds its money stock partly in the form of currency and partly in the form of demand deposits. We assume that the desired ratio of currency to demand deposits also remains constant and denote this ratio by c. In the following arithmetic example, we suppose that r, the bank's desired reserve-deposit ratio, is one-fifth and that c, the public's desired currency-deposit ratio, is one-tenth. Note that the public's desired ratio of currency to the total money stock (including both deposits and currency) is $c/(1 + c)$ and hence is equal to one-eleventh.

Initially, both the banks and the public are in *portfolio equilibrium;*[18] their respective balance sheets are as shown in Table 11.2. The total of currency

---

[13] This conclusion is also true of the other settlement methods described in footnote 12.

[14] As we saw in footnote 12, banks also maintain accounts with other commercial banks. From the point of view of the individual bank, these deposits are a part of its reserves, but they are not reserves for the system as a whole, since a deposit that is an asset to one bank is a liability to another.

[15] These reserves are known as *vault cash.*

[16] Similarly, the authorities make no attempt to control the proportions in which the various denominations of currency are held.

[17] The division of these reserves between currency and deposits at the Fed is unimportant for present purposes.

[18] In the sense that the above asset ratios are satisfied.

Table 11.2 Initial Balance Sheets

COMMERCIAL BANKING SYSTEM			
Reserves	2,000	Deposits	10,000
Loans	8,800	Capital	800
Total assets	10,800	*Total liabilities and capital*	10,800
NONBANK PUBLIC*			
Currency	1,000	Bank loans	8,800
Bank deposits	10,000		

* We include only those items relevant to the discussion. Hence this balance sheet does not balance.

outstanding and bank reserves is $3000: This total is variously described as the *monetary base* or the stock of *high-powered money*.

Assume now that the monetary authorities print $330 in currency and pay it to members of the nonbank public:[19] This increases the stock of high-powered money. To make their currency-deposit ratio equal to one-tenth, members of the public will open new checking accounts in the amount of $300. Hence the balance sheet of a typical bank[20] becomes as shown in Table 11.3. Notice that the bank's reserve ratio now exceeds one-fifth.

Table 11.3 Average Bank Position 1

Reserves	230	Deposits	1030
Loans	880	Equity	80
Total assets	1110	*Total liabilities and capital*	1110

Each individual bank will now wish to purchase earning assets (make loans) in order to increase profits. It will make these purchases by creating new demand deposits. However, it will know that the sellers of those assets are likely to use at least part of these newly created deposits either to obtain currency or to make payments to customers of other banks. In either case the bank will lose both deposits and reserves.[21] For simplicity we will suppose that each bank makes the (pessimistic) assumption[22] that *all* new deposits will be drained away in this manner.[23] Each believes that for every

---

[19] For example, as a tax refund.

[20] Recall that there are ten identical banks in the system so that customers deposit $30 in each bank.

[21] See Table 11.1. When Mr. X makes a payment to Mr. Y, his bank loses an equal amount of reserves and deposits.

[22] This assumption is most likely to be true in areas where there are large numbers of small banks. Thus this assumption might be described as the *small-bank assumption*. States such as Texas and Illinois, which prohibit banks from having branches, are most likely to provide the assumed conditions.

[23] In states such as California and Michigan, where there are a small number of large banks—

dollar of earning assets it acquires it will lose a dollar of reserves and will experience no change in its deposit total. In these circumstances the maximum quantity of earning assets that each bank can safely acquire is equal to the amount of reserves it has over and above that needed to back its *existing* level of deposits. To see that this is the case, consider Table 11.3. The bank has deposits of $1030 and requires reserves equal to one-fifth of that amount: $206. Hence it has surplus reserves of $24. If it makes loans of this amount by creating new demand deposits, its balance sheet becomes (temporarily) as shown in Table 11.4. However, one-eleventh of the new

Table 11.4 Average Bank Position 2

Reserves	230	Deposits	1054
Loans	904	Capital	80
Total assets	1134	*Total liabilities and capital*	1134

deposits will be converted into currency (to restore the public's currency-deposit ratio to one-tenth) and the remainder, on our "small-bank" assumption, will be used to make payments to customers of *other* banks. Thus both its deposit liabilities and its reserves will be depleted by $24 and its balance sheet will become as shown in Table 11.5.

Table 11.5 Average Bank Position 3

Reserves	206	Deposits	1030
Loans	904	Capital	80
Total assets	1110	*Total liabilities and capital*	1110

Comparing Table 11.5 with 11.3 we see that the bank's reserves are reduced by the same amount as its earning assets are expanded: $24. Its deposits are unchanged and all its surplus reserves have disappeared. The reserve ratio is now exactly one-fifth. This result explains why the individual bank feels that it cannot add to its earning assets by more than the amount of its surplus reserves.

However, the preceding argument looks at the situation only from the viewpoint of a single bank. It ignores the facts that all banks have been making loans and hence that customers of all banks have been making payments to customers of other banks. As a result, the customers of any

---

each having many branches—and in small communities that are served by only one or two banks, the banker is likely to assume that a certain proportion of any new deposits will remain at his bank. That is, even though customers use their new deposits to make payments, the payees will in many cases be customers of the same bank so that the deposits will remain at the same bank even though their ownership will change. In this case the details of the money-creation process described below will alter, but the end result is unchanged. You may wish to check this by constructing an example.

single bank will (on the average) be receiving as much as they have been paying out. Thus the customers of any single bank will receive checks (drawn on other banks) amounting[24] to $24 $(1 - \frac{1}{11})$. When these checks are cleared, the average bank's deposits and reserves will each rise by this amount. Thus although each bank expected that its balance sheet would appear as in Table 11.5, it will, in fact, appear[25] as in the Table 11.6.

Table 11.6 Average Bank Position 4

Reserves	$206 + 24 (1 - \frac{1}{11})$	Deposits	$1030 + 24 (1 - \frac{1}{11})$
Loans	904	Capital	80

Once again each individual bank finds that its actual reserves are greater than those required to back its new (higher) level of deposits.[26] A simple calculation shows that surplus reserves amount to $24 $(1 - \frac{1}{11})(1 - \frac{1}{5})$. If each bank again makes loans equal in value to its surplus reserves the whole process will be repeated. Unexpected surplus reserves will appear again and banks will be able to further increase their lending.

At each round of this process the volume of new loans will be less than it was at the previous round. There are two reasons for this, both resulting from the fact that the total stock of deposits increases at each round. First, since the public wishes to hold currency equal to one-tenth its deposit holdings, the banking system suffers a currency outflow at each round. Second, since the banks wish to hold reserves equal to one-fifth of their deposit liabilities, their desired reserves increase at each round. Thus as the process continues, actual reserves decline, desired reserves rise, and hence surplus reserves fall. Eventually surplus reserves disappear and the process stops.

The total volume of loans made by each bank amounts to

$$24 + 24\left(1 - \frac{1}{11}\right)\left(1 - \frac{1}{5}\right) + 24\left(1 - \frac{1}{11}\right)^2\left(1 - \frac{1}{5}\right)^2 + \cdots = \$88$$

Since at each round one-eleventh of the newly created deposits are converted into currency, the total addition to the deposits of each bank is only $80 dollars. Table 11.7 shows the final balance sheet of an average bank.

The consolidated balance sheets of the commercial banking system and of the nonbank public are shown in Table 11.8. In looking at these final balance sheets, we note that the banking system's cash reserves are equal to

---

[24] Recall that bank customers are assumed to withdraw one-eleventh of their newly acquired deposits in the form of currency and to use the remainder, $24 $(1 - \frac{1}{11})$, to make payments to other individuals.

[25] If the banks are not all identical, this statement will not be true. Nonetheless, Table 11.6 will represent the position of an average bank and thus of the banking system as a whole.

[26] If the individual bank had known that all other banks (and their customers) would behave in the same way as itself (and its customers), it could have anticipated this outcome and hence could have bought more earning assets than it did. Most banks will be unwilling to take this risk.

Table 11.7 Average Bank: Final Position

Reserves	206 + 16	Deposits	1030 + 80
Loans	880 + 88	Capital	80
Total assets	1190	*Total liabilities and capital*	1190

one-fifth its deposit liabilities, and the public's currency-deposit ratio is equal to one-tenth. Thus each side has its resources allocated among the various assets available in the proportions that it prefers. Comparing Table 11.8 with Table 11.2, we note that the total money stock has increased by $1210 of which $1100 are in the form of new demand deposits. The public has "purchased" these new deposits partly in exchange for currency[27] ($220) and partly in exchange for their own I.O.U.s ($880).

Table 11.8 Final Balance Sheets

	COMMERCIAL BANKING SYSTEM		
Reserves	2,220	Deposits	11,100
Loans	9,680	Capital	800
Total assets	11,900	*Total liabilities and capital*	11,900
	NONBANK PUBLIC		
Money	12,210	Bank loans	9,680
Currency		1,110	
Deposits		11,100	
Bank equity	800		

This example demonstrates that the banking system as a whole can create demand deposits by purchasing nonmoney earning assets from members of the nonbank public even though the individual bank cannot.[28] When an individual bank purchases an earning asset (such as a personal I.O.U.), this will reduce its reserves by an equal amount and leave its deposit total unaffected. This is because the customer who sells the asset to the bank will, in most cases, use the proceeds of the sale to make payments to customers of other banks. But these payments cause the deposits of those other banks to increase and hence bank purchases of earning assets do add to the total demand deposits of the banking system as a whole.

The Money Multiplier

As we said earlier, the reserves of the banking system and currency in the hands of the nonbank public are known as *high-powered money*. There is a

---

[27] Note that the reserves of the system have increased by $220.
[28] Or, at least, finds it prudent to assume that it cannot.

simple algebraic relation between the stock of money in the hands of the public and the stock of high-powered money.

The public may hold money in the form either of bank deposits (D) or of currency (C):

$$M = D + C$$

High-powered money (H) is held either by the public in the form of currency or by the banks in the form of reserves (R):

$$H = C + R$$

Hence we can write

$$M = \frac{M}{H} \cdot H = \frac{D + C}{C + R} H$$

If we divide the numerator and denominator of this expression by D, we obtain

$$M = \left[\frac{1 + (C/D)}{(C/D) + (R/D)} \right] \cdot H \qquad (11.1)$$

This equation shows that the stock of money is some multiple of the stock of high-powered money. The expression in brackets is known as the *money multiplier*. Equation (11.1) shows that the money stock may be regarded as determined by three factors: the stock of high-powered money, the currency-deposit ratio of the public, and the reserve-deposit ratio of the banking system.[29]

Equation (11.1) is a tautology: It is true by definition. Nonetheless a number of economists[30] have found that it is a useful tool for describing the historical behavior of the money supply. This is because any change in the amount of money outstanding can always be "explained" in terms of changes in H, C/D, and R/D.

An alternative procedure is to begin with the "desired" positions of banks and the public. Desired currency holdings are some proportion c of total deposits.

$$C^D = cD$$

---

[29] Other versions of the multiplier may readily be devised. Since $(C/D) = (C/M)(M/D)$, for example, we can write the multiplier in the form

$$\frac{1 + \dfrac{C}{M} \cdot \dfrac{M}{D}}{\dfrac{C}{M} \cdot \dfrac{M}{D} + \dfrac{R}{D}} = \frac{\dfrac{M}{D}\left[\dfrac{D}{M} + \dfrac{C}{M} \right]}{\dfrac{M}{D}\left[\dfrac{C}{M} + \dfrac{R}{D} \cdot \dfrac{D}{M} \right]} = \frac{1}{\dfrac{C}{M} + \dfrac{R}{D} \cdot \dfrac{D}{M}}$$

In this form the value of the multiplier depends on the reserve ratio of the banks, R/D, and the proportions of the total money supply the public holds in the form of currency (C/M) and deposits (D/M), respectively.

[30] This way of viewing the determinants of the money stock is popular with economists of the monetarist school. However, their views on the role of money in the economy are in no way dependent on the money-multiplier approach.

Similarly, the desired reserves of the banking system are some proportion r of total deposits.

$$R^D = rD$$

The public and the banking system will be in portfolio equilibrium when their desired currency and reserve holdings are equal to the actual amounts in existence:

$$H = C + R = cD^* + rD^*$$

where D^* denotes the equilibrium stock of deposits.

When rearranged, this expression may be written

$$D^* = \frac{1}{c + r} H$$

The money stock comprises bank deposits and currency in the hands of the public. Hence, in equilibrium,

$$M^* = \left[\frac{1 + c}{c + r}\right] H \tag{11.2}$$

This equation is algebraically identical to Eq. (11.1) but is to be interpreted differently; c and r represent the desired values of the currency-deposit ratio and the reserve-deposit ratio rather than the actual values. Moreover, the equation explains the equilibrium value of the money stock (when all parties are content with the distribution of their portfolios) rather than the actual value. As in earlier chapters we generally assume that the financial system is in equilibrium, so that M^* also represents the actual stock of money. In Chapter 12, however, much of our attention will be devoted to the determination of c and r, which were simply taken as given in the analysis of the previous section.

The stock of money may also be related to the stock of bank reserves. If we multiply both sides of Eq. (11.2) by $(c + r)/r$, we obtain

$$M^*(c + r)/r = \frac{1 + c}{r} \cdot H$$

Rearranging this expression yields[31]

---

[31] $M^* = \dfrac{1 + c}{r} H - \dfrac{c}{r} M^*$

$\qquad = \dfrac{1 + c}{r} R + \dfrac{1 + c}{r} C^* - \dfrac{c}{r} D^* - \dfrac{c}{r} C^*$

$\qquad = \dfrac{1 + c}{r} R + \dfrac{C^*}{r} + \dfrac{cC^*}{r} - \dfrac{C^*}{r} - \dfrac{cC^*}{r}$

$\qquad = \dfrac{1 + c}{r} R$

$$M^* = \frac{1+c}{r} R \qquad (11.3)$$

Inspection of Eqs. (11.2) and (11.3) shows that if the monetary authorities can control either the stock of high-powered money H or the stock of bank reserves R, they can influence the stock of money as long as the values of c and r remain relatively stable.[32]

Banks and the Money Stock: The "New View"

In our discussion of the banks' role in the creation of money, we have seen that bank deposits come into existence as a result of the banking system's exchanging new deposits for other types of assets[33] previously owned by the nonbank public. However, the emphasis in our discussion was on the accounting aspects of this exchange rather than the economic aspects. In recent years this traditional (and rather mechanical) approach to the process of money creation has been sharply criticized by a number of monetary economists.[34]

These critics lay particular stress on the fact that although r, the desired reserve-deposit ratio of the banks, and c, the desired currency-deposit ratio of the public, play a key role in the process, the traditional analysis makes little attempt to provide a sound theoretical explanation of how these ratios are determined.[35] Hence they argue that the description of the money-supply process is seriously incomplete.

In our description of the cumulative process of deposit expansion, it was taken for granted that, although the original holder of a new demand deposit might spend it and pass it on to some other individual, it would eventually reach some person who would be willing to hold it. The critics of this approach point out that members of the public cannot be forced to add to their stocks of demand deposits and hence the banking system is powerless to increase the stock of money unless the public can be persuaded to hold it.[36] For example, Mr. X may borrow from his bank and obtain a demand

---

[32] Throughout this section we have maintained the assumption that banks issue only one type of deposits: demand deposits owned by the nonbank public. If this assumption is dropped, other, more complicated, versions of the multiplier may be developed. For examples, see Jerry L. Jordan, "Elements of Money Stock Determination, *Review,* Federal Reserve Bank of St. Louis, Vol. 51, No. 10 (October 1969).

[33] Currency, loans, securities, etc.

[34] One of the earliest and most influential critics of the traditional approach was James Tobin. See his article, "Commercial Banks as Creators of 'Money,' " *Banking and Monetary Studies,* ed. Deane Carson (Homewood, Illinois: Richard D. Irwin, 1963), pp. 408–419.

[35] This does not mean that earlier theorists paid no attention to the determinants of r and c. They did. However, these discussions tended to be somewhat *ad hoc* rather than part of a consistent theoretical scheme.

[36] The same is not true of high-powered money, including currency. If the government pays its bills either in currency or by a check drawn on the Fed, this increases the stocks of both money and high-powered money. Since the government has no commitment to "buy back" outstand-

deposit. However, if he uses this deposit to make a payment to Mr. Y, who promptly uses it to repay a bank loan, the new deposit is destroyed again and no permanent increase in the stock of deposits takes place. This argument implies that the banks cannot increase the stock of money without the cooperation of the public in this process. Generally, the public must be offered some inducement to persuade them to hold more deposits (and less of some other assets) in their wealth portfolios, and hence the stock of deposits will not rise unless the banks are willing to provide such an inducement.[37]

With regard to the behavior of banks, the critics point out that the amount of reserves a bank will want to hold depends partly on the return it can obtain from earning assets. When loan demand is strong, so that the return on loans is high and potential borrowers are plentiful, a bank is more willing to reduce its reserve ratio than when demand is weak and borrowers are hard to find. Thus the proportion of its deposits a bank wants to hold in the form of reserves is closely related to its ability to acquire earning assets on attractive terms.

This view of the money-creation process stresses the fact that bank deposits come into existence as a result of voluntary exchanges of deposits for other types of assets between the banking system and the nonbank public. The creation of a new demand deposit involves a change in the asset portfolios of both the public and the banks. Moreover, neither side can be forced to accept any given portfolio change. Hence in order to understand the economics involved in the creation of money as distinct from the accounting relationships the willingness of both sides to engage in such exchanges must be analyzed. This approach to the creation of money, which emphasizes that both sides must agree to make mutually dependent changes in their portfolios, has come to be known as the "new view." This view argues that since both sides must effect changes in their portfolios if the stock of money is to increase (or decrease), the analysis of the determinants of the money stock must pay attention to the portfolio preferences both of the public and of the banking system. In the following chapter we construct a model of the money-supply process that embodies the principal ideas of this view.

References

Jordan, Jerry L. "Elements of Money Stock Determination," *Review*. Federal Reserve Bank of St. Louis, Vol. 51, No. 10 (October 1969).

---

ing high-powered money, the public cannot get rid of this component of the money stock. However, members of the nonbank public *can* get rid of bank deposits; for example, they can use them to repay bank loans. In Tobin's words, high-powered money is like a "hot potato," which the banking system and members of the public can pass around but cannot get rid of, whereas bank deposits are not.

[37] As we will see in the next chapter, this inducement may take two forms: deposits may be made more attractive by raising the return they yield or nonmoney assets may be made less attractive by lowering their return.

Modern Money Mechanics, A Workbook on Deposits, Currency and Bank Reserves. Federal Reserve Bank of Chicago. Chicago: 1975.

Tobin, James. "Commercial Banks as Creators of 'Money,'" *Banking and Monetary Studies,* ed. Deane Carson. Homewood, Illinois: Richard D. Irwin, 1963.
The reader may wish to glance at this article at this point and reread it after he has completed Chapter 12.

Questions for Classroom Discussion

1. In the text we considered a bank that issued one class of deposits. To check your understanding of the money multiplier, try this problem involving two types of deposits.

   Suppose banks issue two classes of deposits, demand deposits D and time deposits T. The public always wishes to hold two dollars in demand deposits for every one dollar it holds in time deposits. As before, suppose it holds currency equal to one-tenth of its demand deposit holdings. Banks hold reserves equal to one-fifth of their demand deposits plus one-tenth of their time deposits. If the stock of high-powered money is $700, find the money stock ($M = D + C$).

2. Banks can make loans by writing up their deposit liabilities. Saving and loan associations cannot make loans by writing up their share liabilities. Why not?

3. Suppose a bank has surplus reserves. How can it increase its earning assets? What will the effect be on interest rates and asset prices?

4. Suppose a bank has no surplus reserves. Does this mean that it cannot add to its earning assets? Why or why not? Is the same true of the whole banking system?

5. In Part 2 money was treated like a "hot potato." Why are demand deposits not like a hot potato?

The New View of the Money-Supply Process

12

In Chapter 11 we described the *accounting* aspects of the money-supply process. However, in the final section we argued that the banking system can increase the stock of money only if members of the nonbank public are willing to sell nonmoney assets to banks in exchange for money on terms that are acceptable to both sides. In this chapter we develop this argument further. We consider first the factors determining the amount of deposits that banks will want to issue and of assets they will want to hold. Later we discuss the willingness of the public to hold bank deposits and to sell nonmoney assets to the banking system.

The banking system and the public will be in portfolio equilibrium when the amount of deposits the public wants to hold is exactly equal to the amount banks want to issue, and when the amount of assets banks want to hold is equal to the amount the public wants to supply. When the economy is in equilibrium in this sense, these equilibrium conditions will determine the amount of money in existence.

Bank Reserves, the Federal Funds Market, and the Discount Window

Before proceeding with the argument, we need to describe briefly certain features of the U.S. monetary system that were ignored in Chapter 11.

It was assumed in Chapter 11 that the ratio of reserves to deposits is wholly within the discretion of individual banks. In fact, banks that are members of the Federal Reserve System[1] are required by law to maintain certain minimum reserves[2] against their deposit liabilities. The amount of these legally required reserves depends on the bank's size and on the composition of its deposits.[3] Demand deposits are subject to a higher reserve requirement than are time

---

[1] Nonmember banks are subject to similar (but generally less demanding) requirements set by state laws.
[2] Banks may hold these legally required reserves either in vault cash or on deposit at the Fed.
[3] Until 1972 reserve requirements also varied according to the bank's location. Banks in "reserve cities" were required to hold higher reserves than "country" banks. In November of that year this distinction was discontinued.

and saving deposits. Within each category, banks with large deposit totals are required to maintain a higher ratio of reserves to deposits than are smaller banks. Within broad limits set by Congress, the Federal Reserve System may alter these legally required ratios, and it does so from time to time.[4]

Some banks maintain reserves above the legal minimum even when attractive earning assets are available.[5] To see why a bank might do this, assume the legal reserve requirement is 15 percent and Bank X holds reserves exactly equal to the legal minimum. Its balance sheet might appear thus:

BANK X			
Reserves	150	Deposits	1000
Earning assets	850		

If a depositor were to cash a check or make a payment to a customer of another bank, reserves and deposits each would be reduced by the amount of the check, say, $50. The balance sheet would then become:

BANK X			
Reserves	100	Deposits	950
Earning assets	850		

The reserve ratio now is below the legal minimum and the bank must take prompt action to adjust its balance sheet to conform to the legal requirements. This example illustrates that a bank holding no excess reserves[6] may be in a somewhat precarious situation. As a result, many banks find it advisable to hold some reserves over and above those necessary to meet the legal requirements.

Bank X may add to its reserves either by attracting additional deposits or by selling some of its earning assets. However, if it suspects that its reserve deficiency is a temporary phenomenon, it may choose to deal with it by a transaction in the *Federal Funds market.*

When an individual bank finds itself short of reserves, it may obtain additional reserves by borrowing them from other banks. There is a well-established market in which banks may borrow from (and lend to) other banks for short periods of time. The reserves that are traded in this market take the form of deposits at Federal Reserve Banks and hence are known as *Federal Funds.* In the above example, Bank X might enter this market and borrow[7] the reserves it needs from some other bank. When it does so, it will

---

[4] If you are interested in checking the requirements currently in force, you will find them set out in the monthly *Federal Reserve Bulletin.*
[5] For example, when there are customers anxious to borrow on terms that would be profitable to the bank.
[6] Reserves held above the legal minimum are termed *excess reserves.*
[7] If Bank X were already a *lender* of federal funds it might deal with the deficiency by reducing its lending.

obtain the loan in the form of a check drawn on a Federal Reserve Bank. It will pay this check into its own Federal Reserve Bank and have its reserve account credited. It has been estimated that in the late sixties some 350 banks were regular participants in the Federal Funds market. These banks held some 60 percent of total deposits outstanding and included virtually all the large commercial banks in the United States; a much larger number of banks (over 3000) traded occasionally. In December 1969,[8] daily trading volume in the Federal Funds market exceeded $10 billion.

The existence of the Federal Funds market means that a bank with reserves close to the legal minimum is, in fact, in a less risky position than appears at first sight from the example just discussed. This is because it can negotiate to borrow federal funds on very short notice. In fact, some large New York banks are continuous borrowers and rely on the market as a more-or-less permanent source of funds. Conversely, there is little incentive for a bank to hold excess reserves, since these can earn interest if they are lent out to other banks that are temporarily short of reserves. Since these loans are of very short duration, the lending bank can obtain its reserves back very rapidly if its own reserve position deteriorates.

Clearly, the banking system as a whole cannot obtain additional reserves from the Federal Funds market. In that market the available supply of reserves is redistributed from banks that are flush with reserves to those that are short.[9] However, this process cannot increase the aggregate supply of reserves to the system. Hence a general shortage of reserves is likely to be reflected in a rise in the interest rate on federal funds as more banks seek to borrow funds and fewer are willing to lend.

The banking system can obtain additional reserves by borrowing from the Fed. A member bank that finds itself short of reserves may apply for a short-term loan from its Federal Reserve Bank. If granted, the loan will be made by crediting the bank's reserve account. Thus such loans increase the reserves of the banking system.

A bank facing a reserve shortage must choose whether to borrow from the Federal Reserve System or the Federal Funds market. This decision will be based on both price and nonprice considerations. The federal funds interest rate is a market rate that varies continuously in response to supply and demand pressures. The rate charged by the Fed—which is known as the *discount rate*[10]—is an administered rate that is changed infrequently. However, the bank's decision will not be based only on a comparison of these

---

[8] For excellent discussions of the funds market, see Parker B. Willis, *The Federal Funds Market, Its Origin and Development,* The Federal Reserve Bank of Boston, 4th ed. (1970), and James M. Boughton, *Monetary Policy and the Federal Funds Market* (Durham, N.C.: Duke University Press, 1972).

[9] In general, the market acts to channel funds from banks outside the principal financial centers toward the large money-market banks in New York, Chicago, and San Francisco. See Boughton, pp. 11–21.

[10] The department of the Fed, which is responsible for making member bank loans, is popularly known as the *discount window.*

two interest rates. The Fed is not an automatic lender but may impose conditions.[11] For example, banks are expected to borrow only in emergency situations and to repay promptly. A bank that borrows too frequently may find itself subject to closer scrutiny by Federal Reserve regulators and may even have its borrowing privileges suspended temporarily. Hence most banks prefer to borrow federal funds unless the interest rate differential is large or it is clear that their need of assistance is more than a temporary one.

A Portfolio Model of the Banking System

We are now in a position to develop a model of banking system behavior. For simplicity, we will assume that banks issue only one class of deposits (D). Their assets consist of reserves (R), loans to members of the nonbank public (L), and loans to other banks through the federal funds market (F). We ignore the equity of banks and hence the balance-sheet constraint that assets and liabilities must be equal may be written

$$R + L + F = D$$

Since a bank may either lend or borrow federal funds, F may either be positive or negative.[12] There is a legal reserve requirement and hence total reserves consist of required reserves (RR) and excess reserves[13] (ER):

$$R = RR + ER$$

$$RR = kD$$

where k is the required reserve ratio set by the Fed.

Thus the balance sheet constraint may also be written

$$(1 - k)D = ER + L + F \tag{12.1}$$

The term on the left side of this equality represents the bank's *lending capacity*: its total loans—including both customer loans and federal funds loans—cannot exceed this limit.[14] The objective of the bank is to achieve a portfolio of assets and liabilities that satisfies this constraint and provides the optimal combination of risk and return.

A number of theoretical models have been developed that attempt to describe the bank's decision process.[15] We will not review these models in detail. Some represent attempts to apply the standard microeconomic

---

[11] In this respect the Fed differs from certain other central banks, such as the Bank of England.

[12] Thus federal funds borrowed are treated as a negative item on the asset side of the balance sheet rather than as a positive item on the liability side.

[13] We assume that the bank never *plans* to borrow from the Federal Reserve. Such borrowings occur only in emergencies when unforeseen events cause its plans to go awry. This means that planned excess reserves are never negative.

[14] Since F can be negative (that is, the bank can borrow federal funds), it is possible for L to exceed $(1 - k)D$.

[15] Most of these models do not, however, incorporate the federal funds market.

theory of the firm to the special circumstances of the banking business.[16] Other models employ concepts borrowed from the literature on the demand for money. For example, some theorists emphasize the fact that the bank cannot predict its deposit total with complete certainty and yet must always satisfy the legal reserve requirement and be able to meet its customers' demands for cash. By holding excess reserves, the bank can reduce the risk that an unexpected excess of deposit withdrawals over inflows will lower its reserves below the legal limit. However, excess reserves yield no revenue and hence the bank must make a choice between risk and return. These types of considerations lead to a model of the demand for reserves that is similar to the precautionary demand for money by wealth owners.[17] Other theorists focus on the risks associated with bank assets. The division of total assets between loans, which produce a return but also involve some risk of loss, and reserves, which are riskless but yield no revenue, may be analyzed along lines similar to Tobin's mean-standard deviation approach to the demand for money.[18]

The approach used here is consistent with these more detailed models, but is not derived explicitly from them. Instead, we simply present the hypothesis that the bank's portfolio choices depend on the legal reserve requirements set by the Fed and on the various rates of interest it faces. Thus its demands for the three types of assets—customer loans, federal funds loans, and excess reserves—and its supply of deposits may be written as follows:

$$D^S = d[i_D,\ i_L,\ i_F,\ k,\ \eth] \qquad (12.2)$$
$$-\ \ +\ \ +\ +$$

$$L^D = l[i_D,\ i_L,\ i_F,\ k,\ \eth] \qquad (12.3)$$
$$-\ \ +\ \ -\ \ -$$

$$ER^D = r[i_D,\ i_L,\ i_F,\ k,\ \eth] \qquad (12.4)$$
$$-\ \ -\ \ -\ \ +$$

$$F^D = f[i_D,\ i_L,\ i_F,\ k,\ \eth] \qquad (12.5)$$
$$-\ \ -\ \ +\ \ -$$

The responses of the bank to changes in interest rates and in the reserve requirement are indicated by the plus and minus signs. We now discuss these responses in some detail.

---

[16] A good example of this approach is John H. Kareken, "Commercial Banks and the Supply of Money: A Market-Determined Demand Deposit Rate," *Federal Reserve Bulletin* (October 1967).

[17] See, for example, Peter A. Frost, "Banks' Demand for Excess Reserves," *Journal of Political Economy*, Vol. LXXIX, No. 4 (July/August 1971).

[18] J. M. Parkin, M. R. Gray, and R. J. Barrett, "The Portfolio Behavior of Commercial Banks," *The Econometric Study of the United Kingdom: Proceedings of the 1969 Southampton Conference on Short-Run Econometric Models of the U.K. Economy*, eds. Kenneth Hilton and David F. Heathfield (London: Macmillan, 1970).

In these equations, i_L and i_F represent the interest rates on customer loans and federal funds loans, respectively. Equations (12.3) and (12.5) postulate that an increase in either of these interest rates will lead the bank to make more of that class of loan and less of the other class. It will also cause the bank to hold fewer excess reserves [Eq. (12.4)] and also to attempt to add to its deposit total [Eq. (12.2)].

The symbol i_D represents the interest rate on deposits. In the United States banks are forbidden to pay interest on demand deposits. Interest rates on savings and most time deposits are subject to statutory ceilings. In this chapter these regulations are ignored: that is, i_D is assumed free to vary. This case is relevant for two reasons. First, the regulations are widely circumvented by banks paying interest in the form of services rather than in cash.[19] For example, many banks offer free checking accounts or low-cost loans to customers who maintain a deposit balance above some minimum. Second, several proposals have been made to abolish many of these interest-rate ceilings: It is instructive to examine how the system would function if these proposals were implemented. In the following chapter, the economic impact of an effective limit on the deposit rate is examined.

An increase in i_D raises the cost of funds to the bank. Hence it will reduce its deposit total and call in some of its less profitable or more risky customer loans. In addition, it will reduce its federal funds lending and may even become a borrower of funds. Finally, the increased cost of resources will lead the bank to economize on its holdings of excess reserves that yield no revenue to offset their cost.

An increase in the legal reserve requirement (k) means that the bank must divert a larger proportion of its deposits into legal reserves. It can obtain the additional legal reserves it needs by reducing either its earning assets or its excess reserves or by attracting additional deposits. Since reserves yield no return, an increase in k also raises the cost of the bank's lendable funds.[20] This higher cost of resources, combined with the need to add to its legal reserves, will lead the bank to call in some of its less attractive customer loans, to borrow more or lend less in the Federal Funds market, and to reduce its excess reserves if it has any. These effects are analogous to those of a rise in i_D, which also raises the cost of lendable resources. Thus, in Eqs. 12.3, 12.4, and 12.5, the signs on i_D and k are the same.

The effect of a higher reserve requirement on the bank's willingness to supply deposits is less clear. On the one hand, the higher cost of attracting lendable resources will tend to cause the bank to wish to contract its scale of operations: that is, to reduce its lending capacity. On the other hand, an increase in k means that any given lending capacity requires a larger deposit

---

[19] In New England some mutual saving banks offer so-called NOW accounts, which are, in effect, checking accounts that yield interest in cash.

[20] If a bank wishes to increase its lendable capacity by one dollar, it must add to its deposits by $1/(1 - k)$ dollars. Thus the cost of a dollar's worth of lendable funds is $i_D[1/(1 - k)]$ dollars. If k increases, this cost of funds will rise.

total. Equation (12.5) assumes that the second effect outweighs the first: Although the bank obtains some of the additional legal reserves it requires by reducing its earning assets, it also finds it profitable to add to its deposit liabilities.[21] Although this is strictly an assumption, it nonetheless seems a very plausible one.

Excess reserves yield no return so no interest rate on this asset appears in the above equations. However, the Federal Reserve discount rate, represented by $\eth$, does appear. This rate measures the cost to the bank of setting its reserves too low so that it is in danger of having to borrow at the discount window. Thus $\eth$ plays a role that is similar to that of a return on reserves.

An increase in the discount rate will induce banks to add to their reserves in order to reduce the probability of being forced to borrow at the Fed. They may do this either by attracting more deposits or by reducing their loans. It may also induce some banks to borrow in the funds market either to avoid borrowing from the Fed or to repay loans received at the discount window earlier.

Up to now we have been concerned only with the behavior of a single bank. Given the various interest rates and the reserve requirement, Eqs. (12.2) to (12.5) describe the amounts of deposits, loans, and reserves any given bank will wish to issue and hold. These portfolio choices of the individual bank must satisfy its balance-sheet constraint [Eq. (12.1)]. The behavior of the banking system is the aggregate of the behavior of all the individual banks so that Eqs. (12.2) to (12.5) may also be regarded as describing the behavior of the system as a whole. Hence the balance sheet of the banking system will also satisfy Eq. (12.1).

Banks as a group, however, are subject to an additional constraint that does not apply to any single bank. This is the requirement that federal funds borrowing and lending must be equal in the aggregate. The funds market is not a source of additional resources to the banking system as a whole. Thus the balance sheet of the banking *system* must satisfy the following condition:

$$D(1 - k) = ER + L \qquad (12.6)$$

At any arbitrary set of interest rates the portfolio choices of each bank, and hence of the banking system as a whole, will satisfy Eq. (12.1) but may not satisfy Eq. (12.6). However, if Eq. (12.6) is not satisfied in the aggregate, the federal funds market will be out of equilibrium. The interest rate on federal funds will change and banks will be induced to rearrange their portfolios until Eq. (12.6) is satisfied in the aggregate. Of course, even when the funds market is in equilibrium, Eq. (12.6) may not be satisfied by any single bank.

Thus the portfolio choices of the banking system will satisfy the aggregate balance-sheet constraint only when the funds market is in equilibrium: That

---

[21] Since total deposits rise and total lending declines, total reserves (including both required reserves and excess reserves) will increase.

is, when interest rates are such that the volume of funds that lending banks wish to sell is equal to the volume that borrowing banks wish to buy. Algebraically, this equilibrium condition may be written

$$F^D = f[i_L, i_F, i_D, k, \eth] = 0 \qquad (12.7)$$

If funds lenders exceed borrowers, so that F^D is positive, the federal funds rate will tend to decline. Conversely, if borrowers exceed lenders (F^D is negative) the rate will rise.

When the market is in equilibrium ($F^D = 0$), the above equation may be written with the federal funds rate as the dependent variable:

$$i_F = i_F[i_D, i_L, k, \eth] \qquad (12.8)$$
$$+ \quad + \quad + \quad$$

An increase in the rate of return to customer loans (i_L) or in the cost of lendable funds (which may result from an increase in i_D, k, or $\eth$) will lead the average bank to lend less or borrow more in the funds market and hence will tend to drive up the federal funds rate. This conclusion is indicated by the plus signs in Eq. (12.8).

The federal funds market is highly competitive and clears almost instantaneously. Hence we may assume that that market is always in equilibrium: That is, Eq. (12.7) always holds. In considering the behavior of the system as a whole, therefore, Eq. (12.5) may be replaced by Eq. (12.8). Moreover, the latter equation may then be substituted into Eqs. (12.2) through (12.4), thus eliminating the funds rate and reducing the number of equations to three:[22]

$$D^S = d[i_D, i_L, i_F(i_D, i_L, k, \eth), k, \eth]$$
$$= d[i_D, i_L, k, \eth] \qquad (12.9)$$
$$- \quad + \quad + \quad +$$

$$L^D = l[i_D, i_l, i_F(i_D, i_L, k, \eth), k, \eth]$$
$$= l[i_D, i_L, k, \eth] \qquad (12.10)$$
$$- \quad + \quad - \quad -$$

---

[22] The plus and minus signs in these equations follow from the assumptions underlying Eqs. (12.2) through (12.4). In a few cases there are apparent ambiguities. For example,

$$\frac{dL^D}{di_L} = \frac{\partial l}{\partial i_L} + \frac{\partial l}{\partial i_F} \cdot \frac{\partial i_F}{\partial i_L}$$

The first term of this expression is positive and the second is negative so that it appears that their sum is ambiguous. However, the balance sheet constraint implies

$$\frac{dL^D}{di_L} = (1 - k) \cdot \frac{dD^S}{di_L} - \frac{dER^D}{di_L}$$

$$= (1 - k) \left[\frac{\partial D^S}{\partial i_L} + \frac{\partial D^S}{\partial i_F} \cdot \frac{\partial i_F}{\partial i_L} \right] - \left[\frac{\partial ER^D}{\partial i_L} + \frac{\partial ER^D}{\partial i_F} \cdot \frac{\partial i_F}{\partial i_L} \right]$$

which is unambiguously positive. Other apparent ambiguities may be resolved in the same way.

$$ER^D = r[i_D, i_L, i_F(i_D, i_L, k, \eth), k, \eth]$$
$$= r[\underset{-}{i_D}, \underset{-}{i_L}, \underset{-}{k}, \underset{+}{\eth}] \tag{12.11}$$

These three equations determine—as functions of the two interest rates (i_D and i_L) and of the two policy variables (k and $\eth$)—the banking system's desired portfolio of deposits, loans, and reserves.

Equilibrium in the Asset Markets

Up to now we have considered only the willingness of the banking system to issue deposits to and to hold earning assets (I.O.U.s) supplied by members of the nonbank public. However, the essence of the new view is that this is only one side of the story. The willingness of the public to supply assets to banks and to hold deposits created by banks must also be considered. We now turn to these issues.

In Part 2 it was hypothesized that the demands to hold assets depend on wealth, income, and rates of return. So far as money is concerned, this demand was analyzed in some detail in Chapter 9. Throughout the analysis of Parts 2 and 3 it was assumed that there were no banks in the economy and the fact that part of the money stock earns a return in the form of deposit interest was ignored.

In Chapter 4 we also assumed that wealth owners treated all forms of nonmoney wealth (including both government and private I.O.U.s[23] and physical capital) as identical. Although this assumption was dropped in Chapter 6 we will return to it in this chapter: All nonmoney assets[24] will be assumed to be perfect substitutes and hence will yield the same rate of return. This rate will be the customer loan rate i_L. On the other hand, we *shall* take account of the fact that deposits earn interest at the rate i_D. Under these circumstances, the demands to hold currency and deposits depend on wealth, income, and these two interest rates:

$$D^D = D[\underset{+}{i_D}, \underset{-}{i_L}, \underset{+}{Y}, \underset{+}{W}] \tag{12.12}$$

$$C^D = C[\underset{-}{i_D}, \underset{-}{i_L}, \underset{+}{Y}, \underset{+}{W}] \tag{12.13}$$

As before, the plus and minus signs indicate the direction in which these demands will be affected when the variables in question rise. Increases in wealth or income or decreases in the rate of return on nonmoney assets lead

---

[23] Banks hold two kinds of private I.O.U.s: *securities,* which they buy on the open market, and *promissory notes* for bank loans, which they obtain from individual borrowers. For reasons such as those discussed in Chapter 10 (pp. 241–242), we would expect the latter to yield a higher rate of return. For the present all such distinctions between the various classes of bank assets are ignored.

[24] Except federal funds, which are not held by the nonbank public.

wealth holders to hold more of both types of money. However, an increase in the deposit rate causes wealth owners to want to hold more deposits and less currency. In what follows we will assume that the level of income Y remains constant.[25]

Before proceeding, the definition of the wealth of the nonbank public deserves brief mention. In a world that includes a banking system, the wealth of the nonbank public comprises its stock of capital,[26] its claims on the banking system (bank deposits), and on the government (currency and government securities) less the claims of the banking system on it (bank loans plus private securities held by banks). Thus

$$W = q_K K + D + C + q_B B - L$$

However, the net claims of the public on the banking system, $D - L$, are necessarily equal to the total reserves of the banking system and hence

$$\begin{aligned} W &= q_K K + q_B B + C + R \\ &= q_K K + q_B B + H \end{aligned} \tag{12.14}$$

where H represents the stock of high-powered money (the sum of bank reserves and currency outside banks).

Thus, as in the earlier chapters, the wealth of the public consists only of its stock of tangible wealth plus the government debt. However, the government debt now consists of the stocks of government bonds and of high-powered money. Bank-created money is not part of total wealth. This conclusion simply reflects the fact that transactions between the public and the banking system can alter the composition of the public's wealth but cannot change its total amount.

Like the demand to hold money, a wealth holder's willingness to take loans from (that is, sell I.O.U.s to) banks will also depend on income, wealth, and the rates of interest. Thus

$$L^S = L[i_D, i_L, Y, W] \tag{12.15}$$
$$\quad + \quad - \quad + \quad -$$

It is clear that if the loan rate rises, investors will be less willing to borrow from (that is, sell I.O.U.s to) banks.[27] However, the effects of the other three variables (i_D, Y, and W) on their willingness to sell assets to banks may

---

[25] We also ignore the fact that interest rate changes imply corresponding changes in asset prices and hence in total wealth.

[26] This includes bank capital. Increases in bank assets and liabilities will normally be made only when they are profitable. Hence increases in the supply of money generally imply larger bank profits, which in turn imply an increase in the value of bank common stocks owned by wealth holders. This wealth effect is ignored. For a useful discussion of this wealth effect, see Don Patinkin, "Money and Wealth: A Review Article," *Journal of Economic Literature*, Vol. VII, No. 4 (December 1969).

[27] To eliminate any possible misunderstanding, we emphasize that L^S is a stock variable. It represents the total amount of bank loans (promissory notes to banks) that wealth holders wish to have outstanding on any date. It is not the amount they wish to borrow over some period.

be less obvious at first sight. According to the above equation, for example, if either the level of income or the deposit rate rises, members of the public will wish to take more loans from or sell more securities to banks. Why?

The clue to the answer to this question lies in the fact that the wealth holder's holdings of assets and liabilities must satisfy an overall wealth constraint: his net holdings of assets and liabilities must be equal to his stock of wealth. An increase in the deposit rate or in the level of income leads the average wealth holder to want to hold more deposits. If he holds more deposits, however, he must either hold less of some other assets or incur more of some liabilities. Thus if either the deposit rate or the level of income rises, wealth holders will wish to sell earning assets to (or borrow from) banks.

The argument regarding total wealth is similar. If total wealth rises, investors will want to add to their stocks of assets or to reduce their outstanding liabilities. Hence an increase in W will lead wealth holders to wish to reduce their indebtedness to banks.

If both wealth holders and banks are to be satisfied with their holdings of loans and deposits, the structure of interest rates must be such that the supply of deposits (by banks) is equal to the demand for deposits (by the nonbank public) and that the demand for loans (by banks) is equal to the supply of loans (by the public). Thus

$$D^S = d[i_D, i_L, k, \eth] = D^D = D[i_D, i_L, Y, W] \qquad (12.16)$$
$$L^D = l[i_D, i_L, k, \eth] = L^S = L[i_D, i_L, Y, W] \qquad (12.17)$$

Currency and bank reserves together make up the stock of high-powered money. As we will see in Chapter 13, the total supply of high-powered money is controlled by the Federal Reserve System. Hence a further condition for asset-market equilibrium is that the demands for reserves (including both required reserves and excess reserves) by the banking system and for currency by the nonbank public must be equal to the total stock of high-powered money:

$$H^S = RR^D + ER^D + C^D$$
$$= k \cdot d[i_D, i_L, k, \eth] + r[i_D, i_L, k, \eth] + C[i_D, i_L, Y, W]$$
$$\quad - \; + \; + \; + \qquad\quad - \; - \; - \; + \qquad\quad - \; - \; + \; +$$

Note that the effect of an increase in the loan rate i_L on the demand for high-powered money is, in principle, indeterminate.[28] An increase in i_L encourages banks to seek to attract more deposits to be able to make more loans. Since additional deposits entail larger required reserves, this effect acts to increase the demand for high-powered money. However, an increase in the loan rate leads wealth holders to switch out of money into

---

[28] At first sight the effect of k also appears ambiguous: an increase in the reserve requirement increases the demand for legal reserves but reduces that for excess reserves. However, from Eqs. (12.9) and (12.10) we see that a rise in k leads banks to wish to add to their deposits and to reduce their loans, which implies an increase in total reserves.

nonmoney, thus reducing the demand for currency, and also induces banks to economize on their holdings of excess reserves. These two effects act to reduce the demand for high-powered money.

In what follows we will assume that the latter effects outweigh the former so that an increase in i_L reduces the total demand for high-powered money. We make this assumption because it simplifies the ensuing analysis; be aware that several of our later results depend on it. Although this assumption may in some circumstances be unjustified,[29] we choose simplicity (at the possible expense of accuracy) because our objective in this chapter is only to introduce the essential nature of the new view and not to present an exhaustive analysis of every possible set of assumptions. Having mastered the simple case, you should be equipped to examine the effects of choosing alternative assumptions.

Under this assumption, we can write the market-clearing condition for high-powered money as

$$H^S = H[i_D, i_L, k, \eth, Y, W] \tag{12.18}$$
$${-} \;\; {-} \;\; {+} \;\; {+} \;\; {+} \;\; {+}$$

In the United States, the banking system is obligated to supply as much currency as the nonbank public demands. This implies that the supply of currency is demand-determined and that asset equilibrium requires that the demand for bank reserves must equal the supply fixed by the Fed:

$$C^S = C^D = C[i_D, i_L, k, \eth] \tag{12.19}$$
$$R^S = k \cdot d[i_D, I_L, k, \eth] + r[i_D, I_L, k, \eth] \tag{12.20}$$

It is unclear whether the Fed regards the reserve base[30] or the high-powered money stock as its target variable. If the Fed fixes the reserve base and then supplies as much currency as the nonbank public demands, the high-powered money stock is, in effect, determined by the public:

$$H^S = R^S + C^D \tag{12.21}$$

An increase in the demand for currency will draw forth an increased supply from the Fed and the high-powered money stock will rise. If, on the other hand, the Fed fixes the high-powered money stock, an increased demand for currency can be accommodated only by a reduction in bank reserves. In this case, therefore, it is the reserve base that is determined by the public:

---

[29] For example, the assumption may be false if the legal reserve ratio is high so that any rise in deposits entails a large increase in required reserves. For a discussion of this assumption in the context of more elaborate models, see Tobin, "A General Equilibrium Approach to Monetary Theory," *Journal of Money, Credit and Banking,* Vol. I, No. 1 (February 1969), p. 29; and William C. Brainard, "Financial Intermediaries and a Theory of Monetary Control," *Yale Economic Essays,* Vol. IV (Fall 1964), pp. 465–466.

[30] It is sometimes argued that in most cases the Fed is bound to make loans at the discount window when requested to by member banks. Thus it cannot control that portion of the reserve base that represents borrowed reserves. If this assertion is accepted (and it is a dubious one), Eq. (12.20) should be interpreted as referring only to the supply of and demand for "unborrowed reserves."

$$R^S = H^S - C^D \tag{12.22}$$

Monetary economists in the Keynesian tradition generally assume that the reserve base is the exogenous policy variable. Monetarists generally prefer the high-powered money approach. In a few cases, the two assumptions yield different conclusions: For example, an increased demand for currency has no effect on the reserve base under the first assumption but leads to a decline in reserves under the second.

We now have three equations [(12.15), (12.16), and either (12.18) or (12.20)] describing the supplies of and demands for bank deposits, bank loans, and either high-powered money or bank reserves. Full asset equilibrium of both the banking system and the nonbank public requires that all three of these equations be satisfied simultaneously.

The three equations are not independent of one another, however, because both the banking system and the nonbank public are subject to an overall wealth constraint. If we know the amounts of bank deposits and loans outstanding, then we automatically know the total reserves of the banking system. Similarly, given the wealth of the public, if we know its holdings of capital, bonds, and deposits as well as the amount it has borrowed from banks, then we necessarily know its currency holdings. Thus if the supplies of and demand for any two of the assets are equal, then the supply of and demand for the third asset must also be equal. In different terms, if the public and banks are in portfolio equilibrium with respect to any two assets, they must also be in equilibrium with respect to the third asset.

This conclusion is, of course, precisely analogous to those reached in the simpler models of Chapter 4 and 6. In the two-asset model of Chapter 4, for example, equality between the supply of and demand for money implied that the supply of and demand for nonmoney were also equal.[31] Operationally, this conclusion implies that one of the three equations may be discarded. The remaining two equations plus Eq. (12.13), which defines total wealth, then may be solved for the equilibrium interest rates on deposits and loans. Having computed these rates, Eqs. (12.8) and (12.19) may be used to find the equilibrium federal funds rate and the supply of and demand for currency.[32]

At these equilibrium interest rates, the asset and liability portfolios of both the public and the banking system are at their desired levels and satisfy the appropriate balance-sheet constraints. The loan and deposit totals of each bank—and hence of the system as a whole—satisfy the preferences both of the banks themselves and of their customers. In addition, the amount of federal funds that lending banks wish to sell is equal to the amount that borrowing banks wish to buy. Hence the demand for reserves by the banking system is equal to the difference between its total deposits and total

---

[31] See pp. 71–74. The analogous proposition for the three-asset model of Chapter 6 is presented on p. 126.

[32] If the reserve base is treated as the policy variable, Eq. (12.21) will determine the high-powered money stock. Conversely, if H is policy-determined the reserve base is given by Eq. (12.22).

customer loans even though this is not the case for every individual bank. Finally, the public's demand for currency at the prevailing set of interest rates plus the banking system's demand for reserves is equal to the stock of high-powered money set by the Federal Reserve System.[33]

In full portfolio equilibrium, the stock of money (as well as its division between demand deposits and currency) is determined and is at the level desired both by the public and the banking system. However, the essential message of the new view is that this equilibrium with respect to the money stock is only one component of a more general equilibrium situation involving both money and nonmoney assets.

This equilibrium situation is illustrated[34] geometrically in Figures 12.1 and 12.2. In the first of these figures the supplies of and demands for the three

---

[33] If we suppose that the Fed fixes the reserve base rather than the high-powered money stock, this last sentence must be amended slightly, viz: Finally, the banking system's demand for reserves will be equal to the reserve base set by the Fed.

[34] These figures do not derive the equilibrium. A geometric derivation along lines similar to those used in Chapter 6 is provided in the appendix.

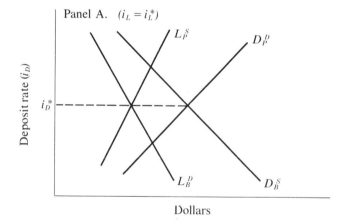

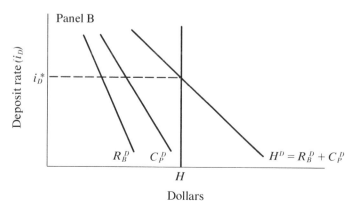

FIGURE 12.1 Asset market equilibrium with banks $(i_L = i_L^*)$

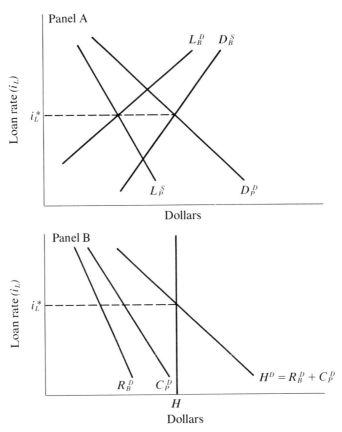

FIGURE 12.2 Asset equilibrium with banks ($i_D = i_D*$)

In the text [Eq. (12.18)] we assumed that the demand for high-powered money H^D was negatively related to the loan rate. This figure embodies the stronger assumption that the demands for bank reserves and currency are each negatively related to i_L.

assets are shown as functions of the *deposit rate*, assuming the loan rate takes its equilibrium value i_L*. In the second figure the roles of the interest rates are reversed: The deposit rate is assumed to take its equilibrium value, i_D*, and the supplies and demands are expressed as functions of the *loan rate*. In both figures, the market for federal funds is assumed always to be in equilibrium.

The banking system's supply of deposits (D_B^S) and demand for earning assets (L_B^D), both of which decline when the deposit rate rises, are shown in Panel A of Figure 12.1. The banks' demand for reserves (R_B^D) is shown in Panel B; the balance-sheet constraint requires that $R_B^D = D_B^S - L_B^D$. Similarly, the public's demand for deposits (D_P^D) and supply of earning assets (L_P^S) are shown in Panel A, while their demand for currency (C_P^D) appears in Panel B.

In equilibrium, the supply of and demand for both deposits and earning assets (loans) must be equal. In Panel A we see that this occurs at deposit rate i_D^*. In addition, at that same deposit rate, the total demand for high-powered money by banks and the public together will be equal to the available stock (see Panel B).

Figure 12.2 illustrates the same equilibrium in terms of the loan rate. This figure is drawn on the assumption that the deposit rate is i_D^*. In Panel A we see that equilibrium in the markets for deposits and loans requires that the loan rate be i_L^*. Panel B shows that at this same rate the supply of and demand for high-powered money are equal.

The "Old" and "New" Views of the Money Supply

In the previous two sections we have developed a model of the behavior of the banking system. This model led to a view of the money supply that differs markedly from that employed in Part 2. In the models of Chapters 4 to 6, the money stock was determined by government fiat. There was no mechanism by which the public could increase or decrease the aggregate money stock. Money was a "hot potato" that *individual* wealth holders could pass from hand to hand but that the public *as a group* can neither add to nor dispose of. As a result, interest rates and asset prices were forced to adjust to the levels at which the available stock of money was willingly held by wealth owners.

In the new view, only the high-powered money stock (or the reserve base) is government-determined. Given that stock, as well as the levels of other policy variables, such as the discount rate and the legal reserve requirements, interest rates and asset prices adjust to the levels at which the balance sheets of the public and the banking system are simultaneously in equilibrium. In that equilibrium the holdings by the public and the banking system of each of the various assets in the economy are at their desired levels. In particular, the quantity of money in existence—as well as the distribution of that stock as between currency and demand deposits—is at a level that satisfies the portfolio preferences of both its producers (the banks) and its holders (the nonbank public). Instead of being fixed by government fiat, the money supply is determined simultaneously with the set of interest rates at which the economy's asset markets attain equilibrium.

At first sight the model of this chapter also differs from the money-multiplier approach to the creation of money presented in Chapter 11. In this case, however, the differences, while they are important, should not be overemphasized. Many of the ideas presented in the last few pages were understood informally by economists[35] who discussed money creation

---

[35] An early example is the work of Pigou. See A. C. Pigou, "The Value of Money," *The Quarterly Journal of Economics,* Vol. XXXII (1917–18). Although he considers a different type of monetary system from ours (one in which gold circulates as currency), Pigou clearly

within the traditional accounting framework.[36] The essential contribution of the new view theorists has been to combine and develop these ideas into a coherent and logically complete theory of the money-supply process.

Within the traditional framework, we saw in the last chapter that the money stock may be regarded as the product of the high-powered money stock and a money multiplier:[37]

$$M = \frac{1 + \dfrac{C}{D}}{\dfrac{C}{D} + \dfrac{R}{D}} \cdot H \tag{12.23}$$

$$M^* = \frac{1 + c}{c + r} \cdot H \tag{12.24}$$

Recall that the first of these equations represents a tautology: It is an identity that is always true by definition. In the second equation, c and r represent the "desired" values of C/D and R/D on the part of wealth holders and banks, and M^* is the equilibrium value of the money stock when these desires are satisfied. Thus in equilibrium $c = C/D$ and $r = R/D$ and hence $M = M^*$.

In its most "mechanical" form this money-multiplier approach treats c and r as institutionally given constants and assumes that the system is always in equilibrium. Banks always maintain a ratio of reserves to deposits of r and the public always allocates its money stock between currency and demand deposits so as to maintain a currency ratio of c. This leads to a model in which the money stock is again determined by government fiat since, with a fixed multiplier, control of H (or R) implies control of M. The banking system plays no independent role and for practical purposes the model is indistinguishable from those of Part 2.

Most exponents of the multiplier approach do, of course, provide some *ad hoc* discussion of the determinants of c and r and also treat informally the possibility that the actual currency-deposit and reserve-deposit ratios may diverge from these desired ratios. For example, many texts point out that banks may hold additional reserves if they cannot find customers for bank loans. However, the multiplier approach fails to provide a coherent framework in which these issues may be examined.

The new view argues that to truly understand the determinants of the money stock we must "go behind" the money-multiplier equations and seek to explain how c and r are determined. Moreover, it asserts that interest rates and asset prices play a key role in the determination of these ratios.

---

recognizes that the asset preferences of the public and of the banks are relevant in determining the stock of money outstanding at any given date.

[36] Regrettably, however, many textbook treatments show little sign of such understanding and are completely mechanical.

[37] These equations were introduced as Eq. (11.1) and (11.2) in Chapter 11.

The stock of money outstanding on any date (as well as the stocks of all the other assets in the hands of the public or the banking system) is determined not by government fiat or historical accident but through the interaction of supply and demand in the markets for assets. This interaction determines a set of interest rates (i_L^*, i_D^*, and i_F^*) at which the public and the banks are simultaneously satisfied with their portfolios of assets and liabilities. When they are satisfied, c and r are determined[38] and hence both the money multiplier and the money stock are also determined. Thus the multiplier is not some constant that, given the stock of high-powered money, determines the stock of money outstanding. Rather, the stock of money and the money multiplier are determined simultaneously as the public and the banks each seek to attain their desired asset portfolios.

As an example of this approach, consider the previously mentioned situation in which banks hold a high proportion of reserves in their portfolios because loan customers are scarce. The multiplier approach would regard this as a *disequilibrium* situation because the reserve ratio is above its "desired" level. The new view theorists would argue that this is a misleading way of characterizing the situation. The scarcity of loan customers implies that the yield on earning assets (i_L in our model) is low relative to the risks involved. Hence banks choose to hold more reserves and fewer earning assets than they would do if interest rates were higher. Thus the high reserve ratio reflects the banks' asset preferences given the interest rates they face and does not imply that their portfolios are "out of equilibrium" in any genuine sense.

Conclusion

Throughout this argument, we have assumed that banks issue only one type of deposit and hold only one class of earning asset. Of course, neither of these assumptions represents the true situation: Banks issue several classes of deposits (saving accounts, time deposits, and certificates of deposit in addition to checking accounts) and hold many types of assets (including government and private securities in addition to customer loans). These facts do not alter the essence of our argument. No matter how many assets and liabilities we find it useful to distinguish, equilibrium in the asset markets requires that the set of interest rates and asset prices be such that the portfolios of the banking system and the nonbank public are consistent with

---

[38] Specifically,

$$c = C[i_D^*, i_L^*, Y, W]/D[i_D^*, i_L^*, Y, W]$$

$$r = \frac{r[i_D^*, i_L^*, i_F^*, k, \mathfrak{d}] + k \cdot d[i_D^*, i_L^*, i_F^*, k, \mathfrak{d}]}{d[i_D^*, i_L^*, i_F^*, k, \mathfrak{d}]}$$

$$= \frac{r[i_D^*, i_L^*, i_F^*, k, \mathfrak{d}]}{d[i_D^*, i_L^*, i_F^*, k, \mathfrak{d}]} + k$$

one another in the sense that for each asset the quantity one side wishes to hold is equal to the quantity the other side wishes to issue.[39]

Thus it remains true that the banking system's ability to obtain any given balance sheet (and thus to supply any given quantity of money) depends on the willingness of the public to make the necessary transactions with the banks. As in our simple model the stock of money in existence is determined by the interaction of supply and demand in the asset markets and is neither a given constant nor determined solely by the banking system.

References

Brainard, William C. "Financial Intermediaries and a Theory of Monetary Control." *Yale Economic Essays,* Vol. IV (Fall 1964).

Tobin, James. "Commercial Banks as Creators of 'Money,'" *Banking and Monetary Studies.* ed. Deane Carson. Homewood, Illinois: Richard D. Irwin, 1963.

This is the classic presentation of the new view. However, much of the article is concerned with the implications of the fact that interest rates on bank deposits are not free to vary, but are subject to statutory and regulatory restrictions. This issue is taken up in Chapter 13.

Tobin, James. "A General Equilibrium Approach to Monetary Theory." *Journal of Money, Credit and Banking,* Vol. I, Number 1 (February 1969).

Questions for Classroom Discussion

1. Use the model of this chapter to show how an increase in the public's demand for currency (assuming it is not accommodated by the Fed) will affect interest rates on money and nonmoney assets.

2. Suppose the Federal Reserve System were to pay interest on member bank reserves. Explain the link between the interest rate on bank reserves and the interest rates on bank earning assets? If the System wished to engage in an expansionary policy, should it raise or lower the interest rate on bank reserves?

3. Why do 10 dimes always exchange for 1 dollar bill? That is, why is the dime price of a dollar bill always 10? Illustrate your answer by showing the supply and demand curves for dollar bills.

4. Why do banks offer free checking accounts when the cost of providing these services is clearly not zero?

---

[39] For examples of new-view models that incorporate a larger number of distinct assets, see the articles by Tobin and Brainard cited earlier.

Appendix   Portfolio Equilibrium with a Banking System

In this appendix we derive the full portfolio equilibrium of an economy with a banking system by algebraic and geometric methods.

Consider first the behavior of the nonbank public. Private wealth holders must choose their holdings of various assets in the system subject to their overall budget constraint:

$$W = q_K K_P + q_B B_P + D_P + C_P - L_P$$

where the subscript $_P$ is used to denote the assets and liabilities of the nonbank public. We will assume that both capital and bonds yield a constant return of one dollar per period. In addition, we continue to assume that wealth holders regard all forms of nonmoney assets as perfect substitutes so that all must yield the same rate of return; we will call this the *loan rate* and write it i_L. Hence

$$q_B = q_K = 1/i_L$$

so that the constraint may be written as

$$W = \frac{K_P + B_P}{i_L} + D_P + C_P - L_P \qquad (12A.1)$$

Deposits yield a rate of return i_D and currency yields no return.

The net demand[1] for nonmoney assets[2] by the public is

$$\frac{K_P^D + B_P^D}{i_L} - L_P^S = N[i_D, i_L, Y, W] \qquad (12A.2)$$
$$\phantom{\frac{K_P^D + B_P^D}{i_L} - L_P^S = N[} - \quad + \quad - \quad +$$

where L_P^S represents the supply of nonmarketable I.O.U.s to the banking system by the public, and $(K_P^D + B_P^D)$ represents their demand for capital and bonds. Similarly, the public's demands for deposits and for currency may be written

$$D_P^D = D[i_D, i_L, Y, W] \qquad (12A.3)$$
$$ + \quad - \quad + \quad +$$

$$C_P^D = C[i_D, i_L, Y, W] \qquad (12A.4)$$
$$ - \quad - \quad + \quad +$$

---

[1] In the text we worked in terms of the public's *supply* of nonmoney assets to the banking system rather than with their *demand* to hold such assets. Since all nonmoney assets must be held either by the public or by the banks, the net demand function $N(\ )$ in Eq. (12A.2) is related to the supply function $L(\ )$ in Eq. 12.15 as follows:

$$[q_K K + q_B B] - N(\ ) = L(\ )$$

The total stock of nonmoney assets less the public's demand for these assets is equal to the public's supply of these assets to the banking system.

[2] In the text a single symbol, L, was used to represent all nonmoney assets. In this equation three types of assets (capital, bonds, and bank loans) are distinguished.

Consider the behavior of the banking system. Suppressing the Federal Funds market, banks must choose an asset and liability portfolio subject to the constraint[3]

$$D_B = q_B B_B + L_B + R_B$$

$$= \frac{B_B}{i_L} + L_B + R_B \tag{12A.5}$$

where the subscript $_B$ is used to denote assets and liabilities of the banking system.

The banking system's supply of deposits and demands for earning assets and reserves may be written:[4]

$$D_B^S = d[i_D, i_L, k, b] \tag{12A.6}$$
$$\quad\quad - \; + \; + \; +$$

$$\frac{B_B^D}{i_L} + L_B^D = l[i_D, i_L, k, b] \tag{12A.7}$$
$$\quad\quad\quad - \; + \; - \; -$$

$$R_B^D = k \cdot d[i_D, i_L, k, b] + r[i_D, i_L, k, b] \tag{12A.8}$$
$$\quad\quad - \; + \; + \; + \quad\quad - \; - \; - \; +$$

Portfolio equilibrium requires that (1) the demand for deposits by the public equal the supply of deposits by the banks, (2) the net demand for nonmoney assets by the public plus the demand for earning assets by the banks equal the total stock of capital and bonds in existence,[5] and (3) the demand for currency by the public plus the demand for reserves by the banks equal the stock of high-powered money provided by the Fed.[6] Algebraically, these conditions may be written:

$$D[i_D, i_L, Y, W] = d[i_D, i_L, k, b] \tag{12A.9}$$
$$N[i_D, i_L, Y, W] + l[i_D, i_L, k, b] = [B + K]/i_L \tag{12A.10}$$
$$C[i_D, i_L, Y, W] + k \cdot d[i_D, i_L, k, b] + r[i_D, i_L, k, b] = H^S \tag{12A.11}$$

It is useful to simplify this last condition to

$$H[i_D, i_L, k, b, Y, W] = H^S \tag{12A.12}$$
$$\quad\quad - \; - \; + \; + \; + \quad +$$

---

[3] Banks do not invest in physical capital or common stocks. Hence their assets consist of their security holdings, their reserves, and their customer loans outstanding. As usual, bank equity is ignored.

[4] These equations are generalizations of those used in the text.

[5] Since the total stock of bonds and capital minus the net demand for nonmoney assets by the public is equal to the net supply of nonmoney assets by the public, this condition may also be stated as requiring that the net supply of nonmoney assets by the public is equal to the net demand for nonmoney assets by the banks. This latter formulation was used in the text.

[6] This presumes that the Fed treats the stock of high-powered money as its target variable. The case in which the reserve base is the target is similar.

These three equations implicitly define three relations between i_D and i_L, which are analogous to the relations between q_K and q_B, which were derived in Chapter 6.[7] By totally differentiating these equations [and using Eq. (12A.1), which defines W] the slopes of these relations may be derived. These slopes are:

From deposits condition, $\qquad\qquad \dfrac{di_L}{di_D} > 0$

From earning assets condition, $\qquad \dfrac{di_L}{di_D} > 0$

From high-powered money condition, $\quad \dfrac{di_L}{di_D} < 0$

These conclusions are summarized in Figure 12A.1. In this figure the *dd* curve represents those combinations of i_D and i_L at which the supply of and demand for deposits are equal. The *hh* and *ll* curves are defined analogously.[8] Since the three markets are not independent—because both banks and the public are subject to overall wealth constraints—the three curves necessarily intersect at the same point. In the figure, equilibrium occurs when the loan rate and deposit rate are i_L^* and i_D^*.

---

[7] These relations were summarized in the *mm*, *bb*, and *kk* curves of that chapter.
[8] The requirement that the slope of the *ll* curve be less than that of the *dd* curve may be derived by a method analogous to that used in Chapter 6, pp. 126–127.

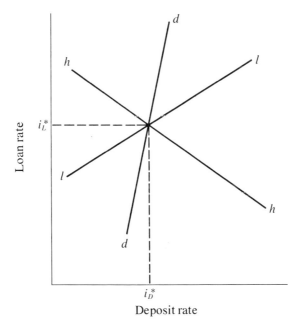

FIGURE 12A.1 Asset equilibrium in an economy with banks

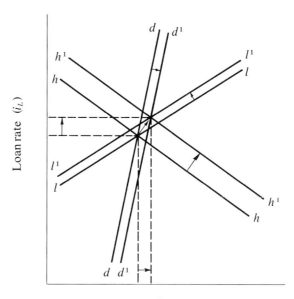

Deposit rate (i_D)

FIGURE 12A.2   The effects of an increased reserve requirement

As an application of this analytical setup, consider the effect of an increase in the legal reserve requirement. Such an increase induces banks to raise their deposit rates in order to attract more lendable funds: Thus the *dd* curve shifts rightward. At the same time it encourages them to cut back on their earning assets, thus lowering asset prices and raising loan rates: The *ll* curve shifts upward. Finally, an increase in k raises the demand for reserves by the banks. Given the fixed stock of high-powered money, the public must be induced to hold less currency by a rise in either i_L or i_D (or both). Thus the *hh* curve shifts rightward.

From Figure 12A.2 we note that these shifts imply an increase in both i_L and i_D. Thus an increase in the reserve requirement is contractionary since it raises interest rates and lowers asset prices.

The model of this appendix may be readily extended by dropping the assumption that capital, bonds, and bank loans all yield the same rate of return. Abandoning this assumption does not alter the essential nature of the model, though it does preclude the use of geometric methods. You are encouraged to experiment along these lines.

Central Banking

In the last two chapters we have seen that the commercial banking system, not the federal government, plays the role of principal money producer in the United States.[1] However, the mechanism through which money is created in an economy with a banking system is essentially the same as in the earlier simple model. Increases in the money stock result from trades between banks and members of the nonbank public in which the former supply new demand deposits in exchange for either claims on governments (including bonds issued by federal, state, and local authorities) or claims on the nonbank public (principally loans and securities of various kinds). The major differences in the model that result from the introduction of banks are that instead of a single money producer there are large numbers of independent and competing banks, and that the motives of these private money producers are different from those of governments. Specifically, commercial banks are profit-maximizing institutions whereas governments are not.

Given the returns that are obtainable on various assets and that must be paid on various liabilities, each bank chooses that portfolio which yields the combination of risk and return that it prefers. Particular interest attaches to its choice of a deposit total since bank deposits function as money. Thus the total supply of bank deposits reflects the aggregate portfolio choices of the banking system.

For the system as a whole, however, the various rates of return are not fixed,[2] but are determined in competitive markets. As a result, the bank portfolios—and hence the stock of money—that emerge at any time depend on the terms on which banks and their customers are willing to trade one type of asset for another.

When the monetary sector of the economy is in equilibrium, neither the banks nor the public wish to alter the makeup of their portfolios at the current set of asset prices

---

[1] Although about one-fourth of the money supply is in the form of currency, the authorities make no attempt to control this portion of the total, but simply supply whatever quantities of notes and coin are demanded by the public and the commercial banking system.

[2] Here we are continuing the assumption of Chapter 12 that the interest rate on bank deposits is not subject to government regulation. Later in this chapter we examine the implications of dropping this assumption.

and rates of return. Specifically, the stock of demand deposits that banks wish to supply is equal to the stock that wealth owners are willing to hold, and the stocks of currency and reserves that wealth owners and banks together wish to hold is equal to the quantity of high-powered money that the monetary authorities are supplying.

This argument, which represents the essence of the "new view," does not mean that the money supply depends *only* on the decisions of the banks and the public. This should be clear from the last sentence of the previous paragraph. An important factor that enters into the decisions of the banks and the public is the stock of high-powered money. This stock is under the control of the monetary authorities, who therefore can strongly influence (many economists would say *determine*) the money-supply process. In this chapter we will attempt to explain how this control of high-powered money is implemented and examine other policy instruments that affect the actions of both banks and their customers.

The Federal Reserve System

The principal agency[3] responsible for the conduct of monetary policy is the Federal Reserve System, which was established by the Federal Reserve Act of 1913. This Act, together with the Banking Acts of 1933 and 1935, set up the central banking structure in existence today.

As its name implies, the Federal Reserve System is a federation of central banks. The principal operations of the System are conducted by regional Federal Reserve banks with overall supervision and control by the Board of Governors in Washington, D.C.

The Board of Governors of the Federal Reserve System consists of seven members appointed by the President, subject to confirmation by the Senate. Each serves a 14-year term and may not be reappointed. All are full-time salaried officials, and their activities are not subject to the day-to-day scrutiny of either the Congress or the Executive branch.

The nation is divided into twelve Federal Reserve districts, each with its own Federal Reserve bank.[4] The Reserve banks are federally chartered corporations. Their common stock is exclusively owned by the commercial banks that are members of the System. However, although the Reserve banks are privately owned, they are operated in the public interest and do not, for example, seek to maximize their profits. Member banks receive a fixed return of 6 percent on their holdings of Reserve bank stock. The remainder of the Reserve banks' profits is returned to the Treasury.

Most decisions on the conduct of monetary policy are made by the

---

[3] The Fed is not the only agency that has responsibilities that affect the money stock. For example, the activities of the Treasury in issuing and redeeming securities, collecting taxes, and making payments also affect the stocks of both money and high-powered money.

[4] Federal Reserve banks are located in Boston, New York, Philadelphia, Cleveland, Richmond, Atlanta, Chicago, St. Louis, Minneapolis, Kansas City (Mo.), Dallas, and San Francisco.

Federal Open Market Committee (FOMC). This body comprises the seven members of the Board of Governors plus the presidents of five of the Reserve banks, who serve on a rotating basis. The committee meets monthly in Washington, D.C. and discusses the current situation almost daily by telephone. The *Federal Reserve Bulletin* publishes the minutes of these monthly meetings after a short delay.

The Federal Reserve System acts as banker both to the U.S. Treasury and to the member banks. In these roles the Fed carries through the monetary policy of the federal government. It also provides banking services to foreign governments and central banks, and performs a number of purely mechanical chores; for example, it is responsible for the issue of notes and coins. A convenient way of describing the System's principal activities is in terms of the balance sheet of the Reserve banks. A recent balance sheet is shown in Table 13.1.

The U.S. gold stock is owned by the Treasury rather than the Reserve banks. *Gold certificates* represent claims on the gold stock and are issued to the Reserve banks by the Treasury. They are a remnant of the gold standard system of earlier days in which gold coins circulated as currency. Changes in the U.S. gold stock normally result from transactions with either foreign

Table 13.1 Consolidated Balance Sheet of the Reserve Banks (September 30, 1975)

	Millions of Dollars
Gold certificates	11,599
Special Drawing Rights certificates	500
Cash	403
Member bank borrowings	283
Acceptances	948
U.S. government securities	86,998
Federal agency securities	6,082
Cash items in process of collection	6,720
Other assets	3,259
Total assets	116,792
F. R. notes	72,562
Member bank deposits	25,913
U.S. Treasury deposits	8,075
Foreign deposits	324
Other deposits	616
Deferred availability cash items	5,829
Other liabilities	1,165
Capital	2,307
Total liabilities and capital	116,792

SOURCE: *Federal Reserve Bulletin*, November 1975.

monetary authorities or international bodies such as the International Monetary Fund. When such an institution sells gold to the U.S. Treasury, the Federal Reserve Bank of New York credits its deposit account and debits that of the Treasury. The Reserve bank obtains the gold and delivers it to the Treasury. In payment for the gold, the Treasury issues gold certificates to the Reserve bank, which in turn credits the Treasury account. Thus the net effect of the transaction is to increase the gold certificate holdings of the Federal Reserve, leaving the Treasury's account unchanged. The rise in the Fed's assets (in the form of gold certificates) is balanced by a corresponding increase in *Foreign deposits* owned by the gold seller.

Special Drawing Rights are an international paper currency issued by the International Monetary Fund and held only by national monetary authorities. They play a similar role to gold in the international payments mechanism and *SDR certificates* are analogous to gold certificates.

Cash represents Federal Reserve holdings of currency other than gold certificates and Federal Reserve notes. It consists mainly of stocks of coin. If a member bank needs to replenish its reserves of coin, it will be supplied out of this stock. The Fed is also responsible for the issue of paper currency. The total volume of notes in circulation is shown in *Federal Reserve notes*. In an accounting sense these notes are a liability of the System, but this is not a true liability, since it can be met simply by supplying new notes.[5]

The Federal Reserve banks act as bankers to the member banks. Their activities in this area show up in two balance-sheet items. First, the total of member-bank checking accounts is shown as *Member bank deposits*. As we have seen, these deposits constitute the bulk of the banking system's reserves. Together with Federal Reserve notes and the stock of coin outstanding, they make up the stock of high-powered money. Second, like the customers of commercial banks, member banks may borrow from *their* banks. The amount of this borrowing is shown in *Member bank borrowings*. We will discuss the role of this borrowing in monetary policy later.

The principal earning assets of the System consist of its holdings of securities issued by the federal government or federal agencies. Most of these securities are purchased in the open market either from banks or from members of the public. Transactions in government bonds are the principal means by which monetary policy is conducted. However, the System also holds a small portfolio of private securities in the form of bankers' acceptances.

The Federal Reserve acts as banker to other institutions besides member banks. The most important of these are the U.S. Treasury and foreign

---

[5] The actual printing of notes is not performed by the Fed but by the Bureau of Engraving, which is located in the Treasury Department. However, the Bureau will supply the needs of the Fed on demand, so this distinction has no real significance. Coins are manufactured by the Mint, which is also part of the Treasury. Coins are sold by the Mint to the Fed at their face value; thus the profit that accrues from the manufacture of coins accrues to the Treasury rather than to the Fed. This profit is known as *seigniorage*.

governments and central banks. A few private U.S. institutions, such as certain large dealers in government securities, are also permitted to own deposits at a Federal Reserve bank.

As we saw in Chapter 11, an important service function of the Federal Reserve is to provide a mechanism by which interbank debts may be settled and thus to reduce the cost of clearing checks. The operation of this mechanism gives rise to the remaining large items on the balance sheet, *Cash items in process of collection* and *Deferred availability cash items*.

When Bank A receives a check drawn on Bank B, it will send it to the Federal Reserve bank for collection. The latter will in turn send the check on to Bank B. Until Bank B receives the check and instructs the Fed to debit its account accordingly, the check represents a claim on Bank B and is shown as a cash item in process of collection on the asset side of the Fed account. The Fed does not immediately credit Bank A's account with the amount of the check, nor does it wait until collection is complete. Instead, it delays credit according to a fixed time schedule. During the interval between the date on which the check is received and that on which A's account is credited, the check is shown as a deferred availability cash item. Since the time required to actually collect checks is often longer than that allowed in the fixed time schedules, the Fed will frequently credit Bank A's account before it debits Bank B's account. As a result, items in process of collection normally exceed deferred availability items. The difference between these two items, which is in effect a loan by the Federal Reserve to the banking system, is known as the Federal Reserve *float*.

Federal Reserve and Treasury Operations

We are now in a position to describe how the operations of the monetary authorities influence the consolidated balance sheet of the Federal Reserve banks. In view of the importance of the stock of high-powered money for the behavior of the banking system, we will pay particular attention to those Federal Reserve or Treasury transactions that lead to changes in either the stock of currency or the volume of member bank deposits at the Fed.

Consider first the situation when a member of the public pays taxes to the Treasury by drawing a check against his commercial bank checking account. Suppose that the Treasury deposits this check into its account at a Federal Reserve bank.[6] The latter will credit the Treasury's account, debit the reserve account of the member bank involved, and pass the check back to that bank. The member bank will in turn debit the account of the taxpayer who drew the check. Thus the parties to the transaction have their balance sheets altered as shown in Table 13.2.

From this table we see that this transaction reduces the stock of high-powered money by the amount of the tax payment. Note that whereas in the

---

[6] This is not the only option open to the Treasury. See the discussion below.

Table 13.2 The Effects of a Tax Payment of $100

	TREASURY		
Tax liability of public	−100		
Account at Fed	+100		
	FEDERAL RESERVE BANKS		
		Treasury account	+100
		Member bank account	−100
	COMMERCIAL BANKS		
Reserve account at Fed	−100	Demand deposits	−100
	NONBANK PUBLIC		
Demand deposits	−100	Tax liability	−100

simple model of Part 2, a tax payment of $100 leads to a reduction in the money stock by the same amount; in an economy with a banking system it leads to an equal reduction in the high-powered money stock and so to a much greater[7] decline in the money stock.

The case of a Treasury payment to a member of the public is similar. The stock of high-powered money is increased by the amount of the payment, and as a result the money supply will probably rise by more than that amount.

Normally the authorities wish to avoid these effects; that is, they wish to make payments to and receive payments from the public without altering the stock of high-powered money. They can do this because the Treasury maintains checking accounts at many commercial banks as well as at the Federal Reserve banks. These accounts are known as *tax and loan accounts*. Normally the Treasury pays checks received from the public into a commercial bank account. When it does, no change occurs in the reserves of the banking system; all that happens is that the ownership of demand deposits passes from the nonbank public to the Treasury. However, since Treasury demand deposits are not regarded as part of the money supply, this operation does reduce the stock of money by the amount of the tax. The Treasury does not make payments to the public by means of checks drawn on its tax and loan account; all such payments are made from the Treasury's Federal Reserve account. However, when the Treasury wishes to make a payment to a member of the public, it will first transfer funds from its commercial bank account into its Federal Reserve account and then write a check against the latter. This combined operation again has no effect on the stock of high-powered money, but increases the money stock in the hands of the public by the amount of the outlay.[8]

The implication of this discussion is that to the extent that the Treasury finances its operations by varying its *commercial* bank accounts rather than its Fed account, changes in the money stock are exactly equal to the

---

[7] This is true if the money multiplier is greater than one, as it normally is.

[8] Check the statements in this paragraph by constructing the appropriate balance sheets.

difference between Treasury receipts and expenditures. In this case, therefore, the introduction of a commercial banking system does not change the analysis presented in Chapters 4 and 5 of the impact of fiscal operations on the financial side of the economy (the *LM* curve).

As a second example of an operation by the monetary authorities that affects bank portfolios, consider a class of transactions that is the principal means by which the Fed acts to change the stock of high-powered money: the purchase and sale of government securities. Such transactions are known as *open-market operations* and are conducted by the Open Market Manager, an official of the Federal Reserve Bank of New York. Policy regarding the volume of purchases or sales is formulated by the Federal Open Market Committee.

Suppose the Fed purchases government securities from a member of the public. It will make payment by drawing a check on itself, which the seller (usually a New York government securities dealer) will deposit into its account at a commercial bank. When the latter sends the check to the Federal Reserve Bank of New York for collection, it will receive a corresponding increase in its reserve account. This increase represents an addition to the stock of high-powered money. The effects of the transaction on the parties involved are shown in Table 13.3.

We see from this table that the initial effect of the transaction is to increase the stock of money and reduce the public's bond holding by equal amounts. However, the banks' portfolios are out of equilibrium. Their liabilities have risen by $100, and the corresponding increase in assets has been exclusively in the form of reserves. They are likely to want to add to their holdings of earning assets, and to the extent that they are able to do so, the stock of demand deposits will increase further.

Since only the Fed initiates open-market operations, it has complete power to control the stock of high-powered money. Other types of transactions that act to change this total (Treasury receipts and payments, changes in the float, member bank borrowing, etc.) can always be offset by appropriate open-market sales or purchases. In practice, the Fed finds itself continuously engaging in operations that are designed to offset the effect of other types of transactions on the stock of high-powered money. Hence it is in general not possible to determine whether a particular purchase or sale is

Table 13.3 The Effects of an Open Market Purchase

FEDERAL RESERVE BANKS			
U.S. government securities	+100	Member bank deposits	+100
COMMERCIAL BANKS			
Reserves at Federal Reserve	+100	Demand deposits	+100
NONBANK PUBLIC			
U.S. government securities	−100		
Demand deposits	+100		

Table 13.4 The Effect of a Currency Withdrawal

	NONBANK PUBLIC		
Notes	+ 50		
Coin	+ 50		
Demand deposits	− 100		
	COMMERCIAL BANKS		
Reserves	− 100	Demand deposits	− 100
	FEDERAL RESERVE BANKS		
Cash	− 50	Member bank deposits	− 100
		Notes outstanding	+ 50

designed to change the stock of high-powered money or to offset some other transaction so that the stock remains unchanged.

As a final example[9] of a transaction that alters Reserve bank balance sheets, suppose the public wishes to increase the proportion of its money stock that it holds in the form of currency. This occurs regularly in the weeks before Christmas when the volume of small transactions increases substantially. Individuals cash checks at their banks, thus depleting the banks' reserves of vault cash.

If the banks decide to restore their vault cash to its former level, they may do so by cashing checks against *their* accounts at the Fed, thus reducing member bank deposits. The effect of this transaction on the Fed balance sheet depends on the type of currency involved. If it is in the form of notes, the liability item, Federal Reserve notes, increases, whereas if it is coin, the asset item, Cash, decreases. Thus if both classes of currency are involved, the balance sheet effect might appear as in Table 13.4 above.

These transactions do not affect the total stock of high-powered money, but they do alter the division of that total: Thus the public has more currency and the banks have less reserves. Unless something else changes, the banks may find it necesssary to reduce their earning assets, and to the extent that they do this, they provoke a multiple contraction of deposits. Normally, however, the Fed will seek to offset such purely seasonal variations in currency demand by increasing the reserve base.[10]

The Discount Window

Banks that are members of the Federal Reserve System may borrow from their Federal Reserve bank if their cash reserves become depleted. Collat-

---

[9] If you are interested in further examples, see *Modern Money Mechanics,* a booklet prepared by the Federal Reserve Bank of Chicago.

[10] In terms of the money-multiplier equation,

$$M = \frac{1 + c}{c + r} \cdot H$$

The case considered here is that of an increase in c, which lowers the multiplier and so provokes a decline in M. Normally, the Fed will seek to prevent this decline by engineering an offsetting increase in H.

eral must be provided in the form of either short-term government securities (normally Treasury bills) or certain "eligible" classes of commercial paper. Interest is payable on such loans at the *discount rate*. This rate is set nominally by the individual Reserve banks, subject to the approval of the Board of Governors. In practice the intiative for change comes from Washington, and alterations in the rate are generally made by all banks simultaneously.

System officials rarely refuse to lend to banks facing a real and immediate shortage of reserves. They do, however, tend to look unfavorably on banks that borrow too frequently. As a result, most banks generally prefer to avoid Federal Reserve borrowing if at all possible. Many banks never borrow from the Fed, preferring instead to rely on the federal funds market to obtain additional reserves if they are needed.

When a bank borrows from its Federal Reserve bank, the stock of high-powered money is increased. Since such borrowing occurs at the initiative of the member banks, and since loan requests are rarely refused, critics of the discount mechanism argue that it reduces the ability of the Fed to control high-powered money.[11] They conclude that the discount window should be abolished. Proponents of the discount mechanism point out that the Fed is not an automatic lender; it can and occasionally does refuse to lend. Hence banks that find their reserves depleted as a result of open-market operations by the Fed cannot automatically undo the effects of the Fed's policy simply by borrowing a corresponding amount of reserves at the discount window. Moreover, open-market operations are undertaken only at the initiative of the Fed. Hence, although other types of transactions—including member bank borrowing—lead to changes in the stock of high-powered money, these effects can always be offset by appropriate open-market sales or purchases. As a result, control over high-powered money is not impaired by the existence of the discount window.

In addition, the proponents point out that the impact of open-market sales designed to reduce the stock of high-powered money may be very uneven. Some banks may suffer substantial reserve losses and be put in real difficulties as a result of an open-market sale by the Fed. The discount mechanism provides a means by which the impact of an overall reduction in reserves on individual banks can be mitigated. As a result, the open-market manager is free to pursue his operations without regard to their effect on individual banks, since he is assured that the officials at the discount window will rescue any bank that is especially hurt by these operations. Hence, argue these economists, the discount mechanism strengthens rather than weakens the Fed's control over the stock of high-powered money.

Since the Fed will provide funds through the discount mechanism only to banks facing emergency situations, it is frequently argued that member-bank

---

[11] See Milton Friedman, *A Program for Monetary Stability* (New York: Fordham University Press, 1959), pp. 30–35.

borrowing is probably rather insensitive to its cost. This has led some economists to recommend that the discount rate be set at a certain level and never varied. However, banks have several alternative ways of dealing with temporary reserve shortages. They may sell short-term securities, call in short-term loans, borrow federal funds, or visit the discount window. It seems unlikely that a bank's decision to visit the discount window rather than to use one of these other options would be totally unaffected by its relative cost. Although visiting the discount window means that a bank must make its difficulties visible to System officials—so that it will generally be reluctant to seek official help in other than emergency situations—it will surely be more inclined to overcome this reluctance if the discount rate on Federal Reserve loans is low than if it is high.

In addition, increasing the cost of borrowing may lead banks to manage their portfolios in such a way as to reduce the likelihood of a reserve shortage. This suggests that a rise in the discount rate will lead banks to reduce their earning assets, add to their cash reserves, and attempt to increase their deposits. Each of these responses will tend to raise market interest rates and so to have a contractionary influence on the economy.

Nonetheless, it appears that the quantitative importance of these effects is quite small, although precise measurement is virtually impossible. The major impact of changes in the discount rate appears to come through their so-called *announcement effect*. An increase in the rate is usually interpreted by the financial community and the media as a signal that the Fed intends to pursue a more restrictive policy in the future. Similarly, a decrease in the rate is usually taken to herald an easier monetary policy. The mere *announcement* of a policy change apparently has an effect on the private decisions of individuals and businesses, which is independent of and operates more rapidly than the policy change itself.[12] However, critics of discount rate policy have suggested that if the Fed wishes to signal its intentions to the world, it could do so more conveniently and with less risk of being misinterpreted by simply holding a news conference.

Other Policy Instruments of the Federal Reserve

In addition to engaging in open-market sales and purchases, setting the discount rate, and managing the discount window, the Federal Reserve has several other powers affecting the operations of private financial institutions. From the point of view of monetary policy, the most important of these are the powers to set legal reserve requirements and to specify the maximum interest rates payable by banks on time and savings deposits.

The power to set legal reserve requirements for member banks was

---

[12] This statement is based on a recent study by Waud. See Roger N. Waud, "Public Interpretation of Federal Reserve Discount Rate Changes: Evidence on the 'Announcement Effect,'" *Econometrica*, Vol. XXXVIII, No. 2 (March 1970).

granted to the Board of Governors by the Banking Act of 1935. Either vault cash or Federal Reserve deposits may be used to satisfy these requirements.[13]

Potentially, this power to set reserve requirements is a very important instrument of monetary control. In terms of the traditional approach to the money-supply process, the Fed, by raising legal reserve requirements, can increase the reserve ratios that member banks maintain and so reduce the money multiplier. With an unchanged stock of high-powered money, this means a reduction in the supply of money in the hands of the public. If the public is to be willing to hold less money in their portfolios, interest rates on nonmoney assets must rise.

In terms of the new-view model, an increase in legal reserve requirements affects the banking system in two ways. First, it reduces the proportion of each dollar of deposits that a bank can use to purchase earning assets, and so effectively raises the (marginal) cost of securing any particular lending capacity. Thus the bank will reduce its lending capacity by decreasing both its earning assets and its excess reserves. Participants in the federal funds market will also reduce their lending or increase their borrowing of these funds. Second, a rise in the reserve requirement increases the deposit total needed to attain any given lending capacity. Because these two effects have conflicting implications for the bank's desired deposits, the net impact of an increase in the reserve requirement on the deposit total is uncertain in theory. In practice, however, the most likely outcome is that banks will seek to attract more deposits.

Each of these responses will tend to raise interest rates. Banks' efforts to issue more deposits will push up deposit rates, and their attempts to sell securities and reduce customer loans will depress bond prices (thus increasing bond rates) and raise loan rates. Finally, the increased demand to borrow federal funds, coupled with the decreased supply of these funds from lenders, will tend to raise the federal funds rate.

In practice, the power to vary reserve requirements has seldom been used. The authorities have argued that any feasible increase in the requirements would cause major difficulties for a large number of banks whose reserves were close to the legal limit, and thus would produce considerable disruption in the banking system. In effect, it is argued that the ability to vary these requirements is too powerful for it to be an effective instrument of monetary policy. However, this argument is valid only if changes in the requirements are large. Since 1935 the reserve requirements have never been changed by less than one-half of a percentage point. This is a large change that will affect a great many banks. But the Fed is not bound to observe such a limitation on its actions and presumably could alter requirements by as little as one-hundredth of a point if it so desired. Such marginal

---

[13] You will find the current requirements in the *Federal Reserve Bulletin*.

adjustments could be used to influence the activities of the banking system and alter the money stock, with very little disruption to individual banks.[14]

In addition to setting reserve requirements, the Board of Governors also specifies the maximum interest rates[15] that banks are permitted to pay on their deposits. Authority for this power derives from the Banking Act of 1933 and is exercised through the Board's Regulation Q. This regulation was originally intended to curb interest-rate competition for deposits that, it was believed, had led banks into making unsafe loans and hence had contributed to the collapse of the banking system during the Great Depression. However, it is now recognized that this power to alter deposit-rate ceilings provides the Fed with an additional tool of monetary policy. By lowering deposit rates, the Fed can impair banks' ability to attract lendable funds and thus force them to reduce their earning assets.

The Effects of Deposit-Rate Ceilings

In the model of banking-system behavior presented in the last chapter we assumed that the rate of interest paid on deposits was determined in a competitive market free of government regulation. We attempted to justify this assumption by arguing that banks are able to evade Regulation Q by devices such as free checking accounts, special gifts for large deposits, and the like. In practice it seems that evasion is far from complete, so that the deposit-rate ceilings imposed by the regulation have a real influence on the behavior of both individual banks and the banking system as a whole. In this section we examine the implications of these ceilings for the model of Chapter 12 and analyze how changes in the ceilings may be expected to influence interest rates and asset prices. A convenient way to proceed is to assume that the banking system is in full portfolio equilibrium and that a deposit-rate ceiling is then imposed.

Such a full equilibrium is illustrated in Figure 13.1. The equilibrium interest rates on deposits and earning assets (loans) are i_D^* and i_L^*. As in Chapter 12 the federal funds market is assumed always to be in equilibrium, so that the funds rate is suppressed. In Panel A S_0^D and D_1^D represent the supply of deposits by the banking system and the demand for deposits by the public when the loan rate is i_L^*. This market is in equilibrium at a deposit rate of i_D^*, at which rate the outstanding stock of deposits is D^*. Similarly, in Panel B, S_1^L and D_2^L represent the supply of and demand for earning assets when the deposit rate is i_D^*. Equilibrium occurs when the loan rate is i_L^* and the banks' stock of earning assets is L^*. Since the net demand for federal funds is zero in equilibrium, the demand for reserves (including both required and excess reserves) is equal to the difference between total deposits and total loans ($D^* - L^*$). This quantity of reserves will be equal to the

---

[14] Any bank that was put into serious difficulties could be assisted through the discount mechanism.

[15] The ceilings currently in force are spelled out in the *Federal Reserve Bulletin*.

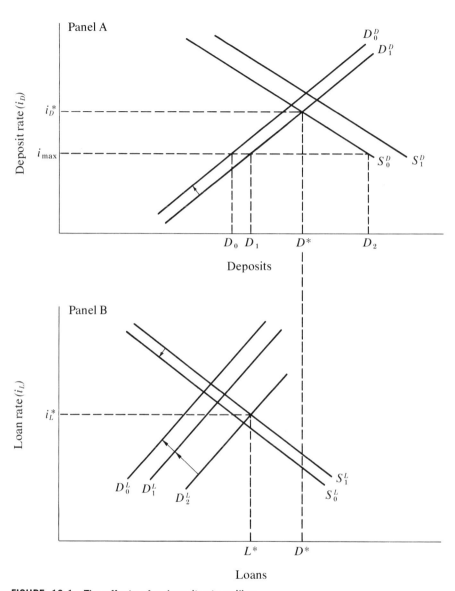

FIGURE 13.1 **The effects of a deposit-rate ceiling**

total stock of high-powered money less the quantity of currency demanded by the public at the equilibrium interest rates.

Assume now that the authorities impose a maximum[16] deposit rate of i_{max}. At this lower deposit rate, bank deposits become a less attractive asset to hold relative to other assets (including both earning assets and currency),

---

[16] Obviously such a regulation will have no effect if the ceiling is set *above* the equilibrium rate. Hence we need only consider the case in which $i_{max} < i_D^*$.

and hence wealth owners will wish to reduce their holdings. In terms of Panel A of Figure 13.1, the volume of deposits that the public is willing to hold declines[17] from D^* to D_1.

Consider now the situation of a typical bank that has been forced to lower its deposit rate and, as a result, has suffered a contraction in its deposit total and hence in its lending capcity. Unless it has large excess reserves, a bank that does not trade in the federal funds market must respond to this contraction by either selling securities or calling in customer loans. Banks that do participate in the funds market may attempt to avoid reducing their earning assets either by increased borrowing or by decreased lending of federal funds. In the aggregate, however, these efforts to reduce the impact of deposit losses on asset portfolios will have the effect of raising the interest rate on federal funds. As a result, these banks will also be induced to decrease their earning assets.[18]

Now turn to the situation of a typical wealth holder. Since the interest rate on bank deposits has declined, nonmoney assets have become more attractive to hold; that is, the public's demand for nonmoney assets has increased. Put differently, this means that the willingness of wealth holders to supply earning assets to the banking system is reduced.

The situation in the market for earning assets is shown in Panel B of Figure 13.1. The argument of the last two paragraphs implies that the effect of the deposit-rate ceiling is to shift both the supply curve and the demand curve for earning assets to the left. Because banks face reduced deposit totals and a higher federal funds rate, their demand for earning assets is lowered: D_2^L shifts to D_1^L. At the same time, since bank deposits are now a less attractive asset, wealth holders will want to hold more nonmoney assets and hence will be willing to supply less of these assets to the banks: S_1^L shifts to S_0^L.

In theory we cannot predict from this simple supply and demand model whether the rate of return on earning assets will rise or fall.[19] In practice, however, the most likely result is that this rate of return will rise. This is the case illustrated in Figure 13.1. Consider what has happened in this situation. Before the introduction of the deposit-rate ceiling, funds were flowing from the lenders in the economy to the borrowers both *directly* (lenders were purchasing securities issued by borrowers) and *indirectly* (lenders were depositing funds in banks, which were passing them on to borrowers). This

---

[17] The reduction in the deposit rate also increases the volume of deposits that banks wish to issue (from D^* to D_2). However, the market for deposits is out of equilibrium: The amount of deposits that banks wish to issue exceeds the amount that wealth owners are willing to hold.

[18] The increase in the funds rate probably will induce some banks to put their excess reserves to work in the federal funds market. To the extent that they do this, the need of the system as a whole to reduce its earning assets is lessened. However, unless the decrease in deposits is quite small or the total amount of excess reserves in the system is large, some reduction in earning assets will be necessary in the aggregate.

[19] Another way of viewing this situation is to say that whereas the demand for nonmoney assets by banks is reduced by the imposition of the ceiling, the demand by the nonbank public is increased, and hence we cannot predict whether the net demand (by the two sectors taken together) will rise or fall. Hence we cannot predict the effect on the loan rate.

indirect route was discussed in some detail in Chapter 10. In that chapter we argued that this *financial intermediation* process increases the amount of borrowing and lending that occurs, since it reduces the amount of risk that any individual borrower or lender has to bear.

The imposition of an effective deposit-rate ceiling causes a reversal of this process: it results in financial disintermediation. Rather than funds flowing from lenders to borrowers via the banking system, they will now flow directly. However, since this is a less efficient and more risky process, the amount of borrowing and lending will be reduced, and the price of a loan (the interest rate) will rise. An example of this occurred in 1966 when a reduction in deposit-rate ceilings—together with the extension of these controls to include a number of nonbank financial intermediaries such as savings and loan associations—was followed by a sharp increase in interest rates.

To the extent that interest rates on earning assets rise, bank deposits become even less attractive to wealth holders. Their willingness to hold deposits declines: In terms of Panel A of Figure 13.1 the demand curve for deposits again shifts leftward[20] from D_1^D to D_0^D, and the outstanding stock of deposits contracts even further to D_0. This contraction will lead to a further reduction in the banking system's demand for earning assets (from D_1^L to D_0^L) and hence to a further increase in interest rates. Finally the system will reach an equilibrium in the sense that given the volume of deposits the public is willing to hold at the ceiling rate, the volume of loans that banks wish to make equals the volume the public is willing to take.

This final situation is illustrated in Figure 13.2. At the new (higher) rate on nonmoney assets, i_L^{**}, the public's demand to hold deposits is represented by D^D in Panel A. At the ceiling rate the public is willing to hold D^{**} bank deposits, which is less than the quantity that banks wish to issue at that rate. Given this stock of deposits and the ceiling rate, the demand for and supply of earning assets are as illustrated in Panel B. Thus the market for non-money assets clears at an interest rate i_L^{**}.

The situation depicted in Figure 13.2 is not a true equilibrium in the sense of that term developed in Chapter 1. It is only an equilibrium subject to the legal restriction that the deposit rate cannot rise above i_{max}. An individual bank would be willing to increase its deposit total at that deposit rate. In traditional "theory of the firm" terms, the marginal revenue from an additional dollar of deposits exceeds the marginal cost of that dollar. However, this situation persists because banks are precluded from raising their deposit rates and thus cannot attract additional deposits.

You are probably familiar with some of the results of this situation. Since banks cannot compete by price, they compete by giving better, cheaper, or a wider variety of services. Thus they lengthen their hours of operation, open

---

[20] If the return on earning assets rises, banks become more anxious to increase their deposits: The supply curve in Panel A shifts to the right from S_0^D to S_1^D. However, since banks are precluded from raising their deposit rates, they cannot translate their desire for more deposits into a reality.

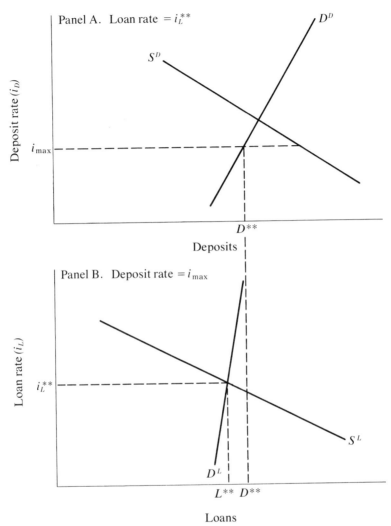

Panel A. Loan rate $= i_L^{**}$

Panel B. Deposit rate $= i_{max}$

FIGURE 13.2 Equilibrium with a deposit-rate ceiling

new branches, provide free checking accounts, supply fancy checks and glamorous banking offices, and engage in various other gimmicks. The objective of all these activities is to shift the demand curve of bank deposits to the right in order to increase the level of deposits that the public will hold at the fixed deposit rate of i_{max}. In addition, some banks attempt to evade the regulation by granting checking privileges for accounts that are legally savings accounts. Finally, many banks attempt to develop other, nonregulated, sources of funds. For example, they borrow from their overseas branches and establish holding companies that issue commercial paper. To the extent that these devices are successful, the impact of the regulation on the flows of funds through the financial system and on the interest rates on nonmoney assets is lessened. Nonetheless, despite the ingenuity of the banking community, it seems almost certain that this restriction does produce some financial disintermediation and thus leads to a misallocation of the society's resources.

In this discussion we have been concerned with the effects of the imposition of a deposit-rate ceiling where none had existed previously. However, the effects of a change in the ceiling rate are analogous. A reduction in the maximum rate, such as was undertaken in 1966 for example, is contractionary. It makes deposits less attractive to wealth owners and induces financial disintermediation. Banks are compelled to reduce their earning assets, and as a result interest rates (on loans, securities, and federal funds) tend to rise. Conversely, a rise in the ceiling rate enables banks to increase their deposit and earning asset totals by bidding up the deposit rate.[21] This increases the extent of financial intermediation and leads to a general decline in interest rates.

Open-Market Operations and the Money Stock

Earlier in this chapter we showed that the Federal Reserve System can alter the stock of high-powered money at will by the purchase or sale of government securities. On the basis of the money-multiplier approach we argued that through such open-market operations, the authorities could influence (or even control) the stock of money in the hands of the nonbank public. In this section we explore the link between open-market operations and the money stock in more detail. We will find that the analysis differs according to whether there is an effective ceiling on the deposit rate.

Suppose the Fed engages in an open-market purchase; that is, it buys securities from a member of the nonbank public. This operation increases the stock of money in the hands of wealth holders while it reduces their holdings of nonmoney assets.[22] As far as the banking system is concerned, it increases the reserve base and the deposit total by equal amounts. How will a typical bank respond to this change in its situation?

In the simple money-multiplier story of Chapter 11, this increase in deposits induces banks to add to their earning assets in order to maintain their reserve ratios unchanged.[23] This leads in turn to a cumulative deposit expansion. The new-view approach suggests that this story, while it captures some of the important factors at work in this situation, is too simple and mechanical. In particular, it fails to recognize that banks are profit-

---

[21] This presumes that the imposed ceiling was previously an effective restriction on banks' behavior, so that when this constraint is relaxed, they are willing to raise their deposit rates.

[22] To induce wealth holders to make this substitution security prices must rise and interest rates fall.

[23] See Chapter 11, pp. 253–256 where we assumed that the bank increased its loans by an amount sufficient to maintain a reserve ratio of one-fifth.

making institutions whose portfolio choices are based not on the desire to maintain certain (essentially arbitrary) asset ratios, but rather on the rates of return prevailing in the various asset markets in which they operate.

Assume first that there is an effective ceiling on the deposit rate. In this case the average bank would obtain larger profits if it could add to its deposit total and acquire more earning assets. The reason it cannot do this is not that members of the public are unwilling to borrow from or sell securities to it. Rather, it is because its deposit customers are unwilling to hold more deposits at the prevailing deposit rate and because, as a result of the rate ceiling, it cannot increase its deposit total by offering a higher deposit rate.[24]

When the Federal Reserve purchases securities, the banking system receives an addition to its deposits. By driving up security prices the Fed induces the public to hold more of its wealth in the form of bank deposits and less in the form of securities. Thus the average bank finds that its deposits are increased. Since the bank's inability to attract additional deposits was previously an effective constraint on its activities, the relaxation of this constraint will induce the average bank to add to its earning assets. It will increase its customer loans and/or purchase securities not simply because it wishes to maintain some arbitrary reserve ratio, but rather because this is the most profitable action to take.[25]

Banks that participate in the federal funds market may also use this increase in their deposits to increase their lending or reduce their borrowing in that market. As a result, the federal funds rate will fall, and this will act as a further inducement to banks to add to their earning assets (loans and securities). In fact, since open-market operations are conducted in New York and most large New York banks are net borrowers of funds, this impact on the funds rate is the most immediate effect of an open-market

---

[24] Nor can it increase its deposits by lowering its loan rate. If a bank reduces its loan rate (or bids up the price of securities), it can induce its customers to sell earning assets to it in exchange for bank deposits; that is, it can persuade the public to increase its deposit-wealth ratio. In most cases, however, the loan customer (or security seller) will use his new deposit to make a payment to a customer of another bank and, as a result, this deposit will not remain with the bank that made the loan. Thus an individual bank cannot increase its deposit total by lowering its loan rate, even though such a lowering would increase the deposits of the banking system as a whole.

If the banking system operated as a monopoly it could expand total deposits by purchasing earning assets and driving their interest rates down. At lower rates of return on nonmoney assets the public would be willing to hold more deposits and less nonmoney, and thus the deposit total of the system could be increased. However, in a system consisting of thousands of competing banks, there is no mechanism by which such an exchange of deposits for earning assets can be achieved, since it is not possible for any single bank to negotiate such a transaction.

[25] We may put this point in "theory of the firm" terms as follows. The marginal cost of a dollar's worth of deposits is i_D. Since a proportion k of this dollar must be allocated to legal reserves, the marginal revenue obtained is $(1 - k)i_L$. The limitation on the deposit rate implies that

$$i_D < (1 - k)i_L$$

so that if the bank is able to increase its deposit total, it will find it profitable to do so.

operation. This change in the funds rate serves as a key link through which the effects of open-market operations—which initially affect only the reserves and deposits of a few New York banks—spread out over the banking system as a whole.[26] In fact, the Fed has in recent years used the funds rate as an indicator of the impact of its operations on the banking system.

As banks add to their earning assets interest rates drop. Indeed, it is this reduction in rates that induces the public to hold more money and to supply nonmoney assets to the banking system. This process is analogous to the reduction in interest rates that occurs in an economy with no banking system when the authorities purchase securities with new money.[27] The principal difference is that in the latter case, the decision by the authorities to purchase securities is a policy decision, whereas in the former case it is the desire to maximize their profits which induces banks to acquire earning assets.

Several factors operate to bring the cumulative expansion process to a halt. First, as bank deposits increase, the demand for currency will rise. Thus for every dollar of earning assets that banks acquire, total deposits increase by less than a dollar. Put differently, although the initial increase in the high-powered money stock accrues entirely in the form of bank reserves, part of this increase will shift into currency as bank deposits rise.[28] Second, each bank must hold more legal reserves as its deposit total increases, and hence the addition to its lending capacity is less than the addition to its deposits. For both of these reasons[29] the addition to the system's lending capacity at each stage is less than the amount of new loans made at the preceding stage.

In addition to these factors stressed by the traditional model of bank behavior, the new view draws attention to another factor, namely, the decline in the rate of return on earning assets that accompanies the cumulative expansion process. At each round of the process, banks add to their holdings of earning assets. If banks buy securities, their prices will be driven up and their rates of return, down. Similarly, in order to make more loans banks must offer more attractive terms; hence the loan rate will tend to decline. In addition, as security prices rise and loan rates fall, banks will find federal funds lending increasingly attractive; hence the federal funds rate will also tend to decline as the number of borrowing banks falls and the number of lending banks rises.

---

[26] It is not the only link. The Fed purchases securities from New York bond dealers so that the initial impact is on the reserves and deposits of the New York banks. However, the dealers normally will rebuild their portfolios of securities by making purchases all over the country. These purchases produce shifts of reserves from the New York banks to those outside New York.

[27] See Chapter 5, pp. 76–78.

[28] However, if the Fed treats the reserve base as its target variable, it will offset this shift by further open-market purchases.

[29] These were, of course, the factors we stressed in our original description of the deposit-creation process in Chapter 11.

As the expansion process continues, this decline in the interest rates on (or rise in the prices of) earning assets makes the public willing to hold more money and fewer nonmoney assets. On the other hand, it makes banks less willing to expand their portfolios of earning assets. The process finally ceases when the public and the banks are again content with their asset portfolios at the prevailing interest rates.

When the expansion comes to a halt, the stock of money may, of course, be represented as some multiple of the new (higher) stock of high-powered money:

$$M = \frac{1 + C/D}{C/D + R/D} \cdot H$$

However, the new view stresses that the money multiplier is not a constant. The public is willing to hold more money only if the interest rate on nonmoney assets is reduced but this reduction also lowers the proportion of its total lending capacity that a typical bank will want to hold in the form of earning assets. Thus the decline in the interest rate on earning assets causes the desired reserve ratio to rise and so lowers the multiplier. In the new equilibrium interest rates must have fallen sufficiently for both the banks and the public to be satisfied with their new situations. At this new equilibrium the multiplier is determined by the prevailing interest rates.

The preceding argument is illustrated graphically in Figure 13.3. As in previous diagrams, Panel A represents the situation in the deposit market, and Panel B represents the market for earning assets. As usual, the funds market is suppressed.

Initially the earning asset rate is $i_L{}^2$; at this rate the supply of and demand for earning assets are equal. However, the market for deposits is out of equilibrium; at the ceiling rate, i_{max}, wealth holders are willing to hold only D_0 deposits, which is less than the quantity that banks wish to issue.

In order to induce members of the public to sell earning assets (securities) in exchange for deposits, the Fed's Open Market Manager must bid security prices up and interest rates down. It is this change in the interest rate that persuades wealth owners to hold more deposits and fewer securities. In terms of Figure 13.3 the demand-for-deposits curve shifts to the right from D_0^p to D_1^p. At the ceiling rate the volume of deposits that the public is willing to hold increases from D_0 to D_1.[30]

This increased stock of deposits leads banks to add to their earning assets.[31] In Panel B the demand curve for earning assets shifts[32] to the right

---

[30] Suppose the Fed bought $100-worth of bonds. This would increase the public's money holding by the same amount. If the currency-deposit ratio is c, the public's holding of deposits would rise by $100/(1 + c)$. This quantity is represented by the distance $D_0 D_1$ in the figure.

[31] Banks will be induced to add to their earning assets not only by the increase in their deposits but also by the decline in the federal funds rate.

[32] This shift also includes the increased demand for nonmoney assets by the Fed, which began the process.

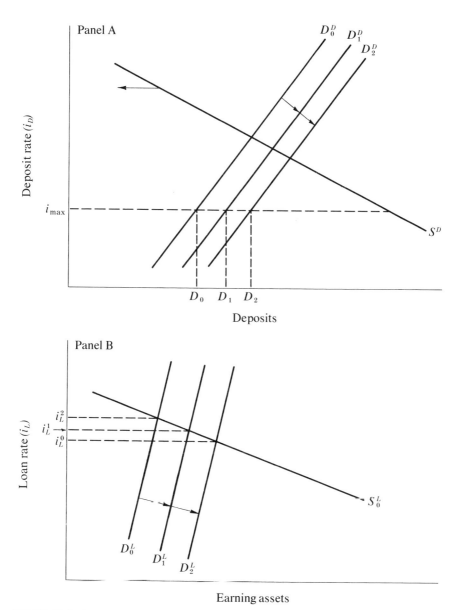

FIGURE 13.3 **The effects of an open-market purchase**

from D_0^L to D_1^L. As a result, the interest rates on these assets decline from i_L^2 to i_L^1. However, this decrease in interest rates induces wealth owners to further increase their deposit holdings, which in turn enables the banks to add to their earning assets a second time. In terms of the figure the public's demand curve for deposits again shifts to the right,[33] thus provoking a second rightward shift in the banks' demand curve for nonmoney assets.

The process finally comes to a halt when the public is no longer willing to add to its deposit holdings at the ceiling rate.[34] In the figure, the new equilibrium is reached when the demand curve for deposits is D_2^D, so that the stock of deposits is D_2. Given this stock, the banks' demand for earning assets is D_2^L, and the market for those assets clears at an interest rate i_L^0.

We now turn to the case in which there is no effective ceiling on the deposit rate either because Regulation Q (and the accompanying ban on the payment of interest on demand deposits) is abolished or evaded, or because the regulatory maximum is above the rate at which the supply of and demand for deposits are equal.[35] Again assume that the system is initially in equilibrium when the authorities undertake their open-market purchase of bonds.

As in the previous case, this purchase adds to the reserves and deposits of the average bank. In that case the marginal cost of an extra dollar of deposits was less than the marginal revenue that could be derived from it. Hence the bank responded to an increase in its deposit total by adding to its earning assets to obtain that extra revenue, and as a result it obtained an increase in its profits. However, in the present case the bank is initially in full equilibrium, so that marginal cost and marginal revenue are equal. This implies that the bank does not obtain higher profits when its deposit and earning asset totals rise.

In these circumstances many banks will respond to the increase in their deposits brought about by the open-market purchase by lowering their deposit rates (in order to drive those unwanted deposits away) rather than by adding to their earning assets. Others will lend their additional resources in the federal funds market or use them to replace funds borrowing. As a result of these responses, the initial impact of an open-market purchase will be to decrease interest rates on deposits and federal funds.

These interest-rate changes will in turn affect both the supply of and the demand for banks' earning assets. First, the decline in the deposit rate will make deposits a less attractive asset and so will increase the demand by wealth owners to hold nonmoney assets. Hence the supply of these assets to the banking system will decline. Second, the decrease in both i_D and i_F will make banks more willing to add to their earning assets. Although banks

---

[33] The decline in the earning asset rate also reduces the willingness of banks to supply deposits: It causes S^D to shift to the left. However, as long as the rate ceiling remains effective, the quantity of deposits that banks wish to issue exceeds the quantity that the public wishes to hold; hence it is the latter which determines the outstanding stock.

[34] This assumes that the ceiling remains effective. It is possible that the return on earning assets may decline sufficiently that the banks no longer wish to add to their deposits at the ceiling rate. In this case the deposit rate will fall below the ceiling level. This is the case where there is no effective deposit-rate ceiling.

[35] An intermediate case is that in which the ceiling is effective when the open-market operation is undertaken, but becomes ineffective as the expansion process proceeds, so that in the final equilibrium the deposit rate is below the ceiling. This was the case mentioned in the preceding footnote.

were generally unwilling to increase their loans and security holdings at the original set of interest rates, they may be more willing to do so when the cost of deposits (i_D) or the yield on federal funds (i_F) declines. However, the combination of a reduced supply of earning assets by the public and an increased demand for them by the banks will tend to raise bond prices (decrease bond rates) and lower loan rates. But this decline in i_L will itself further increase the public's demand for deposits and decrease the banks' willingness to issue them, so that a second round of deposit-rate reductions will occur.

The implication of this discussion is that the primary effect of the open-market purchase is to produce a cumulative contraction in interest rates. Each reduction in the deposit rate increases the banks' demand for earning assets while it decreases the public's willingness to supply them; hence it tends to cause interest rates on those earning assets to decline also. Conversely, each decline in the earning-asset rate reduces the banks' willingness to issue deposits while it increases the public's desire to hold them; hence it tends to cause deposit rates to decline.

However, the decline in interest rates also increases the public's demands for currency and the banks' demand for reserves. Hence the contraction process comes to a halt when interest rates have declined sufficiently for the additional high-powered money created by the open-market purchase to be absorbed into either the currency holdings of the public or the reserves of the banking system.

Once again the money stock in the new equilibrium may be represented by the money-multiplier expression

$$M = \frac{1 + C/D}{C/D + R/D} \cdot H$$

However, the decline in the rate of return on earning assets will cause banks to want to hold a larger reserve ratio. At the same time the reduction in the deposit rate makes the public want to hold more of its money in the form of currency. Hence in the new equilibrium both R/D and C/D will be larger, and the multiplier will be lower. Theoretically it is possible[36] that in the new equilibrium there will be no increase (or even a decrease) in the stock of money; the increase in the monetary base is offset by a reduction in the money multiplier. From the point of view of the public, this means that although the decline in the earning asset rate makes the public willing to hold more money, the simultaneous decline in the deposit rate has the opposite effect. From the point of view of the banks, the decline in the deposit rate makes them willing to supply more deposits, but the lower yield on their assets works in the opposite direction.

---

[36] Since we are discussing a hypothetical economy—one in which deposit rates are free to vary with no government intervention—there are no data against which this theoretical possibility may be tested.

Again the situation may be illustrated graphically, as shown in Figure 13.4. The system is initially in full equilibrium with deposit supply equal to deposit demand when the rate is i_D^1. The open-market operation lowers the earning asset rate and shifts the demand curve for deposits to the right. As a result, the deposit rate begins to decline. However, this decline in the deposit rate leads both the banks and the public to want to add to their stocks of nonmoney assets, which pushes the prices of these assets upward and their rates of return downward. This leads in turn to a second round of reductions in deposit rates.

Finally, equilibrium is restored at new lower interest rates on both deposits and nonmoney assets. The decline in the loan rate has caused the demand-for-deposits curve to shift to the right and the supply curve to shift to the left. The figure illustrates the special case in which the stock of deposits is, on balance, unchanged.[37] Clearly, however, the question of whether deposits (and the stock of money) will actually increase or decrease depends on the shapes of the supply and demand curves and on the extent to which they shift in response to changes in the earning-asset rate.

Several interesting conclusions emerge from the analysis of this section. First, the traditional argument that an increase in the stock of high-powered money leads inevitably to a multiple expansion of the money stock depends

---

[37] Since the currency-deposit ratio has increased, this implies that the money stock has risen somewhat.

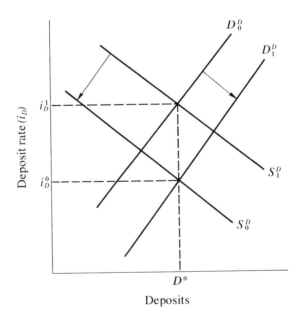

FIGURE 13.4 Open-market operations in the absence of deposit-rate maxima

Note: This diagram illustrates the special case in which the deposit total does not change. Other outcomes are clearly possible.

heavily on the existence of an effective ceiling on the deposit rate. In the absence of such a ceiling an open-market purchase by the authorities may have little effect on the money stock.

In the case of demand deposits, Regulation Q specifies a zero interest rate. However, many banks provide services to their customers below cost and thus, in effect, pay interest on demand deposits. By increasing the charge for these services banks can reduce this implicit interest. Nonetheless, they have relatively little room to maneuver, and hence the traditional analysis is likely to be reasonably close to the true situation. In the case of time deposits the situation is quite different. If interest rates on earning assets are low, so that the interest-rate ceiling is not an effective constraint, a situation in which an expansive open-market policy leads to a reduction in the time deposit rate rather than to an increase in deposit totals would seem quite possible.

However, whether or not an open-market purchase leads to an increase in the money stock, the conclusion that such a policy action is expansionary remains unimpaired. When the deposit-rate ceiling is effective, an increase in bank reserves leads to an increase in the money stock. In order to induce the public to hold the increased stock of money, the rates of return on competing assets (loans, securities, tangible assets) must decline and their prices rise. This rise in asset prices will lead to an increase in spending and hence in output and/or prices. When the ceiling is ineffective, interest rates on deposits, as well as those on other assets, will decline. As a result of this decline in the deposit rate, the public's holdings of money may not increase. However, the general reduction in interest rates will be expansionary regardless of whether the money stock increases.

References

The Federal Reserve System: Purposes and Functions. Board of Governors of the Federal Reserve System, Washington, D. C.: 1974. A useful description of the institutional arrangements of the Fed and of the tools of monetary policy.

Tobin, James. ''Commercial Banks as Creators of 'Money,' '' *Banking and Monetary Studies,* ed. Deane Carson. Homewood, Illinois: Richard D. Irwin, Inc., 1963.

Tobin, James. ''A General Equilibrium Approach to Monetary Theory.'' *Journal of Money, Credit and Banking,* Vol. I (February 1969).

Questions for Classroom Discussion

1. Use the framework of Figure 13.4 to analyze the effect of an increase in the discount rate.
2. What is meant by financial disintermediation? Why does it occur when the maximum interest rate allowable on bank deposits is reduced?
3. In what ways would the conduct of monetary policy differ if banks were permitted to pay interest on checking accounts and Regulation Q were abolished?

4. In some circumstances an open-market operation to increase bank reserves leads to an addition to excess reserves with no expansion in bank lending or securities holding. This situation is described by remarks such as, "You can't push on a string" and, "You can lead a horse to water, but you can't make him drink." Analyze this possibility in terms of the framework developed in this chapter and Chapter 12.

5. Use the model developed in the appendix to Chapter 12 to find the effects of an open-market operation on the loan rate and deposit rate.

Part Five

Prices, Output, and Employment

Up to this point we have assumed an economy that was operating at less than full employment. We supposed that there was a large pool of idle labor and capital that could be brought into use rapidly if required. Hence, if the demand for goods and services had risen, aggregate output would have responded with no increase in prices. Thus the average level of prices (measured, for example, by the implicit price deflator) could be treated as a constant: Changes in the gross national product involved changes in the output dimension, but no changes in the price dimension.

Although this assumption simplified the discussion, it meant that our analysis and results were seriously incomplete. We were unable to answer such important questions as how the division of changes in the GNP between the output and price dimensions is determined, and what the relation is between the amount of unemployment in the economy and the levels of wages and prices. The important subject of inflation obviously could not be treated in a model that assumed constant prices.

In this part of the book we seek to fill this gap. We begin by considering how the analytical apparatus developed in earlier chapters must be modified if the level and the rate of change of prices* are allowed to vary. Then in Chapter 15 we consider the labor market and analyze the reactions of employers and employees to changes in wages and prices. Chapter 16 brings these results together into a complete model to explain prices, wages, employment, and output. In that chapter we are particularly interested in explaining how unemployment and inflation may coexist.

---

* It is important to distinguish between the *level* of prices and the *rate of change* of prices. When we discuss price level, we are concerned with whether prices are high or low. Discussions of the rate of change of prices are concerned with whether prices are rising or falling. You should take care not to confuse high with rising nor low with falling. It is quite possible, for example, to imagine two situations in which the level of prices is the same, but the rate of change of prices is different. Conversely, the rate of change of prices may be the same in two situations, but in one situation prices are high and in the other they are low.

Prices and Aggregate Demand

14

In this chapter we examine the implications for the simple model developed in Part 2 of dropping the assumption that commodity prices are fixed. We first consider the impact of changes both in the *level* and in the *rate of change*[1] of prices on the *IS* and *LM* curves. The results of this analysis are then used to show how such changes will affect the *IS–LM* equilibrium. The impact of price changes on the three-asset model of Chapter 6 is analyzed in the appendix.

Prices, Asset Markets, and the *LM* Curve

Monetary economists generally agree that the demand for money is a demand for *real balances*. Wealth holders are concerned not with the nominal number of dollars, guilders, or yen that they hold, but with their *purchasing power* over goods and services. Moreover, the demand for these real balances is related to the real values of wealth holders' wealth and income rather than to their nominal values. Thus if tangible capital and bonds are alternative assets in which individuals may hold their wealth, the demand for real money balances may be written

$$\frac{M^D}{p} = M[i_B, i_K, Y/p, W/p] \qquad (14.1)$$

where p represents the general level of prices, so that Y/p and W/p are real income and real wealth, respectively, and M^D/p is the demand for dollars of constant purchasing power. Alternatively, we may write the nominal demand for money as

$$M^D = p \cdot M[i_B, i_K, Y/p, W/p] \qquad (14.2)$$

This formulation implies that if the prices of all goods and services double with no change either in the rates of return, i_K and i_B, or in the levels of real income and real wealth, Y/p and W/p, the nominal demand for money will also double. In other words, if the purchasing power of a dollar bill is halved, a wealth holder with the same real income and the same amount of real wealth will want to hold twice as many dollar bills as before.

---

[1] We will often refer to the rate of change of prices as the *rate of inflation*. However, our use of the word *inflation* does not mean that the argument applies only to situations in which prices are rising. The rate of inflation may be negative, in which case prices are falling.

In general, however, if the price level changes, the real value of wealth will not remain constant, but will decline.[2] This is because the stock of wealth includes financial assets whose value is fixed in nominal terms. When general prices rise, the real value of these financial assets and hence of total wealth will fall.

Total wealth consists of tangible capital, (high-powered) money,[3] and government bonds in the hands of the public and the banking system. Thus the real value of wealth may be written

$$W/p = q_K K/p + H/p + q_B B/p$$

For simplicity, let us ignore expected capital gains on nonmoney assets. Then the rates of return on these assets are

$$i_K = r_K/q_K$$
$$i_B = c_B/q_B$$

where r_K and c_B represent the rental on capital and the coupon on securities, respectively.

Suppose that the general level of commodity prices p increases. This means in particular that r_K, the rental of capital, rises. If the rate of return on capital i_K is to remain unchanged,[4] the price of capital goods must increase in the same proportion. As a result, the nominal value of the capital stock rises, but its real value $q_K K/p$ remains unchanged because both p and q_K increase in the same proportion.

The coupon on bonds, unlike the rental on capital, is fixed in nominal terms and therefore does not change when there is an increase in commodity prices. This means that at any given rate of return on bonds[5] the price of bonds does not change when commodity prices rise. As a result, the real value of the bond stock $q_B B/p$ will fall when p increases. The same conclusion holds for the stock of high-powered money. Since that stock is fixed in nominal terms, its real value H/p declines when the price level increases.

The conclusion of this discussion is that the real value of wealth will fall[6]

---

[2] However, real *income* will not be directly affected by a price change, at least in the aggregate. Nominal GNP, Y, has a price and a quantity dimension. Hence real GNP may be written

$$Y/p = \frac{pQ}{p} = Q$$

and thus does not change when prices change.

[3] In an economy without a banking system, money and high-powered money are the same. The arguments of this chapter do not depend on the presence or absence of a banking system. If you wish to examine an economy with no banks, you should simply substitute the symbol M for the symbol H.

[4] The real value of wealth depends on both p and the rates of return on nonmoney assets. To isolate the effects of p, it is necessary to hold i_K and i_B constant. This does not, of course, imply that i_K and i_B will, in fact, remain constant.

[5] See footnote 4.

[6] At given values of i_B and i_K. As shown below, a rise in commodity prices will tend to cause interest rates to rise. This effect, which is separate and distinct from the one being discussed here, will also tend to lower the value of aggregate wealth.

when commodity prices rise.[7] We argued earlier that with real wealth unchanged, a rise in commodity prices will lead to an equal proportionate rise in the nominal demand for money. Since it now appears that real wealth will actually fall, the rise in the nominal demand for money will be less than proportionate to the rise in prices.[8]

The supply of money is not necessarily linked to the price level. In an economy with no banks the government controls the money stock and will not necessarily change it when the level of prices varies. In an economy with a banking system the authorities control the stock of high-powered money, but do not necessarily change it when prices rise or fall. In addition, at any given set of interest rates there is no particular reason to expect either that the public will want to hold more (or less) of its money in the form of currency, or that the banks will want to hold more (or less) reserves relative to deposits when commodity prices are high than when they are low. Hence the money multiplier[9] is also independent of the price level. As a result, in an economy with a banking system there is again no reason to expect the nominal stock of money to change when the commodity price level changes.

This discussion leads to the conclusion that a rise in the general level of prices will not affect the nominal supply of money, but will cause the nominal demand to increase. Hence wealth holders will seek to reduce their holdings of nonmoney assets to increase their money stocks. Since the available supplies of assets are fixed, this attempt by wealth holders to alter the composition of their portfolios will drive up interest rates[10] until wealth owners are again willing to hold the existing asset stocks.

If we adopt the assumption of Chapter 4 that wealth holders regard bonds and capital as perfect substitutes—so that their rates of return are always equal—we may illustrate this result in terms of a shift in the *LM* curve. For simplicity, we again assume that the shares of wealth held in money and nonmoney do not depend on total wealth. Thus the demand for real balances may be written

$$\frac{M^D}{p} = \textbf{\textit{m}}[i, Y/p] \frac{W}{p} \qquad (14.2)$$

where it is understood that Y/p does not change[11] when p changes, and where i represents the (common) rate of return on both nonmoney assets. Since this equation may also be written as

---

[7] The extent of this decline will depend on the relative shares of tangible and financial assets in total wealth. In the United States it has been estimated that government debt comprises approximately one-seventh of the public's wealth. This implies that if commodity prices were to double, real wealth would fall by roughly 7 percent.

[8] Alternatively, we may say that because of the reduction in real wealth, the real demand for money will decline slightly when commodity prices rise.

[9] See Chapter 11, pp. 256–259 for a discussion of the money multiplier.

[10] As we show in the appendix, this statement is not quite accurate since we cannot prove unambiguously that the interest rate on bonds will rise. However, if bonds and capital are reasonably close substitutes, both i_B and i_K will rise.

[11] See footnote 2.

$$\frac{M^D}{W} = m[i, Y/p] \tag{14.3}$$

we note that the desired money-wealth ratio depends only on the interest rate and on real income. It is independent of both real and nominal wealth.

The actual money-wealth ratio may be written

$$\frac{M}{W} = \frac{M}{H + q_B B + q_K K} \tag{14.4}$$

Earlier in this section we saw that if commodity prices rise with no change in rates of return, $q_K K$ must rise in the same proportion but M, $q_B B$, and H remain unchanged. Hence the actual money-wealth ratio associated with any given value of i declines when there is a rise in commodity prices.[12]

The condition for equilibrium in the asset markets is that the actual money-wealth ratio equal the desired ratio:

$$\frac{M}{H + q_B B + q_K K} = m[i, Y/p] \tag{14.5}$$

A rise in the price level causes the left side of this equality to fall; hence the right side must also fall if equilibrium is to be maintained. At any value of real income Y/p, the interest rate must rise. Such a rise implies an upward shift in the *LM* curve.

We may illustrate this argument with the diagram introduced in Chapter 4. In Figure 14.1 the curve labeled $m(i, Y/p)$ represents the desired money-wealth ratio, while $M(p_0)$ represents the actual ratio when the price level is p_0. Asset equilibrium requires that the interest rate be i_0. A rise in prices reduces the money-wealth ratio associated with any given interest rate, and the curve $M(p_0)$ shifts leftward to $M(p_1)$. As a result, the interest rate rises from i_0 to i_1, which implies an upward shift in the *LM* curve.

What happens in this case is that wealth holders find that their total nominal wealth has increased and that the entire increase has come in the form of nonmoney (specifically, in the form of a rise in the value of their

---

[12] If commodity prices rise, capital rentals also rise. Hence the prices of capital goods must increase if bonds and capital are to remain equally attractive to wealth holders. The rise in capital-good prices implies that nominal wealth is higher and hence the actual ratio of money to wealth is lower.

We may show this argument algebraically as follows. Since bonds and capital yield the same rate of return,

$$i = i_K = r_K/q_K$$

and

$$i = i_B = c_B/q_B$$

Hence Eq. (14.4) may be rewritten as

$$\frac{M}{W} = \frac{M}{H + c_B B/i + r_K K/i}$$

An increase in the price level raises r_K in the same proportion and hence lowers this ratio.

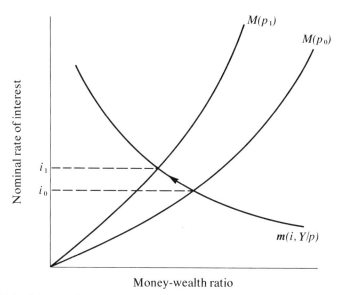

FIGURE 14.1 Prices and the demand for money

holdings of capital assets). As a result, they find that the proportion of money in their portfolios has decreased. Since there has been no change in their real incomes or in the rates of return on nonmoney assets, wealth owners will want to sell nonmoney assets (specifically capital) to restore the money-wealth ratio to its previous level. Their attempts to do this drive the yields on nonmoney assets upward until they are again content with the composition of their portfolios. This rise in yields corresponds to an upward shift in the *LM* curve.

Asset Markets, Inflation, and the *LM* Curve

The preceding argument was concerned with the effects of a change in the price *level* on the demands for assets. Now we consider the effects of a change in the *rate of change* of prices. Specifically, we will ask how the demands for assets are altered if commodity prices are rising rather than constant. We describe such a change as an increase in the rate of inflation. If you master this case, you should have no difficulty analyzing other changes in the rate of change of prices, such as an increase in the rate of deflation.

When commodity prices are rising (or falling), we must draw a distinction between the real rate of return on an asset and the nominal rate of return. If a wealth owner puts $100 into a savings account for one year and receives an interest payment of $5, the nominal rate of interest is 5 percent. However, if the prices of the commodities he buys rise by 3 percent, he would require a nominal return of 3 percent just to stay even in terms of purchasing power. Hence, the real return on his 5-percent savings account is only 2 percent.[13]

Thus the real rate of return on an asset is equal to the nominal return minus the rate of inflation. If the nominal rates of return on money, bonds, and capital are i_M', i_B', and i_K', the real rates may be written

$$i_M = i_M' - \Delta p/p$$

$$i_B = i_B' - \Delta p/p$$

$$i_K = i_K' - \Delta p/p$$

where $\Delta p/p$ represents the proportionate rate of change in commodity prices.

It seems reasonable to assume that wealth holders are more concerned with the real rates of return on their assets than with the nominal rates. After all, most investors ultimately expect to spend the returns yielded by their asset portfolios on goods and services and hence are interested in the real value of those returns rather than in their nominal value. On the other hand, many economists seem to believe that in making decisions about how to distribute their wealth among the various available assets, investors are concerned only with interest-rate *differentials* rather than with the absolute levels of rates. This hypothesis implies that Eq. (14.1) should be written

$$M^D/p = M(i_K - i_M, i_B - i_M, Y/p, W/p)$$

In this case if all rates of return—including that on money—fall by three percentage points, with no change in the levels of real income or wealth, investors will want to hold the same portfolios of assets as before. This assumption implies that the demands for assets may be viewed as depending either on the real rates of return or on the nominal rates. This is because the differential between any pair of real rates is the same as that between the same pair of nominal rates.

Several writers conclude from this that a change in the rate of inflation will have no effect on the set of nominal interest rates at which asset markets reach equilibrium.[14] If asset markets can reach equilibrium at a certain set of nominal interest rates when there is no inflation, then, it is argued, they can reach the same equilibrium at the same set of interest rates when inflation is proceeding. Thus a change in the rate of inflation has no effect on the *LM* curve when it is drawn in terms of the nominal interest rate.[15] The explanation of this result is that although a change in the rate of inflation alters the real rates of return associated with any given set of nominal rates,

---

[13] The argument of this section assumes that wealth holders recognize that inflation is proceeding. That is, it is concerned with anticipated rather than unanticipated changes in prices.

[14] See, for example, Martin J. Bailey, *National Income and the Price Level*, 2nd ed. (New York: McGraw Hill, 1971), pp. 74–75.

[15] This does not, of course, mean that inflation does not affect interest rates. However, it does mean that its effect operates through the *IS* curve rather than the *LM* curve. See Bailey, *National Income and the Price Level*, pp. 74–75.

all real rates are affected equally, and hence differentials do not change. As a result, investors have no incentive to rearrange their portfolios, and hence asset-market equilibria do not change.[16]

However, even if we accept that asset demands depend only on interest-rate differentials, this conclusion is correct only if inflation has no effects on the nominal rates of return that are yielded by the various assets. If inflation affects the nominal returns on some assets but not those on others, then all assets will not be equally affected, investors will be induced to rearrange their portfolios, and the resulting market transactions will produce changes in relative interest rates: The *LM* curve will shift.

The coupons on money and bonds are both fixed in nominal terms and hence do not change when there is a change in the rate of inflation. However, the return on capital includes not only the rental but also a capital gain or loss. Specifically, the nominal rate of return on capital is given by

$$i'_{K\,t+1} = R_{t+1}/q_{K\,t} = \frac{r_{K\,t+1}}{q_{K\,t}} + \frac{q_{K\,t+1} - q_{K\,t}}{q_{K\,t}} - \frac{\delta q_{K\,t+1}}{q_{K\,t}} \tag{14.6}$$

In this equation R_{t+1} represents the nominal return from holding a unit of capital over the period from date t to date $t + 1$, $r_{K\,t+1}$ is the rental received over this period, and δ is the depreciation rate. If, for algebraic simplicity, we assume that there is no depreciation, we can rewrite this equation as

$$i'_K = \frac{r_K}{q_K} + \frac{\Delta q_K}{q_K} = \frac{r_K}{q_K} + \lambda \tag{14.7}$$

where λ represents the expected rate of change in the price of capital goods. Thus an increase in the rate of inflation increases the nominal rate of return on capital. As a result, wealth holders will wish to rearrange their portfolios in order to hold more capital and less money and bonds. Hence the prices of capital goods will rise, and those of bonds will fall.[17]

For the special case in which bonds and capital are perfect substitutes, we may analyze the effect of an increase in the rate of inflation on the *LM* curve. In this case the nominal rates of return on bonds and capital are equal

---

[16] Frequently, writers do not point out that they are assuming that the demand for assets depends only on interest rate differentials. The problem here is that in the United States, the nominal interest rate on money is zero and hence the level of any other rate is always equal to the *differential* between that rate and the rate on money. Bailey, for example, states that the demand for money depends on the *sacrifice* the investor makes when he holds cash rather than earning assets. This clearly implies that it is the differential that matters. On the other hand, he goes on to say that this means that the demand for money depends on the absolute level of the nominal interest rate on earning assets. But this will be true only in the special case in which the nominal return on money is zero.

[17] Strictly speaking this conclusion holds only for the case in which bonds and capital are perfect substitutes. In the more general case the effect on q_B is uncertain. The reason for this is that the rise in capital-goods prices produces an increase in the nominal value of wealth. This wealth effect increases the demand for bonds at the same time as the increased yield on capital causes a reduction in that demand. Hence we cannot predict whether the nominal demand for bonds will rise or fall or whether bond prices will increase or decrease.

$$i_B' = i_K' = i'$$

Thus the prices of these assets are

$$q_K = (r_K + \lambda q_K)/i'$$
$$q_B = c_B/i'$$

so that total wealth may be written

$$W = H + \frac{(r_K + \lambda q_K)K}{i'} + \frac{c_B B}{i'} \qquad (14.8)$$

We see from this expression that at any given nominal interest rate an increase in the rate of inflation λ produces a rise in nominal wealth and thus a decline in the money-wealth ratio. Hence wealth holders will want to shift out of nonmoney and into money, and since the existing stocks of assets are fixed, these attempts by wealth holders to rearrange their portfolios will cause nominal interest rates to rise. This is illustrated in Figure 14.2. In that figure OM represents the actual money-wealth ratio when there is no inflation. An increase in the rate of inflation reduces this ratio at any given interest rate: OM shifts left to OM'. As a result, the nominal interest rate increases from i_0' to i_1'. This increase implies an upward shift in the LM curve.

We can show, however, that this rise in the nominal rate of interest will be

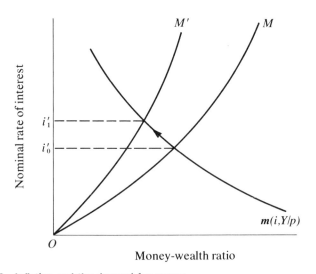

FIGURE 14.2 Inflation and the demand for money
At any given nominal rate of interest, an increase in the rate of inflation implies an increase in total wealth and hence a decline in the money-wealth ratio. However, the resulting rise in the interest rate is less than the increase in the inflation rate: $i_1' - i_0' < \lambda$ and hence the real interest rate falls.

less than the increase in the rate of inflation.[18] Therefore, although the *LM* curve shifts upward, this shift is less than the rise in the inflation rate.[19]

What happens in this case is that the increase in the rate of inflation increases the nominal return on capital. At any given set of nominal interest rates wealth holders experience an increase in the nominal value of their wealth: specifically, in the value of their holdings of tangible capital. Since their money holdings remain unchanged, the proportion of their portfolios held in the form of money declines, and they will want to move out of nonmoney into money. In attempting to do this, they drive up the nominal yields on nonmoney until they are again willing to hold the existing money stock.

Prices, the Demand for Commodities, and the *IS* Curve

We have analyzed the effects of price changes on the demands for stocks of assets. Now we turn to their effects on the demands for flows of goods and services. We wish to analyze the effects of prices on the *IS* curve in terms of the simple model of Part 2.

We consider first the effects of changes in the level of prices on the demand for investment. In Chapter 8 we suggested[20] that the demand to hold tangible capital may be written[21]

$$q_K K^D = k(i_K, i_B)W \tag{14.9}$$

where the rate of return to capital, i_K, is given by Eq. (14.6).

---

[18] The condition for equilibrium is that the supply of money is equal to the demand for money.

$$M = m(i', Y/p) (H + q_K K + q_B B)$$

Substituting for q_K and q_B gives

$$M = m(i', Y/p) \left[H + \frac{(r_K + \lambda q_K)K}{i'} + \frac{c_B B}{i'} \right]$$

This expression implicitly defines the relationship between the nominal interest rate i' and the inflation rate λ. By implicit differentiation, we find that

$$\frac{di'}{d\lambda} = \frac{\dfrac{M}{W} \cdot \dfrac{q_K K}{i'}}{\dfrac{M}{W} \left(\dfrac{q_K K + q_B B}{i'} \right) - m_1 W}$$

where $m_1 = \frac{\partial m}{\partial i'}$.

The numerator and denominator of this expression are both positive, but the numerator is less than the denominator. Thus we conclude that

$$0 < \frac{di'}{d\lambda} < 1$$

[19] If drawn in terms of the real rate of interest the *LM* curve would shift downward.
[20] See Eq. (8.11) on p. 179.
[21] Throughout this section we assume real income (Y/p) is constant and hence omit it from this demand function.

As we saw earlier, a change in the level of commodity prices affects the rental of capital services and hence the rate of return to capital. This in turn alters the demand to hold capital at any given set of asset prices. To simplify our analysis of the effects of this change we will assume a fixed rate of inflation, so that the second and third terms of Eq. (14.6) remain constant and can be ignored.

The conditions for equilibrium in the market for existing capital goods requires that the demand to hold capital be equal to the available stock of capital goods. This requirement may be written

$$q_K K/W = q_K K^D/W = k(R/q_K, i_B) \tag{14.10}$$

How will this equilibrium condition be affected by a rise in the level of commodity prices? We may analyze this question by referring to Figure 14.3.

The left side of Eq. (14.10) may be expanded and written as

$$q_K K/W = q_K K/(H + q_K K + q_B B)$$

As we saw earlier, since the coupon on bonds is fixed in nominal terms, the price of bonds[22] is unaffected by changes in the level of prices. The stocks of assets—H, B, and K—are also independent of prices. Hence for given values of i_B and q_K,[23] the actual capital-wealth ratio is unaffected by a change in the level of commodity prices. Thus the change in prices has no effect on the OK curve in Figure 14.3.

A rise in commodity prices means that the rental of capital services and hence the rate of return on capital goods increases. Wealth holders will want to hold a larger proportion of their wealth in the form of tangible capital. In Figure 14.3 the demand curve for capital shifts to the right.

In fact we can be more specific about the size of this shift. We may invert Eq. (14.10) and write it with the return to capital as the dependent variable,

$$\frac{R}{q_K} = r\left(\frac{q_K K^D}{W}, i_B\right)$$

which in turn may be written as

$$q_K = R/r \, (q_K K^D/W, i_B) \tag{14.11}$$

Since a change in the level of prices has no direct effect on the denominator of this expression, the demand price for capital q_K increases in the same proportion as the nominal return to capital R. For example, if general prices double, wealth holders will continue to demand the same capital-wealth ratio

---

[22] At any given bond interest rate.
[23] In the first section of this chapter we analyzed the effects of a price change on nominal wealth, holding i_K and i_B constant. In that case q_K and hence W rose when the price level increased. In the present analysis it is more convenient to hold q_K constant: hence an increase in prices alters i_K but does not change W.

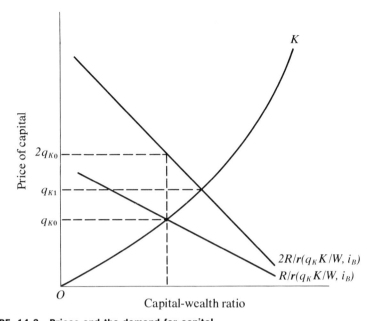

FIGURE 14.3 Prices and the demand for capital

This figure illustrates the effects of a doubling in general prices, which implies a doubling of the return to capital from R to $2R$. Note that the price of existing capital does not double as a result: It rises from q_{K0} to q_{K1}, which is less than $2q_{K0}$.

if and only if the price of capital assets also doubles. The demand curves in Figure 14.3 show this requirement.

Since the demand to hold capital has increased but the available stock is fixed, the price of capital must rise to restore equilibrium in the market for capital. In Figure 14.3 the price of capital rises from q_{K0} to q_{K1}. Note, however, that this increase in prices is less than the increase in the general price level. If, for example, general prices double, the prices of existing capital goods will less than double.[24]

This result implies that new investment (in real terms) will decline when the general level of prices rises. The reason is that the prices of used capital rise relatively less than the prices of new capital. If general prices—and hence the price of new capital—double, the prices of existing capital goods will less than double. Hence wealth holders wishing to add to their stocks of capital will tend to prefer used capital over new capital: Investment in newly produced capital will therefore decline in real terms.

We turn now to the effect of a change in the general level of prices on the flow of consumption expenditures. In Chapter 7 we argued that consump-

---

[24] Another way of seeing this point is to note that $q_K K/W$ is higher in the new equilibrium. This means that the rate of return to capital, R/q_K, has risen. Since R has risen in the same proportion as the general price level, q_K must have increased by a lesser proportion.

tion by the household sector depends on its total resources and on the terms on which it may borrow or lend. Although not stated explicitly, the arguments of that chapter implied that households are concerned with the real rather than the nominal value of their consumption and that this depends on the real value of their resources:[25]

$$C/p = c(\mathcal{V}/p, i) \qquad (14.12)$$

Thus to deduce the effect of a change in the price level we must analyze how $\mathcal{V}/p$ is affected by a change in p, assuming interest rates remain unchanged.

Note that resources comprise human and nonhuman wealth minus the present value of future tax liabilities.

$$\mathcal{V} = HW + NHW - TL$$

Human wealth represents the present value of expected future labor income:

$$HW = \ell_1 + \ell_2/(1 + i) + \ell_3/(1 + i)^2 + \ldots$$

where $\ell_1, \ell_2, \ell_3, \ldots$ represent expected wage and salary income. Nonhuman wealth comprises capital, securities, and money:

$$NHW = q_K K + q_B B + H$$

Governments levy taxes both to meet current expenses and to pay interest on government bonds. Hence we may write the present value of future tax liabilities in obvious notation,

$$TL = TL_G + TL_i$$

Thus total resources may be written as

$$\mathcal{V} = HW + q_K K - TL_G + H + q_B B - TL_i \qquad (14.13)$$

Let us consider these items in turn.

Any rise in the level of prices implies a corresponding rise in labor incomes and thus in human wealth. Therefore if prices rise, nominal human wealth rises in the same proportion. A rise in general prices also implies that the rental on capital increases. With given interest rates, capital good prices and hence the nominal value of the capital stock rises in the same proportion. Finally, an increase in the general level of prices will presumably lead to an equal proportionate increase in tax collections for current purposes. Thus we have established that when general prices rise, the nominal values of the first three categories of resources defined in Eq. (14.13) will rise in the same proportion and hence their real values will be unaffected.

The stock of high-priced money is fixed in nominal terms. Similarly, since the coupon on bonds is set in nominal terms, an increase in prices has no

---

[25] In Chapter 7 we argued that consumption is proportional to total resources. This proportionality hypothesis is not required for the results of this chapter.

effect on the value[26] of government bonds outstanding. Hence when general prices rise, the real values of the money and bond stocks decline.

Finally, consider the value of the tax liabilities associated with the existence of government debt. These liabilities are fixed in nominal terms. If prices rise, therefore, tax payers *benefit* (because the real value of their liabilities declines) to the same extent that bondholders *suffer* (because the real value of their interest receipts declines). If individuals treat their interest receipts from bonds symmetrically with their tax liabilities, these two effects will offset each other. In this case, an increase in prices has no net wealth effect arising from the existence of a government debt. The sole effect comes through the reduced real value of the stock of high-powered money. However, if wealth holders regard government bonds as an asset but neglect the future tax liabilities, which the existence of those bonds implies, there will be a second wealth effect operating through the government debt.[27]

During the late fifties and early sixties these issues were the subject of intense debate[28] among monetary theorists. The main conclusion of that debate was that there probably is a wealth effect operating through the stock of high-powered money but that empirically this effect is small. The question of whether there is any effect via the interest-bearing debt remains open: However, most theorists agree that if such an effect does exist, it too is probably quite small.

We conclude from the above discussion that an increase in the general level of prices will reduce the real value of total resources and hence lower real consumption.[29] However, the effect is unlikely to be large.

Before leaving the subject of the effect of prices on expenditures, brief mention should be made of government spending. Most economists believe that governments are concerned primarily with the real amount of their expenditures. Even if governments do feel constrained by the fact that their budgets must be balanced, these economists point out that when prices rise so do tax revenues. In any event, we will assume in what follows that governments fix the value of their real outlays and real tax receipts without regard to the level of prices.

We may sum up the results of the above analysis as follows. At any given set of interest rates, an increase in the general level of prices tends to reduce

---

[26] At any given interest rate.

[27] This is the assumption we have maintained in earlier chapters. See Appendix B of Chapter 4.

[28] This debate is sometimes known as the *Patinkin controversy,* since it was sparked by the publication in 1956 of Don Patinkin's *Money, Interest and Prices.* In that book Patinkin analyzed, in great detail, the implications for macroeconomic theory of the hypothesis that changes in the level of prices affect expenditure via a wealth effect.

[29] This conclusion raises some minor complications with regard to our earlier conclusion that a price increase reduces investment. If real consumption declines, real saving will rise at any given real income level. According to the arguments pp. 180–183, this would tend to stimulate investment. We assume that this effect is small relative to those tending to lower investment.

real consumption and real investment while leaving real government outlays unchanged. These effects imply that the *IS* curve shifts to the left.

Inflation and the *IS* Curve

We turn now to the effects on spending of an increase in the rate of inflation. First, consider the effect of more rapid inflation on the flow of investment. The analysis is straightforward. If wealth holders come to expect that prices will rise in the future, the expected nominal yield on capital goods increases. This is because the nominal yield includes capital gains on holdings of tangible capital, which become larger when the rate of inflation increases.[30] As a result, the demand to hold capital will increase, capital goods prices will rise, and hence newly produced capital will become cheaper relative to existing capital. This price difference will tend to stimulate investment spending.

The effect of an increase in the rate of inflation on consumption is also expansionary. In Chapter 7 we argued that current consumption responds negatively to the rate of interest. In that chapter no distinction was made between the real and the nominal interest rate, but it was clear from the argument that it was the real interest rate that was relevant. In deciding how to allocate its total resources over its lifetime, the household is concerned with the terms on which consumption in one period may be traded for consumption in another period. These terms of trade depend on the prices of consumer goods as well as on the nominal rate of interest: that is, they depend on the real interest rate.

An increase in the rate of inflation implies a reduction in the real rate associated with any given nominal rate of interest. Hence an increase in inflation implies a rise in the level of current consumption associated with any given nominal interest rate. In common sense terms, if prices are expected to rise, consumers will choose to consume more now and less in the future.

Finally, consider government spending. At any given level of prices the political process will generate a certain flow of spending. In developing our theoretical model, we take these political decisions as given and assume that the spending flow is unaffected by the rate of inflation. This will enable us to predict how the economy will behave in the absence of any overt stabilization actions on the part of the authorities. The role of stabilization policies in the inflation process can then be isolated and studied separately.

The conclusion of this discussion is that an increase in the rate of inflation stimulates both consumption and investment and so shifts the *IS* curve to the right. However, we can go further than this and determine the extent of this shift. Consider Figure 14.4, which shows the *IS* curve before and after an increase in the inflation rate.

---

[30] The second and third terms in Eq. (14.6) become larger.

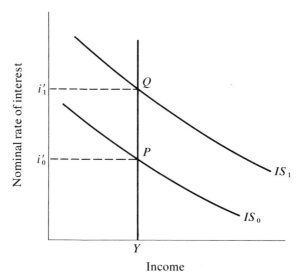

FIGURE 14.4   Inflation and the *IS* curve

An increase in the rate of inflation shifts the *IS* curve upward. In fact, the amount of this shift is equal to the increase in the inflation rate: $i_1' - i_0' = \Delta p/p$.

When there is no inflation, the markets for goods and services can be in equilibrium at a level of output Y when the nominal interest rate is i_0'. If inflation is proceeding, this same level of output will represent equilibrium only if the rate of interest is i_1'. This implies that the levels of consumption and investment spending are the same at points P and Q.

Since real investment is the same at P as at Q, the price of existing capital must also be the same. This price is related to the nominal interest rate:

$$i_0' = r_K/q_K$$
$$i_1' = (r_K + \Delta q_K)/q_K$$

But this implies that

$$i_1' - i_0' = \Delta q_K/q_K$$

Similarly, since consumption depends on the real rate of interest, the fact that consumption is the same at P as it is at Q implies that the rise in the nominal rate is exactly offset by the increase in the rate of inflation. Thus consideration of both consumption and investment implies that the size of the upward shift in the *IS* curve is exactly equal to the increase in the rate of inflation.

Prices in the *IS-LM* Framework

We have now analyzed the effects of price changes on the assets markets and on expenditure flows. In this section these results are brought together.

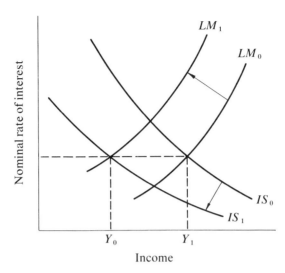

FIGURE 14.5 Prices and aggregate demand
A rise in prices reduces aggregate demand. However, its effect on the interest rate is ambiguous.

In Figure 14.5 the effects of an increase in the *price level* are analyzed. As shown earlier, a rise in prices tends to reduce the flows of consumption and investment spending and hence to shift the *IS* curve to the left. At the same time higher prices lead wealth holders to attempt to shift their wealth out of nonmoney assets (capital goods) and into money, which in turn lowers asset prices and raises rates of return. Hence the *LM* curve also shifts leftward.

We see from the figure that these two effects both tend to reduce aggregate demand. The direct wealth effects of the price increase on consumption and investment spending are reinforced by the contractionary effects of higher interest rates.

Figure 14.6 considers the effects of an increase in the rate of inflation. This tends to stimulate consumption and investment because when prices are expected to rise, it is cheaper to buy now rather than later. On the other hand, an increase in the rate of inflation tends to raise nominal interest rates and this acts to slow expenditures. Hence the net effect appears to be ambiguous: when drawn in terms of the nominal interest rate the *IS* curve shifts to the right and the *LM* curve shifts to the left. However, there is, in fact, no ambiguity because we know the relative sizes of these shifts. We found earlier that whereas the *IS* curve shifts upward by the full amount of the increase in the rate of inflation, the upward shift in the *LM* curve is less than this. When drawn in terms of the *real* rate of interest, the *LM* curve shifts downward while the *IS* curve is unaffected. Hence we conclude that the net effect is expansionary.

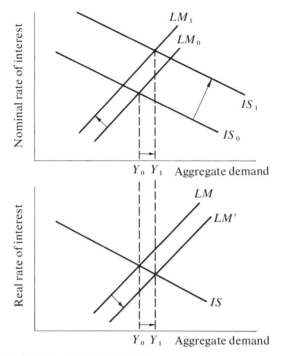

FIGURE 14.6 Inflation and aggregate demand

When drawn in terms of nominal interest rates, both *IS* and *LM* curves shift upward. In terms of real rates, the *IS* curve does not shift and the *LM* curve shifts downward. Thus aggregate demand rises and the real interest rate falls: that is, the nominal rate increases by less than the rate of inflation.

Conclusion

This completes our analysis of the effects of price changes on aggregate demand. However, in contrast to the situation in Part 2, aggregate demand is not synonymous with the level of income and output. This is because producers do not passively adjust their output to the quantity demanded without regard to the levels of wages and prices. Hence it is time now to turn from the behavior of spenders and asset holders to that of producers. This we do in the following chapter.

References

The material covered in this chapter is discussed in most texts on macroeconomic theory. Among the best is the discussion by Martin Bailey in:

Bailey, Martin J. *National Income and the Price Level,* 2nd ed. New York: McGraw-Hill, 1971. See especially Chapters 2, 3, and 4. However, like most texts, Bailey neglects to analyze the implications of the fact that the demands for assets are subject to an overall wealth constraint.

An analysis of the effects of price changes on asset markets in a three-asset model may be found in the Tobin article already cited:

Tobin, James. "A General Equilibrium Approach to Monetary Theory." *Journal of Money, Credit and Banking* (February 1969).

For a classic, but difficult, treatment of the role of prices in the theory of aggregate demand, see:

Patinkin, Don. *Money, Interest and Prices*, 2nd ed. New York: Harper & Row, 1965.

Questions for Classroom Discussion

1. Carefully explain the distinction between an increase in prices and an increase in the rate of inflation.

2. After a long period in which prices have remained constant, they now begin rising at a steady rate of 10 percent a year. Explain how this change will affect (a) the *LM* curve (b) the *IS* curve.

3. Consider the situation in an economy in which the tax system is *progressive*; that is, the share of GNP going to government rises as prices increase. How will this affect your conclusions in question 2? Assume that government outlays are fixed in real terms independent of the rate of inflation.

4. Discuss the issue of whether the stocks of money and government bonds are a part of the public's nonhuman wealth. Why is this issue important for the questions considered in this chapter?

Appendix A   The Role of Price Changes in the Three Asset Model

The purpose of this appendix is to analyze the effects of changes in the level of prices and in the rate of inflation on the portfolio model developed in Chapter 6. This analysis might be conducted by the same graphical methods used in that chapter. In the interest of brevity, however, we will use algebraic techniques.

General equilibrium in the markets for assets requires that the supply of and demand for each asset in the system be equal.

$$M = m[i_K', i_B'] W \qquad (14A.1)$$
$$q_K K = k[i_K', i_B'] W \qquad (14A.2)$$
$$q_K B = b[i_K', i_B'] W \qquad (14A.3)$$

where the primed symbols represent the nominal rates of return.[1] As usual, if two of these equations are satisfied at a given set of asset prices, the third is necessarily satisfied.

The nominal return to capital may be written

$$i_K' = \frac{r_K}{q_K} + \frac{\Delta q_K}{q_K}$$

where r_K represents the nominal rental on capital and $\Delta q_K / q_K$ is the expected rate of capital gains. We assume that the nominal rental is always proportional to the general price level:

$$r_K = p \bar{r}_K$$

Moreover, with no loss of generality we can set $\bar{r}_K$ (the *real* rental on capital) equal to unity so that $r_K = p$. We also define $\bar{q}_K$ as the price of capital relative to the general price level. That is,

$$\bar{q}_K = q_K / p$$

or

$$q_K = p \, \bar{q}_K$$

Finally, we will assume that wealth holders always expect that the prices of capital goods will rise at the same rate as the general price level:

$$\frac{\Delta q_K}{q_K} = \frac{\Delta p}{p} = \lambda$$

With these definitions, the nominal return to capital may be written

$$i_K' = \frac{1}{\bar{q}_K} + \lambda$$

---

[1] Throughout this analysis we treat real income, Y/p, as a constant and hence omit it from our analysis. Also, we assume that asset demands depend only on the differentials between the returns to bonds and capital and the return to money. This enables us to express these demands in terms of the nominal rates of return on nonmoney assets only since the nominal return to money is a constant.

The nominal rate of return on bonds may be written

$$i_B' = c_B/q_B$$

and we can set $c_B = 1$ with no loss of generality.

Equations (14A.1) and (14A.2) may now be written

$$M = m[1/\bar{q}_K + \lambda, 1/q_B] [M + p\bar{q}_K K + q_B B] \qquad (14A.1a)$$

$$p\bar{q}_K K = k[1/\bar{q}_K + \lambda, 1/q_B] [M + p\bar{q}_K + q_B B] \qquad (14A.2a)$$

To determine the effects of an increase in the level of prices, we differentiate these equations with respect to p, holding λ, M, K, and B constant. This gives two simultaneous linear equations that can be solved for the unknown partial derivatives, $\partial \bar{q}_K/\partial p$ and $\partial q_B/\partial p$. These conclusions may then be used to compute the effects of a change in p on q_K and on the two rates of return. The results of this exercise are shown in the left column of Table 14A.1.[2]

An increase in general prices leads to a lesser rise in the price of existing capital goods (q_K rises but $\bar{q}_K$ declines) and so to a rise in their rate of return. However, its effect on the price of, and the rate of return on, bonds cannot be specified a priori. Although wealth holders will wish to switch out of capital, we cannot be sure that they will wish to switch *in to bonds.*

Since new capital will be more expensive relative to existing capital, investment will decline as a result of these developments. However, the effect of the price rise on consumption is, in general, ambiguous.[3] The rise in the rate of return on capital and the reduction in the real value of the money and capital stocks will each tend to cause consumption to decline. However, if bond prices rise so that bond rates fall, the substitution and capital gains effects will each tend to stimulate consumption. Hence, the net effect is uncertain. In practice, it seems probable that capital and bonds are sufficiently close substitutes that their rates of return will move together. In that case, the rate of interest on bonds will rise and consumption will unambiguously decline.[4]

To determine the effects on asset prices and rates of return of an increase in the rate of inflation, we differentiate Eq. (14A.la) and (14A.2a) with respect to λ, holding p, M, B, and K constant. In this case we can, with no loss of generality, assume $p = 1$ so that $q_K = \bar{q}_K$. The resulting equations

---

[2] The remaining rows are derived from the definitions of i_B and q_K given earlier. Since the rate of inflation is constant, there is no distinction in this case between the real and nominal rates of return.

[3] In the text we were concerned with the effect of a price change on the *IS* curve. Hence we analyzed the effects of a price increase holding interest rates constant and concluded that consumption would decline. However, there is a possibility that bond rates may fall, thus stimulating consumption.

[4] As we saw in the text, if bonds and capital are perfect substitutes, their rates of return will both rise: The *LM* curve shifts to the left. In this case consumption unambiguously declines.

Table 14A.1 Effects of Price Changes of Asset Markets

	Increase in Price Level (p)	*Increase in Inflation Rate* (λ)
$\bar{q}_K$	−	+
q_K	+	+
i_K	+	−
i_K'	+	+
q_B	?	?
i_B	?	−
i_B'	?	?

may be solved for the unknown derivatives $\partial q_K/\partial\lambda$ and $\partial q_B/\partial\lambda$. These results can in turn be used to compute the effect of changes in λ on real and nominal rates of return, and they are reported in the second column of the table.

We see from the table that more rapid inflation increases the dollar return from capital, causes its price to rise, and its real rate of return to fall. This tends to encourage investment, since existing capital becomes more expensive relative to newly produced capital. A familiar example of this phenomenon occurs when buyers expect new car prices to rise in the future. The effect of such an expectation is to drive up the prices of used cars and to encourage buyers to purchase new cars rather than used cars.

As in the case of an increase in the level of prices, a rise in the inflation rate has an uncertain effect on the price of bonds and hence on the nominal rate of interest. Interestingly, the same is not true of the real rate, which unambiguously declines.[5] Since all real rates of return decrease, consumption—like investment—will be stimulated by inflation.

Once again we find that the three-asset model yields conclusions that do not conflict with those of the *IS–LM* analysis, though there are some situations in which the conclusions may be ambiguous. In particular, we have shown in the above analysis that an increase in the level of prices tends to be contractionary, whereas the effect of more rapid inflation is generally expansionary.

---

[5] This conclusion cannot be derived algebraically from Eq. (14A.1a) and (14A.2a). However, consider the two possibilities with regard to q_B. If q_B rises, the nominal and real returns to bonds both fall. If q_B falls, we must argue as follows: A decline in q_B means that the bond-wealth ratio also declines. The real rates of return on both money and capital have fallen and, taken alone, these would have caused the desired bond-wealth ratio to rise. Since it has, in fact, declined, the real rate of return to bonds must also have declined. Thus, regardless of whether q_B rises or falls, i_B decreases.

Appendix B Wealth and the *IS* Curve

In the course of this chapter we have used the results from Part 3 that consumption and investment spending depend not only on income flows and on rates of return (which were the only variables considered in Part 2) but also on the stock of wealth. In particular, we have considered how changes in the price level may affect spending through altering the real value of wealth. However, wealth may also be changed in other ways; for example, policy changes that alter the government's budget balance will lead to wealth changes that may shift the *IS* curve. This brief appendix considers these possibilities.

Consider, for example, a reduction in taxes that produces a budget deficit. Such a deficit may be financed by the issue of either new money or new bonds. In either case, nonhuman wealth is increased and this will tend to encourage both consumption and investment. The *IS* curve is shifted to the right by the financing of the tax cut as well as by the tax cut itself.

When a tax cut (or government spending increase) is financed by the issue of new money, monetarist economists generally argue that the ensuing economic expansion is the result of the increased money supply rather than of the fiscal action itself. Often, however, they are unclear whether the expansionary effects of the new money occur primarily because of the resulting decline in interest rates or because of the increased wealth it represents.[1]

It is important to distinguish these two channels of influence. Increases in the money supply *not* associated with budget deficits (and this includes the creation of demand deposits by the banking system) will have no wealth effect since wealth holders exchange one type of asset for another type. Conversely, budget deficits financed by borrowing do have a wealth effect, though no change in the total stock of money occurs.[2]

The emphasis placed by the monetarists on the stock of money per se tends to blur these distinctions. For example, monetarists rarely distinguish increases in the stock of money that represent additions to wealth from increases that do not. Similarly, although they often point out that budget deficits financed by new money have a wealth effect, they tend to downplay the fact that bond issues have an analogous effect.[3]

Budget surpluses and deficits affect the public's total wealth regardless of how they are financed. This wealth effect influences spending directly and

---

[1] Milton Friedman apparently favors the interest-rate route. See, for example, his remarks in his debate with Walter Heller. Milton Friedman and Walter Heller, *Monetary vs. Fiscal Policy*.
[2] Note that when a tax cut is financed by borrowing, the addition to wealth accrues not to the bondholders (who acquire additional bonds in exchange for money) but to the taxpayers. Moreover, although the total money stock does not change, the taxpayers receive their added wealth in the form of money.
[3] A possible explanation is that monetarists assume that taxpayers recognize that increases in the government debt imply larger tax liabilities to pay interest costs. However, such an assumption is empirically somewhat implausible.

shifts the *IS* curve. The method of financing, on the other hand, affects the distribution of wealth, as between the various assets available. This financing effect alters spending by causing changes in asset prices and rates of return: That is, it operates via the *LM* curve. The controversy between the monetarists and Keynesians apparently is over the role of this second effect. The monetarists claim that the method by which a deficit is financed critically influences the economy, while the Keynesians argue that the absolute size of the deficit is more important than the method by which it is financed.

Wages, Prices, and Employment

15

Throughout the analysis of Part 2, we maintained the assumption that producers are always willing to supply more of their products with no increases in their selling prices. Under this assumption, the level of the economy's output depends only on the *demand* for goods and services. The *supply* of goods and services adjusts passively to that demand, and the general level of prices at which output is sold remains constant.

Although such an assumption might have been appropriate as an approximation to the situation in the U.S. economy in the early 1930s, it is plainly not a valid description of our economy in the 1970s. Hence the time has come to develop a more satisfactory theory of producer behavior. This is the purpose of the present chapter, in which we will examine the relation between the *supply* of goods and services and the *prices* at which those commodities are sold. We will find that the level of *wages* plays an important role in this relationship. Moreover, since changes in a firm's output generally lead to the hiring and firing of workers, our model will lead us into a discussion of the determinants of the levels of employment and unemployment. Hence much of this chapter will be concerned with the relations among four principal variables: the general level of prices, the general level of money wages, the amount of employment, and the flow of output.

In the early parts of this chapter our discussion will closely parallel the standard *theory of the firm*, which occupies a central position in traditional microeconomics. If you are familiar with this material, you can regard these sections as essentially a review of price theory. In later sections the so-called *new microeconomics* of employment and output will be discussed. Although this theory is essentially microeconomic in character—being concerned with the behavior of individual workers and individual producers—it has, up until now at least, been used almost exclusively to explain such macroeconomic phenomena as unemployment and inflation.

The Production Function

The total flow of output that an economy produces over a given period of time depends on the quantities of labor services and capital services that are employed by producers. The technological relation between the flow of inputs to the production process and the resulting flow of output is known as the *production function*. Symbolically, we may write[1]

$$Q = F(K, L) \tag{15.1}$$

where K stands for capital services and L stands for labor services.

For simplicity, we will assume that in the short run the stock of capital available to producers in the economy is given. The level of output may be varied only by altering the amount of labor used in conjunction with a given stock of fixed capital equipment; that is, by changing hours of work or by hiring and firing workers. This assumption may be justified by the argument that whereas the amount of labor a firm employs may be increased rapidly by hiring more workers or lengthening hours of work, the manufacture and installation of machinery takes time.

However, the fact that the stock of capital is fixed in the short run does not mean that the same is true of the flow of capital services. In virtually all cases the firm may, if it wishes, employ a flow of capital services that is less than the theoretical maximum that its capital stock is capable of supplying. For example, if the demand for its products declines, a firm can generally either reduce the number of hours per week for which it operates its plant or leave some of its machines completely idle. Thus, although the firm's stock of capital is constant, the flow of capital services it uses may, subject to a certain maximum, be varied upward and downward. An alternative way of describing this phenomenon is to say that reductions in the level of output lead to unemployment of machines as well as of workers. Of course, since workers have families to support and machines do not, unemployment of workers is generally regarded as a more serious social problem than unemployment of machines.

We will assume that the use of existing machines may be altered at no cost[2] so that the only variable costs (that is, costs that vary with the level of output) are wages paid to labor. The situation then may be represented in the well-known isoquant diagram, shown in Figure 15.1.

In this diagram, $\bar{K}$ represents the maximum flow of capital services that can be obtained from a given stock of capital. For output rates below Q_3 the firm will not use all the machine time available to it.[3] For example, it is

---

[1] Note that we draw a distinction between the *stocks* of the factors of production in the economy (measured in numbers of men or numbers of machines) and the *flows* of services these factors provide (measured in man-hours or machine hours). The *flow* of output is assumed to depend only on the *flow* of inputs of factor services.

[2] This assumption rules out the possibility that maintenance costs or depreciation depend on the level of usage of machines.

[3] It is worth pointing out that Q_3 may be a very large rate of output. A firm rarely reaches a

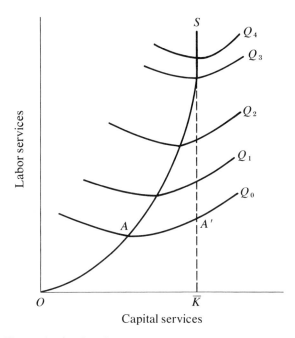

FIGURE 15.1 The production function

cheaper to produce output Q_0 with the labor-capital combination represented by point A than with that given by A'. This reflects the obvious fact that it is rarely economic to operate the complete plant in order to obtain a given level of output. Thus as the firm expands its output from, say, Q_0 to Q_1 it not only hires additional labor but also brings more of its stock of machines into use.

Although the amount of capital services used varies with the level of output, it is clear from the figure that there is a one-to-one relation between the employment of labor and the flow of output. Hence Eq. (15.1) may be simplified to

$$Q = f(L) \qquad (15.2)$$

We assume that this relation between labor input and product output may be represented as in Figure 15.2.[4] At low levels of output, successive increases in labor input yield larger and larger additions to the flow of

position in which the use of capital cannot be increased either by lengthening hours of work or by bringing previously idle machines into operation. Thus most firms in the economy normally operate along the ridge line OS with capital usage below its theoretical maximum.

[4] For a discussion of the conditions under which the relation will take this form, see Ragnar Frisch, *The Theory of Production* (Chicago: Rand McNally, 1965), Chapter 8. The production functions encountered in most price theory texts will generally yield the relation assumed in Figure 15.2.

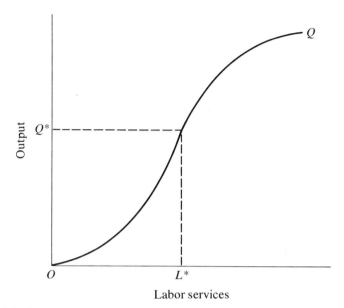

FIGURE 15.2 Output and employment

output, while beyond some critical levels of labor input and product output[5] (L^* and Q^*) they yield smaller and smaller additions.

The Classical Theory of the Labor Market

The slope of the curve OQ in Figure 15.2 represents the increase in output that results from the use of an additional unit (say, a man-hour) of labor services. This is known as the *marginal physical product* of labor. The shape of the curve OQ implies that as the firm expands its output, the marginal physical product at first increases and then, after some point, decreases.

If the firm increases its use of labor by one man-hour, its output will increase by an amount equal to the marginal physical product of labor. If it can sell its output at a given price, its receipts will rise by

Price × Marginal physical product of labor

At the same time the firm's expenses will increase by the amount of the wage paid for the additional man-hour. Clearly, if the addition to receipts exceeds the addition to expenses, it will pay the firm to hire more labor and expand its output. Conversely, the firm should contract its output and reduce its work force if the saving in wage costs is greater than the resulting loss of

---

[5] It may be worth pointing out that Q^* may be greater or smaller than Q_3, the output at which the firm finds it optimal to employ its entire stock of capital.

revenue. This implies that in order to maximize its profits, the firm should choose a level of employment such that[6]

Price × Marginal physical product of labor = Wage of labor

Symbolically,

$$p \cdot MPP_L = w$$

or, using the notation of the differential calculus,

$$p \cdot f'(L^d) = w \tag{15.3}$$

where $f'(L^d)$ is the derivative of output with respect to labor input and represents, approximately, the addition to the flow of output that results from the use of one extra man-hour of labor services.

This equation relates the amount of labor the firm will employ, L^d, to the money wages it must pay, w, and to the price, p, it receives for its product. This relation is illustrated in Figure 15.3. The curves in this figure are *demand curves* for labor services. These demand curves slope downward because, in the vicinity of the profit-maximizing output, the marginal product of labor is declining, and hence the firm will be willing to employ more labor only if the wage of labor is reduced.[7]

A rise in the price of the firm's product causes the demand curve to shift

---

[6] We should add that this is true only for output levels in which the marginal physical product of labor is declining as output expands; that is, in terms of Figure 15.2, for employment and output levels above L^* and Q^*. If you are unfamiliar with this argument, you will find it spelled out in any price theory textbook.

[7] See footnote 6.

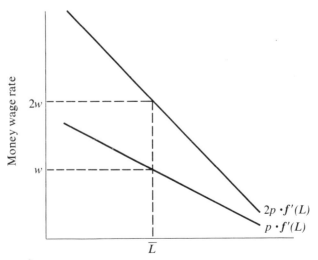

Man-hours of labor demanded

FIGURE 15.3 The demand for labor

upward; that is, the firm will be willing to hire more labor at the same money wages or to pay higher money wages to obtain the same work force. In fact, we can be more specific about the extent of this shift since Eq. (15.3) implies that if, for example, the price of its output doubles, the firm will be willing to offer doubled money wages in order to obtain the same work force. The demand curves in Figure 15.3 incorporate this feature.

Equation (15.3) may be put in an alternative form:

$$w/p = f'(L^d) \tag{15.4}$$

In this form, the equation shows that the demand for labor depends only on the real wage; that is, on the ratio of the money wage to the price of the firm's output. This means that if both wages and prices double, for example, the firm will continue to demand the same amount of labor services.

Up to now we have been concerned with the demand for labor. We turn now to the supply of labor. By this we mean the number of man-hours that workers are willing to provide under various circumstances.

In the classical approach to the supply of labor,[8] it is assumed that individuals work only to obtain the income they need to buy goods and services. This assumption implies that the principal factors affecting workers' labor-supply decisions are the money wages they can earn and the prices of the goods and services they buy. In particular, it implies that if wages and prices both rise (or fall) in the same proportion, the supply of labor will remain unchanged.

Symbolically, this hypothesis may be written as

$$L^s = l(w, p) = l(kw, kp) \qquad k > 0 \tag{15.5a}$$

This equation states that if both wages and prices change in the same proportion, k, workers will be willing to supply the same quantity of labor.

By setting $k = 1/p$ this equation may be transformed into

$$L^s = l(w, p) = l(w/p, 1) = L(w/p) \tag{15.5b}$$

showing that the supply of labor depends only on the *real wage*, w/p. Finally, this equation may be turned around and written with w/p as the dependent variable:

$$w/p = w(L^s)$$

so that

$$w = p \cdot w(L^s) \tag{15.5c}$$

In this form the equation shows that the money wage workers will demand depends on the prices of consumption goods and on the amount of labor they are called upon to supply. In particular, it shows that if prices rise, workers will demand an equal proportionate increase in their money wage.

---

[8] For a lucid discussion of the classical theory of the labor supply, see Kelvin Lancaster, *Introduction to Modern Microeconomics,* 2nd ed. (Chicago: Rand McNally, 1974), pp. 245–249.

The above argument showed only that the supply of labor depends on the real wage. Unfortunately, microeconomic theory is unable to provide any definite hypothesis regarding the *direction* of the effect of changes in the real wage on the supply of labor. We cannot predict, on theoretical grounds alone, whether an increase in the real wage will cause the supply of labor to rise or to fall. This is because changes in money wages and prices have both income and substitution effects on workers' behavior and these effects work in opposite directions.[9]

Consider first the *substitution effect*. When there is a reduction in the real wage (owing either to a rise in prices or to a decline in the money wage), the worker finds that the terms on which he can obtain more consumption goods in return for giving up leisure have worsened. As a result, he has an incentive to substitute leisure for goods: that is, to work less and enjoy more leisure. Conversely, wage increases or price reductions (additions to the real wage) make work more attractive relative to leisure, since an hour of work enables the individual to obtain more goods than before. The individual is encouraged to work more and take less leisure; that is, to substitute goods for leisure time.

In addition to the substitution effect, however, there is also an *income effect*. Declines in his money wage or increases in the prices of consumption goods reduce the material standard of living the individual can obtain from a given amount of work effort. In order to avoid such a reduction in his consumption, he may choose to work more even though the terms on which he can obtain consumption goods in exchange for giving up leisure have worsened. Conversely, if wages increase or prices decline, the worker will be able to enjoy a rise in his material living standard while at the same time working less and taking more leisure. Even though the terms on which he can buy goods by giving up leisure have improved, the worker may choose to take advantage of this situation to enjoy more leisure as well as more goods; that is, he will work less as the real wage rises.

The arguments above indicate that the income and substitution effects operate in opposite directions. An increase (or decrease) in the real wage tends to increase (or decrease) the supply of labor through the substitution effect but to decrease (or increase) it through the income effect. Under these circumstances, it is natural to examine the historical evidence to see whether, in fact, either the substitution or the income effect has tended to predominate. Unfortunately, however, the picture provided by history is not much clearer than that suggested by economic theory.

The evidence indicates that over the last 75 years, the proportion of the population in the labor force[10] has risen only slightly despite a massive increase in real wages. However, this modest rise in the overall participa-

---

[9] The problem here is similar to that encountered in our discussion of the effects of interest-rate changes on consumption. See Chapter 7.

[10] An individual is classified as being in the labor force if he is either at work or actively seeking a job.

tion rate[11] is the combined result of a sharp *increase* in the proportion of women in the work force (presumably reflecting the substitution effect) and an equally sharp *decrease* in the participation of older persons and male teenagers (presumably reflecting the income effect). For the population as a whole, the substitution effect has apparently outweighed the income effect over the long run, but the net effect has been small.[12]

In the short run, however, there is evidence that the income effect frequently outweighs the substitution effect when *declines* in the real wage are involved. For example labor-force participation (particularly of married women and older persons) tends to increase when living standards come under pressure. In the late sixties and early seventies, for example, slowing economic growth and accelerating inflation produced an increase in the number of working wives.

This evidence suggests that household employment decisions are strongly influenced by a desire to maintain accustomed living standards. When there is a reduction in the living standard that can be "purchased" with a given amount of work—either because of a reduction in money wages or because of an increase in the cost of living—households attempt to offset that decline by supplying more labor. Wives and retired persons enter the labor force and begin looking for jobs. When conditions improve, many of these persons withdraw from the labor force.

On the other hand, when the real wage rises to a new high level, the household is under less pressure to adjust its labor supply. The improved terms on which the household can obtain more goods by giving up leisure will encourage it to supply *more* labor (the substitution effect), but at the same time the fact that it can now enjoy the same (or more) consumption of goods with less work will encourage it to supply *less* labor (the income effect). Under these circumstances, the net effect on the labor supply is likely to be smaller and less certain than in the converse case in which the household faces an actual decline in consumption if it does not work more.

We conclude that the responses of households to changes in real wages are likely to be asymmetric. Specifically, the desire to maintain living standards means that a *reduction* in the real wage is likely to lead to an increase in the supply of labor, whereas a *rise* in the real wage, since it causes an increase in workers' real incomes, may lead either to an increase or to a decline in the supply. In what follows we will assume that, in the latter case, the labor supply will rise: This accords with the long-run historical tendency for the overall participation rate to rise as real wages increase.

The preceding arguments imply a labor-supply relation such as that depicted in Figure 15.4. This figure illustrates not only the classical notion that

---

[11] The *participation rate* measures the proportion of the adult population that is in the labor force.

[12] This statement implies that these historical changes were entirely the result of changes in real wages. In fact, there have probably also been changes in workers' preferences: For example, a change in women's preferences as between housewifery and paid employment.

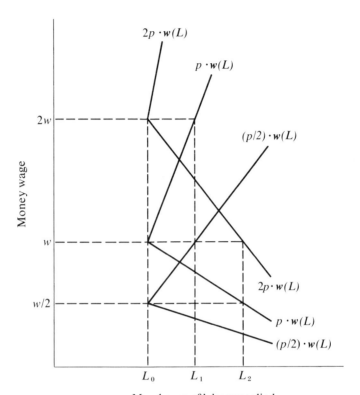

FIGURE 15.4 The supply of labor

the labor supply depends only on the real wage, but also the idea that household responses to changes in wages are probably asymmetric.

In this figure the curves labeled $(p/2) \cdot w(L)$, $p \cdot w(L)$, and $2p \cdot w(L)$ represent the supply of labor when the price level is respectively $p/2$, p, and $2p$. Thus if the current money wage is w and the price level is p, the labor supply will be L_0 man-hours. Since workers are concerned with their real wages, a rise in prices will lead them to demand an equivalent boost in their money wages. For example, if prices rise from p to $2p$, workers will continue to supply L_0 man-hours only if their money wage also rises from w to $2w$.

An increase in the money wage or an equivalent decrease in prices leads workers to increase the labor supply.[13] For example, if wages double to $2w$ but prices remain at p, the labor supply increases from L_0 to L_1. Moreover, this same increase in supply will also result if the price level is halved (to $p/2$) while money wages are unchanged.

---

[13] Remember that we are assuming that when the real-wage rises, the supply of labor increases even though this hypothesis cannot be proven by conventional economic theory and is only weakly supported by historical data.

A decline in the real wage—whether produced by a reduction in the money wage or by an increase in the price level—puts pressure on households' accustomed living standards. We have argued that they will respond to this by supplying more labor. In the figure, the labor supply increases from L_0 to L_2 if either prices rise from p to $2p$ or the money wage declines from w to $w/2$. If the real wage later rises again, the labor supply will decline until the real wage returns to its previous peak level.[14]

Having analyzed both the supply of and the demand for labor, we must now consider the conditions under which the labor market will be in equilibrium (under the classical assumptions). We do this with the aid of Figure 15.5.

The labor market will be in equilibrium at a given configuration of wages and prices if the flow of man-hours that households wish to supply is equal to the flow that businesses wish to employ. In Figure 15.5 this situation obtains if, for example, the money wage is w and the price level of goods and services is p. With a price level of p, the demand curve for labor is given by $p \cdot f'(L)$ and the supply curve of labor by $p \cdot w(L)$. The intersection of these curves indicates that at a money wage of w, employers will wish to employ and households will wish to offer L man-hours of employment. Note that in equilibrium all workers who wish to have jobs at the prevailing levels of wages and prices are able to find them. Thus *full employment* prevails in the sense that there is no worker who would like to have a job at the going real wage but is unable to find one. In addition, there is no employer who would like to add to his labor force at the prevailing real wage but is unable to find suitable workers. Thus there is *no unemployment* and there are *no job vacancies* in this equilibrium situation.[15]

Suppose now there is an increase in the general level of prices from p to, say, $2p$. Such an increase will lead to a rise in the demand for labor: At any given money wage employers will want to hire more workers, since the products of those workers can be sold at higher prices. Alternatively, we can say that since employers can now sell their products at higher prices, they are willing to offer higher money wages to their employees. Specifically, if prices double, employers will be willing to double the money wages they are paying and still employ the same number of workers.[16] Thus the demand

---

[14] Suppose, for example, the wage is w and the price level is p so that the labor supply is L_0. The price level now rises to $2p$. This leads households to increase their participation in the labor force to L_2 as they seek to maintain living standards. At the same time, however, they will press for higher money wages. If they succeed in pushing the wage up to $2w$, participation will fall again and the labor supply will decline back to L_0.

[15] Probably no economist has ever espoused the classical theory of the labor market in the pure textbook form described here. However, before Keynes published his *General Theory,* many economists did argue that full employment was the natural state of affairs, that unemployment was essentially a temporary phenomenon, which could occur only while the economic system was moving from one equilibrium to another, but that, if left alone, the economy would rapidly return to full employment. The experience of the 1930s spelled the end of this comfortable view of the world.

[16] Governments and private individuals also hire workers. Although our discussion of the

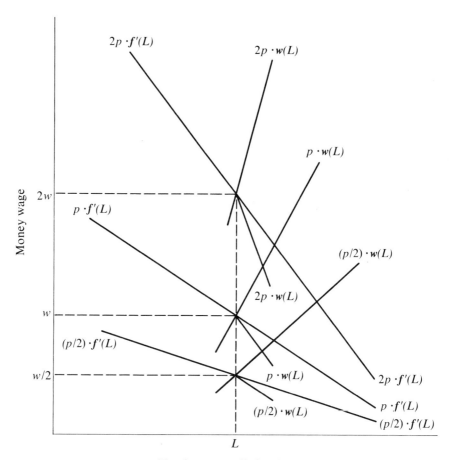

FIGURE 15.5 The labor market

curve for labor shifts upward from $p \cdot f'(L)$ to $2p \cdot f'(L)$. By precisely symmetric arguments, a reduction in prices from p to, say, $p/2$ will cause the demand curve to shift downward from $p \cdot f'(L)$ to $(p/2) \cdot f'(L)$.

Since in the classical model workers are assumed to be interested only in their real wages, a change in the general level of prices leads households to raise or lower the money wages they demand in precisely the same proportion. Thus if prices rise from p to $2p$ the supply curve of labor shifts upward from $p \cdot w(L)$ to $2p \cdot w(L)$. Conversely, if prices decline from p to $p/2$, the supply curve shifts downward from $p \cdot w(L)$ to $(p/2) \cdot w(L)$.

The diagram illustrates a key conclusion of the classical analysis:

---

demand for labor was cast in terms of the behavior of profit-maximizing business firms, it seems plausible to believe that nonbusiness employers respond to prices and wages in a similar fashion.

Changes in prices have no long-term effect on the level of employment. If prices rise, workers demand and employers are prepared to offer increases in money wages. Conversely, if prices fall, employers require and workers are prepared to accept reductions in money wages. Thus full employment is continually maintained. Situations of widespread unemployment—in which many workers want to hold jobs at the prevailing levels of wages and prices but are unable to find them—cannot exist. If a worker is without a job, it must be because he is demanding a wage that is above the equilibrium level; in this sense his unemployment is the result of a voluntary decision on his part—he prefers joblessness to working at the current wage.

The Keynesian Model of the Labor Market

A model of the labor market that rules out the possibility of unemployment was plainly unable to explain the disaster of the Great Depression in which millions of workers remained unemployed for long periods of time. More than any other historical event, it was that catastrophe which led economists to critically reexamine their thinking about how a free-enterprise economy works. So far as the labor market was concerned, this reexamination centered its attention on the classical model of the labor *supply* and particularly on the latter's assertion that workers are concerned only with their *real* wage. That proposition, you will recall, implied that workers will respond in the same way to a reduction in real wages brought about by a cut in the money wage as they will to an equal reduction resulting from a rise in the general level of prices. Maynard Keynes was vehement in his denial of this hypothesis.[17] As a result, the economic model that emerges when this hypothesis is rejected has come to be known as the *Keynesian case*.[18]

Economists who espouse this approach point out that in the real world money wages tend to be rigid in the downward direction. Workers vigorously resist reductions in their money wages and this resistance persists even when such reductions do not imply cuts in their real wage: that is, even when the prices of consumption goods are declining at the same time. This statement implies that workers are concerned both with their real wages *and with their money wages*. Thus although the classical model of the labor supply, as embodied in Eq. (15.4), for example, may correctly describe the response of workers to *increases* in the demand for labor or in the

---

[17] In particular, he argued that workers' responses to a reduction in money wages are generally different from their responses to a rise in the cost of living even though *both* of these events imply a decrease in the real wage. See J. M. Keynes, *The General Theory of Employment, Interest and Money* (London: Macmillan, 1936), p. 9.

[18] Recently several writers have suggested that this so-called Keynesian model is such a gross simplification of the theory put forward by Keynes himself that it does not accurately represent his true thinking. See, for example, Axel Leijonhufvud, *On Keynesian Economics and the Economics of Keynes* (New York: Oxford University Press), 1968.

general level of prices,[19] it does *not* provide a satisfactory description of the situation when either prices or the demand for labor fall. In particular, Keynesian economists argue that workers are generally unwilling to accept cuts in their money wages when the demand for their services declines and this unwillingness persists even if the prices of the goods and services they buy also decline.

If the current level of money wages is w_0, this assumption of downward wage rigidity may be written as

$$w = p \cdot w(L) \qquad \text{for} \quad p \cdot w(L) \geq w_0 \qquad (15.6a)$$

$$w = w_0 \qquad \text{for} \quad p \cdot w(L) < w_0 \qquad (15.6b)$$

Thus the classical assumptions are assumed to hold for increases in money wages above the currently prevailing level[20] but not for decreases. The money wages that workers demand will *rise* if they are called upon by employers to supply more labor or if prices rise, but they *will not fall* in response to declining prices or employment.

Explanations of this phenomenon are typically couched in institutional terms; for example, minimum wage laws and long-term contracts between unions and employers are frequently cited as reasons why money wages do not fall. The new microeconomics provides a strictly economic explanation of the phenomenon of wage rigidity. This explanation will be discussed later: At present, we simply accept the existence of this phenomenon and examine its implications for the classical analysis.

The Keynesian hypothesis of downward-wage rigidity dramatically alters the conclusions of the classical model. No longer is full employment assured. Situations in which workers wish to work at the prevailing levels of wages and prices but are unable to find jobs may persist for long periods. The system does not adjust rapidly to restore full employment equilibrium. Hence government action by either monetary or fiscal policy is required.

The key role played by the rigidity of money wages may be demonstrated by analyzing the effects of a reduction in the demand for labor in the classical and Keynesian models. We do this with the aid of Figure 15.6.

Suppose that, initially, commodity prices are at level p_1 and the supply of and demand for labor services are equal at a level of money wages w_1. There is no unemployment since all workers who are willing to work at that wage will be able to find jobs.[21] That is, with employment L_1 and prices p_1 workers demand to receive and employers are prepared to pay money wages of w_1.

---

[19] That is, if commodity prices rise or if they are called upon to supply more labor at the current wage, workers will demand increases in their money wages.

[20] Note that Eq. (15.6a) is identical to Eq. (15.5c).

[21] In a dynamic and changing economy there will always be some workers who are unemployed because they are in the process of moving from one job to another. However, in labor-market equilibrium there is no unemployment in addition to this so-called *frictional* unemployment. When a worker leaves a job, he will always be able to find another with no undue delay and at a wage which he is willing to accept.

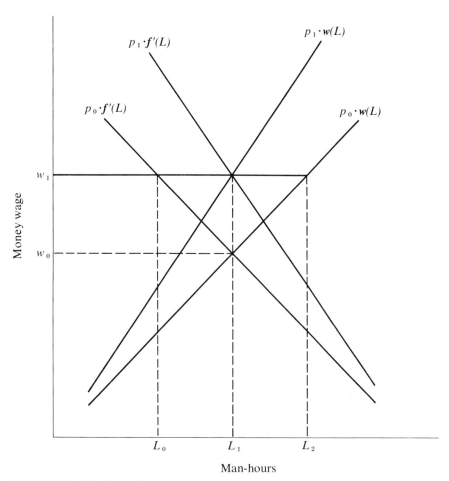

FIGURE 15.6 The Keynesian case

Assume now that the demand for goods and services declines and as a result commodity prices fall from p_1 to p_0. At the prevailing level of money wages w_1, employers will find that the present level of employment L_1 exceeds that at which their profits are maximized. This is because the decline in selling prices lowers the value of the marginal product of the typical firm. Hence firms will begin to shorten working hours, lay off workers, and reduce output.[22] In terms of Figure 15.6 the effect of the reduction in prices is to shift the demand curve for labor downward for $p_1 \cdot f'(L)$ to $p_0 \cdot f'(L)$. If there were no change in the money wages, employers would want to cut the level of employment from L_1 to L_0.

---

[22] Symbolically, the decline in prices from p_1 to p_0 reduces the value of labor's marginal product from $p_1 \cdot f'(L_1)$ to $p_0 \cdot f'(L_1)$. Hence $p_0 \cdot f'(L_1) < w_1$. As a result, the profit-maximizing level of employment is now less than L_1.

Under the classical assumptions, however, workers who are laid off will prefer to work for lower money wages than to remain unemployed. Hence unemployed workers will begin to offer their services to employers at money wages below w_1. Moreover, any unemployed worker who offers his services for a money wage of less than w_1 will promptly be hired, and hence workers who were *not* dismissed will be compelled to accept a reduction in *their* money wages if they are to retain their jobs. On the other hand, these workers will not offer much resistance to such wage cuts because the prices of the goods and services they buy have declined. This is shown by the downward shift of the supply-of-labor curve from $p_1 \cdot w(L)$ to $p_0 \cdot w(L)$.

As long as money wages remain above w_0 there will be more workers looking for jobs than there are jobs available. This is shown in the figure by the fact that at money wages above w_0 the supply curve of labor, $p_0 \cdot w(L)$ lies to the right of the demand curve $p_0 \cdot f'(L)$. Hence unemployed workers will continue to scale down their wage demands and the resulting reduction in wage costs will induce employers to offer more jobs. Finally, money wages will decline to w_0 at which point equilibrium is restored and unemployment is eliminated.[23] This reduction in the money wage (from w_1 to w_0) is not only just sufficient to induce employers to raise the level of employment to L_1 but also exactly equal to the reduction that workers are prepared to accept in order to get their jobs back. In the new equilibrium, employment is at the same level as it was in the original situation. This reflects the fact that both supply and demand depend only on real wages; thus a reduction in the money wage, which restores the real wage to its original level, will cause both employers and employees to be satisfied with a return to the original employment level.[24]

In this classical case, workers who become unemployed find jobs by offering to work for a *reduced money wage*. In the Keynesian case, however, *money wages do not fall* and hence workers who lose their jobs do *not* rapidly find new ones as the classical model predicts. After the decline in prices from p_1 to p_0 employers are willing to employ only L_0 workers at a money wage of w_1. Hence $L_1 L_0$ workers will lose their jobs and will be, in Keynes's phrase, "involuntarily unemployed"; that is, they are willing to work at the prevailing money wage but are unable to find jobs.

Other considerations suggest that unemployment may actually exceed $L_0 L_1$. In the first place, the decline in prices improves the terms of trade

---

[23] Note that the classical analysis only implies the absence of unemployment in equilibrium. While the system is adjusting from one equilibrium to another, there may be some temporary unemployment. However, the classics assumed that this adjustment occurred sufficiently rapidly that this unemployment did not pose a serious social problem.

[24] In this argument we focused our attention exclusively on the labor market. We said nothing about the causes of the initial reduction in the demand for goods and services nor did we analyze the effects of the decline in wages and prices on that demand. Hence we were unable to demonstrate that in the new equilibrium firms will once again be able to sell an output corresponding to full employment. These issues will be taken up in the next chapter.

between goods and leisure. This will induce more workers to enter the labor force and seek jobs. This is illustrated in the diagram by the fact that when the price level is p_0 and money wages are w_1, workers wish to supply L_2 man-hours of employment. As a result, unemployment rises to L_0L_2 since, in the aggregate, these new entrants will be unable to find jobs. Second, the increased unemployment will cut into accustomed living standards and hence will induce many secondary workers (wives, old persons, and teen-agers) to begin searching for jobs. Again, however, these new entrants will be unable to find jobs — at least in the aggregate — unless there is a decline in the money wage. This effect[25] is not illustrated in Figure 15.6 but has been quite important in the United States.

Despite this involuntary unemployment, the Keynesian case assumes that workers are unwilling to accept a reduction in their money wage[26] in order to secure employment. Thus, in contrast to the classical scenario, there is no mechanism in the Keynesian economy by which full employment may be rapidly restored. If we wish to eliminate the unemployment quickly, we must focus our attention on the demand for goods and services; that is, by monetary or fiscal policy, we must increase the demand for firms' output so that they are again willing to employ all those workers who wish to work at a money wage of w_1. This policy conclusion was the essential message of Keynes's *General Theory*.

The New Microeconomics of Wages, Prices, and Employment

Until quite recently, most economists were content to argue that if wages are flexible downward (the classical position), unemployment will be an essentially transitory phenomenon, whereas if wages are rigid downward (the so-called Keynesian position), unemployment may be persistent and there will be no automatic tendency for the economy to move rapidly toward full employment. Most economists[27] paid little attention to the question of *why* money wages might be rigid downward, preferring to focus their attention on the *effects* of such rigidity. In recent years, however, a body of analysis has

---

[25] This is known as the "additional-worker" effect of unemployment. Widespread unemployment also has the effect of inducing some workers to cease searching for a job. This "discouraged-worker" effect reduces the amount of unemployment as measured by the Department of Labor, which only includes active searchers in its unemployment count. However, by any reasonable definition, such persons are truly unemployed: They are jobless because no jobs are available, not because they prefer leisure over employment at the going market wage.
[26] The Keynesian model presented here and in most textbooks assumes that it is the *workers'* refusal to accept reductions in their money wages that causes unemployment to persist. This hypothesis is really quite implausible and a careful reading of Keynes himself suggests that he would not have accepted it. For example, he points out (*General Theory*, p. 9) that "[l]abor is not more truculent in the depression than in the boom—far from it." The search for a more acceptable explanation of wage rigidity has led economists to the theories developed in the next section.
[27] However, Leijonhufvud argues strongly that these strictures do not apply to Keynes himself.

been developed that seeks to provide an economic explanation of wage rigidity to replace earlier institutional and *ad hoc* explanations. This body of economic theory has come to be known as the *new microeconomics*.[28]

In the Keynesian model a worker is assumed to remain unemployed even though he could get a job by reducing his money-wage demands. Why should he behave in such an apparently illogical manner? The answer to this puzzle, says the new microeconomics, lies in the fact that the typical worker (and the typical employer for that matter) has access to much less information than is assumed in the classical model.

To see the crucial role played by the *availability of information,* consider the response of the typical worker who loses his job as a result of a decline in the aggregate demand for labor. The classical model implicitly assumes that this worker has full knowledge of the types of jobs available in the economy and of the money wages they pay. Hence he knows that in order to be reemployed he must lower his asking wage. Moreover, all potential employers are assumed to have full knowledge of the terms on which workers are willing to supply their services. Hence as soon as our typical worker lowers his wage demands, an employer will come forward who is ready to hire him. Thus complete information on both sides of the market ensures that money wages adjust rapidly to their equilibrium level and full employment is maintained.

In any actual situation, however, the newly unemployed worker has very little information on what jobs are available to him or what rate of money wages he can expect to earn. In particular, he generally does not know whether his situation is the result of some circumstance peculiar to his former employer or whether it reflects a more basic change in the economy at large which has produced an overall contraction in the number of jobs available. In these circumstances, he must begin to search for a job; that is, he must devote time, energy, and often money to acquire information about the state of the job market. Moreover, until he has spent some time searching, he is likely to assume that his job loss was the result of some specific factor affecting only his employer (or industry or locality) and was not a reflection of an overall contraction. As a result, the worker probably will begin his search with the assumption that it will be successful in the sense that he will eventually find a new job at the same wage rate he was receiving previously. [As an aside, we might mention that this assumption (or tendency to look on the bright side) is frequently backed up by statements by politicians and other public figures to the effect that "prosperity is just around the corner."]

Since he does not have complete information about available jobs, the worker will realize that it may take some time before he locates an accept-

---

[28] Although it is a recent arrival on the scene, the literature on the new microeconomics is already large and is growing rapidly. A useful collection of some of the more important early contributions is to be found in *Microeconomic Foundations of Employment and Inflation Theory*, ed. Edmund S. Phelps (New York: W. W. Norton, 1970).

able job and that the longer he continues his search the greater is the probability of finding such a job. Probably he will also realize that he will be more likely to find a job rapidly if he scales down his wage demands. Hence the question arises as to why he does not accept a low-paying job immediately while at the same time continuing his search for a high-paying one. The new theories of search provide two possible explanations. First, the search process is more likely to be successful if the worker concentrates on it; that is, it is much easier to look for a job when one is unemployed than when one is employed, simply because one can devote more time and effort to the search. Second, changing jobs is not costless[29] and hence it may not be worthwhile for a worker to accept a low-paying job if he expects to move to a better job in the near future.[30]

The above arguments suggest that it might be quite rational for a worker to hold out for a high money wage even though he knows that this will probably reduce his chances of finding a job quickly and hence will lengthen the duration of his unemployment. Essentially, the argument is that over the long haul the worker believes he will obtain a larger total return if he remains unemployed and devotes time and energy to the search for a high-paying job than if he accepts a low-paying job immediately, which limits his ability to search and also may involve him in additional costs of changing jobs again at a later date.

These arguments explain why workers do not promptly cut their wage demands when they become unemployed and hence why the economy does not return rapidly to full employment as the classical economists assumed. At first sight, however, they do not explain the persistence of high unemployment for long periods of time. Surely workers who are unsuccessful in their search for jobs at their previous money wage will—after a certain period of unemployment—decide that there are no jobs to be found at that wage and hence will reduce their wage demands.

The explanation advanced by the new microeconomics is that persistently high levels of *aggregate* unemployment do not necessarily imply that the *same* individual workers remain unemployed for very long periods. Every month certain workers enter the unemployment pool while others leave it to take new jobs. When the demand for labor falls, the average time spent between jobs lengthens. However, a relatively small increase in the average duration of unemployment implies a relatively large increase in the number of persons unemployed. In recent years, for example, a one point increase in the unemployment rate (say, from 6 percent to 7 percent) has been associated with a rise in the duration of joblessness of only two weeks. Thus many, perhaps most, workers who become unemployed following a decline in aggregate demand do find new jobs. It is true that the search takes

---

[29] Job changes may involve moving expenses, acquisition of new skills, and new tools, etc.
[30] This is particularly true if acceptance of a job means that the worker ceases to receive unemployment compensation or welfare benefits.

somewhat longer than they expected, but not so much longer that they are induced to lower their wage demands. Their search is successful and their expectations of finding a job without reducing their money wages are realized. Moreover, the fact that many workers are successful in their search encourages others who remain or become unemployed not to lower their wage demands but to continue searching in the expectation that they too will succeed.

Even if a job-seeker does decide to lower his asking wage, however, this does not guarantee that he will immediately find a job. This is because the employer faces similar problems of lack of information. If an unemployed person offers to work for a lower wage than his existing workers, an employer will not necessarily find it profitable to hire him and fire one of them. For example, a new worker is to some extent an unknown: The employer may prefer to retain a more highly paid worker whose qualities are known to him than to replace him with someone who, though willing to work for less, is unknown to him.[31] In addition, hiring a new worker involves costs for the employer (for example, training costs) that must be met if the firm replaces an existing employee with a new one.

Similar considerations explain why employers are unlikely to attempt to cut money wages when there is unemployment in the economy. They will fear that any such attempt may lead highly skilled or key workers to quit. To replace such workers will involve *them* in a process of search and in the expense of hiring and training new workers. Even if those workers could be obtained at a lower money wage, the costs of search and employee turnover,[32] plus the added uncertainty as to whether they will be able to find suitable workers, may outweigh any saving in wage costs that results.

This discussion implies that the reason money wages do not fall in the face of unemployment is not that workers and/or employers are irrational but that they lack information. As a result, searching for a new job or a new employee takes time and is not costless. In addition, changing jobs involves costs for the employee and hiring new workers involves costs for the employer. As a result, both sides find it in their best long-term interests not to reduce the level of money wages.

In the classical model, workers and employers respond only to real wages. A decline in the real wage has the same effect on behavior whether it is brought about by a reduction in the money wage or by an increase in prices. In the Keynesian model, by contrast, employers and workers respond differently to these two types of change: The new microeconomics provides an explanation of this asymmetry.

Although unemployed workers will resist a reduction in their real wages

---

[31] In fact, the employer may infer from the fact that the applicant is willing to work for less that he is incompetent. Moreover, if workers recognize that potential employers behave in this way, this will provide an additional reason for not lowering their wage demands.

[32] Including the costs resulting from the disruption to production which occurs when a key worker quits his job.

brought about by a cut in money wages, they will not cease to look for work if their real wages are reduced by a rise in prices. Indeed, they may even react to an increase in the cost of living by raising their wage demands. This is because *an increase in prices is visible to and affects everybody.* As a result, unemployed workers are likely to assume that persons who retained their jobs are receiving wage increases and hence that their chances of finding an acceptable job will not be significantly worsened if they raise their asking prices. Moreover, this assumption is likely to be a correct one. Even when there is widespread unemployment, employers are likely to respond positively to demands for wage increases resulting from a rise in prices. The reason is the same one as that which explains why firms do not attempt to cut wages when unemployment is widespread in the economy. They will assume (correctly) that other firms are facing similar wage demands and hence will fear that, if they do not respond positively, key workers will quit, thus making it necesssary for *them* to engage in a lengthy and expensive search for replacements.

Thus the essential reason for the asymmetrical response of labor-market participants to changes in money wages and in prices is that the information available to them is different in the two cases. Participants know that everyone is affected by a rise in prices; hence workers are not inhibited from demanding a rise in wages and employers are prepared to meet such demands even when there is widespread unemployment. On the other hand, workers are likely to assume that if they accept a reduction in their money wages, their position *relative to other workers* will be worsened. Similarly, employers are likely to assume that if they attempt to lower the wages of their employees, their competitors will not follow suit, and they risk losing their best workers. Moreover, these assumptions will, in most cases, turn out to be correct.

In this discussion we have been concerned with the reasons why money wages tend to be downwardly rigid in advanced economies like the United States. This rigidity of money wages is the essential feature of the Keynesian model that causes it to produce different conclusions from the classical model.[33] However, similar arguments may be made to suggest that commodity prices are also likely to be quite rigid in the downward direction.

Thus consider the situation of an individual firm that experiences a decline in the demand for its product. In many cases the firm will have little definite information to judge whether this decline represents a temporary, essentially random, fluctuation in the market for its product or whether it is signaling a general reduction in aggregate demand, which will affect all the firms in the economy. In the first case, the firm will know that sales will soon pick up whereas in the latter, recovery must await an overall revival in general business. Thus the firm is in a similar situation to the newly unemployed

---

[33] Again, we should emphasize that some scholars would argue that this is not an accurate summary of Keynes's own writings.

worker who does not know whether the loss of his job resulted from some circumstance peculiar to his previous employer or from a general contraction in the economy.[34] In the former case he can be fairly sure that he will be able to find a comparable job without undue delay whereas the latter situation means that there has been an overall reduction in the number of jobs available.

Because of this lack of knowledge, the firm is likely to respond to this situation by maintaining its rate of production and its selling price unchanged while it seeks to acquire additional information. This is because changes in prices and in production levels both involve special costs[35] that the firm will not wish to incur if the reduction in sales is a temporary affair.

However, if production levels are maintained while sales decline, the firm will accumulate additional inventories.[36] Such inventory accumulation involves costs (of insurance, storage, etc.); and hence if the lower level of demand persists, the firm must find some other strategy to meet it. Basically, the firm has two choices: to maintain prices, cut production, and reduce its labor force[37] or to lower prices in the hope that this will stimulate sales and so make an output cutback unnecessary. These choices are analogous to those faced by an unemployed worker between searching for a job at his previous money wage and lowering his wage demands in the hope that he will be able to find a job more rapidly.

If the firm lowers its selling price, sales will probably, but not certainly, pick up, but this does not necessssarily mean that reducing prices is the optimal strategy.[38] For example, the extent to which sales will respond to price cuts is usually quite uncertain and will depend on a number of factors on which the firm will have little or no information. If *all* firms in the industry lower their prices, the net benefit to any single firm will be much less than if it alone cuts prices; but the individual firm can generally only guess at which policy its competitors will adopt. Hence if the firm opts to lower its prices, it is choosing a more uncertain strategy than if it leaves them unaltered. In addition, changing prices frequently involves additional

---

[34] Another possibility is that it represents a permanent decline in the demand for his particular skill. Similarly, in the case of a firm, a reduction in demand may signal a permanent shift in customer tastes away from his product. In the long run, such shifts can be countered only by the worker's learning a new set of skills or by the firm's altering the composition of its product line. Firms that are unwilling to change in this way will suffer a permanent reduction in their profits. Workers who refuse (or are unable) to adapt will suffer either a permanent reduction in their real wages or long spells of unemployment, or both. Such unemployment, which results from permanent shifts in demand away from certain classes of worker, is usually described as *structural unemployment*.

[35] For example, in the case of a temporary reduction in demand, it will generally be uneconomic to fire and later rehire workers.

[36] At first, the firm may be able to take advantage of this situation to run down any outstanding orders it has on hand.

[37] This was the response we assumed in the analysis of Chapter 3.

[38] Analogously, if the unemployed worker reduces his wage demand, he will probably, but not necessarily, find a job more quickly. But this does not mean that cutting the wage is his optimal long-run strategy.

costs for the firm: salesmen must be notified of the change, new price lists must be prepared, and advertisements must be amended. If the reduction in demand proves to be a temporary one, these costs may outweigh any additional revenues that accrue from the extra sales the price cut generates. Also, the firm may fear that if it lowers prices now and the decline in demand proves to be only temporary, it will find it difficult to raise them again later.[39] Finally, frequent price changes also impose costs on the *buyer* and hence the firm may assume (probably correctly) that if it can prevent those costs by maintaining stable selling prices, its sales will be larger in the long run. For example, in a market in which prices change frequently, the buyer must engage in more search activity (shopping around) to be sure he is getting the best deal. Stable prices make such search activity unnecessary and hence may be preferred by the buyer. As a result, the *seller* finds it in his own best interest to maintain stable prices despite fluctuations in his sales.[40] For all these reasons, many firms respond to reduced demand, at least initially, by cutting their output rather than by lowering their selling prices.

These considerations reinforce our earlier argument that firms rarely find it in their best interests to attempt to induce workers to accept wage cuts when the demands for their products decline. In the first place, workers will vigorously resist such cuts. Most will believe that with some search they will be able to find similar new jobs at the same wage.[41] They will prefer to quit rather than take a pay cut. Moreover, this resistance will be even greater if prices have not fallen, since in that case a pay cut implies a reduction in real wages. Secondly, however, if prices are downwardly rigid—so that reductions in product demand must be met by decreases in output—it will be unprofitable for firms to keep workers on the payroll (*even at reduced wage-rates*) if their output cannot be sold.

To summarize this discussion, the "lack-of-information" and "costs-of-search" arguments developed by the new microeconomics imply that both

---

[39] Consider, for example, an auto producer experiencing a reduction in demand. He may feel that by lowering his price he can increase sales to customers who would normally purchase smaller or cheaper cars. But such a change in markets might involve a major alteration in the thrust of his advertising campaign. In addition, he may fear that if his car becomes identified as a "cheap car" he will find it difficult later to raise prices and reenter the high-priced market.

[40] As an example of this phenomenon Armen Alchian cites the case of a restaurant. Frequently one must wait in line or make a reservation in order to obtain a meal. This is inconvenient and imposes a cost on the buyer. By varying prices continually to ensure that demand never exceeded supply, a restaurant could eliminate queues and reservations. But customers would then be unable to predict the price of a meal at any given time. This would probably lead them to do more shopping around. Such searching also involves costs to buyers who might prefer stable and predictable prices even though they lead to queues and to a need to make reservations. The fact that restaurant prices do not fluctuate violently suggests that the costs associated with stable prices (queues, reservations, etc.) are less than the costs of search that would exist if prices were varied continuously. See Armen A. Alchian, "Information Costs, Pricing and Resource Unemployment," in Phelps, pp. 27–52, especially pp. 33–36.

[41] Moreover, even if the reduction in sales reflects a decline in the aggregate demand for labor and not merely a circumstance specific to a particular firm, many workers will be correct in this belief.

wages and prices are likely to be rigid in the downward direction. When aggregate demand declines, firms generally cut output, reduce employment, but maintain their selling prices. Unemployed workers do not seek (and probably could not obtain) work by reducing their money wage rates. Employers do not attempt to negotiate wage reductions in exchange for more jobs because they fear that such reductions would lead key workers to quit, and because it is unprofitable to keep workers on the payroll *at any wage* if their output cannot be sold.[42]

This situation is illustrated in Figure 15.7. In this diagram we assume that the labor market is initially in equilibrium at levels of money wages and commodity prices of w_1 and p_1, respectively. Employment amounts to L_1 workers and there is no involuntary unemployment. Suppose now that the demand for goods and services declines. In the conventional wisdom (of both the classical model and the textbook Keynesian model) this reduction in demand causes a decline in prices, as a result of which the demand curve

---

[42] In this paragraph we have implied that prices and wages may be completely rigid so that the whole of any decline in aggregate demand is translated into a decrease in output. This may not be the case. Declining aggregate demand generally leads to some price reductions or at least to a slowing in the rate of inflation. However, what we wish to emphasize is that the new economics provides a coherent explanation of why prices and wages are considerably less flexible than the classical model assumed and hence of why reductions in demand are generally felt predominantly in the output dimension and only to a lesser extent in the price dimension.

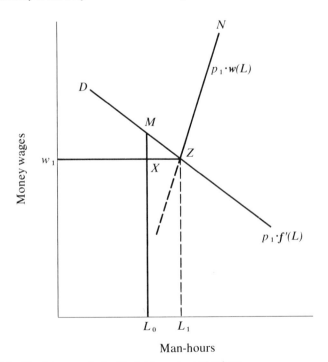

FIGURE 15.7 The labor market with rigid wages and prices

for labor shifts to the left so that at any given money wage firms wish to hire fewer workers. In the classical model this leads to a reduction in money wages whereas in the Keynesian model it produces unemployment. In contrast to both these models, however, the new microeconomics suggests that prices will not fall; nonetheless, firms will wish to reduce employment since at unchanged selling prices, sales of their products will be less. In the diagram we assume that the decline in the demand for goods is such that firms wish to reduce their labor forces from L_1 to L_0; thus the demand curve for labor is the kinked curve labeled DML_0. At the same time workers are unwilling to accept reductions in their money wage below w_1 and hence the supply curve of labor is the kinked curve w_1ZN. The demand and supply curves intersect at point X with employment of L_0 and money wages of w_1. However, although this situation may persist (in economists' jargon, it is a *stable* position) it is not an *equilibrium* in the sense in which that word is usually understood in discussions of supply and demand.

At wages of w_1 with prices of p_1, workers wish to supply an amount of labor L_1 but, in fact, firms only demand an amount L_0. Thus there is involuntary unemployment—in the sense of workers searching for jobs that are not available—of L_0L_1. Similarly, at those wages and prices firms would be willing to supply L_1 jobs *if they could sell the product of that amount of labor*. Since, in fact, they can only sell the product of L_0 jobs, they restrict their employment to that level.[43] Note that, in contrast to the Keynesian model, a reduction in money wages will not increase employment in this model. As long as prices remain rigid downward, firms will be unwilling to hire additional workers, regardless of the level of the money (and hence the real) wage.

Conclusion

We have now completed our discussion of the production side of the economy and the labor market. Our analysis has shown that the behavior of both firms and workers in response to changing demand depends heavily on the amount of information at their disposal and the costs of acquiring that information. Lack of information and the high costs of obtaining it tend to produce stickiness in the response of wages and prices to changing market conditions.

Note that at a number of points in the chapter we have stated or implied that a reduction in the prices of goods will tend to increase the aggregate demand for goods. Although this proposition (that demand curves slope downward) is well known when applied to individual commodities, its validity is less obvious when applied to the aggregate demand for *all* com-

---

[43] Viewing the situation in standard microeconomic terms we could argue that the value of the marginal product of labor is zero when employment is L_0 since no additional output can be sold. Hence employers are unwilling to offer more jobs at any level of the money wage: the demand curve for labor is vertical.

modities. In fact, the proposition is true and was implied, but not stated explicitly, in Chapter 14. In the following chapter we bring the analysis of Chapter 14 and that of this chapter together to show how the supply of and demand for commodities come into equilibrium. An essential part of that discussion will involve the relation between prices and aggregate demand.

References

Branson, William H. *Macroeconomic Theory and Policy*. New York: Harper & Row, 1972.
See especially Chapters 6–8 for analysis of the labor market under varying behavior assumptions.

Microeconomic Foundations of Employment and Inflation Theory, ed. Edmund S. Phelps. New York: W. W. Norton & Co., 1970.
A series of essays on the new microeconomics of search and information theory.

Miller, Roger L., and Raburn M. Williams. *Unemployment and Inflation*. St. Paul: West Publishing Co., 1974.
Chapter 3 contains a model of search behavior that determines the level of unemployment.

Questions for Classroom Discussion

1. At any time there are a number of unemployed workers and a number of vacant houses. The reasons for this unemployment and these vacancies are fundamentally the same: a lack of full information on the part of workers and employers and of home buyers and sellers. Explain this analogy between the market for labor and the market for homes.

2. Owners of apartment buildings usually plan to maintain a certain number of vacancies on the average. If these vacancies were avoided, rents could be reduced. Why don't owners vary rents to keep apartments filled continuously?

3. Suppose an unemployed worker comes to believe that wages in the future will be higher than they are now. How will this affect his search activities?

4. Suppose that the long-run trend of real wages is upward, but that from time to time it declines sharply for a short period and then returns to its trend. Explain how you would expect the participation rate to vary over time in such circumstances.

5. In 1973–1974 auto producers responded to reduced demand by various rebate schemes rather than by cutting sticker prices. In light of the discussion of this chapter, provide an explanation for this behavior.

The Variable-Price Economy

16

In Part 2 we developed a complete model of the fixed price economy and put it through its paces by analyzing the effects of various government policies. In subsequent chapters we added more meat to that bare-bones model. In Part 3 we examined our original intuitively plausible hypotheses more carefully and obtained a deeper understanding of the factors underlying the behavior of spenders and wealth owners. In Part 4 we added a financial system and discussed the role of banks in the creation of money. Finally, in the last two chapters, we examined the effects of changes in both the level and the rate of change of prices on the behavior of households and firms in their roles, first, as spenders and wealth holders and, second, as employees and employers.

It is now time to bring this material together in an attempt to develop a picture of how an economy that has a financial system and in which prices are variable operates. This is the task of this final chapter. Our principal objective will be to examine how the behavior of the economy is affected by our assumptions about the response of workers and employers to variations in aggregate demand. This will lead us into an analysis of the causes of inflation and of the circumstances under which inflation and unemployment may coexist. As in earlier chapters we will carry out this analysis in the form of a discussion of the effects of government policy in such an economy.

Equilibrium in the Classical Economy

We begin by considering how the analysis of Part 2 is altered by dropping the supposition that all prices are constant and replacing it with the assumption that prices and wages are perfectly flexible in both the upward and the downward direction. As we pointed out in the preceding chapter, this classical assumption implies that all buyers and sellers have complete and perfect knowledge of the supply and demand conditions in all the markets in which they participate. It is convenient to illustrate the equilibrium position of such an economy by the diagram in Figure 16.1. This diagram is an amended version of one originally devised by Warren Smith.[1]

---

[1] Warren Smith, "A Graphical Exposition of the Complete Keynesian System," *The Southern Economic Journal,* Volume XXIII (October 1956).

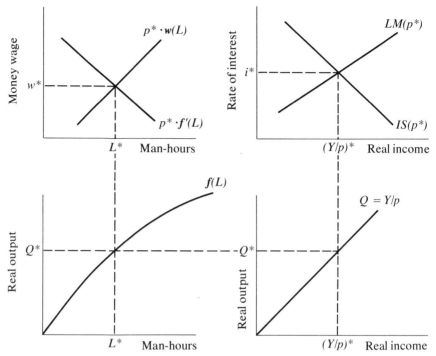

FIGURE 16.1 Equilibrium in a classical economy

The upper left quadrant of this figure represents the labor market. If commodity prices are at level p^*, the demand for labor services is represented by the curve labeled $p^* \cdot f'(L)$ and the supply by $p^* \cdot w(L)$. At a money wage of w^* the amount of labor that employers wish to hire is equal to the amount that workers wish to offer so that the labor market is in equilibrium at an employment level of L^*. In this equilibrium situation, which is usually described as *full employment,* no worker who is willing to work at the going money wage of w^* is unable to find a job and no employer who is willing to hire labor at that wage is unable to find the workers he requires.

The production function in the lower left quadrant represents the technological relation between output and employment. The output level Q^* represents the rate of production that corresponds to an employment level of L^*. Thus if wages and prices are at the levels w^* and p^*, producers wish to supply an output of Q^* units per period, and households are willing to supply the labor required for this level of production.

The fact that output and real income are necessarily equal—by our accounting definitions of Chapter 2—is represented by the 45° ray in the lower right quadrant. From this quadrant we see that when prices and wages are p^* and w^*, real income will be accruing at a rate of $(Y/p)^*$ dollars per period.

The upper right quadrant depicts the *IS-LM* apparatus developed in Part 2 and extended in Chapter 14. Strictly speaking, the use of this apparatus requires that bonds and capital be perfect substitutes so that their rates of return are always equal. We saw earlier, however, that although these rates of return are *not* precisely equal, they normally do tend to move together.[2] Hence, in our verbal analysis of the economy, we will assume that bonds and capital are good but not necessarily perfect substitutes. The interest rate in the *IS-LM* diagram will represent the "general level" of rates rather than the rate on any specific asset.

For each level of the interest rate[3] the *IS* curve represents the real income at which actual and planned expenditures are equal. We showed in Chapter 14 that variations in the level of commodity prices lead to changes in both planned consumption and planned investment, so there is a different *IS* curve corresponding to each level of prices. Specifically, a rise in commodity prices leads to a reduction in both planned consumption and planned investment and hence causes a leftward shift in the *IS* curve.[4] Conversely, a decline in prices leads to a rightward shift. In Figure 16.1, $IS(p^*)$ represents the *IS* curve when prices are at level p^*. If prices are at that level and the interest rate is i^*, planned and actual spending will be equal at a real income of $(Y/p)^*$.

For each level of real income, the *LM* curve shows the rate of interest at which the public is willing to hold the existing stocks of money, bonds, and capital. In Chapter 14 we saw that since the stocks of money and bonds are fixed in nominal terms, but the demands to hold them are real demands, the position of the *LM* curve depends on the level of commodity prices. Specifically, a rise in commodity prices increases the nominal amount of money that wealth holders want to hold at any given rate of interest without altering the actual stock of money in existence. In order to induce wealth holders to acquiesce in this situation, money must become relatively less attractive through an increase in the rate of interest on nonmonetary assets.[5] Thus an increase in commodity prices causes the *LM* curve to shift upward and, by a converse argument, a decline in prices produces a downward shift. In the diagram, prices are at a level p^* and the relevant *LM* curve is $LM(p^*)$. This curve shows that if prices are p^* and real income is $(Y/p)^*$, the asset markets will be equilibrium—with wealth holders willing to hold the existing asset stocks—if and only if the rate of interest is i^*.

---

[2] See Chapter 6. In our discussions of an economy that contains a banking system, we introduced the rates of return on bank deposits and on federal funds in addition to those on bonds and capital. We found that these rates also tended to move in line with those on bonds and capital though this result did depend on certain special assumptions about the demand for high-powered money. See Chapter 12, p. 273.

[3] At present we are assuming that the expected rate of inflation is zero and hence draw no distinction between real and nominal rates of interest.

[4] See Chapter 14, pp. 321–326.

[5] Another way of describing this situation is to say that a rise in commodity prices reduces the actual share of wealth held in the form of money (because the increased prices of capital goods cause a rise in nominal wealth) but does not affect the share which wealth owners desire at given levels of real income and the rate of interest. Hence the interest rate must rise to restore equilibrium. See Chapter 14, pp. 313–317.

The situation depicted in the figure represents an overall equilibrium in the economy. Not only are all three types of markets—the labor market, the asset markets, and the commodities markets—in equilibrium, but these equilibria are consistent with one another.[6]

At wage and price levels of w^* and p^*, producers wish to employ and households are willing to supply L^* man-hours of labor. The labor market is in equilibrium and there is no tendency for wages to change. As a result, there is no pressure on firms from the cost side to alter prices, output, or employment. At an employment level of L^*, gross output is Q^*, and hence real income accrues at a rate of $(Y/p)^*$.

At the same time, given the level of real income $(Y/p)^*$ and the level of prices p^*, the wealth-owning public is willing to hold the existing stocks of money, bonds, and capital assets at a rate of interest of i^*. The economy is "on the LM curve" and there is no pressure tending to alter asset prices and rates of return. Finally, when the price level is p^* and the interest rate is i^*, the amount of real spending that households, businesses, and governments plan to do at a real income of $(Y/p)^*$ is exactly equal to the level of real output. The economy is "on the IS curve," and producers find that they can sell an output of Q^* at prices p^* so that they are under no pressure from the demand side to change either their output or the prices of their products.

Further insight into the nature of this classical equilibrium is obtained by examining how the economy responds to various external changes. We will consider two simple cases: one expansionary and the other contractionary. Having worked through these examples, check that you can develop similar arguments to explain the economy's response to other types of stocks.

The Effects of a Restrictive Monetary Policy

First, consider a policy of reducing the money supply through the sale of government securities by the Federal Reserve System.[7] In Part 2 such an open-market operation was described as a *pure monetary policy*. The reaction of a classical economy to such a policy is illustrated in Figure 16.2. In this figure it is assumed that the economy is initially in equilibrium at levels of wages, prices, output, and the rate of interest of w_2, p_2, Q_2, and i_0, respectively.

In order to induce the public to hold more bonds and less money, the former must become relatively more attractive (that is, cheaper) to wealth

---

[6] Several details have been suppressed in order to make the diagram manageable. For example, if there is a banking system, the market for federal funds will be in equilibrium and either the market for bank deposits will be in equilibrium or the deposit-rate ceiling will be effective. In addition, if bonds and capital goods are not perfect substitutes, their rates of return will differ but the markets for both will be in equilibrium. At the price of capital goods that characterizes these equilibria, the flow of new investment spending will be that which underlies the IS curve in the figure.

[7] The effects of open-market operations on asset markets were discussed in Chapters 4, 5, 6, and 13. Here we only sketch the main outlines of these earlier arguments.

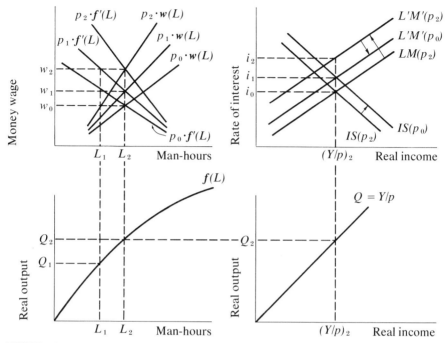

FIGURE 16.2 **Contractionary monetary policy in a classical economy**

owners. In fact, Federal Reserve sales of securities will cause their prices to decline and rates of interest to rise. This fall in security prices represents the immediate impact of the policy action. In addition, however, in an economy with a banking system, an open-market sale lowers bank reserves, raises the federal funds rate, and so induces banks to reduce their earning assets. This will produce a second round of interest-rate increases on both securities and bank loans. Thus interest rates rise as a result not only of the original bond sale by the *Fed* but also of the subsequent actions of the *banks* in selling securities and calling in customer loans. Finally, unless constrained by government-imposed maxima, interest rates on deposits will also rise as banks seek to minimize the impact of the policy on their asset portfolios by attracting additional deposits.

These increases in the rates of return on financial assets make the latter more attractive relative to physical assets. Wealth owners will be induced to shift their resources out of capital and into deposits and securities; hence the prices of capital goods will be driven downward and their rates of return upward.

We conclude that the first effect of an open-market sale is to raise rates of return on both real and financial assets. In the figure, this effect is represented by the upward shift in the *LM* curve from $LM(p_2)$ to $L'M'(p_2)$; the interest rate rises from i_0 to i_2.

A general increase in interest rates leads to a reduction in consumption as households substitute future spending for current spending and are also faced with capital losses on their accumulated assets. In addition, the decline in the prices of existing capital goods relative to the cost of production of new capital reduces the demand for new capital goods and so leads to a decrease in investment spending. Finally, to the extent that spending by states and municipalities is sensitive to interest rates, demand for goods and services by these entities is also reduced.

The argument so far implies that a restrictive monetary policy leads to a rise in rates of return and a decline in asset prices and so to a general reduction in the demand for newly produced goods and services. As a result, producers find that they are accumulating inventories or running down their order books at a faster pace than they had anticipated. Their immediate response to this situation may be to decrease output, to lower selling prices, or to do both of these things. However, although the nature of this response affects the exact nature of the adjustment process that follows, it does not affect the final outcome.

If firms are accustomed to setting their prices in terms of a markup over costs, they may respond initially to the decline in demand by reducing production while leaving selling prices unchanged. As output is cut back, employers will begin to shorten working hours and to lay off workers. However, as unemployment worsens, competition among workers for the reduced number of jobs will cause money wages to fall. This decline in wages will lower costs of production. Finally, reduced production costs— coupled with the stiff competition between firms for shrinking markets[8]— will lead producers to cut their selling prices.

If firms initially react to reduced demand by cutting prices rather than output, the scenario is somewhat different but the conclusion is similar. In this case firms find their revenue per unit of output reduced (because they are selling at lower prices) but their unit costs are unchanged. They will be under pressure to reduce production costs by persuading workers to accept cuts in their money wages. Since the prices of goods and services are declining, workers will generally be willing to acquiesce.

Thus we see that regardless of how firms initially respond to the decline in aggregate demand, the final result is to produce downward pressure on both wages and prices.

In the aggregate, the extent to which output is actually reduced and workers lose their jobs depends on the speed with which money wages are bid downward. Suppose, for example, that firms respond to the decline in demand for their products by cutting prices from p_2 to p_1. From Figure 16.2 we see that the demand curve for labor shifts downward from $p_2 \cdot f'(L)$ to $p_1 \cdot f'(L)$: thus if the money wage were to remain at w_2, firms would offer only

---

[8] This competition might also induce firms to reduce their markups.

L_1 jobs and would produce an output of only Q_1, so that L_1L_2 persons[9] would become unemployed.

Under classical assumptions, however, money wages will *not* remain at w_2. The combined effect of rising unemployment and falling commodity prices is to reduce the money wage that workers are willing to accept. Since employers are seeking to lower their production costs and workers are willing to accept a reduction in their rates of pay, money wages tend to fall. This decline in wages increases the number of jobs that individual firms are prepared to offer. In fact, if money wages were to fall instantaneously from w_2 to w_1, individual firms would be willing to continue to produce an output of Q_2 and to maintain a level of employment of L_2; as a result no unemployment would emerge. However, although the classical economists assumed that money wages are flexible downward, few (if any) went so far as to assume that the reduction in wages occurs instantaneously. To the extent that the decline in wages lags behind that in prices, the classical economists would have conceded that some unemployment may develop in the short run. However, the essence of the classical model is that this unemployment is a disequilibrium phenomenon that will be rapidly eliminated as the money wage falls and the economy returns to equilibrium.

However, the economy will only return to a full-employment equilibrium if the reduction in prices does, in fact, stimulate aggregate demand. As was hinted at the end of Chapter 15, this proposition is less self-evident than it appears at first sight.

We argued above that if prices fall to p_1 and the money wage simultaneously declines to w_1, individual firms will be willing to produce at the full employment level of output. Although this is true of any single firm, however, it may turn out not to be true in the aggregate. In fact, producers may find that at prices p_1 their sales remain below the full employment level of output. Essentially, the reason for this is that although a reduction in its selling price gives an individual firm an advantage over its competitors and enables it to expand its level of output, this competitive edge disappears when the decline in prices is economy-wide. As a result, aggregate sales of firms may not immediately return to the full employment rate even if wages and prices fall together.[10]

The upshot of all this is that the reduction in aggregate demand leads to

---

[9] We remind you that we are speaking loosely. The supply of and demand for labor are *flow* variables having dimension of man-hours per week. When labor demand falls, either the average length of the work week or the number of job holders (or both) will be reduced.

[10] You may be puzzled as to why the decline in commodity prices does not increase aggregate demand directly, in the same way that a decline in the price of bread stimulates sales of bread. The reason is that falling prices also reduce nominal incomes. This follows from the accounting identity between nominal income and the value of output. (Note that it does not depend on whether or not wages fall.) In the case of a single commodity, bread, it is legitimate to assume that a change in its price has no effect on the income of its purchasers and hence that the amount demanded will rise when its price falls. For output as a whole no such assumption can be made: prices and incomes fall together. As a result, there is no direct force causing a rise in the aggregate demand for commodities when the general level of prices falls.

competition between producers for smaller markets and between workers for fewer jobs and hence to steady downward pressure on wages and prices. However, this decline in prices does not directly stimulate aggregate demand. In view of this conclusion, the question naturally arises as to whether there are any indirect forces at work that will tend to stimulate the demand for goods and services and thus restore full employment and bring the decline in wages and prices to a halt. If there were no such forces, prices and wages would presumably fall *ad infinitum*. Fortunately, under classical assumptions, a number of such forces do exist.

In the first place, the decline in commodity prices means that the real value of the public's holdings of financial assets (money and government securities) is increased. This capital gain will stimulate consumption demand though, as we saw in Chapter 14, this effect is probably small. Diagrammatically, it would be represented by a shift to the right in the *IS* curve.

The decline in the price level also influences the demands for the different classes of assets. Since nominal income has fallen, the nominal demand for money will also decline because individuals require fewer dollars to carry on the reduced nominal flow of transactions. Individuals will want to shift out of money and into nonmoney and, as a result, rates of return on both bonds and capital will tend to decline. This reduction in rates of return tends to stimulate both investment and consumption spending. This decrease in interest rates is represented in diagrammatic terms by a downward shift in the *LM* curve, which is expansionary.

The impact of lower prices on the asset markets may be looked at from another point of view. Since the stocks of money and bonds are fixed in nominal terms, the decline in prices has the effect of increasing the proportion of wealth held in financial form. At the initial pattern of rates of return, wealth holders will want to shift out of money and bonds and into capital goods.[11] Since there is an added demand for capital goods, the prices of these goods will rise relative to the general level of prices and as a result the demand for new tangible assets (fixed investment) will tend to increase.[12]

These arguments imply that lower commodity prices stimulate the economy by causing rightward shifts in both the *LM* and the *IS* curves. Moreover, as long as total spending remains below the full employment level of output, wages and prices will continue to fall and the forces tending

---

[11] We have already seen part of this effect from the opposite point of view in the form of the reduced demand for money discussed in the last paragraph.

[12] The argument of these two paragraphs implies that the effect of lower prices on bond interest rates is ambiguous. On the one hand, the reduced level of nominal income leads wealth holders to shift from money into nonmoney (including bonds), tending to drive bond rates downward. On the other hand, lower commodity prices lead investors to want to shift out of financial assets (including bonds) into capital and thus tend to cause bond rates to rise. If bond rates were, in fact, to rise, this would tend to be contractionary. In the text it is assumed that bonds and capital are sufficiently close substitutes that their rates of return both decline: The *LM* curve shifts downward. See Appendix A to Chapter 14.

to stimulate demand will continue to operate. As a result, the economy will gradually expand back toward full employment.

In Figure 16.2 this situation is reached when wages and prices have declined to w_0 and p_0. At these price and wage levels employers will again wish to employ and households will be willing to offer L_2 man-hours of labor. Hence output and real income will be Q_2 and $(Y/p)_2$ as in the original equilibrium. At this full employment income level and with prices p_0, wealth holders will be content to hold the new stocks of bonds, money, and capital when the interest rate is i_1: The economy is on the (new) LM curve $L'M'(p_0)$. Finally, with an interest rate of i_1 and real income of $(Y/p)_2$ spenders will be prepared to purchase the full employment output at prices p_0: the economy is on the IS curve, $IS(p_0)$.

In the new equilibrium very little has changed compared with the situation before the government's policy action. Wages and prices are lower but the *real wage* is unchanged. Output and employment have returned to the full employment level. Only the asset markets have been significantly affected; specifically, the rates of return on earning assets (bonds[13] and capital) are higher[14] reflecting the fact that in the new equilibrium the share of wealth held in the form of nonmoney is larger.[15]

The Effects of an Expansionary Fiscal Policy

As a second example of the impact of a policy shock on the classical equilbrium, we consider a *balanced budget* increase in government spending and tax revenues. We showed in Chapter 5 that such a pure fiscal policy leads to an increase in aggregate demand. In Figure 16.3 this increase in demand is represented by the rightward shift of the IS curve from $IS(p_0)$ to $I'S'(p_0)$.

Faced with this rise in the demand for their products, firms will find their inventories being run down and their order books lengthening. They are

---

[13] Strictly speaking, we cannot predict unambiguously that the bond rate will rise. See footnote 12.

[14] A special case of the argument occurs when bonds and capital are perfect substitutes and there is no wealth effect on spending. In this case bonds and capital yield the same rate of return and there is no shift in the IS curve. In the final equilibrium the interest rate will be the same as in the initial position. Prices decline until the money-wealth ratio returns to the same value as in the original equilibrium. In terms of the figure, the LM curve shifts to the right as prices decline until it takes up the same position as in the original situation.

[15] In the analysis we have just completed, we considered only the effects of changes in the level of prices and assumed implicitly that expected rates of change of prices remained constant. In Chapter 14 we saw that expectations of inflation tend to be expansionary: They shift both the IS and LM curves to the right. By a converse argument, we could show that expectations of declining prices are contractionary. Thus if the reductions in the level of prices lead spenders and wealth holders to expect continuously falling prices, the contractionary effects of these changed expectations might (theoretically) offset the forces making for expansion and thus cause the economy to remain permanently in a less-than-full-employment situation with continually falling wages and prices. Historically, it seems unlikely that such a situation has ever existed. Even if it had, the anlysis of such a case would be of little interest in the environment of the 1970s.

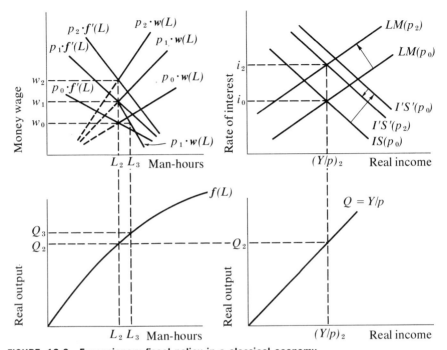

FIGURE 16.3 **Expansionary fiscal policy in a classical economy**

likely to respond to this situation by both raising prices and expanding output.

In order to increase their outputs, firms will find that they must hire additional workers and lengthen working hours. Since, in the initial situation, households were in equilibrium with respect to their labor-supply decisions, many firms will find that in order to attract the workers they need, they must offer higher money wages. Thus wages will tend to rise because of the increase in *demand* for labor by producers. In addition, the rise in prices will lead workers to request increases in their wages in order to maintain their accustomed living standards. As a result, money wages will also be pushed upward from the *supply* side.

Thus we conclude that the increase in aggregate demand generates upward pressure on both prices and wages. As in the contractionary case discussed in the preceding section, the extent to which output and employment actually rise depends on the speed with which wages are bid upward.

Suppose, for example, that as a result of the government-induced increase in aggregate demand, prices rise from p_0 to p_1. In Figure 16.3 the demand curve for labor shifts upward from $p_0 \cdot f'(L)$ to $p_1 \cdot f'(L)$ while the supply curve shifts from $p_0 \cdot w(L)$ to $p_1 \cdot w(L)$. If wages lag behind prices—so that money wages initially remain at w_0 and real wages decline—households will wish to increase their labor supplies to maintain their living standards. Working wives, teenagers, and older persons will begin searching for jobs.

At the same time employers will seek to hire additional workers since the value of the marginal product of labor exceeds the money wage. As a result, employment will rise from L_2 to L_3 and output will rise from Q_2 to Q_3.

This increase in employment will not be permanent, however, because the money wage will not remain at w_0 but will tend to rise[16] toward w_1. As it does so the demand for labor will fall back, secondary workers will withdraw from the labor force, and employment will decline back to L_2.

The conclusion we reach is that the increase in aggregate demand leads only to an increase in wages and prices and to no permanent expansion in output and employment. However, if output does not increase, the increased demand for goods and services remains unsatisfied and hence the question arises of how the rise in prices and wages acts to reduce aggregate demand.[17]

An increase in the general price level reduces the real value of the financial component (money and bonds) of total wealth and this will tend to reduce consumption. This effect is represented by the leftward shift in the IS curve from $I'S'(p_0)$ to $I'S'(p_2)$. The price rise also causes wealth holders to want to hold a larger proportion of their wealth in the form of money (in order to finance the larger value of transactions) and a smaller proportion in the form of capital. These changes in asset demands tend to cause rates of return on nonmoney assets[18] to rise and the LM curve to shift upward to $LM(p_2)$. This rise in interest rates—and the corresponding relative[19] decline in the prices of existing capital goods—will tend to reduce both investment and consumption spending.

As long as aggregate demand exceeds total output, prices and wages will continue to rise and the forces just described will continue to operate. Both consumption and investment demand will fall in real terms, and this contractionary process will continue until the excess aggregate demand is eliminated. In Figure 16.3 equilibrium is restored when prices and wages reach p_2 and w_2, respectively. At these prices firms will wish to produce an output of Q_2 and households will be willing to supply the amount of labor (L_2) that they require. Real income will be $(Y/p)_2$ and at this income level, spenders will be willing to purchase the total output (but no more than the total) when the interest rate is i_2. Finally, at the new higher level of prices and with an interest rate of i_2, wealth holders will be content to hold the existing stocks of money, bonds, and capital.

---

[16] Note that when the price level is p_1 and the money wage is w_0, the demand for labor exceeds the supply.

[17] This issue is the exact opposite of the one raised in the previous section in the case of deficient demand. As in that case, a rise in the general level of prices *does not* directly reduce aggregate demand in the same way as a rise in the price of a single commodity (bread) *does* reduce the demand for that commodity. See footnote 10 above.

[18] As in the previous case, the effect on the bond rate is, in theory, ambiguous. See Appendix A to Chapter 14.

[19] This does not mean that the prices of capital goods actually fall, but only that they rise by less than the general level of prices.

The above discussion parallels almost exactly the analysis of the contractionary policy in the previous section. Hence the reader should now be in a position to trace out the effects of other similar shocks to the classical equilibrium. With flexible wages and prices, the system will always return to a position of full employment.

A somewhat different situation develops when the economy is subjected to a *series* of shocks. The most important example of such a situation is when the government runs a budget deficit (or surplus) that must be financed by continuing issues (or redemptions) of securities or high-powered money. In this case, the equilibrium in the asset markets will be continually disrupted as the stocks of securities and money change so that the system will not return to a static equilibrium. In particular, if there is a budget deficit financed by money creation prices will tend to move steadily upward: A state of true inflation will develop. Before examining such a situation, however, it will be helpful to turn from the classical world of perfect information and flexible prices to the "Keynesian" world where a lack of perfect knowledge causes prices and wages to be somewhat rigid, particularly in the downward direction.

Equilibrium in the "Keynesian" Model

As we saw in the previous chapter the crucial difference between the modern approach to the theory of wages and prices and that of the classical economists is that prices and wages are not assumed to be completely flexible but instead tend to be rigid (or at least "sticky"), particularly in the downward direction. The source of this stickiness is the lack of complete information on the part of employers and employees.

Once we drop the classical assumptions of perfect knowledge and perfectly flexible wages and prices, full employment is no longer assured. However, the precise manner in which the economy will behave depends on what assumptions we make about the extent to which wages and prices are rigid and the amount of knowledge that economic agents possess.

One case that has received considerable attention is that in which prices are perfectly flexible but wages, although they are flexible in the upward direction, are rigid downward. This situation is frequently described as the "Keynesian" case, though it seems very unlikely that Keynes himself would have accepted such a model as a realistic description of any real-life economy.

The implications of this set of assumptions may be analyzed with the aid of Figure 16.4. Assume that the economy is in equilibrium at full employment with wages at level w_2, prices at level p_2, output of Q_2, and employment of L_2. Suppose now that investment, for some unspecified reason, declines so that aggregate demand is below the full employment level of output. In terms of the diagram this decrease in demand is represented by the leftward shift of the IS curve from $IS(p_2)$ to $I'S'(p_2)$.

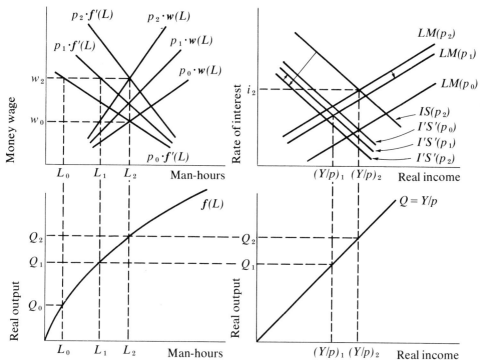

FIGURE 16.4 The "Keynesian" model with unemployment

Firms that have been producing at an output level of Q_2 will find that they are now unable to sell their total production. Inventories build up and firms reduce their selling prices. With no decline in money wages (which are rigid at level w_2) firms will wish to lay off workers and reduce output. In terms of the diagram this is represented by a leftward shift in the demand-for-labor curve. If, for example, prices fall from p_2 to p_1 the demand-for-labor curve shifts from $p_2 \cdot f'(L)$ to $p_1 \cdot f'(L)$, employment declines from L_2 to L_1, and output is cut from Q_2 to Q_1. Thus $L_1 L_2$ workers are involuntarily unemployed in the sense that they would be willing to accept jobs at the going wage of w_2 but they are unable to find such jobs. However, they are, for the reasons discussed in Chapter 15, unwilling to accept money wages below w_2 even though the level of commodity prices (i.e., the cost of living) has declined.

The decline in prices does act to stimulate aggregate demand through the same mechanisms as were discussed earlier in this chapter. Recall that these forces act to shift both the *IS* and the *LM* curves to the right. In Figure 16.4 it is assumed that the decline in prices shifts these curves to the positions $I'S'(p_1)$ and $LM(p_1)$. Thus when prices reach the level p_1, aggregate demand for goods and services is $(Y/p)_1$, which is just equal to the supply of commodities that firms will produce when prices are at that level and wages are w_2. This situation is one of equilibrium, in the sense that the supply of and demand for commodities are equal, but unemployment of L_1L_2 persists.

Why cannot full employment be restored? Basically, the reason is that money wages do not fall. If, for example, prices declined to p_0 the *IS* and *LM* curves would shift further to the right to $I'S'(p_0)$ and $LM(p_0)$. At such a low level of prices, the total demand for goods and services would be equal to the full employment level $(Y/p)_2$. But with wages at level w_2 firms would be unwilling to produce the full employment level of ouput: In fact, with prices p_0 and wages w_2, employers would hire only L_0 workers and produce output Q_0. In order to induce firms to produce at full employment when the money wage is w_2, prices must be at p_2: But at such a price level, demand would be below the full employment level. Thus there is an impasse. At a price level of p_0 aggregate demand is at the full employment level but aggregate supply is substantially below that level. Conversely, at p_2 firms are willing to supply the full employment level of output but demand is below that level. Only at a price level between p_0 and p_2 (p_1 in our diagram) will the supply and demand for commodities be equal. This situation is an equilibrium but not a very attractive one, since many workers are without jobs. Full employment may be restored either by fiscal or monetary policy, which will shift the *IS* and/or the *LM* curves further to the right, or by wage flexibility: If, for example, money wages and prices were to fall to w_0 and p_0, firms would again be willing to produce the full employment level of output and would be able to sell that output. This latter situation is, of course, the classical solution discussed earlier.

The preceding discussion is affected only slightly if we assume that prices, as well as wage rates, are downwardly rigid. We saw in Chapter 15 that in a world of imperfect knowledge firms may find it rational to respond to reduced demand for their product by cutting output but leaving prices unchanged. This is particularly true if wages, the main element in firms' costs of production, do not fall when employment declines.

Consider Figure 16.5. Once again assume that, beginning from a position of full employment, an exogenous decline in investment shifts the *IS* curve from *IS* to $I'S'$. Inventories mount and firms cut production. Workers lose their jobs and begin searching for new ones. However, since they assume that after a time this search process will be successful and since there has been no reduction in the cost of living, unemployed workers continue to demand the same level of money wages. Similarly, firms do not cut prices both because they fear that their competitors will follow suit and because there has been no decline in their labor costs of production. This situation is, to all intents and purposes, identical to that analyzed in Part 2. Wages and prices remain fixed and hence output and employment fall until actual and desired spending are again equal. This occurs when output has declined to Q_0. At the corresponding level of income, $(Y/p)_0$, the economy is "on the *IS* curve." Thus the markets for goods and services are in equilibrium in the

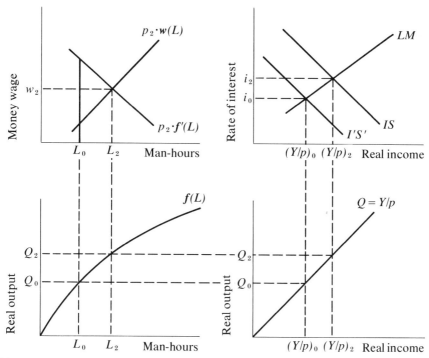

FIGURE 16.5 Unemployment with rigid wages and prices

sense that firms are able to sell the output they produce. However, that output is below that which *could* be produced if full employment prevailed. At prices and wages of p_2 and w_2 firms would be willing to push their output to Q_2 but they are able to sell only Q_0. Similarly, L_2L_0 workers are searching for jobs at a wage of w_2 but are unable to find them. If prices and wages are, indeed, perfectly rigid downward, this unemployment will persist unless there is some exogenous upward shift in aggregate demand or the government takes action through monetary or fiscal policy to stimulate demand.

In the actual American economy, prices and wages are neither perfectly rigid nor perfectly flexible. Reductions in aggregate demand do induce some firms to lower their prices in an endeavor to stimulate production and sales. Frequently, in order to emphasize the temporary and nonaggressive nature of such price cuts, they take the form of special rebates and limited-time "special offers." However, such price reductions often do not suffice to bring supply and demand into balance; that is, at the ruling prices firms wish to increase their sales but are unable to find buyers. Similarly, money wages are not completely inflexible downward, but may be reduced when unemployment is widespread. Often, effective wages are lowered by assigning workers to lower job categories than they would obtain in more prosperous conditions rather than by paying a lower wage for a given category of job.

As in the case of commodity prices, however, such wage reductions are insufficient to restore equilibrium to the labor market. Involuntary unemployment persists in that at these (lower) money wages, many workers do not promptly find jobs: The search process takes longer than workers expect.

Expansionary Policies in the Keynesian Model

Suppose the government responds to the unemployment situations discussed in the preceding section by reducing personal taxes. Such an action will stimulate household spending. However, it will also give rise to a deficit in the federal budget that must be financed. We saw in Chapter 5 that the method by which a deficit is financed is potentially very important in determining the overall effect of the government's policy.

In the United States, the Treasury does not directly control the stock of money. In the first instance, therefore, budget deficits must be met by the issue of government securities[20] that will tend to lower bond prices. The corresponding rise in bond interest rates will reduce the willingness of banks to make customer loans—because securities are a more attractive earning asset—while at the same time it increases borrowers' demands for such loans because borrowing through the issue of bonds has become more expensive. Thus interest rates on bank loans will also tend to rise.[21] Finally, the increase in rates of interest on financial assets will induce wealth holders to shift out of capital, provoking a decline in capital-good prices and a rise in their rates of return.[22]

Thus the initial impact of the issue of government securities to finance a government deficit is to cause a general rise in interest rates. This effect would be summarized in a diagram by an upward shift of the *LM* curve. This rise in interest rates will tend to reduce the expansionary impact of the tax cut. As we saw in Chapter 5, the extent of this "crowding-out" effect is a matter of dispute between the monetarists and the Keynesians.

If the authorities wish to avoid this tendency for interest rates to rise—and so to head off the crowding-out effect—the Federal Reserve must engage in

---

[20] In theory, the Treasury could meet a deficit by running down its balances either at the Federal Reserve or in tax and loan accounts at commercial banks. If it did so, the money supply would rise. In practice, these balances are kept to a minimum so that this is not a viable option for any but a small and temporary deficit.

[21] The rise in interest rates on securities and loans will increase the amount of deposits that the banking system wishes to supply. The effect of the deficit on the demand to hold bank deposits is uncertain in theory since the rise in interest rates on nonmoney assets reduces this demand but the increase in total wealth has the opposite effect. In fact, it seems likely that this demand will fall (or at least not rise by much). Unless it is constrained by an effective ceiling, a reduced demand for deposits combined with an increased supply will cause the deposit rate to increase. Check this result by considering the effect on i_D and i_L of an increase in B in the model presented in the appendix to Chapter 12.

[22] Strictly speaking, this conclusion only holds for the case in which bonds and capital are good substitutes. See Chapter 6, pp. 129–132.

an open-market operation to purchase securities from the nonbank public. Such an operation increases the high-powered money stock and reduces the outstanding stock of government securities. The net effect of the issue of bonds by the Treasury and the open-market operation by the Fed is to increase the stocks of both securities and high-powered money.[23] So far as the public is concerned it is as if the Treasury had financed its deficit partly by printing (high-powered) money and partly by printing securities. The only significant difference is the political one that the decision-making power is shared between the Treasury[24] and the Federal Reserve, with the former determining the size of the deficit and the latter determining the means by which it is financed.

The direct effect of an open-market purchase of securities by the Fed is to limit the increase in interest rates that results from the issue of Treasury securities. In effect, by buying bonds in the open market, the Fed reduces the volume that must be absorbed by the private sector. Hence the increase in the bond rate that is required to persuade wealth holders to hold these securities is lower.

Since the Fed's purchase of securities also increases bank reserves, its direct effect on interest rates is supplemented by the response of the banking system to this change in its situation. Prompted by the increase in their reserves (as well as by the accompanying fall in the federal funds rate) banks will seek to increase their earning assets by lowering loan rates and bidding up bond prices. The decline in rates of return on nonmoney assets will in turn increase the public's demand to hold bank deposits while it reduces the banking system's willingness to supply them. Unless the deposit rate was previously held below its equilibrium level by the ceilings imposed under Regulation Q, this rate also will tend to fall.[25]

The above argument implies that the tendency for budget deficits to drive up interest rates can always be offset by open-market security purchases. No matter how powerful is the crowding-out effect, it can always be overcome by a suitable monetary policy so that the net effect of the combined fiscal and monetary package is expansionary. If the authorities adopt such a package, there will be a dispute between the Keynesians and the monetarists as to whether the stimulation came primarily from the monetary or from the fiscal action, but for our present purposes the source of the expansion is not important.[26]

---

[23] It is, of course, conceivable that Federal Reserve purchases of securities might equal the amount of securities issued by the Treasury so that, on balance, the deficit is financed entirely by the issue of high-powered money. Normally, the Fed finds it unnecessary to purchase securities on so large a scale.

[24] Strictly speaking, of course, decisions over the taxing and spending activities of the government are made by Congress.

[25] Again, check the conclusions of this paragraph by using the model developed in the appendix to Chapter 12.

[26] The dispute is, however, very important to the policy maker. Suppose, for example, he believes that the monetarist view of the economy is correct. He will infer from this view that the primary effect of a tax cut is to raise interest rates. As a result, he will favor an

Let us assume, therefore, that the authorities accompany the tax cut with a monetary policy such that the net effect is unambiguously expansionary. In Figure 16.6 the *IS* and the *LM* curve shift rightward from $IS(p_0)$ and $LM(p_0)$ to $I'S'(p_0)$ and $L'M'(p_0)$. Hence the aggregate demand for goods and services rises.

As a result of this policy action, producers find the flow of new orders increasing, their order books lengthening, and inventories being depleted. Any decline in prices that accompanied the preceding recession will come to a halt and may even be reversed. However, the main response will likely come in the form of increased output. Firms' demands for labor will rise, and workers who were previously unable to find jobs will now be more successful. Employment increases, hours of work lengthen, and unemployment declines. Since jobs are now more abundant, the time required to find a job will be reduced: In other words, the average duration of unemployment will shorten.[27] There may also be some increase in money wage rates.

To the extent that prices do rise, the expansionary effects of the policy actions will be somewhat modified.[28] However, if the policy is sufficiently expansionary, the economy will eventually return to full employment.

Figure 16.6 describes the situation. In the original equilibrium, output and employment are Q_0 and L_0. Prices are p_0 so that aggregate demand just suffices to take this volume of output off the market.[29] Unemployment of L_1L_0 exists but neither wages nor prices fall further because both workers and producers have incomplete knowledge of the markets in which they operate. Unemployed workers are searching for jobs at a money wage of w_0 but are unsuccessful.[30] Despite this unemployment, neither the employed nor the unemployed workers are willing to accept cuts in the money wage. Similarly, at current wage and price levels firms wish to increase their output but are unwilling to cut prices further to stimulate their sales.

The policy action shifts the *IS* and *LM* curves to the right. As a result, demand increases and firms increase their output and employment. As the economy approaches full employment, some firms also raise prices and as they do this *IS* and *LM* curves move back to the left. In the figure the net

---

expansionary monetary policy. However, if he is wrong and, in fact, the Keynesian model more correctly describes the real world, such a policy is likely to be overly stimulating.

[27] Falling unemployment is, in fact, normally accompanied by a reduction in the average duration of unemployment and in the proportion of long-term unemployed persons.

[28] Because higher prices provoke leftward shifts in the *IS* and *LM* curves: That is, they tend to reduce spending both through the wealth effect and through the effects of higher interest rates.

[29] The *IS* and *LM* curves are $IS(p_0)$ and $LM(p_0)$ respectively so that aggregate demand is Y/p_0 which is equal to Q_0.

[30] At least in the aggregate. This does not imply that no searcher is successful. In fact, the pool of unemployed workers will be constantly changing as some workers find jobs and leave the pool while others lose their jobs and begin searching. The fact that many workers are successful in their search—albeit after a longer search than they expected—probably explains why the money wage does not fall. Presumably, if no one found a job at the going wage, the money wage would decline much more rapidly.

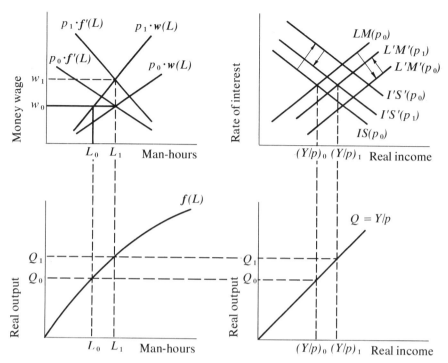

FIGURE 16.6 Expansionary policy in a Keynesian economy

effect of the policy action and the ensuing price increase (if any) is to shift the *IS* and the *LM* curves from $IS(p_0)$ and $LM(p_0)$ to $I'S'(p_1)$ and $L'M'(p_1)$. As full employment approaches, money wages also rise somewhat to w_1. With the new stance of monetary and fiscal policy and the rise in wages and prices to w_1 and p_1, the economy again reaches a full employment equilibrium.

In the preceding description of the recovery process, both wages and prices rose even before full employment was attained. This has been a feature of recent business expansions in the U.S. economy. It is explainable by the fact that workers, jobs, industries, and regions are differentially affected by increases in the level of aggregate demand. Some firms or industries are likely to find themselves operating at full capacity and under demand pressure to raise prices long before this is true for the economy as a whole. Similarly, workers in particular occupations, industries, or geographic areas are likely to find that the demand for their specific services is strong enough to justify a request for a wage boost even though overall unemployment remains quite high.

Thus by the time the economy returns to full employment, both money wages and prices will probably have risen somewhat from their levels at the bottom of the downswing. Whether they continue to rise depends on the course of aggregate demand. Before continuing with the story, however, one characteristic of the full employment equilibrium should be noted.

Although the equilibrium is characterized by a lack of involuntary unemployment, this does not mean that no one is without a job. Even when the economy is operating at a high level of activity, there are always a substantial number of persons who are changing jobs. In fact, when the economy is prosperous, voluntary quits tend to rise as workers seek to take advantage of the strong job market to find more attractive or better-paying jobs. However, these workers do not remain jobless for long: With a strong labor market, workers find that they can locate an acceptable job after quite a short search period.

Expansionary Policies After "Full Employment" Is Reached

Recall that the events of the last section were set off by a government policy of cutting taxes and financing the resulting deficit by an expansionary combination of monetary and debt policy. We assumed that the combined effect of these fiscal and monetary actions was to bring the economy to full employment.

The question now arises as to what happens if these expansionary policies are continued after full employment is reached. Is it possible to increase the level of employment further? To reduce unemployment further? If this is attempted, what will happen to prices and wages? This is the subject of the present section.

If the government's fiscal stance remains unchanged, the economy will receive no further stimulus from the effects of the tax cut. In diagrammatic terms, the shift in the *IS* curve is a once-and-for-all affair. However, if government expenditures and revenues remain unchanged, so will the federal deficit. The authorities may choose to finance this deficit by a combination of security issues and open-market operations, which puts downward pressure on interest rates. In this case, the expansionary effects of the deficit will continue every period. In diagrammatic terms, the *LM* curve continues to move downward, reflecting the fact that if wealth holders and the banking system are to be willing to hold increasing amounts of high-powered money in their portfolios, the rates of return on nonmoney assets must decline and the prices of these assets must correspondingly rise. These interest-rate effects will in turn stimulate the demand for goods and services.

Faced with a steady rise in the demand for their products, firms will wish to raise prices and increase their output. However, although the increase in prices is all but inevitable if the government persists in its expansionary policies, whether output and employment also rise depends on the response of workers to rising prices. Consider Figure 16.7, which shows the situation in the labor market. Initially, we assume that wages and prices are at w_1 and p_1, respectively, and employment is L_1. Although the supply of and demand

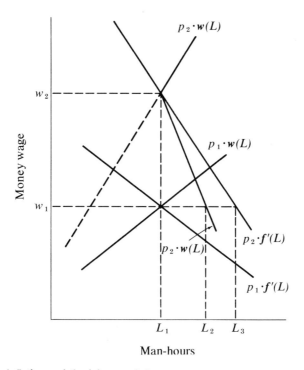

FIGURE 16.7 **Inflation and the labor market**

for labor are equal, some workers are temporarily unemployed as they move from one job to another.

As a result of developments in the asset markets (higher asset prices and lower rates of return), the demand for goods and services rises and firms respond by raising prices from p_1 to p_2. The demand-for-labor curve shifts up from $p_1 \cdot f'(L)$ to $p_2 \cdot f'(L)$. As a result, the level of employment rises.

This increase in the number of persons who are employed comes from two main sources. In the first place, the rise in prices may lead some secondary workers to enter the labor force to offset the pressure on their living standards. This effect is represented by the shift in the supply curve of labor from $p_1 \cdot w(L)$ to $p_2 \cdot w(L)$. If the money wage remains at w_1, the increase in employment from this source will amount to $L_1 L_2$. At a wage of w_1, however, employers will be willing to hire more than L_2 man-hours. Some (or all) of the additional man-hours are made available from the second source of increased employment—the reduction in the average duration of jobless-ness. As a result of the increased demand for labor, persons who are be-tween jobs and are searching for employment at a wage of w_1 will be success-ful sooner than they expected. In addition, the pressure on living standards from higher prices will probably cause some unemployed workers to search more aggressively and may lead them to accept less attractive jobs than they had planned. Finally, the greater availability of jobs and the rise in the cost of living will cause some previously discouraged workers—who had stopped searching because they were unable to find a job—to recommence their search and to be successful. Each of these factors will decrease the time spent between jobs and so reduce the amount of unemployment.[31]

As a result of these factors, employment will rise to at least L_2 and perhaps as high as L_3. However, this increase in employment will not be permanent. It occurs only because workers do not have full knowledge of the situation in the labor market and will disappear as soon as they obtain better information. For example, workers who are unemployed set their asking wage at w_1 since this was the wage they were receiving in their previous jobs. Secondary workers behave similarly. Since the demand for labor has increased, the job-search process is shorter and acceptable jobs come along sooner than expected. Later, however, employees realize that firms are willing to pay wages higher than w_1 and this realization—coupled with increases in the cost of living—leads them to demand higher money wages. As wages rise, the average duration of unemployment lengthens and the level of employment contracts. Secondary workers are unable to find jobs and leave the labor force voluntarily or involuntarily. In terms of Figure 16.7 the money-wage rises to w_2 and employment falls back to L_1.

At the same time the rise in prices from p_1 to p_2 acts to reduce aggregate demand (by shifting the *IS* and *LM* curves leftward) so that it no longer exceeds total output. As a result, the original "full employment" equilibrium is restored at a new (higher) level of wages and prices.

The stage is now set for a steady upward movement in wages and prices. Each period[32] the government finances its deficit in an expansionary manner and as a result aggregate demand increases and prices rise. There is a temporary increase in output and employment. However, after a brief lag, money wages also rise and output falls back to its former level. The increase in prices also acts to bring aggregate demand back down to the full employment level. As a result, there is no permanent increase in employment or output. But then the cycle is repeated again.

Note that the above analysis does not imply that the rate of inflation will accelerate. It is quite possible for the economy to remain continually in a state of full-employment "equilibrium" with prices and wages rising at a constant rate. Each period the government finances its deficit by increasing the nominal stock of financial assets. However, since prices are rising, the real stocks of these assets remain unchanged so that the asset markets remain in equilibrium. The expansionary effects of financing the government deficit are offset by the contractionary impact of the increased price level so that aggregate demand remains constant in real terms. Since wages

---

[31] On the other hand, the greater availability of jobs may tend to increase the number of voluntary quits by workers who believe that by changing jobs they can improve their situation. This factor will tend to increase unemployment. See Bernard Corry and David Laidler, "The Phillips Relation: A Theoretical Explanation," *Economica,* Vol. XXXIV (May 1967).

[32] The length of this period is not important for present purposes.

and prices are rising together, the real wage is constant so the labor market remains in equilibrium.

Once people begin to realize that the rise in prices is a continuing process, a number of changes occur. In the first place, workers recognize that the cost of living is rising steadily and hence, if they are to maintain their standard of living, they must secure regular increases in pay. Moreover, employers do not resist these demands too strenuously since they too recognize the realities of the situation. Hence increases in prices no longer are associated, even temporarily, with increases in employment and output.

Secondly, the change in expectations about the future course of prices influences the markets for assets and the demand for goods and services. That is, it causes shifts in both the *IS* and the *LM* curves. These effects were analyzed in detail in Chapter 14. In that chapter we found that an increase in the rate of inflation produces upward shifts in both the *IS* and the *LM* curves but that the shift in the *IS* curve is greater.[33] Hence when persons come to expect more rapid inflation, aggregate demand is stimulated.

This increase in demand will further raise prices but will again produce no permanent rise in output or employment. However, it is important to recognize that this is a *one-shot* effect which increases the level but not the rate of change of prices. Figure 16.8 shows the course of prices schematically. At date *t* the government begins its expansionary policy. At first prices change little but later, as the economy approaches full employment, the rate of price increase accelerates. Full employment is reached at date *t + s*. From then on, prices rise steadily at constant rate. At date *t + T* expectations change and prices move up sharply.[34] After this change the rate of price change returns to its previous steady upward path. In this new situation the nominal interest rate will be higher[35] because it incorporates an inflationary premium, but the real interest rate, real output, and the level of employment will be the same as before.

Figure 16.9 depicts the steady inflationary equilibrium situation. In the upper panel the *IS* and *LM* curves are shown. Each period nominal wealth increases as the government issues new securities and new high-powered money to finance its continuing deficit. This wealth effect would tend to shift the *IS* curve to the right. At the same time, however, prices rise so that real wealth remains unchanged and, in fact, there is no net wealth effect. Similarly, the expansionary financing policy tends to shift the *LM* curve

---

[33] See Chapter 14, p. 328.

[34] For simplicity we assume in Figure 16.8 that this change in expectations occurs at a single date, and the resulting rise in the level of prices occurs instantaneously. In reality, the change will take place over a period. While this change is occurring, we observe a temporary increase in the rate of price rise rather than the sudden upward jump in prices depicted in the figure. The acceleration in prices during 1973–1974 may be partly attributed to this change in expectations though other special factors (the oil embargo and a series of poor harvests) may also have been important.

[35] See Chapter 14, p. 328. Notice that both the *level* and the *rate of change* have increased.

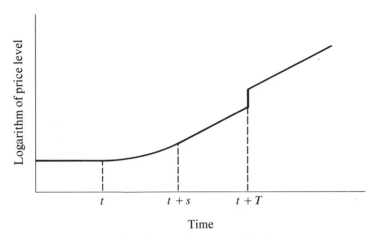

FIGURE 16.8   The course of prices in a business expansion

rightward but this effect is also negated by the rise in prices. As we saw in Chapter 14 the nominal rate of interest is higher under inflationary conditions, but the real rate is not.

The lower panel depicts the situation in the labor market. Each period prices rise so that the demand curve for labor shifts upward and employers demand additional workers at the current money wage. At the same time, however, the supply curve also shifts upward as the rise in prices leads workers to demand higher money wages. Since the demand for labor has increased, employers are willing to grant these wage increases. On balance, all that occurs is that wages and prices increase together and there is no net change in the levels of employment and output. In terms of the diagram, both the supply and demand curves for labor shift upward together, but the level of employment at which they intersect does not change.

Expansionary Policy Changes in an Inflationary Situation

We now consider the effects of an expansionary policy on the inflationary equilibrium discussed in the preceding section. Such a policy might be initiated if policy makers come to the conclusion that the levels of either employment or output were too low for either economic or political reasons. It might also reflect a decision to increase government spending for purposes other than those of macroeconomic policy. The Vietnam build-up of the late sixties is an obvious example.

Assume that the government decides to engage in a more expansionary monetary policy;[36] that is, to finance a larger proportion of its budget deficit by the issue of high-powered money. As a result, the rate of growth of the

---

[36] We choose this example because of its simplicity. The effects of a more expansive fiscal policy would be similar. The points we wish to make in this section do not depend on the type of expansionary policy adopted and hence we choose to analyze the simplest.

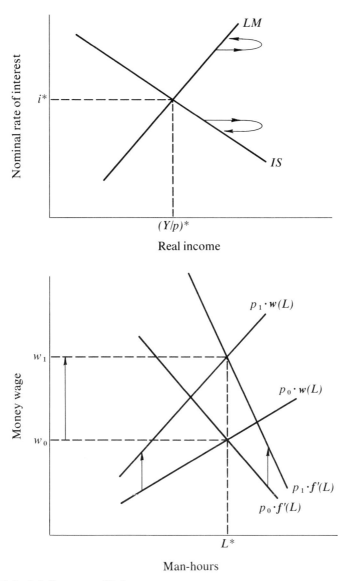

FIGURE 16.9 Inflationary equilibrium

money stock will accelerate. As long as the rate of inflation does not change, such a policy change will cause the *LM* curve to shift to the right and hence will stimulate aggregate demand.

Since the economy is at full employment, the effect of this stimulus is to cause prices to rise more rapidly than they have done in the past. As a result, employment and output will rise temporarily. The reasons for this are essentially the same as those discussed in the previous section.

Consider first the effect of more rapid inflation on persons who are searching for jobs. In determining their asking wage they will have taken account of the previous rate of inflation. If, for example, prices are rising at 10 percent a year, a worker who is unemployed and expects to remain so for six months will be searching for a job that pays 5 percent more than did his former job. A rise in the rate of inflation increases the demand for labor so that such workers find jobs more rapidly than they expected. As a result, total employment increases.

At the same time an increase in the rate of inflation reduces living standards. This induces secondary workers to enter the labor force and may also encourage primary workers who are unemployed to search more intensively and accept job offers more readily. Again, employment and hence output are increased.

Thus the initial impact of the expansionary policy is to cause inflation to accelerate, employment to rise, and output to expand. Over the long haul, however, only the faster rate of inflation will continue: Employment and output will fall back to their previous levels. The reason is simple: After a while both workers and employers recognize that there has been a permanent increase in the rate of inflation. Persons looking for jobs raise their asking-wages and hence the average duration of joblessness increases and employment falls. Since the money wage has caught up with the price level, the incentive for secondary workers to remain in the labor force is removed. The economy returns to a new inflationary equilibrium at the same levels of output and employment as before the change in policy.[37]

The upshot of the preceding discussion is that the levels of employment and output cannot be permanently increased above "full employment" by an increase in the rate of inflation. The only way to permanently lower the unemployment rate is to continually increase the rate of inflation. This proposition—which is known variously as the "natural rate" hypothesis[38] or the "accelerationist" hypothesis—was originally put forward by Milton Friedman and Edmund Phelps.[39] By engaging in a monetary and fiscal policy, which leads to an accelerating rate of inflation, the authorities can produce a situation in which the asking wage of labor continually lags behind the general price level and hence behind the wage that employers are willing to pay. As a result, the duration of unemployment is reduced (because job searchers find acceptable employment sooner than they expect) and there is an increased demand for and supply of secondary workers. We will have

---

[37] Since the inflation rate has increased, there will probably also be a change in expectations. This will provoke another one-shot increase in prices and in the nominal interest rate. See Figure 16.8.

[38] Because the unemployment rate cannot be driven below some natural rate by an increase in the inflation rate.

[39] Milton Friedman, "The Role of Monetary Policy," *American Economic Review,* Vol. LVIII (March 1968). Edmund S. Phelps, "Money-Wage Dynamics and Labor Market Equilibrium," *Journal of Political Economy,* Vol. LXXVI, Number 4, Part II (July/August 1968).

more to say about this propostion in the discussion of the Phillips relation later in this chapter.

Contractionary Policies Under Inflationary Conditions

We now consider the impact of a contractionary policy action on the inflationary equilibrium discussed in the preceding two sections. Specifically, consider the impact of a tax increase coupled with a slowing in the rate of increase of the high-powered money stock. In diagrammatic terms the *IS* and *LM* curves shift to the left.[40]

As a result of this policy, the demand for goods and services contracts. Firms find their order books shortening and their inventories contracting. However, they may not immediately respond by cutting prices: Indeed they may continue to raise prices even in the face of falling demand.

The reasons for this response again reflect the lack of full information. After a long spell of inflation, firms and their workers will have developed expectations that prices will continue to rise. Initially they are likely to assume that the reduction in demand will be a temporary affair. As a result, money wages probably will continue to rise, since workers will continue to demand wage increases in line with the cost of living, and firms will fear that if they do not meet such demands key workers will quit. Individual firms will fear that if they hold the line on prices, their sales will not benefit very much while their wage costs will continue to escalate, causing profits to decline sharply. In such circumstances, firms will respond to reductions in demand by reducing output and laying off workers.

Because of their lack of complete information, newly unemployed workers will commence searching for jobs at money wages at the same levels to which they have become accustomed. Like their former employers, they will assume that the reduction in demand is specific to them and that they will be able to find new jobs after a reasonable period of search.[41] Moreover, they will assume—generally correctly—that workers who retained their jobs are receiving wage increases and hence will be unwilling to accept cuts in their money wages to get their jobs back.

The implications of this discussion are that the initial impact of the contractionary policy will be felt on output and employment rather than on wages and prices. The Nixon "game-plan" of 1968–1971 is an example of this phenomenon. A contractionary policy produced declining output and unemployment over this period, but prices continued to rise.

As output declines and unemployment mounts, the factors stressed so far

[40] A tax increase will reduce the budget deficit and may transform it into a surplus. The volume of Treasury borrowing is reduced. Taken alone, this financing effect would lower interest rates and be expansionary. We are assuming that Federal Reserve open-market operations are conducted to ensure that the net effect of the Treasury and Fed actions is contractionary.

[41] Moreover, for many workers, this prediction will be accurate though typical search times will lengthen. Rising unemployment primarily occurs because the average duration of joblessness lengthens rather than because a substantial number of persons lose their jobs permanently.

are likely to lose some of their force. In particular, firms—faced with falling sales and even sharper declines in their profits—are likely to begin to cut prices. Since this price cutting is unlikely to be economy-wide, however, it at first shows up in the form of a slowing in the average rate of price inflation. Firms are also likely to become more resistant to wage demands. At the same time, workers—reacting to the slowing in the rate of price inflation and the growing unemployment—tend to moderate their wage demands. Thus the rate of wage inflation also slows down.

As inflation slows there will be a downward revision in price expectations. As we saw in Chapter 14, such a change in expectations is contractionary. Thus we may see a sharp upsurge in unemployment and a downward shift in nominal interest rates. The behavior of the economy during 1974–1975 at least partly reflected this phenomenon.

As inflation slows, the decline in output gradually comes to a halt. Whether full employment is restored depends on the setting of government policy. We assumed earlier that the *LM* curve was shifting to the left. This shift reflected both the monetary-debt policy of the Treasury and the Federal Reserve and the rate of inflation. As the inflation rate declines, this leftward shift in the *LM* curve will slow and may be halted or reversed. If it is reversed, the net effect of policy will become expansionary and the system will gradually return to full employment. Frequently, however, a switch to more expansionary policies will be required to achieve this desirable conclusion.

The Phillips Relation

In 1958, A. W. Phillips published an article[42] that profoundly altered the way in which economists viewed unemployment and inflation. Drawing on statistical data for the British economy over a period of nearly 100 years, Phillips showed that unemployment and inflation were inversely related: Low rates of unemployment tended to be accompanied by high rates of inflation and conversely. This relationship—which may be represented by the Phillips curve in Figure 16.10—was later found to exist in a number of other economies.[43]

The Phillips analysis implied that the policy maker faces a dilemma. He wishes to reduce both the unemployment rate and the inflation rate. However, if the Phillips curve represents a true structural relation he cannot do this, since policies to lower unemployment will increase the rate of inflation and, conversely, attempts to reduce inflation will lead to more unemployment. This conclusion leads to the notion of an *inflation–unemployment* trade-off. Since we cannot achieve less unemployment and less inflation

---

[42] A. W. Phillips, "The Relation between Unemployment and the Rate of Change of Money Wage Rates in the United Kingdom, 1861–1957," *Economica,* Vol. XXV (November 1958).
[43] See, for example, P. A. Samuelson and R. M. Solow, "Analytical Aspects of Anti-Inflation Policy," *American Economic Review,* Vol. L (May 1960).

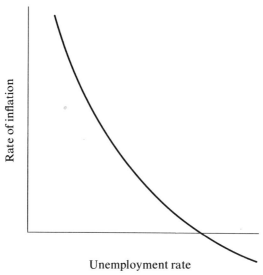

FIGURE 16.10 The Phillips curve

simultaneously, we must choose that combination we like best or dislike least. If we reduce unemployment by one percentage point, we must be prepared to accept more inflation. This increase in the inflation rate represents the price we must pay for a lower unemployment level. Whether we should pursue a policy designed to lower unemployment depends on whether we are prepared to pay this price. Increasingly, during the decade of the sixties, discussions of the objectives of macroeconomic policy came to be phrased in terms of this trade-off between unemployment and inflation.[44]

Much of the early work on the Phillips relation was concerned to establish its empirical existence.[45] Only later did economists turn their attention to the theoretical underpinnings of the relationship and, in fact, the theory of the Phillips curve remains the subject of considerable debate.

One theory of the supposed relation argues that the unemployment rate stands as a proxy either for the level of aggregate demand for goods and services or for the demand for labor. When unemployment is low, this means that demand is strong and hence wages and prices are bid up rapidly. High unemployment, on the other hand, implies a weak demand both for labor and for goods and services; hence wages and prices do not rise much.[46]

---

[44] For an example of a more formal discussion of policy objectives through the application of choice theory to the policy maker's decision process, see R. A. Gordon, *The Goal of Full Employment* (New York: John Wiley & Sons, 1967), pp. 70–71.

[45] A number of writers have asserted that the economics profession has failed in this task and that, in fact, no simple relation of the type proposed by Phillips exists in any actual economy. See, for example, Axel Leijonhufvud, "Comment," *Journal of Political Economy* Vol. 76 (August/September 1968).

[46] An early explanation along these lines was that of Richard Lipsey. See R. G. Lipsey, "The

A more sophisticated version of this approach was presented by James Tobin in his 1971 address to the American Economic Association.[47] Tobin stressed the extreme heterogeneity of a modern advanced economy and the fact that it is subject to a continual series of shocks and disturbances. As a result, even when aggregate demand, employment, and output are approximately stable, the same will not be true so far as individual industries, regions, or occupations are concerned. The economy is in a continual state of microeconomic disequilibrium so that at any time some areas are experiencing excess demand while others are experiencing deficient demand. Moreover, in a world of imperfect knowledge, prices and wages tend to rise in the former but not to fall much in the latter. This means that even when there is no excess demand in the aggregate, the average level of prices will tend to rise.

In such an economy, any attempt to reduce unemployment will tend to generate more rapid inflation. Increases in aggregate demand will increase the number of industries, regions, and job categories in which there is excess demand and reduce the number in which demand is deficient. Although this will reduce the amount of unemployment, it will also increase the number of sectors in which wages and prices are rising and hence will increase the overall inflation rate. Conversely, a reduction in aggregate demand will mean that a larger number of sectors in the economy will experience deficient demand and higher unemployment. However, as long as some sectors continue to enjoy excess demand, prices and wages in these sectors—and hence the average levels of wages and prices in the economy as a whole—will continue to rise.

In these approaches to the Phillips curve, the direction of causation runs from the unemployment rate (seen as a proxy for the level of aggregate demand) to the inflation rate. However, the analysis of the new microeconomics—and especially that of the accelerationists—suggests that the causation may instead run from the inflation rate to the unemployment rate.

We saw in an earlier section that an increase in the rate of inflation may lead to an increase in employment and ouput if it is unexpected. This is because unexpected inflation causes the money wage to lag behind the general price level and hence lowers the real wage. As a result, employers increase their demand for labor. Workers who are in the pool of the unemployed find jobs sooner than they expected, so the unemployment rate declines. In addition, secondary and discouraged workers are able to enter the labor force and obtain jobs. Thus by raising the inflation rate we are able to "buy" an increase in the level of employment.

We argued earlier that this increase in employment will not be permanent.

Relation between Unemployment and the Rate of Change of Money Wage Rates in the United Kingdom, 1862–1957: A Further Analysis," *Economica* Vol. XXVII (February 1960).

[47] James Tobin, "Inflation and Unemployment," *American Economic Review,* Vol. LXII (March 1972).

As workers recognize that the rate of inflation has increased, they will demand (and receive) increases in money wages, and unemployment will return to its former level.

In Figure 16.11 this argument is illustrated in Phillips-curve terms. Suppose that the system has been experiencing inflation at the rate of 5 percent for several years and that workers and employers have become accustomed to this rate. Then the relation between inflation and unemployment is represented by the curve labeled 5%. If the current rate of inflation is also 5 percent, the level of unemployment will be U^*. If aggregate demand is now increased and as a result the rate of inflation rises to, say, 10%, this unexpected increase in the inflation rate will cause unemployment to fall to U_0. However, after a while employees come to realize that the inflation rate has increased. The Phillips curve shifts upward to that labeled 10% and the unemployment rate returns to U^*. To push unemployment back down to U_0, the inflation rate must rise to 15 percent, but again the effect will not be permanent.

The level of unemployment U^* is what accelerationists term the *natural rate of unemployment*. If the authorities seek to push the unemployment rate below this level, they will succeed only in generating accelerating inflation. As shown in Figure 16.11 each "round" of inflation generates a temporary reduction in the unemployment rate. The economy moves through a series of "loops," such as those depicted in Figure 16.12. In each loop an increase in the rate of inflation produces a temporary reduction in the unemployment rate but in the long run the rate remains at its natural level.

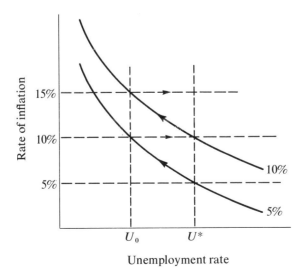

FIGURE 16.11 Price expectations and the Phillips curve

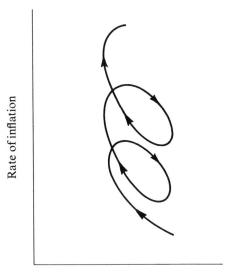

Unemployment rate

FIGURE 16.12 The acceleration hypothesis

There is some evidence that this story gives a fairly accurate description of the U.S. economy over the post-war period. In Figure 16.13 we show the annual rates of change in the consumer price index plotted against annual average unemployment rates. Over the period since 1954, the economy appears to have gone through four loops: 1954–1958, 1958–1961, 1962–1971 and 1972–1975. The natural rate of unemployment seems to have been around 4 percent during the sixties and appears to have risen somewhat since then. This increase may be explained by demographic and social factors that have increased the proportion of young persons and women in the labor force. These groups tend to have higher unemployment rates than do adult men.

The natural-rate hypothesis suggests that it is difficult—if not impossible—to drive the unemployment rate below the natural rate without generating unacceptable rates of inflation. However, it does not necessarily imply that the economy will automatically tend toward an equilibrium at the natural rate. Reductions in aggregate demand—whether produced by mistaken government policies or by outside forces—can lead to unemployment substantially above the natural rate. Given the downward rigidity of wages and prices, the economy may not return to full employment without government intervention on either the monetary or fiscal side.

Tobin's heterogeneity argument also suggests that some annual price increases must be tolerated if the natural rate of unemployment is to be achieved. If we attempt to halt inflation completely, a large number of industries, regions, or job categories will face deficient demand and excessive unemployment. For example, if wages and prices were completely

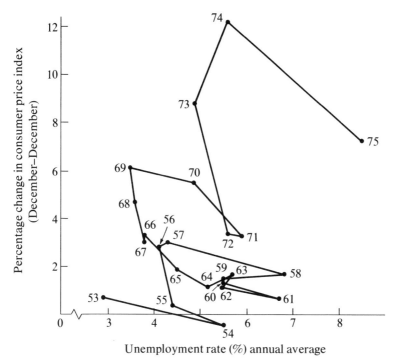

FIGURE 16.13 Inflation and unemployment in the United States, 1954–1975

rigid downward and we achieved a zero average inflation rate, this would imply that wages and prices were not rising anywhere in the economy. Given the fact that demand is continually shifting between industries and regions, this would mean that although some industries were facing deficient demand, none were facing excessive demand. Unemployment would be above the natural rate. By increasing aggregate demand, some areas in the economy could be moved out of the deficient demand category into the excess demand category. This would mean a positive inflation rate, but it would buy a permanent reduction in unemployment.

Figure 16.14 illustrates this argument. The curve labeled 0% represents the Phillips curve when the expected rate of inflation is zero. When aggregate demand is such that the inflation rate is actually zero, large numbers of industries and regions will face deficient demand and hence unemployment will be high (U_2). By increasing aggregate demand, unemployment can be reduced by shifting areas of the economy from the deficient demand to the excess demand category. However, since prices rise in the latter category but do not fall (much) in the former, this increase in aggregate demand also causes inflation to appear. In the diagram we assume that this rate of inflation is 5 percent. Once this rate of inflation has been imbedded in workers' and employers' expectations, the unemployment rate settles down

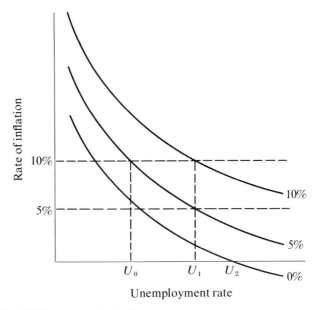

FIGURE 16.14 **Phillips curves in a heterogeneous economy**

at U_1. As shown by the Phillips curve labeled 5%[48] a situation in which the unemployment rate is U_1 and the inflation rate is 5 percent may be sustained permanently. Thus U_1 represents the natural rate of unemployment. Further increases in the rate of inflation cannot permanently reduce unemployment once they become imbedded into expectations. For example, an increase in the inflation rate to 10 percent lowers unemployment to U_0 temporarily, but this effect is lost when expectations alter and the curve shifts upward.

Conclusion

We have now completed our discussion of the variable-price economy. We have seen that the behavior of the economy depends heavily on the behavior of workers and employers in the face of inflation and unemployment. This is an area of continuing research and controversy, with economists divided on the extent to which unemployment can be reduced by fiscal and monetary measures without also producing accelerating inflation.

Some economists infer from the accelerationist hypothesis that government can do little or nothing to alleviate unemployment. This is almost certainly too strong a claim. Downward rigidity of wages and prices means that the economy does not automatically and speedily return to full employ-

---

[48] Of course, unemployment could be pushed even lower if the expected inflation rate remained at zero while the actual rate rose to 5 percent. This is impossible in any but the short run since expectations respond to experience. However, the important point is that some permanent improvement in the unemployment situation can be achieved by increasing the inflation rate from zero to 5 percent.

ment following a decline in aggregate demand. Hence policy action is required. On the other hand, the natural-rate hypothesis implies that there is a definite limit on the ability of the authorities to generate employment increases by macroeconomic policy actions. Once that limit is reached, further reductions in unemployment can be achieved only by *lowering the natural rate*. This can be done by improving the working of the labor market and speeding up the transmission of information about the availability of vacancies and unemployed workers and thus shortening the search processes of both employers and households. However, the discussion of these issues lies outside macroeconomics and thus outside the bounds of this book.

References

Corry, Bernard, and David Laidler. "The Phillips Relation: A Theoretical Exploration." *Economica (N. S.),* Vol. XXXIV (May 1967).

Friedman, Milton. "The Role of Monetary Policy." *American Economic Review,* Vol. LVIII (March 1968).

Lipsey, Richard G. "The Relation between Unemployment and the Rate of Change of Money Wage Rates in the United Kingdom, 1862–1957: A Further Analysis." *Economica,* Vol. XXVII (February 1960).

Phelps, Edmund S. "Money-Wage Dynamics and Labor Market Equilibrium." *Journal of Political Economy,* Vol. LXXVI, Number 4, Part II (July/August 1968).

Phillips, A. W. "The Relation between Unemployment and the Rate of Change of Money Wage Rates in the United Kingdom, 1861–1957." *Economica,* Vol. XXV (November 1958).

Samuelson, P. A., and R. M. Solow. "Analytical Aspects of Anti-Inflation Policy." *American Economic Review,* Vol. L (May 1960).

Smith, Warren. "A Graphical Exposition of the Complete Keynesian System." *The Southern Economic Journal,* Volume XXIII (October 1956).

Tobin, James. "Inflation and Unemployment." *American Economic Review,* Vol. LXII (March 1972).

Questions for Classroom Discussion

1. Suppose the economy is in inflationary equilibrium with a budget deficit being financed by the issue of high-powered money. Assume that this method of financing is replaced by one in which the deficit is entirely covered by the issue of securities. Describe the short- and long-run impacts of this policy.

2. If the authorities engage in an expansionary policy that increases the rate of inflation and lowers unemployment, who gains and who loses? Is it always socially beneficial to reduce the amount of unemployment? The rate of inflation?

3. What is the natural rate of unemployment? Does the economy converge to this rate of unemployment? Why or why not?

Index

1 2 3 4 5 6 7 8 9 0